# THE FINE ART OF *Baseball*

# THE FINE ART OF

**Lew Watts**

# *Baseball*

## A Complete Guide to Strategy, Skills, and System

**second edition**

**Prentice-Hall, Inc.**
**Englewood Cliffs, New Jersey**

*Library of Congress Cataloging in Publication Data*

WATTS, LEW.
  The fine art of baseball.

  1. Baseball.  I. Title.
GV867.W35 1973      796.357'2      72–4247
ISBN 0-13-316968-5

THE FINE ART OF BASEBALL, second edition
Lew Watts

PRENTICE-HALL, INC.
*Englewood Cliffs, New Jersey*

10  9  8  7  6  5  4  3  2  1

Printed in the United States of America

PRENTICE-HALL INTERNATIONAL, INC.,  London
PRENTICE-HALL OF AUSTRALIA, PTY. LTD.,  Sydney
PRENTICE-HALL OF CANADA, LTD.,  Toronto
PRENTICE-HALL OF INDIA PRIVATE LIMITED,  New Delhi
PRENTICE-HALL OF JAPAN, INC.,  Tokyo

*In Memory of*
***SHERMAN P. YOUNG,***
*Gentleman, Scholar, and Greatest of Coaches.*
*Doc Young Taught Me Baseball as a Way of Life*
*and Provided Inspiration*
*That Will Sustain Me for a Lifetime.*

# Acknowledgements

The author would like to make acknowledgement to the many people who have helped make this book possible—

To the Office of the Commissioner of Baseball for permission to use material from the Baseball Rules;

To Hillerich and Bradsby Co. for permission to use material from the Louisville Slugger Yearbook of 1955;

To Scholastic Coach Magazine for the use of most of the photographs found herein;

To Mickey McConnell of the Little League National Headquarters, and Coaches John Herbold, William Hatch, Jack Stallings, Dell Bethel, Ken Dugan, Alan Hale, and Jean McCarthy for additional photographic material;

To Bill Hillman, Athletic Director at The Bordentown-Lenox School for suggestions on training and equipment;

To my wife, Barbara, for her photography and for her help in preparing the pictorial material;

To Herman Masin, Editor of Scholastic Coach, for his ever available advice and encouragement;

To my ballplaying friend, Danny Mays, and my coaching colleague, George Wilson, for many intelligent ideas and stimulating discussions on the game;

To Arthur "Dynie" Mansfield of the University of Wisconsin for his work in reading this material and for his helpful suggestions;

And, above all, to the late Sherman P. Young who started the thought processes that culminated in this book and who was so helpful in its actual creation.

# Preface

The first edition of *The Fine Art of Baseball* had but one aim—to be the most complete book written on the playing and coaching of the game. This it may have been. Yet, the very nature of baseball, despite the fact that a sound approach to it must be based on the tried and true practices developed by the top strategists and performers in the field, inevitably necessitates periodic revisions because of its dynamic quality. The creative refinements that are spawned thereby can mean but one thing—a revised edition, if for no other reason than to validate that one aim anew.

The original book was one written from the viewpoint of a professional ballplayer who happened to have coached at the college level for two years. The revised edition has been written by a long-time high school coach who happened to have played professional baseball for several years and to have profited greatly therefrom. The distinction is important in that points of emphasis and, particularly, of application are quite different at the professional and amateur levels. This is a book which makes a definite effort to differentiate between the two, with specific examples and teaching points. That the author's coaching experience in combination with his professional background has led to a most effective method of teaching the practical approach to good (and correct) baseball is a conviction deeply held. This, then, is a working manual of the way in which professional techniques and tactics can best be applied to the amateur game, providing an approach that is correct from the professional standpoint while being adaptable at all levels of play.

To purport that this is a complete book means that it is comprehensive (every facet of the game is discussed) and detailed (each of these facets is subjected to minute examination). In addition, the mental and psychological factors bearing on all phases of baseball, as well as the mechanics of play and their tactical use, are scrutinized at length.

The first section, "Coaching," discusses teaching philosophy and the educational aspects of the game while at the same time providing a day-by-day guide to the multitude of details implicit in coaching youngsters and developing a team to the point of game-readiness.

Defensive play is dealt with from both an individual and team standpoint and includes an exhaustive diagnosis of the pitching game. Offensive play is given similar treatment and its section on batting is a particularly detailed investigation of the art of hitting a baseball. Special note should be made of the chapter on base-running, a too-often neglected phase of the game, which is duly stressed and thoroughly explained.

The final section embraces rules interpretation and the analysis, pitch-by-pitch, of an actual ball game. The latter, in particular, reveals practical application of the techniques and tactics explained in the preceding text.

The entire volume is replete with new ideas, refinements, and embellishments pertaining to both the mechanics and strategy of individual and team play (quick-pitching the runner, new pick-offs at first and second, making a hitch work to the batter's advantage), with completely revised sections (a meticulous study of the curve ball, both types of double steal, the rundown—offensive and defensive), and several new sections (Reordering Priorities—A New Philosophy of Pitching, The Run-and-Bunt—Key to an Aggressive Running Game, Philosophy for an Effective Defense).

This inquiry into baseball has been done in a manner that might be defined as dissection, examination, and reconstruction. This technique consists of stating well-founded theories as well as developing new ones. The next step is breaking them down into their smallest components, investigating the reasoning behind each of these integral parts, and fitting them together in a unified whole. This method is predicated on the belief that the most effective system of teaching baseball begins with the propounding of basic premises and a thorough explanation of just why these are the most efficient means to good performance. When demonstration and application follow, the learning process should be complete. This, of course, is the role of the coach and, in turn, the player. It is hoped that the presentation of this material is such that these interested parties will be stimulated into effective completion of the whole.

If the primary aim of this book is the most complete study and explanation yet made of the fine art of baseball, its corollary objective is to enable the reader—player, coach, or fan—to derive greater benefit and enjoyment from the game through a more informed, intelligent, and logical viewpoint. If this is accomplished, in even slight degree, our great game will be richer for it.

LEW WATTS

# *Contents*

## *Coaching*

*Offense*

## BATTING—THE MENTAL ASPECT    295

## BASE-RUNNING    313

*Addenda*

# Coaching

# The Role of The Coach

The classical tradition of education has always proclaimed the value of athletics in the development of young people as well as its merit in maintaining sound adults. A coach's role is possibly even more important than that of the classroom teacher, because the instruction that he provides includes practical application. He is truly molding the whole man— the mental, physical, and spiritual being.

Every lasting value derived from athletics revolves around playing to win. Even a losing struggle has worth when it is played to the fullest, with victory as the one objective. Although we cannot win them all, an honest endeavor to do so will give lasting benefit to any participant.

Baseball, perhaps more than any other sport, combines both individual and team effort. The battle between pitcher and batter is an individual one; play in the field is performed by individual players with individual responsibilities; yet each man's own effort must be subordinated to that of the team. A game that can teach youngsters how to win their individual battles within a framework of cooperative enterprise is a remarkable and valuable one. In baseball the good of the group is always paramount, yet completely dependent upon the individual efforts of each man.

The coach should never lose sight of the fact that his teaching applies to the complete development of his charges—their mental, physical, and spiritual betterment. And how better can he do this than by showing each man just how much he *can* do, thus developing confidence, skill, and a spiritual bond between player and coach?

Obviously the main job of a coach is to organize his squad and to formulate his attack and his defense. Yet, because a squad is made up of human beings, through whom the attack and defense function, the psychological factor cannot be overemphasized. Sound knowledge of skills, strategy, and men is the basis of the successful teaching of baseball. Along with imparting correct techniques and tactics to his men, a coach must build a relationship with each of them that will enable the player, and consequently the team, to capitalize fully on his ability—to rise above the purely mechanical.

A healthy atmosphere of mutual respect demands that the coach make a close study of each player and learn as much as he can about his ability, personality, interests, and idiosyncrasies. This will help the coach to pinpoint the areas in which each man should try to improve his play; more importantly, it will build a squad's confidence in the coach. This is absolutely essential in creating a climate in which both individual and team performance flourish to the fullest possible extent.

Each player should be dealt with honestly and fairly. Favoritism and discrimination are absolutely forbidden. Furthermore, in developing a cohesive unit the lowliest substitute is just as important as the .400 hitter —and he should be made to feel that his role, small though it be, is essential to the overall success of the team. In truth, he should feel that the success of his team rests directly on him. This, more than any other single factor, will spur him to top performance.

A coach is, to a great extent, a salesman. His job, in this analogy, is to sell his players on their own ability, as well as on the worthiness of the system of play and teaching that he uses. Unquestionably the greatest factor in successful selling is enthusiasm. The coach must radiate enthusiasm, and he must kindle and rekindle it in every man to ensure consistent peak performance.

Generally, no offensive play should be made unless the coach has ordered it. It is unfair to burden the player with the responsibility for offensive tactics. The coach should also instruct his defense, especially in a close game. This will not affect a boy's confidence in himself. On the contrary, that confidence will be strengthened if he has faith that his coach can and will come to his aid whenever help is needed. Team morale stays at a high level when the coach does not shirk these responsibilities.

Mistakes should definitely be discussed, with a careful explanation of cause, effect, and proper therapy. But only mental errors should be criticized. Moreover, a coach should give credit for heads-up play, try to find something to praise in every boy who has appeared in a game, and periodically laud his bench—the boys who have not played—for their contributions to the team. This is the positive approach and is tremendously valuable in building team morale.

Serious disciplinary problems that demand a severe reprimand should be handled privately. Serious lapses on the ball field should be discussed at a team meeting but should never give rise to public beratement of a player during the course of a ballgame.

## DISCIPLINE

Any discussion of coaching philosophy is replete with the words *morale, cohesiveness, team spirit*—and rightfully so. These are the qualities that lift individual and team performance above the purely mechanical, and a coach should constantly strive for a high degree of this team character. One of the chief factors contributing to this winning atmosphere is discipline.

Good discipline of a baseball squad should not suggest a martinet constantly cracking a whip over his charges. Rather, it presumes the mutual respect of player and coach that is inspired by an air of cooperative helpfulness and that arises most effectively from a truly professional approach to the game; it is this aspiring to the best by using the proven methods of experts at their trade that makes scholastic athletics educational.

When Eddie Dyer was managing a good St. Louis Cardinal team, I was present at a clubhouse meeting during which his main theme was complimenting his squad on the way in which they were helping each other. Great as were the individual performances of such stars as Musial, Slaughter, Marion, and Schoendienst, it was the cohesive unity, the team spirit of this club, that had put it in first place.

An atmosphere of togetherness is absolutely essential to the team that would rise above its normal level of play—whether it be for an inning, a game, or a season. Here is the key to molding a group of individuals into a team—the word *together*.

Everything a ball club does should be done together. In this way the essential spirit of unity can best be built. The members of the squad should associate with one another as much as possible: they should eat together, talk, study, and date together, stick together on road trips, dress together in the locker room, and, above all, they should take the field together—as a team.

The members of a baseball squad can take pride in the fact that they belong to something special—an athletic team that should be representative of their school.

With this justifiable pride must go the responsibility of wearing it well. Appearance and conduct off the field, as well as on, should be exemplary. This is the point at which discipline—the right kind—takes its roots. The members of a baseball squad should act the part of prideful, skilled gentlemen, worthy representatives of their school and their team.

A coach should insist on neatness off the field—good grooming means clean shaves, neat if not trim haircuts, appropriate clothes—and he should absolutely demand it on the field, where it involves sanitation, protection, practicality, and common sense.

It is a great privilege to wear a baseball uniform, and a man worthy of it should wear it properly; that is, with no exceptions or deviations. Furthermore, the uniform is not merely decorative; it has the definite purpose of allowing a man freedom of movement within the bounds of protectiveness.

Here are some suggestions for uniforms, equipment and appearance:

1. All players should dress alike. No extremes will be allowed.
2. No rings or jewelry should be worn. Nails must be cut short at all times.
3. Supporters, inner hose, and undershirts should be changed often and kept clean, for sanitary purposes.
4. Stockings should be rolled into a wide, thick band just below the knee joint, for protective purposes. Supporters should be worn over the undershirt to prevent the latter from pulling out; sliding pads are worn over the shirt and supporter. In this way the uniform will stay in place and provide the most protection.
5. Long-sleeved undershirts should be worn in the spring.
6. Jackets should be worn going to and from the field and be fully buttoned whenever worn.
7. Shoes should fit snugly; cotton inner hose should be worn. Shoes should be cleaned and polished daily. They are a ballplayer's most important tool. Black shoelaces should be worn by all players.
8. No oil should be used on gloves. The slightly shorter wear given by an unoiled glove is more than offset by the fact that a ball hitting the pocket of an unoiled glove does not become slippery. This point is doubly important for pitchers and catchers.
9. Players must look neat. They should stick together, especially when taking the field. Finally, everyone but the game pitcher should run at all times when on the ball field.

Insistence on these rules, or on similar ones, is the first step in building a disciplined, cohesive organization. The second step is to teach properly and in such a way that instructions will be carried out and correct moves made at all times.

Paul Richards was a great disciplinarian and an outstanding manager. It is his theory that during spring training every member of his squad—from the greenest rookie to the most grizzled veteran—must be treated as though he were completely inexperienced. Every mechanical move, every tactical maneuver, every possible play situation must be explained, taught, and practiced until its proper execution becomes almost automatic during a ball game. This method can develop a player who is at once assured, alert, and well disciplined.

The subtle kind of discipline that results in alert play and correct execution stems from an approach in which the coach must follow these practices:

1. Cover every possible play situation in preseason practice sessions.
2. Explain and demonstrate the correct maneuvers: knowing the purpose for and logic behind every drill helps to prevent their being drudgery.

3. Inject competition into practice sessions whenever possible.
4. Avoid overly long, tedious drills and practice sessions.
5. Teach your squad to think in correct patterns, along your own carefully devised lines. This can save much anguish and unnecessary hard feeling during games.
6. Remember that a coach's performance on the field should be as conscientious, systematic, and well planned as a teacher's performance in the class room.

In this way baseball can be made both educational and enjoyable, as it should be.

## THE BENCH

A usually neglected factor in building a winning spirit is the bench. So much effort is devoted to fielding a good nine that the men on the bench are too often neglected—left to twiddle their thumbs, as it were.

On too many occasions reserve players can be seen lolling around the bench area, indulging in horseplay or engaged in a slovenly game of catch. This cannot be tolerated if good discipline and team morale are to be achieved.

Baseball is a team game, and *team* means every man who is in uniform. Every member of a squad should be in the ball game at all times— mentally and spiritually. In this way he can perform four valuable functions:

1. He gears himself for the time when he will be in the game.
2. He lends an air of class to his team.
3. He contributes to the morale of his teammates who are playing.
4. He may uncover valuable information about the opponent that will give his team the winning advantage.

An orderly, alert bench reflects good coaching, the kind that insists upon attention to detail and instills in every squad member the belief that he is an integral part of a successful organization. The bench, individually and as a unit, is the tenth man in the lineup.

The coach who seeks to build a hustling bench will insist that substitutes—

1. keep their attention riveted on the game at all times. Periodic checks help ensure this;
2. lend vocal encouragement to the men on the field;
3. help them whenever possible, by doing such things as informing the

catcher when the runner is stealing ("There he goes!"), informing the pitcher who starts his motion unaware that one of his teammates is out of position, shouting instructions to a player who pursues a fly ball near the bench or home-plate area; and performing similar acts that are to be expected of the "team man";

4. act as housekeepers for the bench area. Retrieving a stray ball, bat or glove may prevent injury to a player whose attention is concentrated on the ball;

5. attempt to discover opponents' signals, unconventional maneuvers, telltale positioning, and pitching "tip-offs";

6. look for lapses on the part of his own team and report them *to the coach* for correction;

7. study the opposing batters. This applies to pitchers and catchers, especially the ones due to go into the game next; with these players the practice should be mandatory.

In this way baseball can truly be a team game, as it should be.

## SCOUTING

A thorough coaching job will prepare every player for any eventuality that may arise on the ball field. Advance knowledge of the time when specific situations will occur would indeed be too good to be true. In absence of it a team should be able to look for the probable, in order to gear itself to cope properly with most of the play situations encountered in a game. It is here that scouting can prove invaluable.

If the opportunity exists to scout an opponent, a coach should, by all means, take advantage of it—along with his catcher and probable starting pitcher, whenever possible.

In my first year of coaching (at the college level) I was able to scout six of our opponents. We defeated them all, although at least two of them had ball clubs superior to ours. Undoubtedly, the psychological effect of knowing what to expect of our opponents had much to do with this success. Also important was the fact that playing strategy could be planned—always better than having to rely strongly on improvisation.

Professional clubs endeavor to compile a complete "book" on their opponents. This is both possible and important in organized baseball, because each opponent will be met numerous times during the season. Naturally, the brevity of an interscholastic season and the annual turnover of players make intensive scouting at the school level neither possible nor practical.

When the schedule of the schools involved permits, an attempt should be made to observe future opponents in game competition. A cursory inspection of a team's style of play and the characteristics of its key players, as well as of any apparent flaws in its game, should be the primary targets of a scouting expedition. Here is a brief listing of the essential points of observation:

## Offense

### Team

1. Do they bunt, steal, or start the runner? If so, when?
2. Is there a particular team strategy? Does the manager favor certain tactics? Do they play for a big inning or go in for a running game?

### Individual

1. Who are their pull, opposite-field, and straightaway hitters? Who hits with power?
2. What pitch does each hitter like? Does he have an apparent weakness? Is he a first-ball hitter?
3. Who are their fast men?

## Defense

### Team

1. What are the strong and weak points of the defense?
2. How do they look against bunts or a running game?
3. Do they bring their infield in any time a runner reaches third base?
4. Do they give the opponent second base on a double steal?
5. Does the third baseman charge the plate whenever a batter squares around?

### Individual

1. What are the strengths and weaknesses of the pitcher? What is his pitching pattern? What are his habits? What does he go to when in the clutch? When behind the hitter? Do base runners upset him? Does he work in a regular cadence with men on base?
2. How does the catcher handle himself? Can and will he throw?
3. How does the outfield throw? Are they fast?
4. How does the second-short duo handle the ball on relays and double steals?

If no opportunity existed to scout a team, there is still one good means of getting advance information: pregame practice (and, to a certain extent, the early innings of the ball game). The field, the weather, and the opponent's players should be taken into consideration.

### The Field (for a road game)

1. If the field is of skin, the ball will skip, and bunts will roll more rapidly. If the field is grass, the ball will roll more slowly but will hop more frequently.
2. An outfield fence demands more careful pitching to men who can reach the short parts of it. Outfielders should test the fences for resiliency and angle of bounce; they should also allow for the carom in backing up one another.
3. How far is the backstop from home plate? Can you run on a passed ball?

### The Weather

1. Wet field: Be prepared for a bunting game. Outfielders should charge ground balls. A base runner must begin his slide sooner.
2. Sunny field: Who should have glasses? The team should be aware of the possible need to assist a man playing a high fly in the sun.
3. Windy day: How will the wind affect the flight of a fly ball or the action of the pitcher's curve ball?
4. Night game: Where are the dark spots on the field? Which players should be made aware of them?

### The Opponents

**Offense.** A complete "book" is not needed. In batting practice look for their pull hitters, for the men who are likely to bunt, those who look weak on the curve ball, those who overstride (pitch them high), those who appear nervous or overanxious (wait on them), and for those who are overly muscular (jam them). What pitches do their good batters hit well in practice—high or low, fast ball or curve?

**Defense.** How does each of them throw? Does the third baseman seem weak on bunts? In the early innings of a ball game one can gain revealing insights into the opponent's pattern of play. For example, a team that bunts early in the game will surely do so in the late innings. Individual weaknesses may also reveal themselves. Important here is the possibility of the catcher's signals being picked up by a base coach, or the pitcher himself tipping his deliveries. Information of this sort can be passed along to any batter who desires it and may also be used to guide a team's use of the steal, a propitious move when a curve or change has been signalled.

## THE BATTING ORDER

A team's batting order should be selected along logical, if not scientific lines. Professional managers give much thought to the choice, and even the development, of the right man for each spot in the offensive lineup. Periodic refinements are made according to individual performance, type of ballpark, and opposing pitcher. A professional manager, with a large squad of well-trained specialists, playing a long season on a daily basis, can afford this approach. With an entirely different set of circumstances facing them, scholastic coaches *cannot adopt the same methods.* Greater thought and different reasoning should govern the selection of the batting order of an amateur or scholastic team, with its prevalence of weak spots.

In general a team's best hitters should be at the top of the batting list in order to assure them a maximum number of times at bat. Furthermore, the strength of the first five hitters should build to a high point with number three and then taper off. There is, however, no formula for selecting the batting order; common-sense rules may guide a coach to the refinements that will give him the most effective offensive lineup possible.

The leadoff man is expected to get on base often, in any way possible. He should have a good eye, be fast of foot, and be a good base runner. Power may be of little moment because of the weak hitters who precede him in the lineup. Yet, a man capable of reaching second base on his own can add greatly to a team's scoring potential because of the men who follow him in the lineup. If the choice is between a lefty or a righty, the right-hander should lead off, with the left-hander in the number-two spot.

The number-two hitter has, as his primary requisite, the ability to get a piece of the ball. Ideally, he is left handed because it is assumed that the leadoff man will get on base often. A left-handed number-two batter will make it easier for the runner to steal, will have a bigger hole to go for with the first baseman holding the bag against the runner, and will be more likely to advance the runner with a batted ball that will, in most cases, go toward right field.

The number-three hitter will probably be the best hitter on the club. He should be faster than number four, because he will generally have more opportunity to score; if one hits left-handed and the other right-handed, he should be the right-hander. Where two or more factors can go into the selection of a hitter, they should be weighed very carefully, with almost equal consideration given them.

The cleanup man should be one of the two best hitters, with the primary consideration (unlike the case of number three) being sheer power.

Number five will generally be the poorest of the big three, but he should, nevertheless, hit well and with power.

Number six is sometimes known as the second leadoff man. Like number one he should have the ability to get on base; but of the two, he should be the power hitter, for he will have more opportunities to drive in runs. If speed is the determining factor, the number-six hitter will be slower than number one. If one of the two is a lefty batter, and the other a righty, the former should fill the number-six slot.

The last three men in the lineup can be taken as a group. At the end of the order, runs should be played for one at a time. Naturally, the hope will be to reach the top of the order with one of the weak hitters on base. Another objective is to avoid leading off an inning with one of the poorest hitters. For this reason a more conservative game should be played when the end of the batting order is reached. It would be wise to have these men try to work the pitcher for a walk. The extra pitches he may have to throw will also leave him with a little less on the ball for the good hitters. The seventh, eighth, and ninth men to bat should also try merely to get a piece of the ball, hoping to reach base on an error.

In professional ball the catcher usually bats eighth and the pitcher ninth, not only because they are often weak hitters, but also because they are not in the lineup every day, and their presence elsewhere in the order would disrupt it constantly. In amateur ball, with far fewer and more widely scattered games, this is not necessary, and good-hitting catchers and pitchers should be spotted where they will bat more often. In the case of a pitcher who, though not outstanding with the stick, is a better hitter than two or three of his teammates, it may be best to bat him ninth so as to conserve his strength for the mound. The fact that colleges play nine innings, rather than seven as in high schools, will also weigh in favor of their having the pitcher bat ninth.

When two or more left-handed batters are in the lineup, the coach should spot them strategically, to help his team's running game. Unless the more conventional considerations weigh heavily against it, a left-handed batter should be placed behind a man who will reach base often, especially a fast one. For example, a lefty is more desirable in the number-two spot than as leadoff man, and at the end of the order he should be placed in the seventh slot rather than the eighth or ninth, where he is less likely to come to the plate with men on base. A deviation that may, with some justification, be preferred by a coach is the placing of a good hitter in the seventh spot rather than near the top of the order, where he would come to bat more often. The idea here would be to break up a possible three sure outs in quick succession. A good-hitting pitcher would fit ideally into this position.

Whatever the lineup, a team must adhere to it carefully during a game lest they lose an out for batting out of order. It is wise to station a scorekeeper on the bench to prevent its happening—and to keep alert for its befalling the opposing ball club.

## MANAGER'S DUTIES

A coach's primary responsibility is the mental and physical preparation of his squad and the direction of its play on the field. The many tasks not directly connected with the playing of the game but necessary to the proper conduct of a baseball schedule demand the delegation of authority. Here is encountered the need for a competent nonplaying manager, usually a member of the student body.

A conscientious, efficient manager is a great boon to any coach; in order to attract the right man, the organization must stress the importance of the job and the prestige that it should carry.

Because a topflight manager is a desirable commodity, the process of selection should be a careful one. Willingness to work and a good degree of capability are the main prerequisites in selection. The system of apprenticeship commonly used, with perhaps two freshmen, two sophomores, and a junior as assistants to the senior manager, serves as a good means of selection for the top position.

The more competent his manager and the more willing his assistant managers, the less gruelling will be a coach's job. Close supervision of the managerial staff is necessary for the smooth running of the baseball program. Nevertheless, a coach cannot have too many extraneous demands on his time if his primary mission is to be accomplished well. For this reason he must select carefully, inspire constantly, and delineate his manager's duties explicitly.

Here is a suggested routine for the managerial staff. Times listed are arbitrary and may be altered to conform with school hours:

## Practice

1. Keep an inventory of equipment on hand and a record of all equipment issued to each player. Keep equipment clean. Get replacements (bats and balls) from the coach when needed.
2. Have all equipment on the field at 2:30 daily (1:00 on Saturdays). See that bases are in place.
3. Keep track of equipment in use, especially balls and bats.
4. Keep a fresh supply of water for use by the players.
5. Have two managers present at all times—one on the field, one near the bench. (A rotating schedule may be used.)

## Game Routine (*for a 2:30 game*)

1. One manager should be assigned to the visiting team upon their arrival.
2. Managers should have all equipment on the field and should be preparing the field for the game by 1:00.
3. Water and towels should be placed in each dugout; a game ball should be delivered to the opposing team's coach; a knife, for cleaning spikes, and spare shoe laces should be placed in the home team dugout.
4. Batter's boxes will be marked just prior to the start of the game (during the pregame conference with umpires).
5. All loose equipment should be removed from the playing area.
6. One manager should be prepared to take notes in the dugout during the game. He should record the coach's comments on each player of both teams as he comes to bat. He should also have the facilities for recording notes on each type of pitch and situation for home team pitchers.
7. Towels should be ready for the visiting team after the game.

## Road Games

1. Submit to the school office a list of all men making the trip. Each name should be checked off as that man reports to the bus.
2. Have all necessary equipment on the bus fifteen minutes before departure time (check with coaches to make a list of all equipment to be taken on the trip).
3. Obtain towels (at least three) and water for your bench and arrange all equipment at the bench. Obtain towels for use after the game.
4. Have a small traveling bag available for checking the valuables of your players, and be custodian of the same.

5. Check all your equipment to see that it is on hand for the return trip. Unload and store the same on your return.

Managers may be delegated the authority for obtaining transportation, handling money, and arranging for rooms and meals on the road. In most cases it is best for the coach or faculty advisor to do so. This decision will depend to a great extent on the reliability of the manager and the coach's faith in him.

## INJURIES AND THEIR TREATMENT

Proper conditioning of a ball club, even before outdoor work is begun, will preclude the possibility of many injuries, certainly most of those that result from sore muscles and poor coordination. Preseason training should include lectures by the coach and trainer on good health habits, personal hygiene, and injury prevention. It is the responsibility of the coach to see that all injuries are recognized and given proper treatment.

A team physician should be retained by the school. Whenever feasible he should administer physical checkups to the squad before the start of preseason work. He should take the additional precaution of ascertaining that all players have had antitetanus inoculations. Having performed these initial duties as team physician, he should serve more in the role of a consultant. He should attend to all apparently serious injuries as well as those that do not respond properly to treatment. He should also instruct and advise the coach and trainer on the handling of minor injuries that may rightfully fall within their province.

In addition to ministering to routine needs of the players and the treatment of minor injuries, the coach and trainer must see that good sanitary habits are practiced. Clean showers, well-ventilated dressing quarters, and clean uniforms are necessities to a well-organized ball club, and the coach should see that this standard of sanitation is maintained. If possible, fresh inner hose, undershirts, and jocks should be provided for each player every day. When economy prevents this, the players should be charged with this responsibility.

### Avoiding Injuries

There are several precautionary measures that should be taken by all ballplayers. Observance of them will help prevent needless injuries. A coach should instruct his squad to observe the following precautions:

1. Don't wear rings or jewelry, and keep fingernails clipped.

2. Always wear clean underclothes—shirts, socks, and supporter.
3. Shower and change immediately after every game or workout.
4. Stretch and loosen up thoroughly before every game or practice session, and condition yourself very gradually early in the season.
5. Never slide unnecessarily, and keep the forward foot in the air when you do slide.
6. Avoid indecision in sliding—once you have decided either to slide or stay up, do so.
7. Avoid the headfirst slide, which causes head and facial injuries.
8. Advise and warn a player who is chasing a fly ball near the fence, screen, or dugout.
9. Keep all bats in the bat rack, where they cannot cause injury.
10. Never turn your back on a play that is in progress.
11. Don't stand in front of a base when a runner is nearing it; this protects the opposing players. It is a coach's duty to see that his men do not contribute to the unnecessary injury of an opponent.
12. Don't stand behind the batter; if lack of space makes this necessary, be sure that you face him.
13. Always keep your eye on the pitcher once you have entered the batter's box.
14. Catch the ball with the fingers slightly bent—never extended.
15. Call all fly balls and obey the call, to avoid collisions.
16. Bunt properly—don't hold the bat directly in front of the body, but keep the fingers of the upper hand behind the bat.
17. Don't try to be a hero if incapacitated—report all injuries. An injured player is of no help to his team.

### Treating Injuries

Certain minor injuries are relatively common and can be treated quite easily and fairly effectively by the coach or trainer. If a doctor is available, he should be consulted for all injuries, and, above all, he should be called on when an ailment persists.

1. *Sprains*: These are serious injuries and should be treated by a physician as soon as possible.
   (a) Ankle: Apply ice or cold pack immediately (ethyl chloride when authorized by the team physician); use a pressure bandage; resume normal movements (not heavy exercise) as soon as possible.
   (b) Knee: Treat the same as an ankle sprain, but stay off it.
   (c) Wrist: Treat the same way; bandage with alternate circular longitudinal layers of tape.

(d) Finger: Apply ice; tape it to the next finger for protection.

2. *Charley horse and muscle bruise*: Apply ice at once; then heat (moist heat is preferable to dry), massage; exercise lightly.

3. *Stone bruise*: Apply ice packs; avoid using injured part; protect with a sponge rubber pad.

4. *Pulled thigh muscle*: Place a band of tape one inch above the injury and one inch below it.

5. *Shin splint*: Apply heat; massage; then use a counterirritant.

6. *Burns*: Apply a disinfectant, then a dusting powder on a vanishing cream base; protect with a sponge bandage—don't use petroleum jelly, which keeps it soft.

7. *Blisters*: Leave unopened; cover with a bandage; if open, treat like a burn.

8. *Jock itch*: Apply dusting powder; place a folded handkerchief inside the supporter.

9. *Sore arm*: Do not work it out—heat and rest are the best remedy; rotation of the limb while under a very hot shower is good; massage is very helpful but should be done only by an experienced "rubber."

10. *Spike wounds*: Cleanse with soap and water; apply a disinfectant and bandage; consult a physician as soon as possible for the advisability of suturing.

11. If the effects of a minor injury persist, a physician should be consulted. Whirlpool baths, infrared lamps, and diathermy have greatly facilitated the treatment of athletic injuries. But they are not for use by the neophyte. An experienced trainer or coach, in absence of a doctor, should supervise their usage and administer treatment.

A well-equipped medicine kit should be available whenever a team is on the field. As a minimum it should include:

| | |
|---|---|
| tape | oral screw |
| gauze | sulfathiazole |
| ace bandages | ethyl chloride (with phy- |
| band-aids | sician's approval) |
| bunion plasters | tincture of green soap |
| sponge pads | smelling salts |
| doughnuts (rubber) | aspirin |
| dusting powder | antacid tablets |
| fungicide | rubbing alcohol |
| vanishing-cream | liniment |
| disinfectant | salt tablets |
| instant cold packs | Vitamin C (cold pre- |
| scissors | ventative) |
| | skin toughener |

## CARE OF THE FIELD

A coach will presumably not have to maintain his own ball field. Yet he must have a rudimentary knowledge of baseball groundskeeping if he is to supervise his caretaking crew in keeping the field in constant readiness for play.

A well-kept field that is, at all times, as level and dry as possible, and without loose stones, roots, or soft spots, not only facilitates better play but also can contribute greatly to injury prevention.

Here is a basic guide to proper care of a ball field:

1. The grass should be cut weekly and the cut grass left on the field. Cutting should be done before rolling.
2. The field should be watered weekly.
3. The field should be rolled weekly.
4. Fences and screens should be kept in constant good repair.
5. The mound, plate, and base paths should be dragged and tamped daily.
6. The recommended composition of the mound and the batter's box is three parts brick dust to one part loam or two and one-half parts clay to one part loam.
7. If the field is too soft, add loam.
   If the field is too dry, add sand.
8. After rain, wet areas can be drained by short lengths of pipe driven into the ground.
   After draining, the damp area should be leveled off and dry sand or dirt applied. This should be raked in and more added as needed.
   All skin areas should be raked; the diamond dragged; the pitcher's box and plate area tamped as well as raked; and the lines re-marked.
9. The recommended minimum equipment includes the following:
   small tarps (5) for mound, plate, and base areas
   rake
   shovels
   mat (for dragging)
   tamper
   dry sand and dirt
   wheelbarrow

# *Practice and Conditioning*

The aim of any coach should be to prepare his team so well that it will build sufficient momentum to carry it successfully through the season. Very often the difference between a good start and a bad one is indoor work.

Gym workouts, in order to be effective, must be purposeful and carefully planned. In fact, indoor practice sessions of a haphazard sort can have a deleterious consequence in two important respects—team discipline can deteriorate to an irretrievably low level, and a sore arm or other crippling injury can be sustained by a key man before the start of the season.

Indoor workouts should be preceded by weekly team meetings, beginning the second week in January. These sessions should cover everything that will be taught to the squad before a condition of game-readiness is achieved, including these points:

1. Approach to the game and educational philosophy
2. Training and discipline
3. Defensive techniques and tactics
4. Offensive techniques and tactics
5. Rules
6. Future plans—schedule, practice, and training routine

The use of a mimeographed study guide is strongly recommended. If all-inclusive, it can save much valuable time on the practice field because the material covered when actual physical work begins will not be completely unfamiliar to any squad member.


## PITCHING READINESS

Because a baseball team's entire operation revolves around its pitching staff, its training period should do so too. The section on pitching includes several suggestions on the individual conditioning of pitchers. It would be wise to review this material for the edification of the coach who will supervise the overall training procedure. With this as a guide to conditioning devices, a day-by-day schedule of throwing activity will be outlined. It is assumed that training work of a more general nature will be added to this regimen in an attempt to integrate the preparation of the pitching staff with that of the entire squad.

Weekly squad meetings will begin the second week in January. They should be conducted regularly until the middle of February, at which time pitchers (and catchers) will start their actual physical work. The entire squad will report on a full-time basis two weeks later.

The routine outlined below pertains only to the conditioning of the arm itself. Other activity should be added by the coach.

Calisthenics are only incidental to the physical preparation of a base-ball squad. Conditioning of the legs by running, and of the arm by throwing, are the most important facets of preseason workouts—especially for pitchers. For that reason it is recommended that calisthenics be engaged in for only the first two weeks—not in an excessive amount and never in a way that is contrary to baseball's regular muscular actions. Loose muscle exercises are the most effective ones.

Before any physical work is attempted, common-sense precautionary measures should be formulated as mandatory rules for the squad. Suggested ones are as follows:

1. Workouts will be carried out only under the direct supervision of the coach.
2. No throwing should be done until a player has thoroughly loosened his muscles by stretching exercises. In order to fully lubricate the bursar tendon of the shoulder it is strongly recommended that the arm be allowed to hang limp from the shoulder and be rotated counterclockwise for ten to fifteen seconds.
3. Hard throwing should be attempted only after a player is fully warmed up.
4. All injuries, including sore arms, must be reported to the coach immediately.

### Pitching Schedule

This sequence of arm conditioning assumes a hypothetical opening date of April 7, with the second game scheduled for April 10. It is presumed that Saturday workouts will be held—at least for pitchers—and that indoor sessions will be conducted during inclement weather.

The routine is designed to prepare two pitchers for starting duty. Until they are definitely selected (by March 1), all pitching candidates should follow this schedule. Relief men and added starters may be trained similarly and at the coach's discretion. Once the entire squad has reported, there should always be a batter in position during these

```
            Pitcher A                                    Pitcher B

Feb.18(Tu) - 5 minutes throwing          Feb.18(Tu) - 5 minutes throwing
    19(W)  - 5      "        "                19(W)  - 5      "        "
    20(Th) - 5      "        "                20(Th) - 5      "        "
    22(S)  - 10     "        "                22(S)  - 10     "        "
    24(M)  - 10     "        "                24(M)  - 10     "        "
    26(W)  - 10     "        "                26(W)  - 10     "        "
    28(F)  - 10     "        "                27(Th) - 5      "        "
    29(S)  - 5      "        "                29(S)  - 15     "        "

Mar. 2(M)  - 15     "        "           Mar. 2(M)  - 15     "        "
    4(W)   - 15     "        "                4(W)   - 15     "        "
    6(F)   - 15     "        "                7(S)   - 3  innings pitching
    9(M)   - 3  innings pitching                          (51 pitches)
               (51 pitches)                  10(Tu) - 3      "
    11(W)  - 3  innings                       12(Th) - 3      "
    13(F)  - 3      "                         14(S)  - 3      "
    16(M)  - 3      "                         17(Tu) - 5  innings
    18(W)  - 5  innings                                     (85 pitches)
               (85 pitches)                   20(F)  - 5      "
    21(S)  - 5      "                         23(M)  - 5      "
    24(Tu) - 5      "                         26(Th) - 5      "
    27(F)  - 5      "                         30(M)  - 5      "
    30(M)  - 6  innings
               (102 pitches)             Apr. 2(Th) - 6  innings
                                                        (102 pitches)
Apr. 3(F)  - 7  innings
               (119 pitches)                 6(M)   - 7  innings
    6(M)   - 5  minutes light throwing                   (119 pitches)
    7(Tu)  - GAME                           9(Th)  - 5  minutes light throwing
                                            10(F)  - GAME
```

(a)  Timed throwing is an overall figure, representing total throwing.

(b)  Innings pitched is in addition to a thorough warm-up.

(c)  Part of every workout should be devoted to pitching from a stretch.

(d)  A pitcher should always throw for strikes. When the full squad reports and
     a batter is assigned to a pitcher, his catcher should serve as umpire.

(e)  A pitcher should know his own arm and make sure that his coach also does.

pitching drills. When outdoor work commences, this plan may be integrated with batting practice and intrasquad games.

Squad meetings will have been held on Mondays throughout January and up to, and including, February 17. The last of these sessions should be followed by physical work for batterymen, including calisthenics (continue these for two weeks) and leg work (running and "pick-ups," which should be continued by the pitchers all season, except on days when they pitch).

## THE FULL SQUAD

Pitchers and catchers will have been working for two weeks when the other players report for duty and should be in a fair state of readiness. Calisthenics are no longer necessary for them. The rest of the squad should engage in them during the first week of their conditioning period.

The various phases of conditioning a baseball team and the devices for achieving readiness in each of them while the squad is confined to the gymnasium are as follows:

## Indoor Phase

### Calisthenics

ERECT: Jumping jack, windmill, trunk twister
SITTING: Alternate toe-toucher
PRONE: Stomach rocker, up-and-down (to standing position and back)
SUPINE: Sit-ups, toe-toucher, bicycle

### General Exercise

Volley ball is an excellent conditioner and can occupy the entire squad at one time. Furthermore, it adds a competitive element to an otherwise tedious routine.

Pepper games are valuable for the accomplishment of several things. Fielding, batting, throwing, and good bodily exercise are being practiced at one time. Several pepper games can be held simultaneously if the ball is hit down one alley with the fielders taking turns. The man who has fielded the ball goes to the end of the line, and the others move up, in turn.

*Conditioning: pick-ups for the pitchers*

### Leg Conditioners

**Running.** Much running should be done by all players. This is doubly necessary for pitchers. Running should be in the form of wind-sprints.

**Pick-ups.** This is one of the most beneficial of conditioning devices, excellent for the legs and good for the entire body. It is done by having one player, stationed about eight feet away, roll a ball to another player —first to one side, then the other, in an arc of about ten feet. The latter must pick up the ball with two hands and return it with an underhand toss. (Actually, this can be done by one man, by simulating the pick-up and toss.) This exercise should be started with about twenty-five pick-ups and be increased until fifty is reached on a once-a-day basis. Along with their running, the pitchers should continue this exercise all season.

### Batting

**The Still Head.** One of the most important factors in achieving good batting performance is the maintaining of a still head (and level eyes) throughout the entire hitting action. Its accomplishment should be acquired in gradual steps, the first of which is merely swinging a bat. An effective way of checking on head movement is to have a strong light (the sun, when outdoors) behind the hitter. The coach or another player then places his foot on the shadow of the batter's head. A full swing is taken, the object being to take the cut with the "head remaining underfoot." This should be repeated many times, until the head remains consistently still, and should be checked daily throughout the training period and whenever game performance indicates a possible lapse in the practice of this basic.

**Batting Tee.** The next step in acquiring good batting habits is to swing at a ball—stationary in this case. Indoor use of a batting tee may require using sponge rubber balls. This gadget, easily constructed, enables a coach to check the batting form of each player and to apply corrective therapy as needed. Hand position, distribution of weight, stride, swing, follow-through, and the level head are things to watch, for possible correction.

**Batting Practice.** When a coach is satisfied that his players have achieved effective individual hitting form, they should progress to regular batting practice.

Sponge rubber or tennis balls, can be used. A pitching machine, if available, should serve as batting practice pitcher. In the absence of one, players can be used—but never a pitcher.

A regular batting cage can be set up with nets. If this is impractical, a heavy curtain of asbestos or similar material can be stretched across the gym at the midway point. Balls hit into this drop harmlessly to the floor. The batter, practice pitcher (if used), and three men waiting to hit should be the maximum number in the batting area at one time. The rest of the squad should be engaged in regular practice activity in the other half of the gym.

If no such equipment is available, one method of batting practice remains—the use of a whiffle ball. This enables players to swing at a moving ball while in no way endangering fixtures or persons. Furthermore, two groups can engage in batting practice simultaneously, one at either end of the floor, since a whiffle ball travels with little force. No player should throw a whiffle ball; a manager or other nonparticipant should do the pitching.

**Ball-on-a-String.** This is a tool useful in helping a player learn to cope with the curve ball. Because indoor batting practice pitching will consist of nothing but straight throws, this method can be valuable as a preparation for the breaking balls that will be encountered when outdoor work is begun.

The necessary equipment includes a high jump standard, a ten-to-twelve-foot length of cord, and a rubber ball. One end of the cord is affixed to the top of the standard, the other to the ball. The batter stands in hitting position, the length of the cord removed from the standard. Another player propels the ball in whip-like fashion. As it nears the batter, he attempts to meet the ball squarely. This provides practice in hitting a ball that is breaking as it nears the plate.

**Hip Pivot.** A good batting swing is given its impetus by a hip pivot. The hips should begin to rotate into the ball before any other bodily move takes place. Hip action carries the entire body through the swing. For this reason it is wise to begin all phases of batting practice with a hip-turning drill.

**Bunting.** This vital phase of batting can be fully perfected indoors. The value of bunting practice is that the batter, though confined to a gymnasium, can accustom himself to facing actual pitching—with a baseball.

A fully equipped catcher should assume his normal position behind the plate. The pitcher should throw fairly hard from about forty feet away, thereby helping the bunter acquire skill in performing this difficult maneuver. The batter should practice the sacrifice (bunting only a good pitch), the squeeze (bunting the next pitch); and the bunt-for-a-hit. Foul lines should be chalked on the floor, and a bunt will be considered a good one when it is in fair territory, near the foul line.

If there is enough room, infielders should be in position. In this way the men who will handle bunts under game conditions can practice fielding them. Throws to the bases should be "lobbed."

Even when space is limited, the pitcher should be required to capitalize on this opportunity to practice handling bunts.

### Base-running

The vital contribution that running can make to the conditioning of a ball club in general, and to pitchers in particular, has already been emphasized. Valuable purpose can be given to running by combining it with practice in base-running.

Whether done individually or in groups, it should be performed as though a base runner were tagging up on a fly ball or breaking for the next base on a steal. The two starting positions can be used alternately for wind sprints.

Tagging up: The left foot should be on the bag and the weight forward; a full start made as soon as the ball hits the glove of the coach, who simulates a catch.

Steal: Players should take a lead by backing off the bag; face the pitcher with feet spread and weight evenly distributed on the balls of the feet; a pivot and crossover step permit the most effective start, the signal being a simulated pitching motion performed by the coach.

Sliding: Those fields that have a field house or cage provide outdoor conditions for this phase of practice. Nevertheless, a sliding pit should be used to prevent leg injuries.

The intricate technique of correct sliding can be perfected even when no better facilities than a gymnasium floor are available. Indoor sliding practice should be done only at half speed and in stocking feet in order to lessen the possibility of injury. Furthermore, only a short run should be used.

### Individual Drills

Although the primary purpose of indoor workouts is the overall conditioning of the entire squad and the perfection of skills that pertain to all players, many phases of individual position play can be covered and practiced to a degree of perfection. The greater the mastery of these maneuvers achieved indoors, the greater a team's state of readiness when it takes the field.

*Pitcher*: In addition to arm conditioning and the handling of bunts, work should be done on covering first base, the pick-off move, and the fielding of ground balls.

*Catcher*: The catcher, too, will have practiced fielding bunts. He should also be drilled in shifting, handling low pitches, hiding signs, proper handling of his mitt (bringing the ball toward his belt buckle), cocking his arm, and throwing to a base (if space permits).

*First baseman*: Added to his work in fielding bunts should be ground balls, feeding the pitcher, correct footwork, holding the runner, and much practice in handling low throws.

*Second-Short*: The second baseman and shortstop should be given much work in fielding ground balls. The first few grounders each day should be fielded with the right hand held behind the back, in order to ensure correct glove position. Even more time should be devoted to making the double play, with emphasis on feeding the ball properly and on learning the several patterns of footwork involved in making the pivot.

*Third baseman*: Fielding ground balls is of importance, and the hand-behind-back routine is recommended here. Special stress should be placed on the handling of bunts and slow rollers, the initial work each day being performed with a stationary ball.

*Outfielders*: Outfielders should be drilled on footwork, hand technique, ground balls, flies (moderately thrown), and their most difficult play—the line drive (thrown).

In any preseason work, indoors or out, the coach's main concern should be to keep everyone busy with (and interested in) purposeful activity. Provided every man undergoes thorough conditioning, the squad, when selected, will be at close to playing readiness.

### Outdoor Phase

Planning a definite timed schedule for preseason work is difficult because springtime weather is so uncertain in much of the country. Thus, any set routine or, for that matter, any single practice device must be worked into the overall preseason schedule as the weather permits. The step-by-step execution of a comprehensive training routine will be possible only if there should be an early stretch of good weather. Improvisation, then, is important in the achievement of a condition of game-readiness. Yet a master plan of complete squad training must be used as a guide to each segment of any given workout.

#### Batting Practice

Although the conditioning of a baseball team rightfully revolves primarily around the pitching staff, the greater part of any workout centers on batting practice. This, too, is correct, because batting is the one activity common to every player. Fortunately, a well-organized batting drill enables every player to practice his individual position play. Conversely, a slovenly hitting session accomplishes little of real value and is the sign of a poorly coached team.

The first step in every session of batting practice should be to divide the squad into two teams. This results in two definite assets to both coach and team—(1) an uncluttered field with every player engaged in purposeful activity and (2) more and better practice for each player.

**Corollary Activity.** Supernumeraries, if any, should be kept busy at all times and must be given their turns at bat and in the field. While otherwise unoccupied, they should be engaged in warming up pitchers, hitting fungoes (or retrieving for the fungo hitter), and playing pepper. Except for the batter and man on deck, members of the offensive team should busy themselves playing pepper and performing still-head and hip-turning drills. In absence of an adequate managerial staff they should be responsible for retrieving foul balls.

A pitcher is the logical man to back up the batting practice hurler. For safety purposes balls should be rolled to him. This has an additional purpose—forcing him to exercise with constant bending. The feeder should be stationed at the midway point, between second base and the mound.

**Defensive Value.** During batting practice valuable time is available; the coach should capitalize on it by hitting to his infield. The correct position for him during this operation is in the home-plate area, close enough so that he is protected by the batting cage, yet far enough removed so that batter and catcher will not be hit by a ball returned to him. As in the case of the pitcher, the ball should be rolled or bounced to the man hitting to the infield or his catcher. As a further precaution this catcher should remain well behind this batter so as to be out of danger from a ball batted from home plate.

A strict adherence to system should be demanded by the coach during batting practice, which can be hazardous, indeed, with several baseballs flying in several directions. The rule for hitting to the infield during batting practice is that the ball shall be hit to an infielder only after a pitched ball has passed the batter and before it has been returned to the pitcher. Furthermore, the infield ball—not the one used in batting practice—is the only one that is to be thrown to another infielder.

Supernumeraries may be used to hit to the outfield. One thus engaged should be stationed behind first or third in foul territory—preferably one man and a retriever at each of those spots. When two men are so stationed, only one of them should hit to the center fielder (this being decided before a ball is fungoed); the man behind third base will hit to right field and the one behind first to left. Although the rule need not be adhered to so strictly by this group, wisdom still dictates that a fly ball should be fungoed only after a pitched ball has passed the batter and before it has been returned to the pitcher.

Three general regulations for this portion of a batting practice session should be imposed:

1. Warn any teammate who is in danger of being hit by a thrown or batted ball.
2. Never turn your back to the plate until a pitched ball has passed the batter or been hit in another direction.
3. Always call a player's name before hitting fungoes to him.

### The Pitcher and Batting Practice

This phase of a pitcher's activity is valuable for the opportunity it affords him to work from the mound and face batters, thereby simulating, to a certain degree, the conditions that will be encountered in game competition.

The time and extent of his work in batting practice should be integrated with his overall conditioning routine.

Batting practice is intended primarily for the benefit of the hitter. Only in competitive batting drills should the pitcher work at full speed or endeavor to fool the man at the plate. He should seek to perfect his control, polish his footwork and delivery, and react to and field batted balls.

Every pitch delivered in a ball game should have a purpose. This also pertains to batting practice. Here the intention should be to throw nothing but strikes. In short, the fewer pitches per batter and the more batters faced in the allotted time (number of pitches, when innings are calculated), the greater the benefit derived from batting practice.

A pitcher can further profit from this type of work by close observation of each batter—of his stance and of his swing—in the hope of discovering any weakness that will properly guide his pitching strategy for each hitter. Although he will not utilize this knowledge during batting practice, the habit of close observation of the batter will carry over into actual ball games, wherein (in absence of a "book") he may be able to spot telltale signs of weakness in a moment's time.

The batting practice pitcher should work from a stretch when the batter is about to bunt and should field the ball just as he would in a game, but without throwing to a base. He should signal his intentions when throwing a curve ball and should not do so until the batter "has his eye on the ball."

A pitcher must not be used for batting practice duty simply because he is a pitcher. His schedule for this work should conform with his over-all conditioning routine. With relatively small pitching staffs other players will occasionally have to be assigned this task, particularly during the playing season.

Nonpitchers who throw batting practice should be selected primarily for their ability to get the ball over the plate. A wild hurler wastes time and can contribute to a batter's tendency to go for bad balls.

A coach who is hard pressed for pitchers may resort to a pitching machine. This assures the rapid completion of each round but is not particularly desirable, because the batter should learn to time the pitcher's motion as well as the ball and should accustom himself to facing different angles of delivery. The use of a pitching machine in addition to regular batting practice can, however, be invaluable for the extra practice it affords the hitter. For example, a hitter, after taking his regular cuts, can take a dozen or more swings against the machine. Even a batting tee can provide this kind of extra practice. Sufficient space is of the essence if this type of routine is to be followed.

Once a ball club gets into its actual playing schedule, a different routine will have to be developed for assigning pitchers to batting practice duty. The pattern of this activity will then be an individual matter, dependent upon how each pitching arm responds to work and requires rest. For a guide to sensible routines for an individual pitcher, consult the section on pitching.

### The Batter's Practice

Although batting practice is essentially for the benefit of the batter, he must approach it with the realization that every one of his team-mates should reap full value from it. The most good will come from a hitting session that is well organized. Each man should comply with the agenda and with the rules that are laid down by the coach.

Game conditions should be approached as nearly as possible within the framework of conventional batting practice in two principal respects:

1. The batter should learn his strike zone by swinging only at good pitches.
2. He should not "take strikes." Being overly choosy not only fosters the habit of passing up good pitches but also is harmful to the morale of the pitcher and to the purpose of the entire undertaking, which is to give every man the fullest opportunity to bat within the allotted time. Having the catcher serve as umpire can help make the batting practice snappy and beneficial.

A definite batting order for the practice should be picked and then followed faithfully. In the case of one of the two teams into which the squad has been divided, this will more than likely be the game lineup. When a substitute replaces a starter who may be detained or injured, he should be inserted in the regular's normal spot in order to retain the day-by-day continuity that builds cohesion.

There are several alternatives in the routine that should be followed, as well as variations that can be profitably inserted once the session is underway. The one condition dictated by common sense is that the course established should provide definite benefit to every player. In batting drills, as in every other phase of baseball practice, moves that will not be used and conditions that will not be encountered in a game should not be permitted.

During the early phases of preseason work more time should be given to bunting, both to perfect skill at it and to help a man get his eye on the ball. In fact, an occasional abbreviated round devoted exclusively to the bunt may be in order, both early in the year and later, should poor bunting show itself as a team weakness. The pitcher should throw hard from a distance of no more than fifty feet for all practice bunts.

A thoughtful coach will call for a certain type of bunt at specific times. Such action is in order when he feels that his club's attack may have to include a more frequent use of the squeeze play (here the next pitch must be bunted), or if he has a man who may help the team by occasionally bunting for a hit (here he should indicate whether the ball is to be dragged or pushed and whether the batter should try to beat it out).

The routines suggested below may form a basic guide to proper procedure, and each coach may adapt them to the needs of his squad.

*Early Season*

> ROUND 1
>> Two bunts—one down each foul line
>> Three swings—all fast balls
>
> ROUND 2
>> One bunt—where the ball is pitched
>> Three swings—the last a curve ball
>
> ROUND 3 (time permitting)
>> Two swings—the last a curve ball

*Intermediate*

> ROUND 1
>> One bunt

Four swings—the last a curve ball
Round 2
    One bunt
    Three swings—fast ball, curve, and batter's choice
Round 3 (time permitting)
    Two swings—batter's choice, then pitcher's choice

## Mid-Season

Round 1
    One bunt
    Four swings—two fast balls, curve, and batter's choice
Round 2
    One bunt
    Three swings—fast ball, curve, and pitcher's choice
Round 3 (time permitting)
    Two swings—fast ball and curve

## Game

Round 1
    One bunt
    Four swings—the last a curve
Round 2
    One bunt
    Three swings—two of them curves
Round 3 (time permitting)
    Two swings—both fast balls

## Explanatory Notes

1. For young ballplayers, unless otherwise noted, bunts should be aimed according to where the ball is pitched.
2. A particularly good batsman need not be required to bunt, especially on game days.
3. The catcher should serve as umpire when the pitcher has the choice.
4. The batter should run out his last swing. He then takes his lead at first as the pitcher delivers for the next batter's bunt. Occasionally, he can break, as on a steal, to give the catcher practice. The same procedure can be followed at second. Any work simulating a game situation that is incorporated into the regular routine can be of great value and add interest to the workout.
5. A catcher should always be used.
6. The next pitcher should be warmed up and ready when scheduled to take over.

### *Further Variations*

**Competitive.** The pitcher tries to retire the batter, and the catcher serves as umpire. As long as the batter "hits safely," he continues to bat.

### Next Pitch.

1. The batter must hit the ball no matter where it is pitched.
   The pitcher must try to throw a strike.
2. The coach may call this play after the pitcher has begun his delivery.
3. The coach may order the ball hit to right field.

In each case a successful effort should be rewarded with an extra swing.

**One Pitch.** The batter must swing at the ball no matter where it is pitched. This is often used when time permits only a last, very rapid round of hitting.

**Practice Game.** An attempt is made by all defensive players to retire the batter. The offensive team goes through its batting order. An umpire calls balls and strikes. The chief difference between this and a game is that the teams do not change sides every three outs.

**Long Round.** This is an entirely different overall batting practice routine, in which each hitter takes his full batting workout (for example,

*A well-organized batting practice*

two bunts and ten swings) in one time at the plate. Some coaches prefer this method because of the time saved by eliminating frequent changes of batters. Its primary drawbacks are that it makes the simulation of game conditions relatively difficult and that it does not allow the pitcher to face a sufficient number of different batters and vice versa.

Whatever routine is selected, batting practice should be carefully planned and smoothly run if it is to have real value.

### Base-running

This is a sadly neglected phase of the game because too much is taken for granted. It should not be assumed that base-running comes naturally to a youngster, that instinct alone will assure his practice of correct method and techniques. The ultimate goal of the offense is to score runs. To facilitate the accomplishment of this objective, coaches and players should leave little to chance. Base-running can be taught, and it is the coach's duty to see that his ballplayers learn the proper way to do it by covering the subject completely. His order of instruction should include these points:

*General*

1. The start toward first
2. Rounding the base
3. Taking a lead (at each base) and getting the jump
4. Going from first to third; going from second to third
5. The steal—straight, delayed, and double steal
6. The squeeze—breaking for the plate correctly
7. The hit-and-run
8. Tagging up—both how and when to do it

*Sliding*

1. Bent leg slide—right and left
2. Hook slide—right and left
3. Sliding back to the base
4. Breaking up the double play

A sliding pit should be used to prevent injuries. A good one will be about twelve feet by sixteen feet and 3½ feet deep—filled with fine sand topped with sawdust and shavings. It should be raked constantly while in use.

A rope stretched across the front of the pit at a height of 2½ to three feet, with instructions given to slide under it, can be of definite help in making a man learn to hit the dirt properly.

*Base-Running Signals*

1. When to look for them
2. How to take them when leading off the base
3. What they are

All base-line coaches should use standard signals to indicate to the runner when he should hold up, make a turn, stay on the bag, slide (left, right, or straight in), or keep going.

### Team Offense

The lessons imparted to each player must be fitted together as a whole to achieve maximum team results from game-to-game individual performance.

Through a definite set of offensive plays a team's attack can gain proper cohesion. A coach should make certain that his players understand each offensive maneuver, the theory behind it, its strategical use, and their own roles in its effective execution.

Offensive plays are relatively few in number; yet because every player may be called upon to fulfill one of the roles that each includes, considerable work must be done in perfecting them. Every player should be drilled in each of the various parts.

The basic repertoire of an amateur team should include the sacrifice and the steal—straight and delayed, single and double—as warranted by the type of squad.

Not essential yet always desirable in the offensive arsenal are the squeeze—safe, suicide, and double—and the hit-and-run, with its variations—the bunt-and-run and, more favorable for use by amateur teams, the run-and-hit.

Thorough knowledge of offensive signals should be taught to every member of the squad.

### Defense

If thorough knowledge of baseball techniques and tactics is a prerequisite to good coaching, meticulous instruction in every phase of the game is essential in the full development of the team and its players.

Before a team has reached a condition of game-readiness, it should have a working knowledge, if not complete mastery, of the following vital defensive plays:

1. Infield depths
2. The cut-off (including relay assignments)
3. The force play
4. The double play—with runners on first base; first and second; first and third; first, second, and third; and the fake and throw to third
5. The sacrifice—with runners on first; first and second; first and third; and on second
6. The squeeze
7. The hit-and-run
8. The steal
9. The double steal
10. The pick-off play
11. The run-down
12. Covering the bases
13. Backing up the bases

Special emphasis should be placed on the force play, the relay, the double steal, and the run-down as essentials for a good defensive ball club.

From an individual standpoint, a team's defense can be considered well prepared when the following points have been thoroughly practiced:

*Catcher*: Giving the signal; glove position; catching the ball "toward the belt buckle"; shifting with the pitch; blocking low throws; removing the mask; catching pop flies; backing up first; covering third; cocking the arm; the one-step throw to the bases; the pitch-out; the double steal; fielding bunts (and throwing to first); calling the play; and blocking and tagging the runner.

*Pitcher*: Covering first; pick-offs; holding the runner; stepping off the rubber; the double play; playing slowly hit balls; making the play at third at the right time; handling bunts; backing up bases; covering the plate; taking the signal; and the pitch-out.

*First Baseman*: Shifting and stretching; handling low throws; leaving the base to catch the ball; taking a throw from the home-plate area; holding and tagging the runner; the pick-off play; handling bunts; the double play to second and back to first; feeding the ball to the pitcher; pop flies; cut-off and relay; following the runner; and the run-down.

*Second-Short*: Base-covering assignments; the tag; the steal; the double steal; the bunt; the hit-and-run; the double play; pop flies; cut-off and relay; the pick-off play; the run-down; and making the play to third.

*Third Baseman*: The bunt; slowly hit balls; the cut-off play; steals; the tag; the pick-off from the catcher; pop flies; and the throw home (and following the runner).

*Outfield*: The crossover step; handling ground balls; playing line drives; relays; throwing to bases; backing up the play; calling the play and taking the ball; playing the sun field; using glasses; and playing the fence (where applicable).

The role of the coach in drilling his squad has been presented in the form of a check list. A detailed description of the various maneuvers, both tactical and mechanical, will be found in appropriate sections of the text.

### Infield Practice

Infield practice is the backbone of a team's defensive practice. Except on game days, each period spent on the field should conclude with a spirited infield drill.

Considerable preseason time should be devoted to combatting the various situations that can arise in a game. The outfielders ought to be included in this work, as well as base runners. Game conditions should be duplicated in all respects save that the coach sets up the play he wants practiced and changes it at his discretion. He should call the play, just before hitting the ball, according to the game situation and the position of base runners; for example (after placing runners at first and third): "Eighth inning; no outs; we're leading by three runs."

Routine infield drills should be based on game-day procedure. The everyday workout, of course, is not limited in time, and a coach may conduct it to accommodate more than his starting team. Furthermore, he should include practice on pop flies for each of his infielders and the catcher, especially early in the spring. When proficiency is achieved, less practice is needed but should be continued throughout the season. The player who is to field it should call for each fly ball, even in practice. In addition, an occasional long ball should be hit past the outfielders (by way of surprise) to see that the relay is executed instinctively. A ball rolled behind the catcher to simulate a dropped third strike should also be employed. In short, all possible game situations should be worked on during practice sessions.

It is game-day infield practice that should most concern a coach, because it reflects the discipline and mood of his ball club. Furthermore, a snappy infield drill can boost a team's morale and have a definite psychological effect on the opposition.

The following routine has been devised as a logical one, conducive to spirited effort, smart appearance, and good game preparation. It is based on two fundamental principles: no play should be made that will not be encountered in a game; and fumbles should be played to first base (as in a game) unless, of course, the misplay precludes any possibility of retiring a runner:

**Outfield Round.** (Batter should hit hard grounders; cut-off men are in position.)

1. *Throw to second*: Hit to left fielder near the foul line.
   Hit to center fielder in left center.
   Hit to right fielder near the foul line.
2. *Throw to third*: Hit straight at them.
3. *Throw home*: Hit straight at them—they should charge the ball
4. *Throw home*: Hit a fly ball (to test wind and sun).
5. Outfielders then go to deep center field. A pitcher hits to them.

**Infield.** A warm-up round consists of a throw to each man from the catcher.

*Round 1* To first: The ball is hit directly at each man (first baseman plays ball to second and takes return throw); first baseman returns ball to catcher who throws to the man who started the play—at his bag; ball returned by way of third; catcher fields ball rolled near third base line, plays it to first, receives return throw from first baseman.

*Round 2* To first: The ball is hit to each man's left; same procedure is followed except that ball for catcher is rolled toward mound.

*Round 3* Double play: The ball is hit to left of third baseman and shortstop, to right of second and first basemen, and rolled toward first for the catcher. Return throw routine is the same.

*Round 4* Double play: The ball is hit to right of third baseman and shortstop, to left of second and first basemen (latter steps on first and shouts "tag" as he throws to second), and dropped near the plate for the catcher. Return throw routine is the same.

*Round 5* To first: The ball is hit to each man's right; first baseman plays ball to third and receives return throw; catcher plays ball to third on his roller; catcher's throw to shortstop and second baseman is taken in cut-off position and returned home.

*Round 6* To first: A slow roller is hit to each man, who charges the ball, plays it to first (the first baseman throws home), and returns to a position at the edge of the infield grass; on his grounder, first baseman takes a position as though holding a runner, coming off the bag to field the ball; there is no throwing by the catcher, nor does he field a roller.

*Round 7*   To home: A slow roller is hit to each man, who plays the ball to home and returns to his normal position. Throws should be knee high. No throwing by the catcher.

*Round 8*   A high pop fly is hit to each man. No throwing.

To save time, the batter should use two balls and hit the ball to the next man as the catcher receives the final throw from the previous play. Players should make their moves with precision and with a concentrated effort to make each throw perfect.

### Game Preparations

*Day Before The Game*

1. Pitchers throw lightly, do pick-ups, run; shower and dress.
2. Batting practice in the form of a game.
3. Game-day fielding drill; practice relays and cut-offs.
4. Run; shower and dress; brief talk.

*Day Of Game*

A 2:30 starting time is used. Plan A assumes that facilities are available for the teams to take batting practice simultaneously. Plan B is for fields on which the teams must take turns.

*A*

1:00   Meet in squad room; announce lineup; brief talk.

1:10   Take the field together; warm-up.

1:20   Batting practice for starting lineup and regular substitutes; try to use a pitcher similar to their starter; starting pitcher and catcher should watch opponents bat.

1:50   Visitor's infield; home squad should watch it, allowing a few minutes for warming up prior to home practice.

2:05   Home infield; starting pitcher begins warming up between 2:10 and 2:15, depending on the weather and his arm.

2:25   Work on diamond; meet with umpires; squad on the bench; starting catcher should handle last three minutes of pitcher's warm-up; pitcher should allow time to sit down for two or three minutes to dry himself and catch his breath.

*B*

12:40   Meet in squad room; announce lineup; brief talk.

12:50   Take the field together; warm-up.
 1:00   Home batting practice.
 1:30   Visitor's batting practice; squad on the bench, watching the first
        fifteen minutes of it; then play pepper and catch.
 1:55   Visitor's infield; home squad should watch last five minutes of it.
 2:10   Home infield; same routine for pitcher.
 2:25   Same routine.

A copy of the ground rules and line-up should be given to the umpire and the visiting team. If a field has dugouts, the ground rules should
be posted in both of them, avoiding the need to give the visitors a copy
during the home-plate ceremonies.

Those obligations, which a first-rate organization owes its visitors,
are detailed in the section on manager's duties. These are matters that
ought to be given scrupulous attention.

# Umpires

The competence of the umpires hired by a coach, and his team's
behavior toward all umpires are definite marks of character—individual,
team, and school. The coach who tolerates incompetent umpires and
hometown decisions when his club is host, or who abuses the arbiters
on any occasion, is not worthy of his charge.

Umpiring at all levels of competition has improved tremendously
since prewar days, and, as a class, today's men in blue are competent
gentlemen of unquestioned integrity. Conference requirements and umpires' associations have made good officiating the rule in today's game.
Clinics and lectures by outstanding practitioners have made rule interpretation, knowledge of the game, standards of conduct, umpiring techniques, and, above all, uniformity of officiating the prevalent qualities in
our umpires.

The importance of good appearance, bearing, and conduct for players is stressed repeatedly by the outstanding men in the coaching profession. Certainly, then, these attributes, along with technical competence,
are imperatives for an umpire.

The best umpires invariably reflect one desirable trait. When they
take the field, they encourage the feeling that the game will be com-

pletely under control and that decisions will be correct and inviolate. There is no arrogance or show behind this, only an air of unmistakable authority and competence. This is the attitude that a first-rate umpire should inspire. Every umpire cannot fit this mold, but men of the highest degree of competence and impartiality should constantly be sought as officials. They ensure well-run ball games and the good disposition of the coaches—things that we owe our players.

Dignity and courage should be added to competence and impartiality, as essential qualities in umpires. In short, a coach should engage the services of officials who demonstrate the characteristics he is trying to instill in his own players.

An umpire need not have been an outstanding ballplayer to be sought as an official, but he should definitely have a feel for the game and for the intricacies of position play. An understanding of what a player must do in a given situation, and of the mechanics involved, cannot help but make him a better umpire. It may even be said that an appreciation of the player's task is a requisite for a topflight arbiter.

How concerned should a coach be about an umpire's complete integrity? Let him merely ask himself whether he desires an impartial umpire when his club is the visiting team. Obviously he wants impartiality on the road; consequently, he is expected to provide it at home. A coach who would look to the "home" type of umpire to assure his team an advantage should not be entrusted with the leadership of young men.

A proven maxim for salesmen is "win the argument, lose the sale." For a baseball coach the admonishment should be, "Lose the argument, lose the decision anyhow"—not well put, but sufficient to show the basic folly of arguing with umpires. Win, lose, or draw in the argument, no good can come of it, for the decision on a judgment play, once made, must stand.

Harassment of umpires by a coach is not only fruitless but also detrimental to squad morale. The players look upon the coach not only as an instructor but also as an example of correct behavior. If he constantly "jaws" at umpires, his players, and often the spectators, tend to follow suit. Only chaos can ensue.

A coach should make it an ironclad rule that no player abuse or even argue with an umpire. If a legitimate complaint on a matter of interpretation (not judgment) seems warranted, the captain, and possibly the coach, are the only members of a squad legally authorized to discuss the matter with an umpire. In the absence of strong league control and proper punitive measures for flagrant offenders, it is the duty of the coach to enforce conformity with this rule.

The exception to the rule of questioning an umpire's decisions is in the matter of balls and strikes. The vast numbers of these calls in the course of a game and the continual stress confronting ballplayers are reason enough to allow an occasional lapse. Disputing an umpire's decisions, however, must not be encouraged; in fact, it should definitely be discouraged. Baseball's outstanding stars rarely question an umpire's judgment. They realize that he is human and, furthermore, accept the bad with the good and go about their business like true professionals.

There is a correct way in which to talk to an umpire, based on a conscious effort to avoid making him look bad in the eyes of the crowd, for an umpire is never "at home." When an occasion arises in which the umpire's judgment may justifiably be questioned, the catcher or batter should address him without turning in his direction. A pitcher who feels the need to speak up should meet his catcher in front of the plate, turn his back on the man in blue, and address him in a dispassionate manner.

Abuse of an umpire should not be tolerated by a coach. He and his players should aspire to the best. In order to earn it, they should deserve it.

# The Captain

The captain of a baseball team can be of tremendous value to coach and squad alike—if he is the right man for the job. He is the coach's alter ego (on the field) and can be the proverbial "second right arm" to the mentor (both on and off the field). Thus, his selection must not be taken lightly, nor should it become a popularity contest.

The qualities expected of a man worthy of being team captain are several, but they revolve around one quality—character. The man chosen to lead his teammates should be a player of ability who knows the rules of baseball and of proper conduct. He should be a man of good moral fibre, even temperament, courage, and clarity of mind. He should be the type of man whose deportment will serve as an example to his teammates whether they win or lose.

His game duties start with the pregame ceremonies, at which he hands the lineup to the umpires and clarifies the ground rules—for the visitors when his is the host club, for his own team when they are on the road. He then advises his teammates of the ground rules and leads them into battle. During the contest he keeps the umpires informed of lineup changes and handles any necessary discussion with the umpires. The latter's judgment should never be questioned, his interpretation being the only justifiable topic of argument—pursued in a gentlemanly manner by the captain alone.

The captain's duties as an intermediary between coach and players embrace both on- and off-the-field activity. He represents his coach on the field through his personal example and his oral direction relating to the coach's orders. He should report to the coach any pertinent information that may otherwise go unnoticed by the bench.

During practice sessions his value can increase vastly if he helps oversee and keep in operation the many groups of players. He should be given formal authority to assist in the conduct of practice sessions.

Off the field he should not only set a good example for his teammates but also serve as advisor and counsellor to them when the need arises. In this role he should act only on the authority of the coach and in a manner that will reflect only the coach's philosophy and system of play. This phase of his responsibilities further includes the pacifying of gripers. The captain should bring directly to the coach legitimate complaints and any moot point put forth by a squad member. Covert criticism of coach, teammates, or school must not be tolerated.

Obviously, an exceptional man is needed to fill the captain's role properly. Furthermore, because he will be delegating authority to this emissary of his, a coach should have the type of man he wants. For that reason, and to avoid a mere popularity contest, the coach should choose the captain. It is sufficient to allow the team to elect its own honorary captain at the close of the season.

Some coaches prefer game captains. With the possibility of finding more than one real leader on a squad quite rare, a season captain seems more logical. Should more than one man have outstanding qualities of the sort desired, co-captains may be a better solution than alternate ones because the authority involved cannot have significance if it is transferred continually.

Another possible solution, if one outstanding leader has not made himself manifest, is to have co-captains for, say, the first two games and then to select either the man or men deemed outstanding as team leader for the balance of the season.

Whatever course is followed, the coach should pick his own captain —with care.

# Arranging the Schedule

The designing of an intelligent schedule is a difficult feat, for carefully laid plans often must be modified by practical considerations. In practice the ideal can rarely materialize, but it can be approached— though only if common-sense principles are diligently applied.

Financial and academic matters are primary considerations in scheduling. The amount of money allocated to baseball and the scholastic standards that the players must meet should be determining factors in both the number of games arranged and the travel involved in playing them.

The most important consideration from the standpoint of the boy on the squad is his academic well-being. Baseball (or any sport) is not an end in itself. Rather, it should be made an integral part of his education. Baseball can serve as a wholesome outlet for the vigorous youngster. Its demands on a boy should promote health, purpose, and a budgeting of his time, which can all serve as a stimulus to his education. For this reason it should be carefully integrated with the academic program. If scholastic demands are exceptionally high, the number of games and the travel involved should be held down, so that no player's academic standing will be adversely affected by his obligation to the team. A boy in academic difficulty should be made to concentrate on his books—at the expense of the ball club. The only philosophy that can be justified is that, although we should strive for a strong mind in a strong body, the development of the mind must come first.

Merely because of his familiarity with his athletes, a coach should have the final say in schedule-making. Whenever possible he should arrange for relatively easy games early in the season, especially if his squad is an inexperienced one. It is experience in actual competition that breeds confidence, and nothing can boost a squad's morale better than some easy victories.

Of course, compromise with and accommodation of other teams are inevitable. Above these demands stand conference commitments. Within this framework a balanced schedule must be worked out, one in which natural rivals should be met near the end of the season (preceded, if possible, by an easy game and sufficient rest).

The first rule of thumb is that good equipment for the players should not be sacrificed for an overly-ambitious schedule. It is far better to travel first class on a short trip than to ride the rods on a long one.

Squad strength is a factor to be respected. Baseball loses its educational value when victories are unduly easy or hopelessly difficult. Although team strengths are often unpredictable at the time schedules are being fixed, the coach should, nevertheless, endeavor to send his squad against an opponent with whom they have an even chance in at least eighty per cent of their games.

A sensible schedule at the secondary school level is two games a week, properly spaced. College men, because of their greater maturity and need to experience the full development of the game, should be given more competition. Distribution of playing dates, however, is still a matter for consideration. The size and strength of the pitching staff and, to a slightly lesser extent, of the squad constitute the chief temporizing element.

Rain will, of course, curtail the number of games played. Because the weather is completely unpredictable, it should not bear direct influence on schedule-making. Rather, it should promote balance—sufficient games to ensure that a rainy spring will not cause too little competition, few enough games to ensure that a dry spring will not find a team's manpower overburdened.

Secondary schools will normally confine their activity to a localized area. Colleges must usually go further afield for suitable opponents; but budgetary limitations may preclude long trips. Whenever they can be arranged, however, they can provide a worthwhile experience. Logically, a long jaunt should include more than one game and should be followed by a day of rest. It follows that the ideal arrangement for an extended road trip would conclude with a Saturday game.

The most satisfactory mode of transportation is by bus. Here, again, finances may enter the picture and force travel by automobile. Whichever method is used, long journeys should be arranged so that the time of arrival will allow a good night's rest before a game is played. If necessary, automobile transportation is acceptable when its use will enable a squad to have the financial means for an extra night's lodging. If this basic requirement of rest cannot be met, long road trips should not be taken.

For the team that is poorly financed, a preponderance of away games in a localized area is justifiable, for they often cost less than home games, in which the expenses of umpires, balls, and visitor's guarantee are involved.

The ideal schedule at various levels of scholastic competition would be something like this:

High School:   Tuesday and Friday
Prep School:   Wednesday and Saturday

College:   (Two games) Wednesday and Saturday
           (Three games) Tuesday, Thursday, and Saturday
           (Long Trip) Friday and Saturday.

## FALL BASEBALL

A recent development in college baseball circles in the New York area is the playing of an abbreviated schedule in the early fall. The practice has met with success among the handful of schools trying it, and for good reason—physical conditioning of the squad and inclement weather are relatively minor problems.

With a summer of activity behind them, the players will need no preseason conditioning. Two weeks should be sufficient for the achievement of playing condition. Then, with at least four weeks of better-than-April weather at his disposal, a coach can play an eight-to-ten-game schedule.

Booking two games a week will enable a team to make up rain outs with no great strain on the players. Tuesday and Friday are the logical game days, the latter to avoid a conflict with football, the former to allow a proper spacing of the contests.

In many cases, particularly in smaller schools, a number of baseball players will be engaged in football and, thus, will be lost to the baseball squad. Yet fall baseball is a worthwhile undertaking, valuable in itself and of great merit for the carryover effect that will be gained for the regular season.

An autumn schedule will be of particular advantage to teams in the northern section of the country. The month of October almost invariably affords more favorable baseball weather than does April, and its seems reasonable to profit by the opportunity thus presented.

## MULTI-SPORT MEN

Because many baseball players are all-around athletes, occasional conflicts with other sports are inevitable. This problem primarily affects participants in winter sports and concerns the inroads that these activities make on their baseball conditioning program.

Because there is no season conflict involved, football players need concern us here only in so far as possible injury is involved. The school and its football coach should not be deprived of the services of a good performer because he happens to be a baseball player. It is only in the case of a boy who is an outstanding ballplayer but only mediocre in football that a choice is called for. In this case his value to his school, and his potential in higher levels of baseball, should determine whether he should play on the gridiron. This determination should be weighted also by the possible effects of *two-sport participation on his health and his schoolwork.* Football should generally be discouraged if a boy's contribution to that sport will be a minor one, especially if he needs the extra time for study, is not overly robust, or is a baseball player of exceptional ability.

The same standards are the basis (though to a lesser degree) for deciding whether a ballplayer should participate in winter sports. Basketball players, for example, pose a problem to the baseball coach, primarily because of the loss of valuable preseason baseball work that can be involved. This stems not only from an overlapping of seasons but also from the need for a period of recuperation from the basketball season.

A boy's health and his academic status far outweigh the need to report early for baseball. The winter sport participant should be required to take a definite period of rest between seasons. A reasonable period at the high school level would be one week (no less)—for essentially physical reasons. College men should have a mandatory two-week respite—for physical and scholastic reasons. The baseball routine for them may then have to be condensed. This is the proper approach—closely observing the master plan and not eliminating any of it.

Obviously, the only rational guide to follow is a careful consideration of the possible consequences of dual participation on the health and scholastic standing of the boy; his contribution to the school and to baseball are contingent factors.

# *Equipment*

In order to fulfill its educational function, baseball should contribute a worthwhile experience to the maturing youngster. As with the schedule, the equipment for the squad should be first rate if the sport is to serve its desired purpose. Here, once again, we enter the realm of fiscal affairs, and a careful calculation and weighing of objectives is demanded in the case of all but the most affluent budgets.

Regardless of the size of the budget, the key to its proper management is the economical use of available funds. This means good quality at a good price. Certain equipment will be expected to last longer (uniforms, jackets, etc.); thus, a little extra expenditure for superior quality will pay dividends over the years: good equipment lasts longer and looks better; hence it is more economical.

Rather than completely outfit a squad with inferior equipment, the coach should omit nonessentials and buy well-made essential items.

Because price, quality, and service are the major considerations in outfitting a ball club, a coach should seek a reputable firm. Local merchants often handle the best line, cooperate financially, and are available for service. If none are readily at hand, the major manufacturers have centrally located agencies, and their representatives can be called on, with little difficulty, to visit a school.

Equipment has priority in the budget and should be the last item to suffer if financial difficulty is encountered. Wise buying, can help greatly in avoiding financial distress. Its practice implies the observance of several basic rules:

1. Buy with the future in mind.
2. Purchase the best quality within your means.
3. Plan carefully and buy early.
4. Don't overstock.
5. The coach, not the player, should select all equipment. In the case of bats, gloves, and shoes, his recommendations should be followed; the player should try these items for size.

The stockroom is of utmost importance. One that is properly maintained can be a great aid as a guide to purchases and in the preservation of equipment.

The stockroom should be neatly shelved with all equipment immediately accessible. Good ventilation and temperature control are essential. A stockroom that is overly hot tends to harm the leather products, and one that is too damp promotes mold, which injures all other materials.

Before discussing the several items of equipment needed for a well-run baseball club, a word is necessary on two topics of a more general nature.

*Textiles:* Cleanliness is imperative. Uniforms should not be worn in practice—they are for games only; woolen goods (jackets, uniforms, and stockings) should be stored in the off season with one of the firms that specialize in equipment storage and that also take care of necessary repairs. If this cannot be afforded, woolen goods should be cleaned, packed in mothballs, and stored in a dry place.

*Personal equipment*: If budgetary limitations preclude the possibility of equipping the squad with gloves, shoes, and any desirable though un-essential item, two methods of approaching the problem bear investigation.

(a) *Share the cost*: The school and the player split the cost of any piece of equipment he wants.

(b) *Player bear the cost*: The most sensible way to do this is to have the school purchase the equipment (at discount prices, to which it is entitled) and sell it to the player at cost.

Items of equipment range in classification from essentials to luxuries. All will be listed, with the method of supply given for each of three categories—ideal, fair, and good.

| Item | Ideal Situation | Fair | Poor |
|------|-----------------|------|------|
| 1. Uniforms (and stockings) | A | $A_1$ | B |
| 2. Jackets | A | $A_1$ | B |
| 3. Caps | D | E | B |
| 4. Sweatshirts | D | E | B |
| 5. Supporters | D | E | E |
| (a) Cups (for pitchers, catchers, infielders) | E | F | F |
| 6. Inner Hose | D (three pairs) | D (1 pair) | F |
| 7. Sliding Pads | E | B (regulars only) | G |
| 8. Rubber Shirts | E | B (regulars only) | B (pitchers only) |
| 9. Gloves | E–B | G | F |
| 10. Shoes | D | E | G |
| 11. Traveling Bags | B | F | F |
| 12. Bats | C (new) | B–C | B |
| 13. Balls | C (new) | B–C | B–C |
| 14. Catcher's Equipment | B (two sets) | B (one set) | B (one set) |
| 15. Sunglasses | B (7 pairs) | B (three pairs) | B (one pair) |

#### CODE

A = Four new ones per year   $A_1$ = Two new ones per year   B = Replace as needed
C = Order according to number of games   D = Order yearly   E = Provide for new men
F = Not supplied by school   G = Share the cost

## Hints on Equipment

1. *Uniforms and jackets*: Buy the best. Keep clean and in good repair. Wear only during games. (Jackets may be used for practice.) Wear correctly (see *Discipline*). Mend rips and tears immediately (a stitch in time does save nine here).

2. *Caps*: Buy the best. Caps alone can make a team look good. Supply new ones yearly, if possible. Avoid crushing. They should fit tight to avoid blowing off.

3. *Sweatshirts*: Ideally a player should have three—heavy wool for cold weather; medium weight, long sleeves for normal wear; short sleeves for hot weather. Keep clean and wear one at all times. The same color should be worn by all players.

4. *Inner hose*: Must be worn (no sweat socks allowed). Keep clean.

5. *Sliding pads*: Advised for regulars.

6. *Rubber shirts*: Recommended for early-season wear for all players. An essential item for pitchers.

7. *Gloves*: Today's gloves are made so that little breaking-in is necessary. Keep clean. Do not oil. A player's glove should be worn by that man exclusively.

8. *Shoes*: Ideally a player should have a practice pair (last year's) and a game pair; shoes should be two sizes smaller than street shoes and worn only with cotton inner hose; can be kept clean with saddle soap, soft and pliable with waterproof oil. Should be cleaned immediately after use on a wet day. Leather toe plates are mandatory for pitchers. Wear black shoelaces only.

9. *Bats*: Buy the best. Each regular should have his own bat. Rub with bone or bottle to harden surface. Don't overstock, because bats dry out with age. Use last year's leftovers for early season workouts when many are split. Bats should be light enough to be easily handled, but not so light that they cannot be well controlled. Thin, whip-like bats are for experts. Inexperienced players should have thick-handled bats, which produce better bat control, fewer broken bats, and more safe hits when the ball is hit off the handle or other nonhitting surface.

10. *Balls*: Good ones must be used in games. Allow for use of one per inning. "Seconds" may be used in practice as an economy measure. Pitchers should not be permitted to throw a ball that has become heavier than normal.

11. *Catcher's equipment*: When not in use, handle it as a valuable item. Keep clean, dry, and in good repair. This equipment should be lightweight. The glove should be easy to handle but not small, since it is used as a target and to block wild pitches.

Good equipment is essential to a well-run ball club. Because it represents a large investment, careful planning and close observance of preservative measures are essential. The correct handling of the equipment problem involves detailed attention to procurement, care, and storage.

# Defense

# Pitching

## TECHNIQUES—THE FUNDAMENTALS OF GOOD PITCHING

If a pitcher were physically capable of overpowering every hitter, his battle would be won as soon as he stepped on the mound. Demonstrably, such is not the case, and although exceptional speed or a baffling curve will enable him to get by at some levels of competition, he will somewhere along the way to the big leagues encounter hitters who are physically his peers. He will then have arrived at the point at which he must become a pitcher rather than a thrower.

Many qualities, both physical and mental, contribute toward the making of a polished performer. Physical ability and the development thereof; knowledge of the hitters; poise, confidence, and the desire to win; and courage are the most important of these qualities.

### The First Fundamental

Probably the most important rule that should be followed by all pitchers is that every pitch should have a purpose. There should be no such thing as a waste pitch, if the term is taken literally. Regardless of what delivery is used, the pitch should have a meaning and aim behind it. It might be a quick strike to get ahead of the hitter; a change of pace to keep him off balance or set him up for the fast ball; or a calculated bad ball, a pitch that is not too good but will induce the batter to swing at it for an out. But whatever the pitch, it should never be a random throw.

Furthermore, every occasion on which a pitcher throws the ball should be one in which he has a definite purpose in mind. This pertains to warming up, pitching batting practice, or even a game of catch—as well as to actual game competition.

## *MECHANICS*

The basic objective of every aspiring pitcher should be to capitalize to the utmost on his physical equipment. He should not only acquire a sound tactical background and develop a good method of operation but also learn to put all his mechanical ability to effective use in the actual throwing of the ball. In short, learning to pitch includes the development of maximum stuff within the limits of a man's physical capabilities.

### Method

We should first consider, from a strictly physical standpoint, some of the theory that lies behind the act of delivering the ball to the batter with the most telling effect. Strategy, tactics, and the development of operational proficiency will be covered in subsequent chapters. At this point we will explore the mechanical means that have contributed greatly to the success of baseball's finest pitchers.

At the outset it should be realized that overpowering stuff requires muscular adaptation to a greater degree than it does sheer muscular strength. Size and power, although a great asset to any pitcher—particularly in regard to endurance and sustained stuff—are not the predominant factors enabling a man to throw hard and to break off a good curve ball. Men of short stature, slight build, and moderate strength have possessed exceptional stuff. To a great extent this is so because the muscular control necessary for pitching involves every part of the body—fingers, wrist, arm, and legs, as well as the entire physical being. What these men have developed is the knack of putting something on the ball without exerting maximum effort. The key to this mastery of ideal pitching coordination is relaxation. It not only enables a man to get maximum stuff on the ball but also allows him to conserve his strength and to call upon the little bit extra that is needed in any clutch situation.

One of the main factors that go into the making of a good pitcher is balance. It is, in fact, an essential at all stages in the delivery of any pitch. A slight imbalance at any point in the pitching motion is greatly magnified in the full sequence of motion and in the resultant effect on the course and action of the pitch. Thus, it follows that all pitchers should strive for good balance and the maintenance thereof from the time that they take a stance on the rubber until the follow-through is completed and the squared-away fielding position is assumed. A simple means of testing one's balance is to wind up, rear back with the striding foot in the air, and then hold the position on one leg for several seconds. When this can be done consistently with good equilibrium, a pitcher can be reasonably sure that his balance is proper at the start of his delivery; this balance will, in most cases, carry through to the end of his motion.

There are two distinct schools of thought on the physical effects created by the amount of time taken to deliver the ball. The first of these holds that a pitcher should work fast and waste little time on extraneous movements and undue deliberation, the belief being that taking excessive time will keep him on his feet longer and add to his fatigue as the game progresses.

The other theory maintains that a pitcher should work slowly. The reasoning is that working fast does not allow the arm muscles to contract sufficiently after the severe stretching they undergo in a hard throw. Consequently, the toll of working fast is too heavy on the arm.

The problem of which method to adopt is probably best left to the individual, because he is qualified to judge his own physical capabilities and limitations. A combination of the two methods could supply the most effective solution, provided that consideration were given to the game situation and, in particular, to the hitter. An unusually hot day requires deliberate movements, which allow the pitcher to conserve his strength for the full nine innings, as well as for any tough situations which may arise in the course of a ball game.

## Preliminaries

Before he even toes the rubber, a pitcher must concern himself with certain considerations that will leave him fully prepared to work with the greatest possible effectiveness. First of all, there is the matter of equipment.

*Shoes:* The most important tools of the trade to any ballplayer are his shoes. They are, literally, the foundation from which he must work and are possibly of even greater moment to a pitcher than to any other man on the field. The extra few dollars required to equip himself with high-quality footwear will be worthwhile in the long run. A lightweight kangaroo-skin shoe is predominant among professionals, who correctly assume that their base of operations is vital enough to their performance to demand both high quality and good condition. New shoes should be about two sizes smaller than ordinary footwear. They stretch considerably, and a snug fit is necessary to assure a pitcher of good balance, a powerful push-off, and the ability to start quickly and cleanly when fielding duties so require. New shoes should be worn only a few minutes at a time until they are properly broken in; that is, until they feel comfortable and have become almost molded to the foot.

A toe plate is essential because the shoe of the pivot foot is subject to great wear and tear. A piece of thick leather stitched over the inside of the toe of the shoe is recommended. This simple and economical device can be obtained from and applied by any shoemaker.

Every ballplayer should give his baseball shoes the care that their importance warrants. This includes regular cleaning and polishing for the maintenance of good condition. Either shoe polish or saddle soap is an effective ingredient for this chore. As an extra precaution wet shoes should be rubbed dry immediately after use, and mud should not be allowed to remain on them overnight.

Every ball club should keep extra shoelaces in its medicine kit. In the absence of them, a pitcher should carry an extra pair in the pocket of his jacket and should never allow himself to be handicapped by a broken shoelace.

Another on-the-field precaution is the removal of any excess mud or dirt from the spikes. Its presence can prevent a pitcher from getting effective purchase in both his push-off and stride. The spikes should be cleaned before the start of each inning and at any time that an accumulation of dirt appears.

Above all, a pitcher should see to it that his game shoes are in good condition. They should fit snugly, be in good repair, and have spikes that are long and held tightly in place. The only place for old, worn baseball shoes is in practice sessions—if not the trash heap.

*The Glove*: Size is the main essential in selecting a glove. It should be of good quality and should, by all means, be large—the larger the better, within the rules of the game. The reasons for this are twofold and fairly obvious: (1) to permit the pitcher to hide the ball; (2) to aid him in fielding his position (a big glove enables him to stop or deflect many balls that may otherwise go through the box for hits).

One precaution should be observed by ballplayers in general and pitchers in particular. Oil or greasy solutions of any kind should never be applied to a glove. Oil that is rubbed into a glove is exuded by it and will get on any ball that is caught. Controlling a baseball is difficult at best, and the slipperiness caused by oil imposes an extra handicap on the pitcher. The slight amount of extra life afforded by the preservative qualities of the oil are far outweighed by the harmful effects on a pitcher's control.

When a glove becomes dirty, it can be cleaned with a damp cloth. When it becomes too loose and "floppy," an application of water will help it regain the desired condition.

*Protective Equipment*: A pitcher should wear a long-sleeved undershirt at all times. On cold days this should be a woolen one; in warmer weather a lighter material—cotton, for example—can be used. When the temperature soars into the nineties a short sleeve can be worn on the gloved-hand arm, but the sleeve of the pitching arm should always be long enough to cover the elbow. This is vital to proper protection of the pitching arm. Furthermore, a long sleeve will absorb much perspiration and prevent it from reaching the hand and causing the ball to become slippery.

A pitcher should keep an extra undershirt on the bench so that he can make a change whenever his shirt becomes saturated with perspiration and uncomfortably heavy. This is particularly applicable to night games, during which the pitcher will invariably stop perspiring and be in danger of cooling off from about the fifth inning on. At this point it should be compulsory that he change shirts.

It is also advisable for pitchers to carry a washcloth or extra-large handkerchief in their pockets, to permit a thorough drying of the hands and forehead. All teams should keep at least one towel on the bench, primarily for between-innings use by the pitcher; in cases in which this is not done, the pitcher should attend to the detail himself.

An essential for every pitcher is a warm jacket; its use should be mandatory at all times when he is not on the mound or at bat. Even in hot weather or when running the bases, he should wear his jacket. A pitcher's arm cools off too quickly to allow him to run any foolish risks.

It is in the cool temperatures of early spring that the danger of contracting a sore arm is at its height. For that reason it is wise for a pitcher to wear a rubber or nylon shirt (in addition to the undershirt) during preseason workouts. A rubber shirt not only promotes quick and relatively easy warming up but also keeps the warmth inside the uniform once a sweat has been worked up, and affords good protection against the chill winds that are so prevalent in the early part of the season.

Of a more personal nature but, nevertheless, worthy of mention is the protective cup. This simple device can save a pitcher from serious injury, and its use, from both a physical and psychological viewpoint, is highly advisable.

### Taking the Mound

The impression will be given many times in this book that a pitcher's job starts long before he faces a batter. Even in a ball game he should not wait until he toes the rubber to concern himself with the task at hand.

As stated above, good balance is imperative to a pitcher, and this starts from the ground up. It follows that consideration should be given to the condition of the mound from which the hurler must work. Outside of professional ball there is wide divergence in the height and the material composition of pitchers' mounds. Because of the many varieties, we cannot concern ourselves with the mound per se—that is up to managers, coaches, and groundskeepers. The working condition of the mound is a different matter.

No two pitchers throw in identical fashion. All of them dig holes in the mound with their spikes. For these reasons every pitcher should smooth the mound at the start of every inning. He should take care to fill in the hole dug at the rubber and the one made by the stride of the opposing moundsman. Furthermore, when his own stride marks become too deep, they can throw him off stride; so these should be filled in when conditions warrant. In other words, for proper working conditions, the mound should be smooth at all times.

To take the signal from the catcher, the pitcher should stand on the rubber. To speed up the game, the rules require the pitcher to take the signal while in this position. To further accelerate action, he is required to deliver the ball to the batter within twenty seconds after he receives it. For this reason alone it is advisable to take the signal while in position to proceed into the windup. The same rule applies with men on base, with the exception that the pitcher is allowed to straddle the rubber while getting the sign. In addition to complying with the rules of the game, this practice prevents the pitcher from walking around the center of the diamond and indulging in various extraneous actions which do nothing more than use up his energy.

The pitcher ought also to examine the condition of the baseball in use. When its surface becomes blemished in such a way as to impair the pitcher's ability to work with it effectively, he should request a different ball from the umpire. If, on the other hand, a new ball is too slick, it should be rubbed until the sheen is removed. This duty is assigned to the umpire as a pregame task, but if it has been neglected, it can be done by the pitcher or one of his teammates as long as no foreign substance is applied. A little saliva, added to the dirt that is normally present on a ballplayer's hand, should suffice. When a pitcher uses this method, he should step off the mound before going to his mouth, lest he violate the rules of the game.

A rosin bag should always be on hand for the pitcher's use. At any time that his hand becomes slippery or does not supply the desired resistance in releasing the ball, the pitcher should dust his hands by gripping the rosin bag and squeezing it several times. Two words of precaution should be added: rosin may not be applied directly to the ball, because the rules consider it a foreign substance; and the application of rosin should be done judiciously, because an excess of it can cause the fingers to adhere to the ball sufficiently to impair one's control. In the absence of a rosin bag, a pitcher should use dirt or dust to dry his hand.

The observance of these seemingly minor, but actually highly important preliminaries will assist any pitcher in making his task an easier one.

### Grip

At this point we will not concern ourselves with the nuances of gripping the ball for various pitches or for the several styles of delivery. Instead, we will devote a few words to the grip on the ball, in general terms.

*Pitching grip (across the seams)*    *Pitching grip (with the seams)*

Regardless of how the moundsman holds the ball for his several pitches, he should strive for sameness of grip each time he throws a certain pitch. This similarity in grip helps a pitcher take advantage of the balance of the ball. By so doing he will be giving valuable assistance to his control, while lending uniformity to his stuff, thereby allowing him to gauge more accurately the probable action of the ball.

That is, every pitcher should strive to get into a groove that will facilitate his overall operations, for each facet of his pitching action enters into the total picture.

### Stance

The basic stance for a pitcher is one that finds him squarely facing the plate. To comply with the previously mentioned rule (requiring him to take his signal while on the rubber) and to enable him to go into his motion more effectively, he should place the front spike of his pivot foot over the edge of the rubber. This foot should be angled slightly toward the side from which the ball is thrown in order to facilitate the pivot and help get the body weight behind the throw. In fact, on the pitch the foot must be in front of the rubber (not on top of it) if a pitcher is to reach peak effectiveness.

The striding foot should be kept a few inches behind the rubber, and the weight should be forward. The body should be kept fairly erect, and the shoulders should be level. While taking the signal, the pitcher should hide the ball from the batter. Holding it behind the thigh or in the glove will accomplish this.

With men on base the same general principles apply. The main exception is that the stance is now a sideward one. The pivot foot can be angled along the inside of the rubber or placed as in the basic stance. The striding foot should be placed forward, with the toe slightly to the left for a right-hander and pointed normally for a lefty. The body must remain motionless, although the head can be moved back and forth. The hands must come to a complete stop before the ball may be delivered to the plate (this does not apply to the pick-off throw to a base). The pitcher should watch the runner out of the corner of the eye. This phase of pitching is dealt with in detail in the section on working with men on base.

## The Windup

The term *windup* is actually a misnomer. A windmill-like flailing of the arms is rarely employed by pitchers, probably because it accomplishes little aside from tiring the arms. This phase of the motion can be more aptly termed the pump since that is the nature of the actions used by most successful pitchers.

The pump serves a twofold purpose. It loosens and relaxes the arm and shoulder muscles, and it helps the hurler to get his weight properly behind the pitch.

Complete relaxation is essential until just before the ball is delivered. Intentness of purpose is, of course, a vital factor in successful pitching; yet it should not interfere with physical relaxation. The pitcher can help his cause by "breaking" his wrist in the forward and backward pump of his windup. This maneuver also permits greater flexibility of the wrist and arm and should be practiced until it becomes automatic in those cases in which it is not done naturally.

Another purpose accomplished by a pumping motion is the loosening of the shirt and undershirt around the arm and shoulder. Inconsequential though this may seem, it can bear heavily on a pitcher's effectiveness, for a shirt can, at times, bind his shoulders and arms to the extent of impairing his normal delivery. For this reason the pitcher should fully stretch his arms when going into his windup. With men on base he can employ a full stretch in order to loosen the shirt and undershirt thoroughly.

The pumping motions employed by pitchers vary considerably. One thing that most good pitchers have in common, however, is that their windup or pump is done above the throwing shoulder. There are exceptions, but in most cases the hands and arms never actually cross the face —meaning, among other things, that the view of home plate will not be obscured at any time during the windup. Indeed, some pitchers manage to get all the benefits of a full pump without ever raising their hands above their faces.

As the pitcher starts his windup, he should shift his weight forward. The primary purpose of the windup, however, is to move the body weight back and into the "rearing back," which puts power into the pitch. To facilitate this necessary transfer of body weight, many good pitchers take an initial step back on the striding foot. This process may be thought of as "gathering the weight" in preparation for the start of the windup. It is recommended as a means of getting increased power into the delivery. The entire pattern of action can be likened to a pendulum.

This pattern of action is highly important when one considers that salient but rarely emphasized point: you can't add speed or stuff to a pitch after you let go of the ball. "Reaching way back" is one extreme of the pendulum-like motion that ends in the follow-through. It is, moreover, the more important of the two extremes. The follow-through is essential to a good delivery and is a sign that all other phases of the delivery have probably been performed correctly. "Reaching way back" provides the explosive charge that actually propels the ball and, thus, is a must for all pitchers.

### The Pivot

The windup or pump leads quite naturally into the pivot. Momentum for the proper shifting of body weight has been started by the pump, and it reaches its "point of recoil," or of forward "detonation," at the rear extreme of the pivot. It is this phase of the motion which provides the real source of power and in which the very important "reaching way back" takes place. It is here that complete bodily relaxation is transformed into intense physical action—not by strained effort, which will impair a smooth-flowing delivery, but by the controlled and natural actions that will impart maximum power.

As the pitcher brings his arms up in his pump, he should shift his weight backwards. It is then that the pivot actually begins. The pivot foot slides diagonally forward, and the body turns toward the throwing side. As the pivot to the rear takes place, the pitcher should swing his striding leg up and around toward the pitching arm. At this stage of his motion the pitcher should be eyeing home plate and his target over the shoulder of his gloved hand. The kick itself should be moderate because an exaggerated one can throw the pitcher off balance, hindering his stuff and ruining his control.

During the windup and at the start of the pivot, the legs should be relatively straight—not rigidly so, but straight enough to eliminate purely extraneous movements that do not contribute to the desired pendulum effect but are primarily of a vertical nature.

At the start of the pivot the pitcher's stance should be slightly open; that is, the toe of his pivot foot should be pointed out (slightly toward third base for a right-hander, toward first for a lefty). This will minimize excessive body action on the pivot while still allowing it to be a good pendulum-like one. The pitcher will thereby have better control without an impairing of the power that can be imparted to the throw.

The pivot should be a relatively short one that can be fully controlled. The upper body should remain straight during this phase of the delivery, and the ball should be removed from the glove quickly—before the push-off. Also, a very important consideration is that the pitcher should concentrate intently on his target at this point, as well as at all times during his entire motion.

### The Stride

The obvious purpose of the stride is to shift the weight forward and into the delivery. It is the central link in the chain of physical movements making up the overall pitching motion. It is a key factor in giving impetus to the ball. Nevertheless, the pitcher needs to observe moderation.

The stride should not be exaggerated. It should be long and strong enough to provide full power, but not to the extent that it interferes with good coordination, damaging both stuff and control.

As the pitcher's arm swings back, his striding foot comes straight forward and hits the ground with the toe pointed directly at the plate. The arm comes through as the body drives hard off the pivot foot.

There are three points in the last paragraph that bear elucidation: (1) The striding foot should hit the ground almost flat, or even slightly on the ball of the foot. When a pitcher lands on his heel, he jars himself, hindering his balance and, consequently, his control; he also offers too much resistance to the forward shift of his body weight, thereby cutting down on his power—he should actually slide smoothly into his stride. (2) The toe should be pointed directly at the target. This simple device is a great boon to good control. (3) The body must drive hard off the pivot foot. A powerful push-off is an essential to getting the full weight behind the pitch and to adding greatly to its power.

As the pitcher takes his stride, he should keep his arm back of the rear shoulder, which, in turn, lags behind the stride. The arm should start forward as the foot hits the ground, and the stride should be completed before the top point of the delivery is reached. Not until this point in the delivery has been reached should the wrist snap take place. Perfect balance is demanded during this entire series of actions if good stuff and adequate control are to be achieved.

The pitch should be made against the front leg, which serves as a form of anchor in this case. This leg must be bent at least slightly to prevent the jarring effect that can hinder a pitcher's control, and so that it will not serve as a brake that checks the smooth flow of motion that leads into the follow-through and that inhibits the power behind the pitch. To assure this essential smoothness and power, the pitcher must absolutely avoid a stiff or locked front leg. The knee should be bent as the foot hits the ground; as the arm, body, and rear foot follow through to complete the motion, the knee should continue to bend, and the weight should be transferred to the ball of the foot.

Consider the correct stride from the viewpoint of a right-hander: the stride, in order to assure a pitcher of his most effective delivery, should be not only forward but also slightly to the left. A left-hander's stepping foot should move forward and slightly to the right. In order to ascertain the correctness of this move, the pitcher should draw a straight line in the dirt pointing from the pivot foot toward home plate. The striding foot should land at a point three to six inches to the left of this line for a right-hander and three to six inches to the right of it for a left-hander, the only exceptions being those occasions when a crossfire delivery is employed. The value of this is that it prevents a pitcher from throwing across his body and thus creating unnecessary resistance, which decreases the power behind the pitch, hinders control, and can damage the arm by placing an unnatural strain on it. By using a good pivot and stride, the pitcher will show the batter his "tail" as he reaches back and his "belly button" as he strides.

### The Delivery

There are four basic types of pitching delivery common to baseball. They can be categorized generally as overhand, three-quarters, side-arm, and underhand. All pitchers use one of these methods, and some employ a combination, usually adding an occasional sidearm pitch to a normally overhand or three-quarters style.

Overhand pitchers generally throw a fast ball that rises and a curve

*Good pitching form, right-hander, overhand delivery—note two-way hip pivot, squared away follow-through, and how eyes remain on target throughout entire delivery*

that breaks down. They release a fast ball off the ends of the fingers and employ a full downward sweep of the arm, which passes close to the head. By raising himself up on his toes during the delivery, an overhand pitcher will gain the added leverage that puts more hop on his fast ball.

The three-quarters delivery is, as the term implies, halfway between overhand and sidearm, and is used by most pitchers. Pitchers who employ this style throw a curve ball breaking down and to one side. Their fast balls vary according to the method of release, rising when the ball is released off the ends of the fingers, but moving in and down (the sinker) when the ball leaves the hand off the middle finger while the wrist is rotated toward the body.

Sidearm pitchers almost invariably throw a sinking fast ball and can add to this effect by rotating the wrist to the inside ("turning it over" as the arm comes through) and releasing the ball off the side and tip of the middle finger. The curve ball thrown by a sidearmer is usually a "flat" one. For this reason, and because the ball can be so well hidden from the batter, the sidearm pitcher is more effective against a batter who swings from the same side; that is, righty versus righty and lefty versus lefty.

Underhand pitchers are few, possibly because it seems to be more difficult to get good stuff on the ball in this way than by another means of delivery. An underhand fast ball will sink, and an underhand curve ball will rise and move to the side when thrown with sufficient power.

*Good pitching form, left-hander, overhand delivery—note how back bends in follow-through*

The crossfire is a variation that is occasionally used by pitchers who employ a sidearm delivery. It is the one method in which the striding foot crosses the line between the pivot foot and home plate. Consequently, it can cause considerable strain on the arm and for that reason must be used judiciously. Because the stride is made toward a point behind the batter and the sweep of the arm makes the ball appear to be coming from somewhere near third base for a right-hander and first base for a lefty, the batter can be both intimidated and deceived. In this case, the angle of delivery rather than the action of the ball is the key factor.

It is the angle of delivery that marks the difference in these several styles of pitching. Each has its definite strong points. Perhaps the prime consideration in employing a particular style should be consistency of delivery. This refers to the motion used in throwing different pitches and pertains to the important element of deception, which adds to their effectiveness. For example, a pitcher who uses a three-quarters delivery should throw his fast ball and curve from the same angle so as not to tip off the batter. If every fast ball is thrown three-quarters and every curve sidearm, an opposing batsman will know exactly what is being thrown on each pitch. A smart hitter will be able to pick up even slight variations if they exist. Furthermore, in those cases in which a combination of deliveries is used, a pitcher should throw his entire repertoire from each angle used; that is, every type of pitch he throws overhand he should throw sidearm, and he should let the opposition know that he can do so.

One of the important requisites for sustained pitching success is smoothness of delivery. Although ungainly moves and jerky actions are not a serious deterrent, the actual throwing motion should be smooth enough to allow a pitcher to fall into an easy, natural groove. All aspects of his pitching will be improved, and, most important, his arm will be subject to much less wear.

Regardless of the style used, certain basic qualities are imperative. In any type of delivery there must be balance, the proper pivot, correct stride, and a good follow-through—plus the rapid coordination that comes with practice.

### The Release and Follow-through

In breaking down the pitching motion into its various distinct segments, we have reached the point at which the body drives hard off the pivot foot and the arm comes through with a good wrist snap. In the continuity of action the arm should then proceed naturally through its arc of motion, the hand reaching a point below the knee opposite the pitching shoulder. The body should be bent sharply at the waist. At the finish of this sequence of action, the pitcher should find his pivot foot slightly ahead of the striding foot and his body in a crouch.

An important factor in achieving maximum stuff with a minimum of effort is getting the shoulder behind the pitch and leaning the weight into the delivery. An example of the ideal execution of this technique is provided by Tom Seaver. This trait has contributed strongly to Seaver's endurance and his ability to call on the needed something extra in clutch situations.

Wrist action and the release of the ball are primarily responsible for imparting stuff to the pitch. For best results the ball should be released in front of the pitching shoulder. This not only provides necessary power but also has a strong effect on control. Both will be at peak efficiency only when the ball is released in front of the pitching shoulder.

*Good pitching form, right-hander, three-quarter delivery—note how striding foot points straight at target*

It has already been stated that a pitcher cannot add stuff after he has let go of the ball. This lends emphasis to the importance of "reaching back" and then observing all the fundamentals that have been discussed thus far. Nevertheless, the follow-through is extremely important to good pitching. It is at least a sign that all other basic essentials have been performed correctly.

One of the first pieces of advice given to youngsters in any athletic endeavor is to follow through. Its importance in throwing a baseball can be observed in practice. A pitching motion that stops abruptly upon release of the ball hinders rather than contributes to the speed and control of the pitch. One that is only partial in its follow-through achieves only mediocre results. On the other hand, a full sweep of the arm and a complete follow-through will produce markedly better results in all respects. Merely by experimenting with these three methods in practice, a pitcher will readily come to appreciate the value of a good follow-through.

A simple method of checking on the completeness of the follow-through is to observe whether or not the pitching hand is below and to the outside of the knee of the striding foot upon completion of the throw. If the heel of that foot can be touched with no conscious effort, the follow-through is a good one.

At this final point in the delivery the pivot foot will be slightly in advance of the striding one. In order to be squared away properly and in good position for his fielding duties, the pitcher should employ a short shuffle step with his striding foot to bring it in line with the other. He will then be fully prepared to move in any direction to field the ball.

## CONTROL

It is generally agreed that control is the main essential in successful pitching. Without it the most overpowering of pitchers cannot rise above

mediocrity. Ability to throw hard and to make the ball do tricks will go for naught if the ball cannot be controlled.

Its importance being widely accepted, let us try, first of all, to determine exactly what control is.

The prime requisite of good pitching is to throw strikes consistently. Although getting the ball into the strike zone is an imperative for the pitcher, this is perhaps too broad a definition of control, in view of the ability of some batters to hit with authority balls in most parts of the strike zone.

The best definition of a successful pitcher's control is "the ability to put the ball *close to* the target with good stuff on it." The italicized words emphasize that simply getting the ball into the strike zone is not sufficient in the long run, although it must, of necessity, be the pitcher's initial objective.

### Acquiring Control

Because control is the most essential factor in good pitching, it is very fortunate that it is a quality that can be acquired. The observance of certain basic principles, the avoidance of several prevalent faults, the adoption of a sound mental attitude combined with the application of good common sense, and, above all, practice, practice, and more practice will help any pitcher to gain improved if not outstanding control. There, of course, has never been a pitcher who could afford not to better his control.

The first rule for the observance of all pitchers is to have a definite target. Although pinpoint control—the ability to thread the needle—is not, in itself, essential, the attempt to achieve it is a must. Every pitcher should pick out a specific target (not merely a general area in the strike zone), should concentrate on it intently, and should make a determined effort to hit that target on every pitch. Its benefits for a pitcher's control

*Pitching targets (the four corners)*

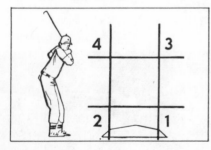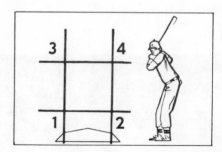

will come as a pleasant surprise to those who have not followed this practice.

Obviously, the catcher's glove is an ideal target. But in the higher ranks of baseball, observant hitters will take advantage of this type of advance information. If the catcher's glove is used as a target and moved from pitch to pitch, they will be able to tell where a pitch is being aimed. Fixed targets should therefore be employed. There are four of these that can be used to advantage by every pitcher—the catcher's knees and his shoulders. For a low, outside pitch to a right-handed batter, for example, the target will be the catcher's right knee; for a high, inside pitch to a right-hander, his left shoulder; and so forth.

Other targets can be used, depending upon what suits the pitcher's purpose most effectively. Two things, however, must definitely be borne in mind: his target must be within the confines of the strike zone unless a pitch-out or waste ball is being used; and he must remember to keep his eye on one fixed target during his entire motion.

One final word on this phase of the problem should be added. A pitcher, though he should strive for pinpoint accuracy, must definitely avoid aiming the ball if good control is to become an asset. Aiming the ball actually means that it is being held too long, in an effort to point it at a certain spot. This causes full energy to be lost and a natural motion to be ruined. The result is both an impairment of a pitcher's stuff and an even greater loss of control than that which has caused him to aim the ball in the first place.

The first step in acquiring control is a simple but effective practice technique. In throwing to a catcher, a pitcher should start by trying to throw every ball "through the middle." The pitcher should repeat this practice, using only a fast ball at three-quarters speed, until control to this particular spot is nearly perfect. Once this has been accomplished, the target should be shifted to low and "through the middle," with repetition until perfection is reached. The same method can then be used at the letter-high level; finally, when satisfied with his ability to hit these targets, the pitcher should follow the same procedure in throwing the ball over the inside and outside corners of the plate. This routine should be followed at frequent intervals, particularly during the preseason training period, with the catcher offering a steady glove target for each pitch. This simple drill will greatly benefit the control of any hurler and can be employed with each of his various deliveries—but only after nearly perfect control of his fast ball has been mastered.

The stride is very important in achieving control, and it should be given careful consideration by a player who is attempting to perfect this essential phase of pitching technique. There are three facets of the stride that bear heavily on control of the ball—its direction, the part of the foot on which it lands, and its length.

As previously stated, the striding foot should land at a point three to six inches to the side of an imaginary line running from the pivot foot to home plate. This assures the pitcher of greater freedom of movement by preventing his throwing across his body, a practice that locks his arm and chest in such a way that both power and control are affected. At the same time the striding foot should be pointed directly at the pitcher's target. This last point is extremely important. Simple though this suggestion may appear, an analysis of pitching styles shows that it is unfortunately too often overlooked. The improvement in one's control will be quite noticeable if this idea is carried out faithfully.

In taking his stride, the pitcher should land on the ball of his foot. The man who lands on his heel jars his entire body sufficiently to upset his balance and temporarily blur his vision. These handicaps can be eliminated if he lands on the ball of his foot, a practice ensuring both better stuff and improved control since it leads directly to a good follow-through.

The length of the stride should be moderate—of sufficient length to get power behind the throw, but not so long that it upsets the delicate balance essential to a good pitching movement. Overstriding is a serious deterrent to good control, for it is usually accompanied by the above-mentioned landing on the heel, which jars one's vision. Furthermore, it prevents that proper bending of the back required for a good follow-through.

The follow-through itself is vital because it maintains control through the last body movement of the pitching motion.

Good control is obviously dependent upon a repetition of actions for each type of pitch. This means that the fingers will be the same distance apart, the ball will be held the same distance from the crotch formed by the thumb and forefinger, the angle of delivery will be similar for each throw, the finger pressure applied to the ball will be alike from pitch to pitch, and the feet will go in the same spots on each follow-through. A fraction of an inch difference at the rubber can mean inches at the strike zone.

In short, control can be acquired by constant, systematic practice and by applying the principles of the fixed target, the well-controlled stride, and similarity of actions.

### The Causes of Wildness

Granted that some pitchers are inordinately wild and that all of them can afford to improve their control, what are the basic, underlying reasons for wildness in any degree? Under analysis the fundamental causes of this affliction seem to resolve themselves into nine distinct categories, each of which will now be listed and touched upon briefly.

1. *Changing finger pressures on the ball*: The finger pressure for each kind of pitch—fast ball, curve, change, and so forth—must be kept the same each time it is delivered. This rule reflects the principle of similarity of actions. Inconsistent action in this case means that more pressure is applied on one side of the ball. This causes a general imbalance in grip and results in a different release of the ball from pitch to pitch. The resulting absence of a consistent release will hurt control and compound any wildness that already exists. Thus, it is imperative that every fast ball, every curve, every change-up, and so forth, be gripped in identical fashion.

2. *Failure to concentrate on a fixed target*: The need for a pitcher to keep his eyes focused on a definite target is so important that it can bear frequent repetition. Even when a fixed target is selected, it is often lost from view during the pitching motion. This failure is almost invariably caused by the turning of the head and eyes during the pivot. This means that the eyes must refocus on the target as the pivot is completed.

3. *Excess rocking*: This is closely allied to the second category. The most effective motion is the pendulum type. When the body is rocked excessively during the pivot, the head and eyes will move and lose sight of the target. The suggested remedy is a shortened pump and a concentration on restricting the shifting of the weight to backward and forward movements, thereby eliminating extraneous and harmful body actions.

4. *Throwing across the body*: This habit locks the hips and shoulders to such an extent that a good follow-through is impossible—meaning, also, that a smooth continuity of motion will be absent from the delivery. It can be corrected by a practice already explained; namely, by drawing a line from the pivot foot to home plate and planting the striding foot about four inches to the side of this line (first base side for a right-handed pitcher, third base side for a left-hander).

5. *Lack of proper follow-through*: A partial follow-through interrupts the continuous control that should be maintained throughout the pitching motion. In addition, it means that the body is not completely behind the throw and can give rise to the sore arm to which "arm-throwers" are prone. The partial follow-through is characterized by a relatively straight back and can be remedied by a full bending of the back and the effort to complete the delivery with the pitching hand below and to the outside of the knee of the striding leg.

This problem is closely related to poor balance on release of the ball, a habit equally injurious to control. This is caused by an uneven follow-through, which, in turn, arises because the pitcher does not "follow the ball" with his motion. It can be corrected by striving for a squared-away follow-through, which can be achieved in most cases by a short shuffle step with the pivot foot upon completion of the delivery.

6. *Overstriding*: This has already been discussed. It prevents the proper bending of the back in the follow-through and leads to the landing of the weight on the heel—the cause of the ruinous jarring of the vision. It can be corrected only by the use of moderation in striding.

7. *Improper footing*: This is harmful to all aspects of pitching form. It can be caused by poor shoes or an accumulation of mud on the spikes. More often, however, the improper planting of the pivot foot is the contributing factor. The spikes should not be placed on the rubber and the push-off made from that spot. Rather, the front spike should extend over the rubber at the start of the motion; the foot should pivot toward the pitching side; and the shoe should slide from the rubber and be braced against and parallel to it for the push-off.

8. *Poor physical condition*: This is definitely harmful to a pitcher's control, particularly in the late innings when fatigue begins to take its toll. A pitcher's control is no better than his wind and legs—and, of course, a pitcher without control has nothing. Plenty of good hard running is the logical solution.

9. *Mental factors*: A pitcher conclusively demonstrates lack of self-control when he becomes upset by poor support from his teammates or infuriated at his own failings. Lack of courage, or, more accurately, lack of confidence, can be caused in the vast majority of cases, by an unfamiliarity with game conditions or a lack of faith in one's ability to get the ball over the plate with something on it. Aiming the ball is another fault that is essentially mental in nature, because it stems primarily from lack of confidence.

Experience under game conditions, a full realization of the percentages that lie in his favor, and the resultant faith in his own ability favor the proper mental outlook that will help a pitcher overcome these difficulties.

The faults listed in this section are the most common causes of wildness. The existence of one of them is usually inadvertent and unconscious on the part of the pitcher. Careful self-analysis may uncover such a root of evil, but cooperation from a coach, manager, catcher, or another pitcher is a more certain method of detecting a flaw. If none of these basic faults are present in one's pitching style, the control problem will be greatly minimized—perhaps eliminated entirely.

### Correcting Wildness

When a pitcher's control is faulty, he must adopt an attitude that is simultaneously realistic and optimistic. Mere hope and a dogged persistence in his present style are not enough. The pitcher should seek informed outside help and diligently apply the proper advice, once the cause of the trouble is discovered. The pitcher, in setting out to improve his control, should realize that (1) his wildness is almost invariably caused by a flaw in his delivery; (2) he must discover the source of his trouble and work hard to remedy it; and (3) the situation is far from hopeless—control can definitely be improved by a sensible approach and a determined effort.

Experienced baseball men, in appraising the control problems of many pitchers over a number of years, have arrived at the conclusion that when wildness is consistent, it can be corrected, usually by an alteration in bodily movements that has the effect of adjusting the sights. Thus, if a pitcher's wildness results in his throwing the ball consistently to one general area outside the strike zone, his trouble can be rectified. If, on the other hand, his throws go "all over the place," he is releasing the ball differently on all of his deliveries, because of his changing finger pressures. Unfortunately, this is a serious situation, one that demands a complete change of style—a fresh start, as it were—if the situation is not to progress to a point beyond all hope.

Wildness is either horizontal or vertical in nature. In other words, a bad pitch is primarily inside, outside, too high, or too low. Of course, combinations of two of these difficulties do occur frequently, but wildness on pitch after pitch will be predominantly in only one of these general areas.

The pitching rubber is six inches wide by twenty-four inches long. This twenty-four-inch length provides a pitcher with sufficient space in which to make the adjustments needed to correct horizontal wildness. By moving to either side of the rubber, he can correct this horizontal wildness, the exact amount of the shift being determined through experimentation. Both overall wildness and temporary loss of control on a horizontal plane should be treated in this fashion. For example, if a right-handed pitcher finds that he is consistently wild inside in relation to a right-handed batter, he can eliminate this trouble by moving to his left on the rubber. A comparable application of this basic principle can be used to correct other instances of horizontal wildness in its varied forms.

Vertical wildness is primarily due to a flaw in the follow-through and is greatly affected by the length of the stride. A good follow-through, with the back bent and the pitching hand below and outside of the knee of the striding leg, is vital to good control and should be practiced continuously. Specific adjustments can be effected by alterations in the length of the stride. If a pitcher is wild high, he is releasing the ball too soon and can remedy the fault by shortening his stride. This move brings his body weight forward more quickly in relation to his arm motion, allowing a lower point of release and promoting a better follow-through, both of which will help him to bring the ball down. Conversely, when he is plagued by being wild low, a lengthening of his stride should offset the faulty equilibrium that is causing him to release the ball too late and making his pitches consistently low.

Similarity of actions has already been noted as imperative to good control. Wildness is often caused by a lack of this desired sameness in the stride. The striding foot should come down in the same place and in the same manner each time one of various pitches—fast ball, curve, change, and so forth—is thrown. A check of footprints can reveal when this is not being done, and an effort to stride in the same place for each pitch should bring about the necessary cure.

A pitcher should always have a specific mark at which to throw, and he should keep his eyes focused on that spot throughout his entire motion. Above all, he should have his eyes focused on his target prior to any forward movement of his body; otherwise his pitching will be tantamount to throwing at a moving target. One method to ensure the performance of this vital act is to hesitate momentarily at the top of the windup. This allows for applied concentration on the target, free from any distracting movements, and is a definite boon to control in the case of a pitcher whose wildness is due to his eyes wandering from the target.

Control is sometimes affected by the presence of runners on the bases. The chief cause of this is the failure of the pitcher to sight his target properly. The sideward stance provides a less complete view of home plate than does the normal delivery, in which the pitcher faces the batter squarely. Two things should be indelibly impressed on a hurler's mind when he works with men on base: (1) he should look at his target with both eyes (the tendency in working from a stop position runs counter to this); (2) he must never pitch from memory—in other words, he should take a good look at his target before delivering the ball, even at the cost of allowing the runner an extra step or two of lead. If these two precautions are observed, a man's control should be no worse with men on base than it is with the bases empty.

A further word of advice on correcting wildness concerns the desirability of acquiring a pendulum-like motion, in which movements are primarily backward and forward in relation to home plate. Excessive rocking moves the head and eyes and causes temporary loss of the target. An effective method of steering the ball toward the target without disrupting the smooth, pendulum movement, is to turn the body further in the direction in which the pitcher intends the ball to go. The ball should, moreover, be released in the same way; the striding foot should point directly at the target; and the ball should not be aimed.

Acquiring proper techniques for good control and applying the corrective therapy when wildness exists can best be accomplished on the sidelines during practice sessions. When throwing for control, the pitcher should work from a mound. Having a batter standing in hitting position is also desirable and is, incidentally, beneficial to the hitter, too, in his efforts to learn and familiarize himself with the strike zone. The use of strings erected to outline the strike zone is also of great value. Any of these devices can be fruitfully employed; a combination of all is ideal. Attempts at correcting wildness should further emphasize the need to give every pitch a definite purpose—even in simple warm-up sessions.

The performance of any of these measures that may apply to a particular case, the repetition of similar actions for each pitch, and the development of the proper mental attitude should help any pitcher who hopes to achieve good control.

### The Mental Side of Control

Some pitchers seem to have good control naturally; others succeed in developing it; still others never acquire it. Yet it is one of baseball's truisms that *anyone* can improve his control unless he is convinced that he cannot.

A pitcher's frame of mind is of tremendous importance to his overall performance and to his control in particular. Confidence, poise, and, to a certain extent, competitive spirit are increased by the assurance that comes from familiarity with the job. All of these influence a pitcher's control and, paradoxically, are at the same time influenced by his control. There is a very close interrelationship between them.

The successful pitcher takes keen delight in outsmarting the hitter. He also realizes how strongly percentages will work in his favor if he throws strikes. Even if he cannot overpower a batter, he is fully aware that the best of them do not hit safely more than once in three times at bat. Thus, if he gets the ball over the plate with good stuff on it, the law of averages is definitely on his side. If he can stay ahead of the hitter and then put the ball in the area of that man's weakness, he will be on his way to significant success.

Yet there are pitchers who are actually afraid to put the ball over the plate. This is, of course, a sign that they lack confidence in their stuff. It also indicates that they are not fully aware of the way in which percentages favor them. Even in batting practice, when the ball is "laid in there" for the hitter, more balls are hit that would be outs than would be base hits. Obviously, this fear can lead to nothing but trouble.

A pathetic and too often heard description of pitching ineptitude is, "He got behind the hitter and had to come in with a 'fat' pitch." A survey has shown that in the major leagues, a .250 hitter becomes a .350 hitter with the pitcher in the hole, and, just as conclusively, a .350 hitter becomes a .250 hitter when the pitcher has him in the hole. These are not exact figures, but they are approximations accurate enough to demonstrate that the pitcher who consistently falls behind the batter in the count is committing a grave error.

Occasional and usually inexplicable wild streaks will arise to plague every pitcher. These are all but inevitable occurrences, and the surest way to prolong one is to fall prey to excessive worry. A pitcher must never allow himself to ease up and aim the ball in order to get it over the plate. Instead, he should combat a spell of wildness by firing away naturally until he once again finds the proper groove.

Pressure can also take its toll on a pitcher's control. There is actually no need for him to allow the situation to become too big for him. He must bear in mind that the hitter is in an equally tough spot and that a pitcher, furthermore, has the odds in his favor. He has eight other men waiting to help him, and the law of averages dictates that even when the batter does hit the ball, it will fall in safely only a small percentage of the time.

The conclusions should be obvious. The pitcher who realizes that the advantage lies with him, who exhibits poise and assurance at all times, and who has confidence in his ability to get the ball over the plate with something on it will have little difficulty with his control and can reasonably expect to be a winner.

## THE BASIC PITCHES

Baseball's basic pitches are three in number. They are the fast ball, curve, and change of pace. More accurately, it may be said that there are four of them, since the change of pace includes a change-up on both the fast ball and curve.

The basic pitches, along with control of each of them, are all that any pitcher needs in order to be successful. At the same time, all four pitches must be perfected if a pitcher hopes to reach real stardom.

The slider has become prevalent in recent years and is a valuable addition to a pitcher's arsenal. The knuckler, screw ball, palm ball, fork ball, and so forth are the so-called off pitches and all have their staunch advocates. For the time being, however, we should concern ourselves with the basic three, the ones that are essential in making a pitcher. They should be mastered one at a time and, when each is perfected, will combine to give a pitcher an effective repertoire. Only after mastery of the basic pitches has been achieved should any thought be given to the other deliveries; even at that time, their acquisition is not vital to success on the mound.

When thrown at different speeds and, if possible, when delivered both overhand and sidearm, the basic pitches will furnish a pitcher with the material needed to inject an almost unlimited amount of variety into his method of operation.

### The Fast Ball

A good fast ball is, of course, a gift of nature. The ability to throw exceptionally hard cannot be learned. Any natural attributes, however, can and should be exploited fully. There are certain techniques that if perfected, will enable a pitcher to get the maximum benefit from his physical ability and will actually increase the speed of his delivery. Those we will consider at this point. Later, in the section on tactics, we will explore the strategy that makes possible the judicious use of various pitches in such a way that a fast ball can be made to seem considerably swifter than it actually is.

**Defining the Fast Ball.** A fast ball is, by literal definition, the swiftest pitch that a hurler is capable of delivering. More precisely, it is a normal, hard throw delivered with a full sweep of the arm and a completely natural motion.

The laws of physics have demonstrated that force cannot exist without resistance and that resistance will be nonexistent in the absence of force. In other words, one must be present in order for the other to develop. In relation to velocity, it has been conclusively proved that the speed of any object will be greater when resistance is built up against the propelling force.

These statements sound highly technical in the light of a discussion on pitching, but they certainly apply to this phase of baseball. Furthermore, an understanding of them may furnish the means for the development of an effective fast ball.

Force in pitching is provided by the long, whip-like action of the arm combined with a snap of wrist and elbow. Resistance, in this case, is furnished by finger pressure against the ball and the shifting of body weight brought about by the stride and push-off. The application of our physical laws to the act of throwing a baseball leads to the conclusion that the greater the resistance provided by the fingers and the momentum (not the sheer bulk) of the shift of body weight, and the longer the arc of the arm, and the stronger the wrist and elbow snap, the greater the velocity of the pitched ball. Most important of all contributing factors is the speed with which the arm comes through and the wrist is snapped.

The term "good fast ball" applies both to the actual speed of the pitch and, even more so, to the movement of the ball in flight. Mere velocity is generally not sufficient to nullify the ability of good hitters. The most effective fast ball is one that is not only swift, but also "live." That is, it deviates slightly in course, or "moves."

The movement of the ball in flight varies according to the spin imparted as it leaves a pitcher's hand. A fast ball that "moves" can deviate on either a horizontal or vertical plane and often does so in a combination of the two. Generally speaking, a "live" fast ball delivered overhand has a tendency to rise; thrown sidearm, it usually sinks; and hurled with a three-quarters delivery, it may do either. In addition, sideward deflections in course will be present in a great many cases. Through experience a pitcher can tell what tendency his fast ball has and can gauge himself accordingly in his use of it.

Pitchers who compile impressive strike-out records invariably possess an exceptionally good fast ball. It is their "strike-out pitch." Even in the case of pitchers who are not overpoweringly swift, a good, well-controlled, judiciously used fast ball is the one most likely to be their "out pitch." This leads to the idea that a pitcher should have two broadly defined types of fast ball—a good one, which is thrown naturally and with no extra effort, for use in getting ahead of the hitter and in what might be called normal situations; and an extra-fast one, which is held in reserve for those instances in which the pitcher finds himself in a tight situation or in which he has two strikes on the batter.

A further breakdown of fast ball types can be made and would include a sinker, a slider, and a power pitch. Some pitchers are fortunate enough to have developed all three. They can be employed for different purposes: the sinker, which breaks down, can be used when it is desirable to induce the batter to hit the ball on the ground; the slider, which moves to the side, can prevent the batter from getting good wood on the ball when he is set for a normal fast ball; and the extra-fast pitch, which should overpower a batter, can be used to "drive it" in on the batter when he has been properly set up for it. The pitcher who possesses all three has a valuable weapon with which to combat the hitters—variety in his most basic pitch sufficient enough so that the one pitch can be used in several widely differing situations.

**Throwing the Fast Ball.** The ultimate objective of a pitcher who is working to perfect his fast ball should be the development of maximum speed with minimum effort. Relaxation is the psychological basis for this. The bodily actions that produce maximum speed are a firm grip, a good push-off with the pivot foot, full utilization of the body weight, getting the shoulder behind the throw, a strong wrist and elbow snap, and a good follow-through. All these are absolutely necessary.

All deflections from a horizontal or vertical line and all changes in speed are caused by varying the spin and pressure. It is the grip on the ball and the snap of the wrist that are responsible for this.

For best results the first two fingers should be close together in gripping the ball. This provides a firmer grip and a more fluid wrist action, which, in turn, give greater rotation to a pitch. (A wide grip, on the other hand, can help one's control.) The ball should be placed as far out from the crotch formed by the thumb and fingers as is possible while still permitting control over the ball. Furthermore, the ball should be gripped firmly in order to provide resistance for the propelling force of the arm sweep, but not so tightly as to create a tense wrist. A grip that is too tight has a tendency to lock the muscles; conversely, a loose wrist supplies the rapidity of rotation that gives the ball its "life."

Adopting the proper grip is sometimes an involved matter and often calls for experimentation. This experimentation is occasioned, to a great extent, by the need to employ a grip that is just right—not too loose, not too tight; firm, yet fluid. Obviously, "feel" is an important factor. It cannot be taught in lectures or books but must be arrived at by the pitcher himself. The position of the thumb should not be overlooked during the period of trial and error. Its role is vital in contributing the delicate balance that provides maximum results.

Getting the weight and pumping power correctly behind the pitch is accomplished by three elements of the pitching motion—the pivot, the push-off, and the stride. It is desirable to use a full body pivot. This will transfer the weight, in balance, to the rear leg, which should be rigid though bent, like a coiled spring. Then follows the push-off, which is extremely important in imparting power to the throw. A pronounced push—slightly up as well as forward—should be employed off of the rear foot. This not only provides power but also serves to prevent the arm from coming through too late in the motion. This push leads naturally into the stride, which should not be so exaggerated as to dissipate all the force and leave none for the throw itself. Landing on the ball of the foot (not the heel) lessens resistance to the body's momentum and facilitates the continuous flow of motion that ends in the follow-through.

The direction in which the body weight should move warrants at least passing mention. The push-off and stride help to get the shoulder and body weight properly behind the throw. Only when the momentum imparted is directed in a straight line toward home plate will the full propelling power be brought into play. The throw must never be made across the body. For this reason previous reference has been made to the advisability of pushing off and striding directly toward home and planting the lead foot slightly toward the side opposite the throwing arm. To ensure the channeling of the body weight in the proper path, a pitcher should extend this principle to the pumping motion, which is the inception of a pitch. Preliminary moves of this nature will lead to a more effective utilization of a man's bodily capacities; that is, they will help him to throw a better fast ball.

The necessary good follow-through is the natural culmination that stems from reaching way back. It is actually a result rather than a cause and furnishes proof that the other fundamentals have been properly observed.

Reaching way back and the follow-through are closely allied and represent the start and finish of the prescribed pendulum-like motion. The delivery should be in the form of an arch having as its initial lowpoint the end of the backswing, its highpoint the release of the ball, and its concluding lowpoint the follow-through.

Each pitcher can tell what tendency his fast ball has and can take steps to improve its action. The guiding principle is to hold the ball in the way that will bring it into the position in which it will be subject to the fullest degree of air resistance. For instance, in order to impart maximum backspin to a rising fast ball, the pitcher should use an across-the-seams grip. He should grip a sinking fast ball, on the other hand, with the seams. The former applies primarily to overhand pitchers, the latter to sidearmers.

By releasing the ball off the ends of the fingers with a strong wrist snap, an overhand pitcher can impart the backspin needed to make his

*Release of the ball (fast ball)*

fast ball "hop." The heavy backspin exerts an opposite rising force, which at a certain point succeeds in overcoming gravity for a split second, enabling the ball to rise slightly in its flight.

Much publicity has been given the "sinker." In most instances this is not a separate pitch, but merely a fast ball that has a natural tendency to sink rather than rise. This is a regular characteristic of a sidearmer's fast ball and is common to a number of hurlers who deliver the ball in three-quarters fashion. A downward follow-through is one of the chief factors in making the ball sink, and this should be emphasized in the case of a pitcher who throws this type of fast ball. When combined with an inward roll of the wrist and the release of the ball off the side of the middle finger the effect of the downward follow-through will be more pronounced. This is known as "turning the ball over"; at the finish of the delivery, the back of the hand is turned in toward the head.

Because the middle finger is longest and is the last one in contact with the ball at the point of release, the fast ball also has a tendency to move toward the side from which it is thrown, particularly in the case of a pitcher who rolls his wrist to the inside. A different spin can be imparted simply by moving the tip of the middle finger back or by gripping the ball off center. Thus, the fast ball can be made to move to either side. This is the underlying principle of the slider, which is, in reality, a variation on the fast ball and will be discussed later.

In brief, the factors that create a good fast ball are a firm grip, a good push-off on the pivot foot, getting the shoulder and body behind the throw, a strong wrist and elbow snap, and a complete follow-through.

**Improving the Fast Ball.** The most effective method of throwing the fast ball, as well as the varieties thereof, has been rather thoroughly covered in the last section under the general heading of *Mechanics.* Yet one problem remains. What should be done in the case of a pitcher who is not blessed by nature with a good fast ball or in the case of one who feels that he is properly observing all the fundamentals but whose fast ball is still ineffective?

One part of this question concerns pitching strategy and is the subject of a later chapter showing how to put all these principles to correct use. The other concerns itself with ironing out flaws that may be present in the delivery and with learning some of the tricks of the trade that accomplished moundsmen have discovered through hard work and experimentation.

The first step to an improved fast ball is the uncovering of any basic flaw that may be hindering its delivery or the lack of that little something that will make a big difference in quality. Self-appraisal, though always helpful, is not the complete answer. Close observation, analysis, and instruction by an interested party are needed. A coach, manager, or experienced teammate can often provide the solution to the problem and should be consulted.

Several simple measures that can be of help in developing a good fast ball will be discussed briefly in the following paragraphs. Some of them have been mentioned in the preceding material; any or all of them may possibly provide the means by which a pitcher can acquire a more effective fast ball.

1. The fast ball is improved by practice while a pitcher is young. The muscles most important to throwing well will develop along with a youngster's physical growth. Plenty of free and natural throwing is a boon to the development of a pitcher and should be indulged in to the fullest extent—but should not exceed that point at which any undue strain on the arm is felt.

2. The grip is basic in importance. The pressure of the two fingers increases the rotation of the ball; the seams aid the grip and should be utilized to the fullest extent. In his eagerness to throw hard, a pitcher may allow himself to grip the ball too tightly or to "choke the ball" (allowing insufficient space between the ball and the crotch of the hand). The former causes a tension that locks the muscles and wrist; the latter cuts the speed of a pitch by decreasing the leverage provided by the wrist and arm motion.

3. Body movement should not be expended in any direction other than toward home plate. One of the chief causes of a lack of speed (and of sore arms) is throwing across the body. The motion should be directly toward home plate and be given impetus by a powerful push-off. Swinging the front hip and leg into the stride can add force to the delivery. It is, furthermore, of the utmost importance that the front knee be bent and flexible. The push-off should be slightly up as well as forward, particularly in the case of overhand pitchers, who will find that this gives a better angle of delivery and increased leverage, both of which help impart the "hop" that makes this pitch so effective.

4. The gloved hand and arm help bring the weight correctly into the pitch. They should be thrust toward the plate (thrown at the batter) in such a way that the action will start a good body movement.

5. One practice may promote relaxation and contribute to the value of the pump: when bending forward, the pitcher should exhale; when going up and back, he should inhale; he should have his lungs full on the "reach-back."

6. Rosin can be helpful when properly used. In hot weather it dries the hand; on a cold day it offsets the prevailing dry, smooth condition. It definitely helps provide the needed friction. For most telling results, it should be applied only to the first two fingers.

7. The condition of the ball can contribute to the effect achieved by a fast ball. A slick, new ball has a tendency to sail. A cut ball will break in the direction away from the cut as it is prior to release. (With a blemished surface facing to the right, the ball breaks down and to the left.) A rough spot will add to friction, thereby increasing the ball's rotation. When present, these conditions should be fully exploited.

## The Curve Ball

It is not only a consensus of informed baseball opinion but also a proven fact that a curve ball can be learned, improved upon, and perfected by almost any pitcher with average physical abilities. Its mastery depends on aptitude, flexibility of wrist, suppleness of arm, and the determination evidenced by the man who is endeavoring to acquire an effective curve ball.

Yet a first-rate curve rarely comes easily. The pitcher must practice it assiduously until he can throw it with a consistently sharp break and with the degree of control that will enable him to "move it around" as well as he can his fast ball. He should also bear in mind that even a fair curve ball is often sufficient to keep hitters off balance: the very knowledge that it is included in his repertoire will inevitably enhance the effectiveness of his fast ball.

**Theory.** Two basic methods exist whereby a pitcher can retire a batter—on a horizontal or on a vertical plane. Included in the first category are the fast ball, which either overpowers or sneaks by the hitter, and changes of speed, which are designed to upset his timing. The curve ball is the principal method of applying the vertical-plane theory because, quite obviously, it is the one pitch that changes course most radically and usually on a predominantly vertical plane.

Before suggesting specific curve ball techniques and in an attempt to lend greater appreciation of them to the reader, we will introduce the rudimentary scientific aspects of this pitch.

First, let it be clearly understood that a curve ball is dependent on forward spin for its action—unlike the fast ball, which derives its "life" and attendant effectiveness from its backspin. Having imparted sufficient forward spin to the ball, a pitcher can rest assured that air resistance will cause it to change course. This is a natural physical reaction of air to any object moving through it at high speed. The air resistance that builds up will cause a deviation in the course of a ball that is rotating at an exceedingly rapid rate. The spin of the ball meets resistance from the air on its top side, but because the spin at the bottom as the ball rotates is accelerating, there is less resistance or air pressure at that point. This causes the air to "give way," as it were, and makes the ball break in the direction in which it is spinning. It follows that the faster the rotation the greater the resistance on top and the give on the bottom (or side, according to the angle of delivery) and the bigger, if not sharper, the curve.

One can appreciate the significance of air resistance in making a curve ball break by considering that a good curve is exceedingly difficult to throw at high altitudes (light air), but a damp day (heavy air) facilitates the throwing of a good one. To lend emphasis to this premise, one should note that, paradoxically, a curve ball pitcher can obtain good results when throwing into the wind. Here, again, increased air resistance is responsible since a better "bite" can be achieved when nature provides a rotating ball with added air resistance.

It is estimated that a ball spinning at 1800 rpm will provide optimum results. Obviously, then, the aspiring curve-baller should first adopt techniques designed to provide maximum rotation, the key to a good curve ball.

### Technique

The proper technique for throwing an effective curve ball can be divided into several segments. Each facet is of prime importance and should be approached separately—regardless of the pitcher's familiarity with the pitch—until mastered. Putting them together into a single delivery will then come much more easily.

**Grip.** Any grip that feels comfortable and that, above all, produces maximum spin is the correct one. Although it is preferable to use the same grip for both fast ball and curve, the value of achieving the best possible curve far outweighs any benefit that the opposition may derive from recognizing a difference in grips. It is unlikely that a batter will be able to take advantage of advance knowledge of the pitch if his discovery of a curve ball grip does not take place until the pitcher's arm is well into its forward motion. The time interval in this case is too minute for the difference in finger position to bear heavily on the situation. Thus, the best policy is to use the grip that produces the best curve, keeping it concealed from the batter long enough to nullify the effect of possible discovery and hiding it from the base-line coaches until the actual throwing motion has begun.

In order to facilitate fluid wrist action, the pitcher should not grip the ball as tightly for the curve as for the fast ball. Most of the pressure is applied with the middle finger. The actual gripping of the ball is done

(a) Grip: Ball held comfortably, not choked, with ample space between thumb and forefinger, thumb tucked under, last two fingers bent into palm, pressure with middle finger. (b) Curve takes form; elbow and wrist bend in toward head as elbow comes up to shoulder level. (c) Forward motion: hips open, left foot strides toward plate, elbow stays high, head moves out of way; fingers on top, thumb under. (d) Snap: Elbow leads, wrist is on outside of ball and rolls toward hitter, release will be in front of head; back of hand is thrown at catcher with ball being pulled down and across body. (e) Release: Ball comes out of hand between thumb and index finger; thumb is now on top with fingers underneath, rotation of hand completed as ball leaves it. (f) Follow-through: Arms come across body and hand winds up below knee with knuckles pointed toward ground; back is bent.

primarily with the ends of the fingers—with the admonition that the strong tendency to wrap the fingers as far around the ball as possible should be avoided. (This is known as "choking the ball" and can impede both the rotation and the speed of the pitch.)

Another matter that may be left to individual preference is whether to release the ball off the ends or sides of the fingers. The former allows greater wrist movement but, being used primarily for an overhand curve, limits the possible angles of delivery. The latter allows greater use of the elbow in imparting snap to the ball and is adaptable to all angles of delivery. There are effective pitchers utilizing each of these methods, their decisions being based on maximum effectiveness of the curve. Nevertheless, this study of curve ball techniques will be limited to the side-of-fingers release, for it is far more widely used, and its adaptability to different angles of delivery enhances the tactical uses to which the curve ball may be put.

Perhaps the most important, yet neglected, aspect of the curve ball grip is the position and use of the thumb. Too often there is insufficient space between thumb and forefinger. These two digits should "bisect the ball." This means that, in relation to the thumb, the middle (or pressure) finger will be more than halfway around the ball. Tucking the thumb under the ball by bending it at the knuckle will add to this effect. The object here is to ensure that the release of the ball will be *between* the thumb and forefinger—not over the thumb, a flaw that impedes the speed of rotation and the length and strength of the wrist and elbow snap. Furthermore, when the thumb is tucked under the ball, it can be brought into play to give extra impetus to the spin of the ball. This quick flip as the ball is being released will help impart enough additional rotation to increase the sharpness of the break.

Only the thumb and first two fingers should be used in throwing a curve. The ring finger, too, should be bent (into the palm) as should the little finger. The use of the ring finger in gripping the ball is another deterrent to both speed and rotation.

Finger position in relation to the seams is still another matter of personal preference. Some good curve-ballers use an across-the-seams grip; others hold the ball with the seams. Although greater spin is provided by the rotation of all four seams, the pitcher's comfort and success are the best criteria to follow. It should be emphasized, however, that whatever grip is employed, having the first two fingers close together, not spread, is essential to imparting maximum rotation to the ball.

**Arm Movement.** The curve ball should not begin to materialize at the beginning of the motion. Too often, young pitchers have a tendency to "crook the arm" and bend the wrist at the very outset, a clear give-away to the hitter that a curve is coming. No matter how good the curve, deception is still a highly important element in its effectiveness. When correctly done, the pitcher brings the arm back and down as in the normal throwing motion. When the elbow comes up to shoulder level and the arm reaches a position behind the ear, the curve ball delivery begins to take shape. At this point, where the arm begins it forward motion, the forearm and wrist should be turned in toward the shoulder and head until muscular tension is felt. The elbow precedes the hand in the forward sweep so as to "pull" the ball through. It should also be kept away from the body to assure the full-arm sweep that is an essential factor in throwing a good curve. The elbow should remain up (at shoulder level) until the wrist snap has started; in this way the pitcher can "stay on top of the ball" and also make it appear more like the fast ball at this stage of the motion. All this will bring the wrist and hand into position to release the ball with a rolling motion ("throw the back of your hand at the catcher") between the thumb and forefinger.

**Stride.** The proper stride for the curve is several inches shorter than that used in throwing a fast ball. This is of the utmost importance because the shorter stride produces a lower point of release for the ball and a better follow-through (the back must be bent), both of which help to impart greater spin. The proper stride will also facilitate bringing the arm *across* the body, another essential in throwing a good curve. Other measures beneficial to the stride include a good push-off with the rear foot to aid the follow-through and opening the stride (stepping more to the side than on the fast ball). The latter device is especially helpful in making the break of a curve less flat (a good one should move down as well as to the side) and is particularly recommended as a means of improving a sidearm curve ball.

**Release.** The budding moundsman should be advised that, on all pitches, an effective maneuver in both hiding the ball from the batter and imparting greater force to it is to show the hitter his tail as the ball is brought back and his belly button just before the release. At the latter moment the toe of the striding foot should point straight at the target. Facing the hitter directly immediately before propelling the ball plateward takes on added significance when the curve is being thrown. This is so because it is essential to open the front shoulder and, in fact, to move the head to the side, because the arm must come across the body if the curve is to be a good one. Finally, the pitcher's head is, in effect, being pulled out of the way of his arm as it comes through in its forward motion.

The pitcher can provide the curve ball with additional propulsion and spin by "pulling" it to the side with the front hip and leg and "pushing" it through with the rear hip and leg. The shoulder, too, enters the overall picture and should be as much as possible behind the throw. In essence, then, practically all parts of the body should be brought into the act in order to apply maximum *pull* to the ball, thereby achieving as much rotation as can be imparted to the development of a first-rate curve.

At this stage of the delivery the pitcher's arm motion has brought the elbow to shoulder level, preceding the hand in its forward path. The wrist and elbow are bent in toward the head, the first two fingers on top of the ball, the thumb under it.

A powerful wrist snap, also utilizing the elbow to a great extent, is the principle objective at this stage of the motion. Timing also takes on added significance in achieving optimum effectiveness in the break that the ball takes. In fact, the timing of the wrist snap is a delicate matter, deserving repeated practice until properly executed. The pitcher should seek a late snap, though not so late that the ball will be delivered low and with insufficient spin. Conversely, the curve ball will be completely ineffective if the wrist snap is completed before the hand is in front of the head.

The wrist snap should start when the hand has reached a position at which it is even with the body in its full sweep—but still behind the head. This is the point at which the pitcher should be most conscious of the need to throw the back of his hand at the catcher. His fingers have been on top and his thumb beneath the ball, but now their relative positions should be reversed. The wrist is rotated toward the plate, the index finger goes down, the thumb rolls up, and the ball leaves the hand with the fingers beneath it. Stated differently, this means that the back of the hand should be toward the ground, the palm toward the sky. In addition, correct execution and best results are most likely when the ball is released in front of the head.

### Improving the Curve Ball

Although an aspiring hurler may observe these rudiments of the curve ball, he may still lack an effective one. It is here that the therapeutic approach should be applied. The coach should generally check the man's grip, stride, and release for the proper performance of the techniques just outlined.

Other points also warrant inspection. It is important not to attempt to throw the curve ball too hard. This practice can cause a stiff wrist, whereas, in order to break off a good curve, the pitcher must keep his wrist relaxed and its motion fluid. The curve ball is, by nature, a slower pitch than the fast ball, and no pitcher should strive to alter that fact. It is the wrist and elbow snap that should be as hard as possible, not the throwing motion itself.

Every device used to develop an effective curve is connected with the important practice of "pulling the ball" through the motion. This cannot be overemphasized. In fact, the overwhelming majority of poor curves are caused by the pitcher's *pushing* the ball. Pushing the curve violates two essential techniques: (1) the hand is too far ahead of the elbow before the ball is released; (2) the front, not the back, of the hand is going toward the catcher.

The correct wrist action for throwing a curve is similar to that used in hammering a nail, with the obvious exception that the elbow and hand are rotated until the back of the hand would be used to apply the blow to the nail. The pitcher should feel that he is bringing his hand over the ball. Furthermore, it is imperative that the *wrist* be *outside* of the ball. The arm makes a full sweep until it is alongside the knee of the striding leg, and the back must be bent to a great degree.

All these observations, with repeated emphasis on "pulling the ball," arise from one of our previously stated irrefutable physical premises; namely, that a curve ball is dependent on *overspin* for its action.

### Coaching Points

There are several useful teaching devices designed to improve the curve ball. The first is a simple exercise to improve the wrist snap. It consists simply of snapping the wrist with a curve ball rotation while holding the elbow stationary. After this has been done for a few minutes, the wrist and elbow should be snapped with the shoulder serving as fulcrum. Finally, the hand is brought to a position behind the ear and bent as in the curve ball motion, while the elbow is raised to shoulder level but kept ahead of the hand. Now a full curve ball arm motion is repeated several times, with emphasis on correct observance of the fundamentals. A few minutes a day spent in this fashion would be beneficial to any pitcher striving to develop a good curve ball. The wrist-snap phase of the routine can be done often—between classes, walking to school, and so on. Squeezing a tennis ball or handgrip is an additional measure that will strengthen the wrist itself.

The problem of learning to throw a curve ball should be approached in stages, the pitcher working from gradually increasing distances until he reaches the full sixty feet, six inches. He should start at perhaps thirty feet, spinning the ball with a full curve ball motion. After he has achieved a satisfactory "feel," he should repeat the process at forty-five feet; finally, he can work from the regulation pitching distance. The idea behind this method is to develop the curve ball motion that will impart maximum spin to the ball. Primary consideration should be given to how fast the ball can be made to spin. Once he has mastered maximum rotation, the break of the ball will take care of itself, and the pitcher can concentrate on the curve ball as a pitch.

An excellent means for improving one's curve ball on any given day is related to the manner in which the pitcher delivers his first few curves during his warm-up. He should throw them with his rear foot anchored. In order to get any significant rotation and action on the ball, he must observe all the correct fundamentals of arm movement and release. In particular, he is forced to throw the back of his hand at the catcher, pull the ball down, and bend his back. After a few preliminary deliveries in this manner he can employ his normal curve ball motion with much greater likelihood of his throwing a good one. It is also a good idea to use the anchored-leg technique for one of his curve balls during his warm-up pitches before every inning.

An additional effective coaching point is the use of two admonitions, repeated whenever necessary. These take the form of continually reminding a pitcher to "*pull* the ball" and to "bend his back." So important are these factors that it is incumbent on a coach to issue a warning to a pitcher any time he spots a violation of either, whether it be in a game, during batting practice, or simply during a sideline warm-up.

### Controlling the Curve

For effective tactical use of any pitch, good control of it is essential. The pitcher who can throw strikes seven out of ten times with each of his deliveries has taken the first and most important step toward becoming a real craftsman. To categorize, we may term this stage of development *control*. Projecting this to its more desirable point, let us say that good control means the ability to throw the ball *close* to one's target with consistency. Good control of even reasonably good stuff is sufficient to win at almost any level of competition—certainly at the level of scholastic baseball.

The importance of the curve ball having been advanced and its techniques acquired, developing control of it is the next logical step. (It is assumed that this has already been done with the fast ball.) Getting it into the strike zone 70 percent of the time is the first objective. Moving it around as desired is, of course, the ultimate goal.

The idea that a curve ball is more difficult to control than a fast ball is not necessarily so. It should not be if it is thrown as often as the fast ball and cultivated with care. In addition, more precise mechanical techniques are used in delivering the curve ball. Thus, the greater physical discipline involved here should serve to make the curve ball more easily controlled. In fact, once mastered, its action and its line of flight should be more predictable on a given day or in a particular inning than are those of the fast ball.

The suggestions propounded in the section on *Control* are applicable to the curve ball and should be followed carefully. Emphasis on throwing low strikes takes on added importance when the curve is used, for a curve ball is most effective when thrown low, whereas a high, or "hanging," curve is the most likely candidate for the home run ball. Ability to keep the curve ball low is often sufficient in itself for winning. Once this has been mastered, the knack of hitting the corners should be sought. Acquisition of this type of proficiency all but assures one of outstanding success on the mound.

The mechanics previously mentioned are essential for the control as well as the action of the curve ball. With primary regard to control, emphasis should be on the stride—having the proper length, having it slightly open, landing on the ball of the foot (not the heel), and pointing the striding foot directly at the target. Moving around on the rubber and adjusting the direction of the stride are beneficial to aiming for spots. "Pulling to the side" with the front foot and hip can, for example, provide a more sweeping break and/or move the ball out of the strike zone when desired. Incidentally, moving to the side of the rubber from which he throws will provide a pitcher with a sharper angle for his curve.

The best feature of the practice-makes-perfect routine is that the curve ball and the control of it are being improved simultaneously. All this leads to the question of when a boy should start extensive use of the curve ball and of what possible damage can arise from throwing it too often. Any youngster who is ready for high school varsity competition should be mature enough physically to become a curve ball pitcher. As for frequency of use, many good pitchers have relied heavily on the breaking ball for years without unusual adverse effect on the arm. In fact, the curve ball may be less damaging to the arm than the fast ball. The latter seems to place more strain on the shoulder and is thrown harder, whereas the heavy load borne by the wrist and elbow seems to allow for a more even distribution of the strain when a curve is thrown. Bursitis of the shoulder seems to be the most common crippler of pitchers, and the sufferers thereof generally believe that this source of discomfort stems from trying to get too much on the fast ball too many times, rather than from throwing curve balls.

### The Change of Pace

The change of pace, employed judiciously, can be the most valuable weapon at a pitcher's command. This is due to its dual purpose in serving as a good pitch in its own right while making his other deliveries more effective by preventing the batter from getting set for them.

Changing speeds in such a way as to keep the hitter off balance and upset his timing is an example of retiring him on a horizontal plane. In other words, the batter can be fooled by differing velocities in the pitches that are delivered to him even though they involve no deviation in line of flight, the idea being to nullify his power by making him swing too soon or too late to hit the ball with authority. Added to breaking stuff and a live fast ball, the change of pace will give a pitcher sufficient equipment to cope with any hitter.

**The Value of the Change-up.** Every pitcher will sooner or later encounter batters whose physical ability equals his own and whom he cannot overpower. It is here that he must become a pitcher rather than simply a thrower. At this point the change of pace proves valuable and really becomes a necessity. Taking something off a normal delivery can completely upset a batter's timing and make him relatively easy prey for a smart moundsman.

A pitcher should use no fewer than three different speeds. First come his normal fast pitches; second, the extra something that he should hold in reserve for tight spots; and third, the slow pitch, or change of pace, with which he keeps the hitter off balance. The pitcher must avoid firing away with everything he has on every pitch, thereby getting in an operating rut that will enable the batter to adjust his timing to every delivery of the ball. The objective is to acquire the ability to retire the batter on a horizontal plane.

Every pitcher should strive to develop a change of pace. It has strategic value in giving a man a wider variety of pitches with which to operate, psychological value in making the batter realize that he must not allow himself to be set for only one speed, and physical value by imposing little strain on a pitcher's arm and by being less tiring than his fast pitches.

**Mastering the Change of Pace.** The most effective change-ups are those that most closely resemble the fast pitches in everything save velocity of the ball in flight. Exaggerated movements or differences in method of delivery should be avoided. To give the pitch its maximum of deception, the pitcher should not only use the same motion but also expend the same amount of effort in making that motion. The objective

*Release of the ball (change of pace)*

is to make the batter swing at the pitcher's motion rather than at the ball itself.

The means by which professionals lend similarity to the appearance of their fast and slow pitches are several in number and involve either the grip or the stride. They are as follows:

1. Probably the most commonly employed method is one in which the ball is held well back against the crotch of the hand, gripped loosely, and thrown with a tight wrist. The fingers remain crooked to serve as a brake.

2. The finger tips are raised and the ball is gripped as though the fingers were cut off at the second joint. Pressure is applied at that point (the middle joint), and the ball is thrown with a stiff wrist and no snap, the motion being closely akin to that used in pulling down a window shade. The raised fingers mean that the ball is shoved in shot-put fashion.

3. A more effective method is a combination of these two and should be tried when the pitcher feels that he is capable. Here, a fast ball grip is used, but the ball is held back in the crotch of the hand. As the release is made, the finger tips are raised. This manner of throwing the change is more deceptive because it imparts a backward rotation that makes the pitch more closely resemble a fast ball.

4. Another way in which something can be taken off the fast ball is by lengthening the stride and dragging the rear foot, thereby slowing the weight shift and lessening the force put into the pitch. This is particularly helpful in throwing a change of pace curve ball, for which a good wrist snap is necessary for getting significant break on the ball; consequently, the arm motion and grip should be practically the same as that used for the fast curve.

5. Gripping the ball with three fingers (rather than two) will also serve to detract from the speed of a pitch, no matter how hard it is thrown.

6. Simply taking something off one's fast pitches can be effective, the main idea still being to lend variety to the repertoire and to upset the hitter's timing.

One thing about the change-up that should always be borne in mind is that the looser the grip, the slower the pitch will be.

The change of pace is the most difficult of the three basic pitches to control and requires constant practice for mastery. Accomplished mound artists develop it to the point at which they can move it around at will, not merely get it over the plate. This is a goal well worth aspiring to.

The change should not be thrown too slow lest the batter succeed in double-timing it. Neither should it be so fast as to offer too little variation in speed from the regular pitches. Above all, the ball should be kept low if the pitch is to be effective.

No man will ever become an accomplished pitcher until he has learned to throw a deceptive, well-controlled change of pace with complete confidence.

### The Slow Curve

Baseball's better pitchers throw a change-up off the curve as well as off the fast ball. This immediately gives them one more pitch with which to work on the batter. A thoughtful approach will show that the slow curve can be, in itself, the most effective pitch in a hurler's repertoire, because it will provide him with a single delivery that can fool the batter on both a horizontal and a vertical plane.

Several of the principles used in throwing a straight change-up apply to the slow curve. Using a longer stride and dragging the rear foot is a method that has already been mentioned in connection with this pitch. Its great value lies in the fact that it allows a normal curve ball arm motion and wrist snap to be used while decreasing the speed of the pitch, thus promoting a slow curve with a good break.

The slow curve can also be thrown by employing a loose grip, the rule of thumb being the looser the grip, the slower the pitch; by keeping the elbow relatively close to the body for an overhand delivery, preventing the full-arm sweep that imparts speed to a pitch; by using more body motion, thereby dissipating most of the force in this action rather than in the sweep of the arm; and by raising the fingers and tightening the wrist action, just as in the straight change.

Any of these ideas may prove adaptable and helpful to a pitcher in acquiring the knack of throwing a change curve. Regardless of the technique used, this pitch should be practiced diligently in the same manner advocated for developing a good curve ball; that is, the process should be gradual, with the pitcher spinning the ball from a short distance and working back to the full sixty feet, six inches, striving for a deceptive motion and maximum rotation while doing so.

An aspiring pitcher should, quite naturally, use the method that he finds will give him the best results, keeping in mind that the slow curve should be gripped well back in the hand since this technique prevents a man from throwing the ball fast while still enabling him to impart good spin to it.

## The Slider

Emphasis has been placed on the three basic pitches, with the firm conviction that mastery and control of them are difficult in themselves and should provide any pitcher with the necessary equipment to cope with the best of hitters.

As he advances through the various stages of baseball, a pitcher may find it advisable to add an extra pitch—but only after the basic three have been perfected.

The most favored of the off pitches that hurlers strive to develop as added equipment is the slider. It is relatively simple to throw and control, having great deception in that it resembles a fast ball, yet behaving like a quick, sharp curve as it nears the plate.

**What It Is.** The slider is often referred to as a "nickel curve." Nevertheless, it can be more accurately classified as a variation on the fast ball. It is thrown with a normal fast ball motion, refined by a minor alteration in grip or by a slight twist of the wrist as the ball is released.

In the section on the fast ball we mentioned that the ball can be made to move to the right or left by altering the grip or by moving one of the finger tips back, the theory being that by applying pressure at a different point, the pitcher will impart a different spin to the ball.

This principle assuredly applies to the slider. The basic idea in its development is to provide sufficient spin to make the ball move to the side (slide), rather than change courses in pronounced fashion (curve). The great advantage in using this pitch is that it approaches the batter almost as swiftly as a fast ball (which it will resemble), while moving in the same direction as the curve ball—but with a quicker, smaller break.

**How It Is Thrown.** Unlike the curve ball, the slider is thrown with the index finger controlling its release and being the last digit in contact with the ball. (In this respect it can be likened to passing a football.) The pitcher should experience the feeling of pointing his index finger at home plate as he throws the slider.

The first finger is the one with which pressure is applied. In further contrast to the curve ball delivery, the slider is thrown with a very late wrist snap (immediately before the release), which is just enough to impart the rotation that will make the ball veer to the side opposite that from which it is thrown.

With these ideas to help him in developing a good slider, a pitcher should give consideration to the two principal methods of delivery and should then adapt one of them to his own use, along with any refinements that may be needed to achieve good results.

One of the techniques that can be used involves a fast ball grip and motion, modified by a slight outward rotation of the wrist as the ball is released. It is analogous to shaking hands with the ball—the hand is brought down, more or less to the side of the ball, which slides off the fingers as it is let go. The pitcher imparts sufficient spin to make the ball move to the side, though not enough to slow it up and make it break in a big arc, like the curve.

The other principal method is one that enables the pitcher to achieve the same effect by gripping the ball off center, with the greater part of it being toward the side to which it will move. It is thrown with a fast ball motion, the off-center grip giving it the desired rotation.

The slider should be kept away from the middle of the plate. When thrown to a man who bats from the same side (righty versus righty) and aimed for the outside half of the plate, it will veer away from his bat. It is probably most effective however, when it can be made to break in on the hands of a man who bats from the opposite side.

One word of caution should be interjected at this point. The slider can impose an extra strain on the elbow and for this reason should not be attempted unless the arm is in good condition and until it is thoroughly warmed up.

## The Other Off Pitches

The deliveries mentioned above generally suffice to provide a pitcher with all the equipment he needs. However, if deficiencies exist in his command of the more conventional pitches and their effectiveness, he may find it advisable to develop one of the so-called off pitches. It must be understood that pitchers of limited experience should use them only as a last resort. More accomplished hurlers who employ them often do so because their fast ball or curve is of inferior quality, and they usually rely very heavily on whichever of these off pitches they include in their repertoires.

### The Knuckle Ball

The knuckler has enjoyed much popularity, no doubt because of its sometimes baffling actions. It can be so unpredictable that at times it will fool batter, catcher, and pitcher alike. Furthermore, it is not only difficult to control but also easy to run on, consequently allowing base runners to take liberties at the pitcher's expense.

The knuckler is held with the ball cradled against the first joints or fingernails of either the first two or first three fingers, which are bent for this pitch. The thumb and remaining finger(s) encircle the ball in a tight grip and serve primarily to control it.

A spinning ball is held on course by its rotation and can be likened to a bullet fired from a gun. The knuckle ball, on the other hand, because it revolves slightly if at all, does not hold its course and derives its erratic actions from the resistance of the air or wind against the seams of the ball. For this reason the knuckler will have a better break when thrown into a wind blowing toward or across the path of the ball. A good one floats toward the plate, breaking suddenly, just before it reaches the batter. Variations in the cleanliness of the seams cause the inconsistency in the actions of this pitch.

There are two principal types of knuckle ball: (1) the floater, or butterfly type, which is thrown at half speed with a stiff wrist and seems to dance as it approaches the plate, reacting to each shift in air currents; (2) the fast knuckler, or "dry spitter," which is thrown at full speed. As the ball is released the fingers are snapped outward (extended), giving the ball extra velocity and sufficient downspin to make it dip sharply as it nears the batter—"rolling off the table," as it were.

A pitcher will find it next to impossible to hide this pitch from the batter and coaches. Its success is due to its actions, not to any element of surprise.

### The Screw Ball

The screw ball is, in effect, a reverse curve. Its grip is similar to the fast ball's and it is thrown with an inside-out twist of the hand and wrist. It is spun out of the hand between the middle and ring fingers and is given its rotation by the reverse quarter turn of the wrist, the middle finger release, and the thumb, which is used to increase the reverse spin by giving the ball a last-second flip as it is released.

The screw ball is usually thrown overhand and breaks down and toward the side from which it is thrown. It is a relatively slow pitch, and its break is far less pronounced than that of the curve ball.

Because of the manner of delivery, the fingers go through first, then the ball, creating the effect of a change-up. In fact, the screw ball is sometimes used as a change of pace, not so much for the action of the ball (although this does add to its effectiveness) but because it simply cannot be a fast pitch, even when thrown hard. The reverse twist of the wrist and the dragging action of the hand in releasing the ball serve to take away much of the speed that is normally provided by natural arm and body action.

This pitch often proves a great strain on the arm because of the unnatural motion used in throwing it. If for no other reason, its use by inexperienced pitchers should not be encouraged.

### The Fork Ball

The fork ball is so named because of the manner in which it is gripped. The index and middle fingers form a fork that encircles the ball. This pitch is thrown with a forward wrist snap, and the ball slides from between the spread fingers.

The fork ball, like the knuckler, has little rotation and, consequently, floats toward the plate. Its break is almost invariably downward and is more predictable than the knuckler. Furthermore, it can be much more easily concealed than the knuckle ball and, for most pitchers, is less troublesome to control. Achieving effective action of the fork ball, however, is far more difficult.

The fork ball cannot be thrown with great speed, no matter how intense the effort, and for that reason can be used as a change of pace.

### The Palm Ball

This pitch is gripped with all the fingers on and around the ball and spread slightly. The ball is held back against the palm of the hand and slides from the thumb and palm with little wrist action, the fingers resting very lightly on the ball and acting primarily as a guide.

The palm ball revolves very little and floats in with a slight downward break, much like the knuckler and fork ball. It is an even slower pitch than those two.

This pitch can also be thrown with the two-finger, second-joint grip delineated under the heading *change of pace*. In this case the ball is slid from the hand with the palm to the side (as for a curve ball) or down (as for a fast ball). The former is known as the *slip pitch*.

Let it be emphatically stated to all young pitchers that they should give no consideration to the off pitches until the basic three can be delivered with control, consistency, and effectiveness.

## *FIELDING FOR THE PITCHER*

According to an old baseball maxim, a successful pitcher is one who rarely, if ever, hurts himself. One part of his job in which a pitcher can definitely help himself is fielding his position. Too often the pitcher's job is thought of as simply throwing the ball, and his defensive play is left to instinct and natural athletic ability. The study and practice of correct techniques and tactics relating to this phase of the game can contribute immeasurably toward making a pitcher's main task much easier, while also making him a well-rounded ballplayer who contributes in all respects to the success of his team.

### On Being Prepared

A pitcher should literally be a fifth infielder. Through fielding dexterity and knowledge of the correct move to make, he will prevent many base hits and possible runs should he be involved in a play.

In order to be that fifth infielder, he must make certain essential preparations. First is the matter of equipment. A big glove is a requisite for a pitcher, not only in covering his pitches but also in enabling him to stop many batted balls that would otherwise go for hits. In addition to being able to field batted balls with a large glove, he will succeed in deflecting many otherwise unstoppable balls, making them playable for the other infielders.

Next, the pitcher must have the correct play in mind any time the ball is hit. This includes knowing what to do with the ball when he fields it, carrying out his duties as a backup man when the batter drives one to the outfield, being fully aware of the responsibilities involved in any situation demanding that he cover a base, and filling his role in lending vocal and occasional physical support on foul flies. He should be prepared to make the right play before the occasion actually arises, taking into consideration the game situation and all possible plays and ramifications thereof. He should also include in his mental preparations a definite plan of action in case of an error.

Finally comes the physical preparation entailed in the completion of the act of delivering the ball. The pitcher should be in a squared-away position in his follow-through, with his feet relatively parallel and his weight evenly distributed. This will give him better balance and enable him to move quickly in any direction. In cases in which, after the natural motion, the pivot foot is in advance of or dragging behind the striding foot, an extra shuffle step or hop (a short one in either case) is a good method of achieving a balanced, squared-away position. Bringing his glove into position in front of his body can also prove very helpful when quick reactions are demanded.

Although not particularly germane to the subject of preparation, we should mention the act of receiving the return throw from the catcher. It is advisable, in this instance, to catch the ball with one hand (one of the few times when this is advocated) in order to offer proper protection to the fingers of the pitching hand.

### Playing the Ball

The outstanding fielding pitchers are men who possess great agility and quick reflexes. These traits are, of course, inherent to a great degree. They can, however, be improved in the case of anyone who is willing to work at becoming a better fielder.

The seemingly unimportant pepper games in which major league pitchers engage during pregame practice actually have a definite, twofold purpose. They not only serve as a fine conditioner but also help greatly a pitcher's fielding, because they promote good balance, agility, and sharp reflexes. A pitcher cannot play too much pepper.

*Fielding a bunt*

Another drill that can be engaged in during practice sessions and that helps a pitcher become accustomed to handling ground balls under game conditions goes as follows: with a batter at home plate, the pitcher throws to the catcher; simultaneously with each pitch, the batter fungoes grounders through the box. This drill gives the pitcher experience in fielding batted balls after going through his complete motion, while helping him develop a balanced follow-through and agility.

The pitcher should keep his eye on the ball while fielding it; in fact, he should follow it visually right into his glove. This statement seems almost superfluous but is necessary in that, because of his proximity to the batter, the pitcher is often liable to a tendency to go for a batted ball without full concentration; or, on a bunt or slow roller, he may pay too much heed to the runners. Obviously, he cannot make a play until he is in complete possession of the ball, and that should be his primary consideration.

The pitcher should try to block any ball hit through the middle. Every precaution should be exercised to make sure of the stop, for the ball comes to him so quickly that he will have time to make a play even if he does not field the ball cleanly.

A good moundsman does not wait for the ball to be on the ground before he breaks for the plate; he does so as soon as the batter shows his intentions, because the least delay will allow the bunter to beat it out for a hit.

Occasionally a bunt or slow roller must be played to first base very quickly; the pitcher must field the ball as best he can, throwing underhand or sidearm from a bent position, as an infielder does on a close play. However, bunts and slowly hit balls should generally be played with two hands, the safest way usually proving the surest. When the play is not hurried, he should use his normal throwing motion.

After fielding a ground ball, the pitcher should make the shortest possible pivot to throw to first or second base. For example, a left-hander fielding a grounder to his left should turn to his left to throw to first; when he fields the ball in the home-plate area, he should turn to his right after handling the ball in front of his left foot. If the play is at second base, he should turn to his right on any ball fielded in front of him. A right-handed pitcher should make his turn to the left when throwing to either first or second.

A left-hander turns to his right on any throw to third base. When a right-hander fields a ball close to the third base line and his back is toward third, he should pivot to his left for the throw. If, on the other hand, he is partially facing third as he fields the ball, he should turn to his right.

The throw itself depends, to a great extent, on the distance involved.

Long throws should be hard for the sake of both carry and accuracy, while shorter ones can be slower so as to make the catch easier for the receiver. The lob throw should be avoided if at all possible; it generally lacks accuracy and is often confusing, because of the change in speed, for the receiver.

The ability of the pitcher to handle batted balls and diagnose play situations can be as important to his success as the stuff and control with which he delivers the ball. Conceivably, in the course of a single play, he can be required to pitch to the batter, handle a batted ball, throw to the appropriate base, cover another base, and finally back up the play. His failure to do any of these things properly may completely destroy the effect of throwing the right pitch in the first place. He must be a fifth infielder.

### What to Do and When to Do It

Fielding, as all phases of pitching, demands far more than mere mechanical ability. Common sense, an awareness of all possible play situations and the duties that they entail, and quick thinking are requisites to a good-fielding pitcher. He not only must know where to throw the ball when he makes a play himself but also must recognize the need for performing other fielding duties, and should have a knowledge of the correct techniques involved in carrying out these maneuvers with efficiency and dispatch.

**Indecision—a Pitfall to Avoid.** Baseball is literally a game of inches. Defensive plays must be carried out with split-second rapidity if they are to succeed. Along with his teammates a pitcher must think ahead and take quick, decisive action when the occasion for it arises.

Among the general points that will help the pitcher to avoid indecision are three that warrant mention: (1) A slowly hit ball or fumble should be played to first base. The delay caused by a fumble or a slow roller will make it all but impossible to retire a base runner who has taken a lead and, in many cases, enjoyed a running start. The batter, on the other hand, must complete his swing before setting out for first base and must run a full ninety feet to reach his objective. (2) The catcher is the field general and has a much better view of the play. His advice should be heeded and, when contrary to the first point, is the only time that that rule should be ignored. (3) Any time that a runner is hung up between bases while the pitcher is in possession of the ball the latter should run directly at the runner, waiting until he commits himself before making a throw.

**Working With the First Baseman.** A pitcher must coordinate his efforts with those of the first baseman on any play involving both of them. This includes not only ground balls to the right side of the infield on which the pitcher must cover first base but also ones that he fields himself.

When a pitcher fields a hard-hit ground ball, he should take two or three steps toward first before making his throw to that base. This will give the first baseman time to reach the base and set himself for the throw. It will also ease some of the tension that can build up during this period of waiting and impair the accuracy of the throw. The throw should be made to the inside of the base to facilitate the first baseman's handling of the ball and to eliminate the possibility of a collision with the oncoming base runner.

The pitcher's role in covering first base is highly important and, because it is an intricate maneuver, is the subject of many hours of practice by major league teams. The pitcher should break toward first base on all balls hit to the right side of the infield. Covering first is necessary on every play, and there are times when this duty falls to the pitcher.

There are two methods of performing this play. On a ball hit to the first baseman's left, or straight to him, the pitcher should go to the foul line about twenty feet in front of the base and cross the bag, running parallel to the line. As he nears the base he should slow down slightly and bring his speed under control. This manner of making the play reduces the danger of collision with the runner and its attendant fumble and, at the same time, permits the first baseman to time his throw more accurately.

On a ball hit to the first baseman's right, or on a slow roller, the pitcher should go directly to the bag and anchor there. This also applies to the first-second-first double play with the shortstop. In these instances the throw to first will be delayed, and there will be no time for a carefully timed play.

In those cases in which doubt arises as to who should field the ball or cover the base, the play should be called: "I've got it" and "You take it" are the initiating and answering calls that should be used. When the

(a) *Ball hit straight at 1B or to his left*    (b) *Ball hit to 1B's right, or slow roller*

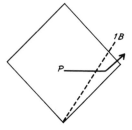
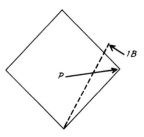

first baseman makes the play himself, the pitcher should get out of the way.

If there are other runners on base, the pitcher, after taking the throw at first, should take care not to continue running down the base line toward right field. Instead, he should stop quickly, turn, and run the ball back toward the plate in order to check the advance of any other runner or to catch him rounding the base too far.

**Covering an Unguarded Base.** On many plays one of the bases is left unprotected, and some player must leave his normal position to cover it. Quite often this is the pitcher's responsibility.

In addition to covering first base on some ground balls, the pitcher should go to that base in readiness to handle a throw whenever the first baseman tries for a fly ball. This is particularly important when there is more than one runner on base and the first baseman makes the play on a foul fly. Here, the pitcher not only covers first base but also serves as a relay man should more than one runner try for the next base or bluff an attempt to do so in an effort to draw a throw.

The pitcher should cover second base when both the second baseman and shortstop go for a fly ball in short center field—unless either the first or third baseman can leave his position to do so, in which case the pitcher should go to whichever base has been vacated.

There are two occasions on which the pitcher should cover third base. One of these occurs when both the third baseman and shortstop go after a fly ball with a runner on base. The other occurs when, with a runner on base, the third baseman fields a bunt or slow roller for which both he and the pitcher have tried and the catcher or shortstop is unable to get to third base in time to cover it.

Home plate is the runner's ultimate objective. It should be covered at all times. Whenever home plate is left open with men on base, the pitcher should cover it. This duty should be performed any time a pitched ball gets away from the catcher and whenever he leaves his position to catch a pop fly. In taking a throw from the catcher for a play on a runner attempting to score, the pitcher should take a position in fair territory just in front of the plate, facing the catcher. If he receives a good throw, he should turn to his right for the tag, clutching the ball in his bare hand and holding his gloved hand between the ball and the runner for protection. If the throw is a wide one and there is still a chance to retire the runner, the pitcher should dive for the third base side of home plate after catching the ball.

**The Pitcher's Role on Pop Flies.** We have mentioned the need for the pitcher to cover a base that has been left unguarded when the man who usually protects it must leave it to field a pop fly. There are other considerations to be observed when a pop fly is hit over or near the infield.

The pitcher should let the infielders handle any fly ball in the vicinity of the mound. They are in better position and are better equipped to play such balls. Consequently, the only fly balls that the hurler should field are popped-up bunts and weak taps not high enough for the infielders to reach.

On a foul fly the pitcher should go toward the ball and call the play, lending both aid and encouragement to the player(s) involved. In this case he has a better view of the play than a player who is concentrating on the ball. The exceptions to this are the above-mentioned instances in which he must cover a vacated base.

A foul fly, because of its drift and the fact that it is easily lost in a bright sun, is one of the most difficult plays for a catcher to make. For this reason the pitcher's help is needed. He not only can lend valuable assistance in calling the play and giving encouragement but also may be in position to catch the ball should the catcher lose it in the sun or wind.

Still another advantage to the pitcher's going toward a foul fly is that he will be in position to serve as a relay man when base runners make a move toward the next base after the catch. This is especially important on a fly ball to the first or third baseman with men on first and third. The pitcher as cut-off man in this situation can prevent the success of a bluff move by either runner intended to draw a long throw that will enable the other to advance.

**The Double-play Throw.** The double play is the pitcher's greatest aid in breaking up scoring threats when the opposition has runners on base. The throw to start a double play is of paramount importance; the cardinal principle behind a double play is to make sure of the first out, for without it the play will go for nought, and the pitcher will be in additional trouble.

On a ball hit back to the pitcher, the double-play throw should always go to the shortstop unless a decided right-hand pull hitter is at bat and the shortstop is stationed in the hole, far out of his normal position. On any ball hit through the middle, he will be going toward the bag and should be in good position to take the throw and complete the double play.

In making this play the pitcher should pivot quickly and throw after deliberating long enough to allow the shortstop to get in proper position. He should take a look at the base before getting rid of the ball, taking care, above all, to make sure of the first out.

The throw should be chest high and about one-half step to the left of the bag, to facilitate handling of the ball and to allow continuity of motion on the part of the shortstop. The only exception to this occurs when the shortstop is out of position and the play must be handled by the second baseman. In this case the throw should be chest high and about one-half step to the right (first base) side of the bag.

This maneuver should be worked on during batting practice on balls hit back to the pitcher. Then he should practice his pivot and throw— even when no one is covering second base. Simulated game conditions are always best for developing successful mound techniques.

With the bases loaded a pitcher's double-play throw should go home, then to first (this is a relatively easy double play on a ball hit directly to the pitcher).

At the higher levels of baseball, the double-play throw with men on first and second goes to second base unless the batted ball is a slow roller between the mound and third base, in which case a play at third is logical and easy. In scholastic ball, with its scarcity of double plays, retiring the lead runner seems more important than attempting to go for two. Getting the force-out at third not only keeps a runner from advancing to that base (from which there are many more ways to score than from second) but also eliminates the first-and-third situation, which can prove so troublesome to youthful ball clubs.

**Looking the Runner Back.** Lest this term prove confusing, consider the following situation. With a runner on third base, or runners on second and third, a ground ball is hit to the pitcher. Unless the runner on third makes a foolhardy break for home, the play is obviously to first base. To prevent the runner from scoring while the play is being made on the batter, the pitcher should "look him back" to third before throwing to first. A mere glance at the runner will usually succeed in driving him back, and the pitcher who neglects this sensible move deserves no better than to lose the run with which the opposition will occasionally be gifted.

The same thing applies with a runner on second base. He should be driven back to his base before the play is made on the batter. As an added benefit, this slight delay will allow the first baseman sufficient time in which to reach the bag and position himself to receive the throw.

When the glance at the runner reveals that he is foolishly trying to advance to the next base, the play should be made on him.

**Defensing the Sacrifice.** The sacrifice bunt presents two problems— the mechanical and the tactical aspects of the situation. Because the sacrifice can often be anticipated, the mechanical phase of defending against it is simplified. The pitcher should not wait for the ball to be on the ground to break toward home but should do so as soon as the batter shows his intentions.

For safety's sake the ball should be fielded with two hands—even if it is rolling very slowly. The throw should be made to the base to which the catcher directs the play, since he has a better view of the situation. However, if the bunt is a hard one, directly back to the mound, there is little cause to wait for the catcher's call—a force-out will be relatively easy to achieve, and the throw should be made for it.

With a right-hander at bat, most sacrifice attempts will go toward first base. This is the easiest bunt for a right-hand batter and is, strategically, a wise move against a right-handed first baseman, because he must turn to make a throw to second.

The sacrifice bunt with a runner on second will usually go toward third in an attempt to draw the third baseman in to field it, leaving the base unprotected against the advancing runner.

The accepted technique for fielding a bunt has been worked out quite logically from a physical standpoint. A left-handed pitcher should overrun the ball slightly so as to field it to the inside of his left foot and in front of him. A right-hander should overrun the ball slightly so as to field it to the inside of his right foot and in front of him. This will lead to an easier pivot, which results in a quicker, more accurate throw. Regardless of the base to which the throw should be made, a left-hander's pivot should be to his right, while a right-hander should turn to his left. In effect, this means that the pivot will always be made toward the infield.

On a sacrifice with runners on first and second, the pitcher should charge toward the third base line as soon as he releases the ball, in order to give proper coverage to that area and allow the third baseman to remain at the bag to receive the throw for a force-out. Let us repeat for clarification: for a throw to third, a right-hander pivots to his left, a left-hander to his right; for a throw to first, a right-hander once again pivots to his left and a left-hander to his right. If it is apparent that the runner is "in" at third base, the throw should go to first, not second, for the other runner will have enjoyed an even bigger lead than the one who is already safe.

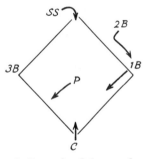

The setup is the same for the sacrifice with a runner on second base only.

**The Squeeze.** The *suicide squeeze* is a play in which the runner at third breaks for home with the pitch and the batter simply has to bunt the ball on the ground in fair territory in order to score the run. If properly executed, it is almost impossible to stop. The only defense against it is early detection and an unbuntable pitch. Therefore, when a squeeze situation exists, the pitcher should watch the runner closely for an indication of the play because, in many cases, he will tip his hand by a premature start. It may even be wise to work from a stretch at a time like this. (The most logical time for the squeeze is with one out in a close ball game and with someone other than a power hitter at bat.)

When the squeeze is detected, the pitch should be made unbuntable. Regardless of what the catcher's signal has been, the pitcher should deliver a fast ball—high and well outside the plate to a left-hander; at the head of a right-handed batter. The latter act does not constitute a bean ball, for this is one occasion on which the batter can expect to be "knocked down." Pitches delivered to these spots will be both unbuntable and easy for the catcher to handle in making a play on the runner.

When a squeeze play is worked successfully with runners on second and third, the throw to first should be made quickly, and the runner on second must not be allowed to score when the play is made at first.

With runners on first and third the opposition will occasionally attempt a safe squeeze, in which the runner holds third until it is apparent that he can score. This should be played like an ordinary sacrifice, with two exceptions: the catcher must cover home, putting greater responsibility for fielding the ball on the pitcher; a defensive player who has fielded the ball should glance at the runner on third before making his throw to first. If the runner is far off his base at third, the play should be made on him.

Any time that a bunt is played to first base, the throw should be to the inside of the base, so that the runner will not obstruct the first baseman's view of the ball and, quite possibly, interfere with the throw. A throw to either second or third should be directly over the base.

**Backing Up the Play.** One of a pitcher's primary duties is backing up the right base on any ball hit to the outfield. He should know which base to back up under any circumstance that may arise, and should never hesitate to get into position to do so.

An alert moundsman will be one base ahead of the lead runner, so that he can prevent him from taking an extra base on any ball that may have to be retrieved. When he is the backup man, the pitcher is generally in foul territory, and he should station himself about forty feet behind the base that he is backing up. Being too close to the play is ineffective because it will not allow him to cover sufficient ground to retrieve most overthrows.

Deciding which base to back up is dependent upon where and how the ball has been hit, the strength of the outfielder's arm, the speed of the runners, the inning, and the score. Nevertheless, staying one base ahead of the lead runner is a safe rule of thumb and will, in the vast majority of cases, provide the correct solution.

Another principle that the pitcher should follow in backing up a play is to get off the mound and into position quickly, so that there will be no possibility of interfering with the cut-off man, who also has a definite station to take.

An overthrow that must be fielded by the backup man should be blocked. To eliminate any danger of the ball's getting through him, the pitcher should drop to one knee to stop it.

The pitcher's duties in his backup role also include run-down plays. On a run-down between first and second he should cover first base unless there is a runner on third, in which case he should back up home plate. On a run-down between second and third the pitcher should cover third —with the same exception. On a third-to-home run-down he should cover the plate—with no exceptions.

Many of these situations involve the cut-off play; consequently, all pitchers should understand this important maneuver. Briefly, the cut-off play, by means of an intercepted throw, enables a team to prevent another runner from advancing when the lead runner is obviously safe at his destination. At times, it makes possible the *sure* out.

The shortstop is the cut-off man on plays at third base. When the throw should go home, the third baseman acts as cut-off man on a hit to left field, while the first baseman assumes that role on hits to center and right field. The cut-off man stations himself about forty feet from the base at which the play is made, in a direct line between the throwing player and that base. On a good throw he listens to the baseman for instructions; on a bad throw he intercepts the ball on his own, without hesitation.

In all such situations the pitcher backs up the play, with two possible exceptions. The first arises when the game is being played on a field on which the backstop is very close to home plate. Here, because there is little need for the pitcher to back up the play, he can serve as cut-off man, allowing the first and third basemen to cover their bases.

The other exception is more in the nature of a tactical variation, and its use can be left to the discretion of each team. When a single is hit to either center or right field with a runner on second base, the first baseman assumes the cut-off position. In such instances the pitcher can cover first base. This is a relatively unexpected move and can result in a putout on the batter, who almost invariably takes a wide turn at first base when the throw goes home. Any team can use it to good effect—especially teenage teams, with whom there is little danger of a powerful throw that will sail over the catcher's head.

Visualize the following situation as a good example of how important the pitcher's backup role is. With a runner on first base a single is hit to the outfield. The runner will probably try to reach third; so a play will probably be made at that base. Should the ball go through the third baseman, the runner will score, and the batter will reach second base—meaning one run home and another in scoring position—unless the pitcher is in position to back up the play at third.

## WORKING WITH MEN ON BASE

To be realistic about his situation and to be successful, a pitcher must learn how to work effectively with men on base. This means not only that he should be able to hold the runners close to their bases and foil such offensive plays as the sacrifice, squeeze, hit-and-run, and steal, but also that he should be able to get good stuff on the ball and control it despite the presence of base runners.

### The Approach to the Problem

Although it is true that no pitcher can get his best stuff on the ball while working with men on base, and that few hurlers can keep every runner from getting a good jump on the ball, the fact remains that this obstacle is not insurmountable.

A realistic approach acknowledges that the problem will always exist at frequent intervals and that the situation is not conducive to peak efficiency. Yet the smart pitcher accepts this set of circumstances, works hard to learn the most efficient method of operating under them, and, in the case of the real mound artist, looks on the situation as a definite challenge. The true competitor is often a better pitcher with men on base, because he does not allow himself to become upset and bears down even harder when the opposition confronts him with a scoring threat.

The problem of working with men on base necessitates a twofold task—preventing the runner(s) from taking undue liberties on the base paths and maintaining a high degree of effectiveness in dealing with the batter.

Two basic principles should be advanced in order to give reassurance and the proper attitude to all pitchers: (1) Relax. The runner is probably more keyed up over the situation than you are. (2) Don't forget the batter. He's still the man you want.

## The Right Moves

The first fundamental is, of course, to assume a proper stop position. Although minor differences exist in this phase of the pitching motion, a strong similarity must (according to the rules) and does (in practice) exist.

The rear foot must be in contact with the rubber; the only movement of the feet permitted, other than in delivering the ball, is a lateral movement of the front foot preparatory to coming to an actual stop. After he takes his stretch, and before the delivery, the pitcher must come to a complete stop and must not take his hand from the ball or make a perceptible movement of any part of his body except his head. After the stop he can deliver the ball to the plate, throw to an occupied base, fake a throw to second or third if it is occupied by a runner, or step from the rubber and call "time." He can, however, throw to a base *before* coming to a stop. As long as his foot is in contact with the rubber, he cannot make a move toward first base without throwing the ball there. If, on the other hand, he steps back off the rubber before making any move, it is almost impossible for him to balk. Thus, though not practicable in throwing to first, this is a good policy to follow in coping with base runners.

A good pick-off move is a great asset to a pitcher and should be practiced diligently until perfected. The reputation of having a good one is in itself often enough to keep runners close to their bases.

In developing a good pick-off motion, the pitcher should assume a position that will enable him, with a quick glance, to keep an eye on the runner, yet not cause him to "lose" home plate. In fact, he should never "pitch from memory." Rather, he should always take a good look at home plate before delivering the ball to the batter.

**Assuming the Stop Position.** The basic stop position should quite naturally be developed in relation to a runner at first base. Its primary purpose is to hold the runner close to his base, making it as difficult as possible for him to advance to scoring position. Also, with fewer than two outs, it facilitates a double play. A left-hander, of course, enjoys a big advantage in holding the runner close because he faces in that direction. A right-hander, to offset some of the natural disadvantage under which he must work, should assume a slightly open stance—one that will enable him to see the runner out of the corner of his eye without turning his head completely toward first.

With men on base all moves on the part of the pitcher must be faster, and, because of the natural loss in power that results from working out of a stretch, the push-off from the rubber is even more important in contributing to speed and stuff. A long, slow stretch is not necessary, but enough of one should be used to relieve tension and loosen the uniform around the shoulders and armpits.

When the hands are held in a relatively high position (at the letters) upon completion of the stretch, excess body motion will be cut down, and movements will be quicker and more deceptive. In order to hold the runner(s) in check, the striding foot should pass closer to the ground in delivering the ball to the plate from a stop position. A well-balanced stance is advisable for centering of the weight because the placing of too much weight on the rear foot will slow the move to a base, while too much weight on the front foot takes stuff off a pitched ball. All these ideas are designed to help speed up a pitcher's moves and enable him to hold the runner close to his base.

### The Pick-Off at First

**A Right-hander's Move.** A right-hander's main hope is a quick motion and a low, hard throw that should be aimed at the first baseman's knee to allow him to catch the ball and apply the tag quickly, with little lost motion.

Although a right-hander should watch the runner, he will need less body movement for the pitch if he faces third base. However, if he finds that this technique allows the runner to get a big lead, he should move his front foot further to the side (first base) and place a little more weight on it. This will lead to a quicker move to first. This slightly open stance may, however, slow down the motion of his delivery to the plate, enabling the runner to get a good jump on the pitch. In this case he should close his stance so that less time is devoted to the backward body pivot. Furthermore, a righty should not lean back toward first in his stretch, and whether a right- or left-hander, he should bend his knees in the stretch because they must bend before the ball can be delivered.

The initial move in throwing to first should be the lifting of the rear

*Right-hander's pick-off at first*

*Left-hander's pick-off at first*

heel, for this properly launches the pivot that is made on the ball of the rear foot. A right-hander can add effectiveness to his move by making his throw to first a so-called deception move—one that involves a feint of the head or movement of the knee closely resembling that used in delivering the ball to the batter.

A particularly deceptive move (though difficult to master) that has been developed by some astute practitioners involves a "drop-step, underhand motion." It stems from a normal stop position, but the first move is a backward step with the left foot, which places it in line with and facing the same direction as the right foot. The hips open toward first while both feet pivot on the toes at the same time the arm is propelling the ball toward first in a low sidearm motion (below the hip.) All these actions are almost simultaneous. Obviously, this provides a very quick and deceptive move but one that must, because it can easily cause a wild throw, be practiced assiduously before being attempted in game competition.

**A Left-hander's Move.** A left-hander can be more deceptive in his move to first base because he faces in that direction when working from a stop position and can easily keep an eye on the runner.

According to the rules, he must step toward a point at least halfway between home and first when throwing to that base. If he steps more toward home than toward first, he can be charged with a balk. Nevertheless, some left-handers succeed in getting away with half-balks by the simple expedient of stepping quickly toward first after making a pick-off throw with a step that is almost directly toward home. These steps follow one another so rapidly that detecting a balk is very difficult, and when performed in this fashion, the move to first is, of course, very deceptive.

There are two basic ways for a left-hander to pick off a runner at first. (1) In the *head move* he looks alternately at home and first, turning his head ninety degrees to do so. Then, after looking at first, instead of completing a full ninety-degree turn to "go home," he stops halfway, turns back, and makes a quick throw to first. (2) In the *swing move*, used primarily to hold the runner close to his base, he swings his body and leg toward (but not further than) first before delivering the ball to the plate. If the swing move is employed, the hurler can throw the ball to first if he sees that the runner has strayed too far off his base.

**Making the Move Effective.** The secret of picking a runner off first is to catch him off balance and to throw when he is leaning toward second and needs extra time to get back to the base. To catch the runner leaning, the pitcher should vary his move. Occasionally he should throw to first without taking a full stretch. He can render the move more deceptive by varying the interval between pitches, the interval between throws to the base, and the length of time consumed in the stretch itself.

A device that is used with occasional success by experienced moundsmen makes good use of changes of speed in the throw to first. By means of half-speed throws, the pitcher can lure the runner into taking an extra-long lead. A quick, hard throw may then catch him off base. The pitcher should make sure to allow the runner to get back to first easily several times in order to "bait the trap."

The habits of base runners should also be taken into consideration. A man who moves off the base with a jump can occasionally be caught while taking the jump. A player who crosses his legs while taking a lead is easy prey for a pick-off throw when caught with his legs crossed. For the nervous runner who dances around in an effort to rattle the pitcher the latter should stand and wait, causing the runner to tire of his own exertions and making him less likely to attempt a steal. A jumpy runner

*Right-hander's pick-off at second*

is rarely able to get off to a fast start and can be combatted by simply pitching to the hitter.

As long as the runner must slide to get back safely, the pitcher should keep throwing to first. This is an indication that his lead is too big and that he may be planning to steal.

Although the pitcher should be aware of and practice these pick-off moves, he must never forget that the batter is the man on whom to concentrate. He should never deliver the ball to the plate until he has looked at his target with *both* eyes.

The most effective move to first is the one in which the pitcher appears to be making his usual pitch to the batter—to the very point at which the pick-off throw is made.

## The Pick-Off at Second

There are two basic methods of working the pick-off at second base —by a signal from either the shortstop or the catcher and by the *daylight play*, in which the pitcher uses his own judgment. Random throws to second base are risky—and are rarely effective.

The shortstop is the proper man with whom to work for the pick-off at second. The second baseman serves only as an additional nuisance, for the runner can detect his moves too easily for him to be effective.

The time to throw is when the pitcher sees daylight between the shortstop and the runner, with the shortstop closer to the bag—otherwise there is little chance to get him. This, then, is the daylight play.

A count play, worked out and practiced with the shortstop beforehand, is the preferred method. A signal from the shortstop starts the play, which can be executed as follows. While the pitcher is looking at the runner, the shortstop flashes the signal. He breaks for the bag as the pitcher turns back to face the batter. As the pitcher turns toward the

*Left-hander's pick-off at second*

plate, he counts "one-two"—and turns and throws on "three." The throw should be knee high and directly over the bag in order to facilitate a sure catch and a quick tag for the shortstop. When the runner takes an extra-large lead, he is fair game for this maneuver.

A turn to the left is more deceptive and effective for a right-hander because it creates the illusion that he is delivering the ball to the plate before the pivot is completed and the pick-off throw made. A left-hander, for the same reason, should turn to his right. In either case the correct technique is a quick pivot and a deliberate, but hard, throw. The pitcher should always look before he throws.

The pick-off at second can also be made on a signal from the catcher, who directs a throw to the base when he sees the shortstop break for it. Because this involves one more player and the additional room for error that follows, a coach should not highly recommend it.

The *block play* may succeed if the shortstop pick-off fails. In it, the shortstop, after leaving the base to return to his position, passes in front of the runner, gaining the latter's attention by so doing. The second baseman, meanwhile, has edged over to the bag to take a quick throw from the pitcher that can catch an unwary runner napping.

A jump-turn allows for the necessary pause after the pivot and before the throw. Furthermore, the throw will be more natural (and accurate) when the striding foot is brought past a direct line to second base; that is, the pivot is one of slightly more than 180 degrees.

The first move, for both left- and right-handers, should be the lifting of the rear heel. This move properly starts the pivot, which is made on the ball of the rear foot.

One exception to this move can exist in the case of the sidearmer: he will often find it easier to pivot toward his throwing side.

Regardless of the technique employed, there are several tactical points that should be borne in mind:

1. A pitcher should not get into the habit of turning to look at the runner only once, then pitching. All moves should be varied to prevent a smart runner from gaining an unwarranted advantage.

2. Runners can be categorized as *head-turners* (shifting the glance from pitcher to shortstop) and *leaners* (placing the weight on the right foot to get a good start toward third). They should be studied for these habits, which will aid in picking them off base.

3. A pick-off throw to second is most likely to succeed on a 2-1 or 3-2 count, in which case the runner is more likely to take liberties. This is especially so with a left-hander at bat, because the shortstop will be playing closer to the base.

4. The pitcher should step off the rubber before throwing to second, so as to eliminate any danger of a balk.

5. The throw will be an unnecessary one and should not be risked if it is apparent that the play will not succeed. The rules do not require that a move to second be completed by a throw.

6. The ball should never be delivered to the plate after an infielder has made a move toward the base. He should be allowed to return to his position before a pitch is made.

7. Don't pitch from memory; take a look at the plate before delivering the ball, even if it permits the runner to get a big jump.

8. The pick-off play must be practiced diligently until timing, including the meter of the count, is synchronized and the throw can be made quickly and with accuracy.

### The Pick-Off at Third

A pick-off throw to third base is risky and should be attempted only by experienced players who have practiced it many times. It is a prearranged play, signalled by either the pitcher or third baseman, and demands an accurate throw that arrives at the base simultaneously with the third baseman, if not slightly after he has reached the bag. Here, again, the rules do not require completion of a throw to the base, and a needless one should not be made. Because the main object is to drive the runner back to his base, a fake throw or stepping off the rubber is equally effective as and far less hazardous than a throw to third base.

A pick-off with men on first and third or (especially) on second and third is more feasible than one with only a runner at third base. In operation it works as follows: The pitcher, *after stepping off the rubber*, pivots toward second (or first, as the case may be), continues around to third, and throws. This move can be worked effectively only by a right-hander and should not be attempted until it has been practiced to the point of perfection.

A situation with runners on first and third presents another possibility for the offense that must be guarded against by the pitcher. The man on first base will occasionally break for second while the pitcher is holding the ball, hoping to force a balk or to draw a hurried throw allowing the runner on third to score. After being warned by the first baseman ("Step off"), the pitcher should step off the rubber to avoid a balk, pivot to second by way of third (thereby freezing the runner at third), and throw to the shortstop at second base. The latter drives the runner back to first, keeping an eye on the man at third for a possible play at home.

### Holding the Runner

The idea of developing an effective method of operation with men on base stems from the need to hold the runner close to his base. Because a pick-off play is rarely successful, extra consideration should be given to preventing the runner(s) from gaining a big lead, which will allow him to advance to the next base with comparative ease.

The first time a man gets on base, the pitcher should "look him back," and it is a good policy to do so more than once. This will let the runner know that he is being watched and cannot afford to take too big a lead. A left-hander can add to this effect by using the swing move, which was previously described and which may enable him to drive the runner back to the base while in the process of delivering the ball to the plate. A right-hander must rely more heavily on a head move ("looking him back") and, at times, a throw to the base. The pitcher should definitely make an occasional throw when a dangerous runner is on base.

One thing in particular that should be avoided is allowing the runner to get a walking lead. He should be made to stop before the ball is delivered to the batter. The first step in preventing a walking start is to wait on the runner. If this fails, the pitcher should step off the rubber to ensure that the man returns to his base. This involves correct technique. The pitcher should step back off the rubber with his rear foot. Any other movement prior to lifting the rear foot and placing it behind the rubber can be construed as a move intended to deceive the runner and may result in the pitcher's being charged with a balk. Furthermore, he is not permitted to step off once he has started his pitching motion.

Still another method of holding the runner close is to take a deep breath while at the stop position. In this case the runner will have difficulty in deciding whether the pitcher is breathing or moving to pitch.

Two additional precautionary notes that deserve consideration deal with the same phase of the problem; one applies to a right-hander, one to a left-hander. When a right-hander, having reached his stop position and made a half-turn of his head toward first base, finds that the runner has vanished from his field of vision, he should make a throw. The same principle pertains to a left-hander working with a man on second. When the runner can't be sighted by means of peripheral vision, his lead is too big, and he should be forced back to the base.

The following are tactical points to remember in holding the runner close to his base:

1. If the pitcher is working with more than a two-run lead, he need pay little heed to the base-runner—he's not going anywhere; that is, he should not be going anywhere, since it is bad baseball to take chances when you are more than one run behind.

2. If the pitcher at all suspects a hit-and-run or steal, he should throw to first base. When the automatic run-and-hit is in order (a 3-2 count with a force play possible), he must not allow the runner to get too big a jump on the ball. A well-timed pick-off throw may catch him off base in this situation.

3. If the bunt is in order but not certain, the pitcher should take his stretch, then step off the rubber. When this is done, the batter may give away his intentions.

4. With the hit-and-run in order, a right-handed batter should be pitched tight, and a left-hander should be pitched outside. This will make it difficult for either to hit behind the runner.

5. With a fast man on third in a tight game, the pitcher may consider working from a stop position. This is particularly applicable to a right-hander. It seems more logical for a left-hander to work out of a short pump, from which he can keep an eye on the runner, rather than from a stretch, which will require him to have his back to the man on third.

6. With a man on third base the pitcher should employ a short pump and a quick delivery regardless of the circumstances. A right-hander can actually take a glance at the runner while in his pitching motion.

7. If a teammate shouts a warning while the pitcher is taking his stretch or after he has reached the stop position, he should immediately step off the rubber and quickly size up the situation. Only then should he take positive action.

8. A special move that can often be used in scholastic ball is for the pitcher, after throwing to first, to take the return throw while on the rubber. Then, simply coming to a stop before delivering his pitch will leave the runner on or close to the base (that is, with little or no lead). This might be called "quick-pitching" the runner and is perfectly legal. A smart hitter, of course, will prevent its use by calling time whenever a pick-off throw is made.

To condition himself to working with men on base, the pitcher requires experience. The simplest means of achieving this is to put a man on first base during batting practice and have him jump around in an effort to disconcert the pitcher. This will serve to acquaint the hurler with operating under these game conditions.

### The Pitch-Out

A pitch-out is a device resorted to with two purposes in mind—to pick off a runner who has taken too big a lead or to foil an attempted hit-and-run, steal, or squeeze. It generally calls for a fast ball, letter high and wide of the plate (as the term implies), permitting the catcher to make an unobstructed throw. To permit easy handling and to afford the catcher a good chance to get the runner, the pitcher should not make his throw too wide. Although useful in checking runners, the pitch-out is not for pitchers who are experiencing control problems, for they cannot afford to waste a pitch. In fact, at the scholastic level it makes good sense to ignore the pitch-out and utilize a high, fast strike when the steal seems likely. This pitch is actually easier for most amateur catchers to handle and gives the pitcher a strike in a situation in which the batter, aware of the planned steal, is extremely unlikely to hit the ball.

If a pitch-out does seem propitious, one refinement should be considered. With a runner on first base and a left-hander at bat, some catchers prefer an inside pitch in order to make a pick-off throw to that base. Their throw is then made sidearm, around the batter. This is a matter of personal preference, and the pitcher should deliver the ball in accordance with his catcher's wishes.

When a waste pitch is thrown with men on base, it should be a pitch-out. A curve ball pitch-out is a good maneuver with a bunt in order, because the batter will lean with the pitch and may lure the runner(s) into straying far enough off base to fall victim to a pick-off throw. This is especially so with a runner on second base—even if a bunt is not suspected.

Combatting the squeeze play has already been discussed, and the unbuntable pitch called for in that situation is, in essence, a pitch-out.

The beginning of a steal of home looks so much like the squeeze play that the same tactics should be used in coping with it. When it can be distinguished from the squeeze, the pitcher can throw a low fast ball in the strike zone, allowing the catcher to be in good position for the play; at the same time the pitcher gains a strike because the batter is unlikely to be swinging.

A special situation for which the pitcher should be prepared is an attempted steal of home with two strikes on the batter. Here, the fast ball should once more be automatic; the pitcher should make it a strike since the oncoming runner may interfere with the batter's swing.

The pitch-out per se should be employed only in a close game in which the out at stake is a big one. It can occasionally be used in an attempt to discover the intentions of the offensive team; once it has been signalled by the catcher, it should actually be thrown, because at least one infielder will have left his position to handle the pick-off throw, and the infield will be inadequately defended should the pitch be hit by the batter. Consequently, it should be unhittable.

## CONDITIONING

Warming up is an extremely important phase of pitching that is too often taken for granted. It is a positive measure, not simply something that has to be done, and a pitcher should take full advantage of it to prepare himself properly, whether it be with a single inning, a specific game, or an entire season in mind.

Proper warm-up procedure varies for different pitchers just as do individual physiques. A man's muscular structure, his pitching style, his temperament, and other less personal factors, such as the weather, must be considered and dealt with according to what past experience has shown to be necessary. For example, a thick-muscled pitcher needs a longer warm-up than one who is loose and smooth muscled; a "junk ball" artist needs less time to be ready than a fast-baller; and a cold day necessitates a slow, careful warm-up, whereas on a very hot day a pitcher can be ready with only a few loosening-up throws.

With the premise that it is better to be overly warmed up than insufficiently so, this section will consider various aspects of this important fundamental of good pitching.

### Preseason

This phase of conditioning should be done slowly and with care. The first consideration should be a pitcher's legs and wind—they are closely allied and must be in shape before his arm will be ready.

Legs, as well as the arm, should be strengthened gradually. Overexertion at too early a date can result in a pulled muscle, and consequently can disrupt the entire training schedule. Long walks during the off season will serve as a good preparation for the hard work that follows. Squeezing a handgrip or rubber ball, snapping the wrist in a curve ball motion, and swinging an Indian club in an easy throwing motion will help in developing a strong, supple wrist.

Jogging, to condition the muscles, is the second phase of preseason work. Calisthenics in general and leg builders in particular are also very beneficial. The routine should include running; squatting, for the calves and thighs; twists and bends, to loosen and develop the trunk; and bicycling, to strengthen the back. Ten minutes of calisthenics is not enough to harden the muscles, and it will promote stamina and looseness.

When his legs have begun to grow strong, the pitcher can engage in harder work. Wind sprints—short dashes at full speed—are the most effective of all conditioners. He should continue these all season and combine them with shagging flies in batting practice and chasing fungoes hit by a coach.

"Pick-ups" are another boon to good conditioning. It is done with the aid of a partner, who takes a position about eight feet away. He rolls a ball, first to one side, then the other. The subject of the drill picks up the ball, bending fully to do so, and tosses it back to his partner while straightening up. This is continued at a rapid pace while moving from side to side. About fifty of these pick-ups daily will prove highly beneficial.

Wind sprints are still the cornerstone of a good conditioning program. No fewer than ten good, hard ones per day should be the rule for every pitcher, the only exception being on the day of a game that he is scheduled to pitch.

Leg conditioning should be accompanied by daily throwing, with a gradual increase in the speed of the pitches. The pitcher should get the arm attuned to the curve ball motion almost at the outset of the training period. He should start by simply spinning the ball—with a full-arm motion—but attempt no hard curve balls until his arm is fully prepared for it.

The arm will round into shape along with the legs and should be ready to respond to hard work when the ball begins to feel light. Once a pitcher is ready to throw at top speed, he should begin working up to a full-game routine, starting with two- or three-inning chores and gradually building up to a full nine innings. He should be ready for a complete game in about four weeks' time (see the section on coaching). After this period of preliminary work has been completed, emphasis should be placed on the improvement of skills, as well as the maintenance of good physical condition. When the arm is sound, the more throwing for accuracy, the better.

When he does commence hard throwing and working up to his game routine, the pitcher should begin to take a day of rest (running, but no throwing) between his pitching stints, taking care to forego all throwing whenever his arm feels tired or heavy. Some experienced pitchers believe in throwing every day until the arm feels a strain—then abstaining for a day.

At the same time that he is gradually conditioning himself for his full-game routine, he should also be working up to his full between-games rest period, usually consisting of three or four days interspersed with only running and light throwing.

All pitchers should observe three important precautionary moves:

1. A damp sweatshirt should be changed immediately after throwing.
2. In early preseason conditioning, a pitcher should throw hard enough to loosen the kinks but not so hard that his arm will be strained.
3. Soreness should not be pitched out; rest and heat are the best cures.

The overall preseason conditioning period should be conducted with the basic idea in mind that poor physical shape results in fatigue, which in turn ruins coordination and can cause injury to the arm. The pitcher should in all respects be ready to go at full speed for nine innings by the time the training period has been completed.

## Pregame

A pitcher's pregame warm-up should be taken slowly and include plenty of bending and stretching. Calisthenics should not be indulged in, but exercises of the stretching variety are very helpful when performed just before the actual warm-up. It should be a scrupulously observed rule that no ballplayer attempt to throw unless he has taken the time to bend and stretch until his muscles are loose. For a pitcher this should include revolving his arm above his head (to loosen his shoulder muscles), letting his arm hang down and rotating it counterclockwise (to lubricate the bursar), and massaging his elbow (to stimulate circulation).

Each pitcher will come to know just how much and what kind of warm-up he needs in order to be ready. The weather is a factor to be considered, a cold day necessitating a long, slow warm-up and a hot day demanding only a few minutes of throwing. Moreover, in hot weather the pitcher should begin his warm-up early enough to assure himself a few minutes' rest before the game starts.

When ready to throw hard, a hurler should try each of his pitches until satisfied that all are working properly. The curve ball should simply be spun at first, then thrown several times with the pivot foot anchored.

All these and, of course, all subsequent efforts should include concentration on a full-arm sweep and follow-through, as well as a good wrist snap.

A certain portion of the warm-up should be devoted to throwing from a stop position, with each of the deliveries being tried this way, as well as with a full wind-up.

Every pitch should be in the strike zone. By striving for this during his warm-up, a hurler will be practicing the correct pitching habits that will get him in the proper groove for the game.

Each time he draws a starting assignment, a moundsman should be sufficiently warmed up to begin the first inning at peak efficiency, but, at the same time, he should take care not to leave his game on the sidelines. Careful study has shown that the first inning and the last three are the most difficult for a pitcher, hence the need to draw a fine line between too little and too much warm-up. Eight to ten hard throws at the close of the full warm-up should prove sufficient for readiness, and under normal conditions, about fifteen minutes of throwing should prepare a pitcher adequately for the game.

The warm-up throws should be made in the same direction as those he will throw in the game. Wind can be a very important factor in affecting the action of a thrown ball, and a pitcher should become accustomed and adjusted to the wind before he starts the game.

### Between Innings

There should be a definite purpose to the between-innings warm-up. Every pitch should be thrown for a strike and with a full motion, and the last two should be thrown hard so that the pitcher will be fully prepared to start the inning.

Eight throws are permitted by the rules and are the standard used by most pitchers. If the preceding half-inning has been a long one, the pitcher should make the full number allowed—and in unhurried fashion. Under normal circumstances, however, five throws should prove sufficient. The extra three per inning will add up to twenty-seven for nine innings, and that constitutes an extra inning or more of pitching to which the arm will be subjected. This can take its toll over the course of a complete game.

The pitcher, for his own protection, should always wear a jacket between innings. On an oppressively hot day it need not be donned fully, but even under these conditions, the pitching arm and shoulder should be covered. During a night game a pitcher, for the same reason, should change his sweatshirt *before* he stops perspiring, something that generally occurs in about the fifth inning.

### Bullpen Routine

In the major leagues each club carries on its roster pitchers who are relief specialists. As we go down the ladder to the other levels of baseball, the trend is to a combination of starting and relieving for all pitchers. Every pitcher will be called upon for bullpen duty at some time during his career, and because it calls for a different warm-up technique, he should have some knowledge of this deviation from standard procedure so as to be prepared to provide his club with effective relief pitching.

The pitcher who excels in relief is distinguished by two major attributes—his ability to get the ball over the plate with something on it, under pressure, and his knack of warming up quickly at a moment's notice.

A reliever may find it advisable to loosen up in advance, at the start of the game. To save valuable time when the call comes, either he or his catcher should be equipped with a baseball from the time the game begins.

A pitcher who gets the sign to warm up in the bullpen must be ready in a hurry. He should take about ten tosses and then throw hard. Once he is warmed up thoroughly, he should just lob the ball to stay ready for the call to action that may come at any time.

### Between Games

One of the problems confronting every pitcher is the adoption of a between-games routine by which he will be able to maintain good physical condition and, at the same time, arrive at his pitching assignments with the desired degree of sharpness. There is no formulated schedule that is correct for every pitcher. Rather, each one will respond best to a pattern tailored to his own physical makeup and peculiarities. Experience and observation will enable him to determine his own conditioning program.

A three-day rest between starts is standard; yet some hurlers work more effectively with an extra day's rest, while others are sharper, at times, with only a two-day rest. Using three days as a norm, a sensible routine might go somewhat like this:

Game

First day:     Light exercise, such as backing up the batting practice pitcher, which involves much bending and stretching; running; *no* throwing.

Second day:  Throwing for control, possibly one round of batting practice; pick-ups; running.

Third day:    Running; a light warm-up.

Game

The day before a game is highly important and warrants further mention. Calisthenics should be eliminated so as to avoid a source of possible game-day stiffness. Much good, hard running should be done. Five minutes of throwing should suffice to tune up the arm; hard or prolonged throwing will rob the pitcher of the edge that he should have for the game itself. This easy warm-up will loosen the muscles properly and should be followed immediately by a shower.

The routine above is flexible; it is presented simply to serve as a guide. As stated above, each pitcher should develop the routine that best serves his purpose. The watchword should be, "Know your own arm."

## TACTICS—GENERAL STRATEGY

The mechanical phases of the pitching game having been covered quite thoroughly, the applied study of them should succeed in the making of an improved thrower. What remains is to transform the thrower into a pitcher.

The natural attributes of any pitcher, if fully developed and properly applied, should suffice to make him a winner. It is the application of the previously discussed principles that is the topic of this section on tactics.

Without delving into the technique of working on batters in general or the various types that will be encountered (these facets of the game are included in subsequent chapters), we will here present several basic ideas on pitching tactics.

### The Science of Pitching

The science of pitching is developed primarily to upset the batter's timing. No pitcher can overpower every hitter; his primary objective should be to nullify the power of his adversary so that the ball will not be solidly hit. The best method of accomplishing this is to give the batter the pitch for which he is least prepared at a given time.

Later on, the means for keeping the hitter off balance will be investigated thoroughly. Since we are here dealing more with generalities, suffice it to say that a pitcher should avoid getting into too rhythmical a groove, the cadence of which can be easily timed by the batter. Rather, he should vary his working speed. This does not refer simply to the velocity of a pitched ball. It also involves the time interval between deliveries. For example, on one pitch he can take fifteen to twenty seconds before delivering the ball; on the next one he can fire away as soon as he gets the catcher's signal; and on the following pitch he can get the signal, take a deep breath, pump once, and throw. Such a routine will keep the hitter from getting too well set at the plate and help make the pitcher's task easier.

Changing speeds is, of course, a very effective method of upsetting the batter's timing. In more general terms it serves an equally valuable purpose. A pitcher should not invariably fire away with everything he has on every pitch, particularly in the early innings. He should save his very best stuff for the tight spots when he must call on that extra something to get him out of trouble. This is what is known as "pacing one's self"; it is a knack that has been mastered by almost every successful hurler in the game. And, quite naturally, if a pitcher has not saved something extra for the tight spots, it will not be there when he most needs it.

Trying too hard to put everything on a pitch and straining himself in the process is never good practice for a pitcher. This bad habit actually works negatively in that it does not allow him to deliver the ball with his best possible stuff; furthermore, it can have a definitely harmful effect on his control. Every pitcher should strive for a quality that may be called "controlled relaxation."

Much emphasis has been placed on the value of getting the ball over the plate with something on it. This will always stand as one of the keys to mound success. Getting a batter out on a minimum number of pitches lessens a hurler's problems in every conceivable respect. Staying ahead of the batter is the secret to this, particularly in view of the fact that study of the game has demonstrated conclusively that the percentage of batters who hit safely with two strikes is quite small.

Low-ball pitching is generally the most effective. The pitcher who can throw low strikes consistently will be successful. Yet each hurler should learn to take advantage of his natural stuff. The pitcher with the big fast ball that rises and tails in on the batter can do well when he keeps the ball high and tight, particularly on a pitch on which a definite attempt is made to retire the batter. Nevertheless, even when following this theory for the key pitches, he will do well to be essentially a low-ball pitcher.

A curve ball should always be kept low because it will have a better break when thrown below the waist and because it generally breaks down as well as to the side. A sinking fast ball should be aimed at a low spot for the same reason. A fast ball that rises and, especially, a change of pace on which the batter must supply his own power are also effective when kept low, for, when thrown around the knees, they are more difficult to drive for distance.

The physical aspect of a ballpark is another factor that enters into the tactical side of the pitching game. Short fences demand careful work and spot pitching. A big ball park permits more freedom of operation, and the batter can, at times, be allowed to hit the ball more freely because percentages alone will account for many "long outs." A short fence in one field will dictate pitching away from the power of a batter who hits in that direction, with occasional variations in tactics when he is attempting to offset this strategy by crowding the plate. A park with short fences down both foul lines demands that the pitcher make a determined effort to keep the batter from pulling the ball. He must make judicious use of slow pitches and keep the ball away from most hitters. As a general rule, a pitcher can expect to be reached for more extra base hits in a small park and a greater number of singles in a big one.

Since a smart coach at first or third base can often "read" a pitch from some telltale movement by the pitcher, the latter must constantly guard against tipping off the opposition as to what pitch is coming. He should not only try to use the same grip for his fast ball, curve, and change of pace and throw them all with the same motion but also must take care to cover the ball from the view of the coaches and the batter. A right-hander should cover his pitches from the third-base side and a left-hander from the first base side, and both should cover the wrist as well as the hand in order to prevent a coach from "reading" the pitch and relaying this vital information to the batter. Peculiar mannerisms should also be masked from the probing eyes of clever coaches.

Naturally, the ball should be hidden from the batter as much as possible. Some pitchers with an abundance of stuff are not successful because they are too "true" in their deliveries. An extra turn or twist of the body during the pitching motion can be very helpful in overcoming this difficulty. The wisdom of concealing the ball from the batter until the last possible moment is proved by the effectiveness of a sidearm pitch to a batter who hits from the same side that the pitcher throws (right-handed pitcher, right-handed batter, and so forth). The fact that the ball is hidden by the pitcher's body until the instant it is released makes this pitch effective. The same principle can be applied in concealing any pitch and, well done, will add greatly to the success of the pitcher.

In probing into the intricacies of strategic pitching, one fact stands out above all others. To develop a good command of sound tactics and to facilitate maximum utilization of his natural abilities, a pitcher should definitely acquire the habit of observing, asking, and listening. No matter how polished a performer he may be, he will never "know it all," and there is always someone from whom he can learn something new and valuable.

**Working With the Team**

Baseball is essentially a team game, and the efforts of each player must be coordinated with those of his teammates. Because no pitcher can strike out every batsman, he must design his pitching strategy to work in close harmony with his team's defensive alignment; by so doing, he will be assured of the good fielding support that he needs in order to be a winner. There is a psychological as well as a physical aspect of the situation. When a ball club has confidence in the ability of a pitcher to work in close cooperation with them, the many players will perform exceptionally well. If the pitcher has faith in the support of his teammates, his performance will be improved. This close cooperation and mutual confidence can produce an almost unbeatable combination.

Fielders will station themselves according to the way in which the batter will be pitched. Likewise, a pitcher should work on the batsman in such a way as to make him most likely to hit the ball to the section of the field that has the best coverage. Thus, when an exaggerated defensive alignment is employed against an exceptionally strong pull hitter, he should be pitched tight, to make hitting to the opposite field, all but uncovered in this case, very difficult.

When the game situation demands the use of a tight infield to cut off a run at the plate, the pitcher should keep the ball low, so that it is most likely to be hit on the ground. The same principle should be applied when a double play is anticipated. When the first baseman is holding a runner close to the base, the pitcher should refrain from giving a left-hander slow or inside pitches, which will be easy for him to pull through the hole left by the first baseman. These are a few of the instances in which a pitcher should operate according to his team's defensive alignment.

Conversely, a team's defensive positioning depends, to a great extent, on the pitcher himself. For example, a batter will be played to pull the slower pitches; or, with two strikes, the batter will be "guarding the plate" and be less likely to pull the ball, so will be played accordingly.

Thus, if a team is to function at peak efficiency, the pitcher should pay close attention to the defensive setup behind him and should operate in such a way that his teammates will be aware of his methods and intentions; in this way they will often be enabled to get the jump on a batted ball that will allow them to turn base hits into put outs. This, incidentally, is the underlying motive behind the strategy worked out during pregame clubhouse meetings.

There are certain pitchers who seem to enjoy exceptionally good defensive support. There is a definite reason for this—the confidence in them manifested by their teammates. An old baseball saying states that a team can go "up on its toes" only so many times. In other words, when the pitcher stays ahead of the hitter, they will play much better defensive baseball behind him.

### Working With the Catcher

A smart catcher, by properly utilizing a pitcher's stuff on a given day, can guide him through a game with telling effect. If a pitcher follows his partner's lead closely, adding knowledgeable embellishments of his own, a really smooth-working battery will be the result.

The basic strategy should be dictated by the manager or coach. He should not, however, go so far as to call each pitch. Rather, he should teach his pitchers and catchers to think along certain lines and to evolve (and improvise on) a plan of operation that is basically sound while also allowing room for the sudden changes of tactics often dictated by alert observation. Doing this adds to a hurler's effectiveness by taking advantage of every possible opening as it arises. This will ensure the best results, for in dealing with the batter, feel and touch are far more important than pure theory. By close observation, the batterymen can detect slight changes in grip, stance, and even in the air of determination shown by the hitter, all of which can always be put to good use.

The only definable guide that the pitcher and catcher possess is the instinct and courage to gamble. The fact that the unaided reasoning of one man can often lead him into a rut makes it logical that the pitcher and catcher should both do some thinking in the calling of pitches. Indeed, the catcher gives the signals and, by reason of proximity, can better observe the batter; yet the pitcher knows his own arm and has a different perspective of the situation. Thus, he not only can, but should, shake off the catcher when he feels that his own instincts and ideas have merit. Between the two of them, sound tactics can be developed.

It is of the utmost importance for the catcher to know what pitch is being thrown. This statement is so obvious as to seem ridiculous. But the fact remains that such is not always the case, and when the catcher is crossed up or caught unawares, a passed ball and possibly even a broken finger can result. For this reason the pitcher should give extra consideration to his batterymate (and the welfare of his team). At times the game situation may demand especially intense concentration, or the pitcher may be unable to read the signs. Nevertheless, the pitcher should never allow himself to be so preoccupied that he will either miss altogether or fail to interpret correctly the catcher's signal.

## Developing Strategy

Evolving a plan of operation at any stage of the contest depends on several factors: knowledge of the batter, his habits, and peculiarities; the game situation, including the inning, score, count, number of outs, position of runners, weather conditions, and physical characteristics of the ball park; the tactical approach generally employed by the opposition; the alignment of the defensive players; the condition of the pitcher, including the stuff and control at his command at a given time; the intangibles that bear on the degree of alertness to rapidly changing conditions; and gambling instinct, modified by a sound knowledge of baseball percentages.

First, the pitcher should be fully aware of who is at bat. Past experience will furnish at least the beginning of a book on each batter. In the absence of previous encounters the pitcher can obtain at least a sketchbook by studying the opponent in batting practice, observing his general physical characteristics and his stance and attitude at the plate. An additional factor that can shed light on the situation is the hitter's position in the batting order and what can reasonably be expected of a man who occupies that spot.

One of the basic principles of good pitching is to give the batter the pitch that he is least expecting and to make him hit the one that the pitcher wants him to hit. This involves the establishment of a sequence of pitching (variable, when advisable) that will set up the batter. It also allows development of a strategy that will permit the hurler to use his best pitch in the clutch.

The last sentence should be reminder enough of the importance of pitching to one's own strength. Regardless of how well a batter's weakness may be known, there are occasions when this knowledge can be ignored. One such case is general in nature: in a tight spot it is usually best to rely on one's most effective pitch. Another is the dilemma of strength against weakness, which has only one logical conclusion. Consider a pitcher with a good overhand curve and a sinking fast ball. Obviously, he is most effective when he keeps the ball low. It follows that even with a low-ball hitter at bat, he will probably be more successful by keeping the ball low, since the value of pitching to his own strength outweighs putting the ball in the batter's strong zone.

There are times when a moundsman will find that one of his basic pitches is not up to par. If one pitch is working well and another is not, he should merely *show* the batter the one that is not working, but should make him *hit* the one that is. For example, on a day when his curve ball is behaving poorly, he should use it as a waste pitch, letting the batter know that he has a curve—but without putting it in the strike zone. The fast ball is the one that should be thrown for strikes and that the batter should be made to hit. Actually, this is simply a variation of the idea that a hurler should rely on his best pitch or, in other words, pitch to his own strength.

Setting up the hitter by developing an effective sequence of pitches is an art in itself. Its mastery should be an aspiration of every pitcher. Yet using a predetermined method of setting up a batter is not always good practice. The idea in occasionally avoiding it is to keep the batter from learning exactly how a pitcher operates and to prevent him from getting set for a certain pitch. What this amounts to is staying out of a rut. It also accomplishes the purpose of keeping the hitter off balance.

An oft-repeated maxim for success on the mound is to "stay ahead of the hitter." To achieve a first-pitch strike, a pitcher should occasionally try something a little unusual. The time to go to the "pattern" or to one's best pitch is when the batter must swing. If a hurler finds that the opposition is consistently hitting the first pitch, he should resort to pitching to the batter's weakness on his first delivery.

### The Game Situation and Strategy

As mentioned above, several factors influence the development of sound pitching strategy. Among these, and of great importance, is the game situation. Every ballplayer should, at all times, be fully aware of the score, the inning, the number of outs, the count, and the position of base runners. The pitcher should base much of his strategy on the game situation.

Following is a brief listing of specific factors that come under the general heading of game situations and that should be taken into consideration when deciding on the proper pitch at a certain time.

1. When the pitcher is behind in the count, he should concentrate primarily on getting the ball over the plate.

2. The time to pitch to spots is when the pitcher is ahead of the batter.

3. A pitcher should try to "thread the needle" only occasionally. Attempting to have pinpoint control of every pitch can only lead to trouble for all but the very few who possess this control.

4. When the pitcher is one or two runs behind with men on base, he should throw no "fat" pitches. A base hit, in this case, could put the game beyond control.

5. No "fat" pitches should be thrown with first base open and either or both of the other two occupied. Here, a pitcher can afford to be extra careful since a walk will do little additional harm. Furthermore, with a

man in scoring position, a batter is more likely to go for a bad ball because of his anxiety to bring home a run.

6. Close consideration should be given the weather. On a hot day the pitcher should try to conserve his strength by throwing a minimum number of pitches. In damp weather he should rely heavily on his curve. When it is dark, he should place special emphasis on the use of his fast ball.

7. It is easier to pitch with a used baseball than with a new one. The catcher, and the first and third basemen should retrieve foul balls in an effort to keep the same one in play.

8. When a slick, new ball is introduced into the game, a curve is more difficult to throw. For this reason and because a new ball has a tendency to sail that adds to its effectiveness, the fast ball should be relied on heavily.

9. A 3-2 curve ball is an effective pitch and will often catch the batter looking at a called third strike, because he rarely anticipates such tactics.

10. With the bases loaded, the pitcher should throw a 3-2, two-out pitch from a set position, for the base runners, who will be moving, should be held close to their bases so that all will not be able to score on a base hit.

11. With a runner on second base and no outs, the pitcher should apply extra effort to prevent the batter from hitting toward right field, since this will probably move the runner to third base, from where he will be able to score on a fly ball.

12. If a first-strike bunt attempt is fouled off or missed, the next delivery should be a pitch-out. A curve ball pitch-out is especially effective in this case since the batter leans with it, and the runner is more likely to take a few extra steps.

This, by no means, covers every possible game situation. However, it can serve to channel a pitcher's thoughts in the right direction and aid him in the development of sound strategy and tactics.

## The Intentional Pass

The intentional pass is a highly controversial part of the game but a tactically important one to the pitcher. No matter how much scorn and ridicule it may arouse, there are certain situations in which its use is wise, others in which it is all but mandatory. Although the pass is generally called for by the manager, the principles and theory behind it should be thoroughly understood by the man who puts it into execution —the pitcher.

The catcher must remain within the confines of the catcher's box until the ball is on its way to the plate; thus, care must be exercised in throwing the four wide ones that constitute an intentional pass. The catcher stands at the extreme outside limit of his box and extends his bare hand to the side with a right-hander at bat and his glove with a left-hander at the plate. Either of the two is the target for which a pitcher should aim, the catcher stepping to the side to receive the ball as it leaves the pitcher's hand.

No signals are necessary for separate pitches once the intentional pass has been decided upon. A medium-speed fast ball should be delivered from a stop position to carry out this maneuver. When it is employed with fewer than two out and a runner on third, the catcher should squat behind the plate and give a conventional signal for the first of the four pitches in order to discourage an attempt at a squeeze play.

The intentional pass is generally dictated by sound strategy rather than fear of a particular batter. The intentional pass is used when it appears strategically more logical to pitch to the next batter in the order; it also sets up a force or possible double play. It is used only with first base open since there would be no sense in moving an important run nearer to home. With a runner on third it sets up a double play; with a runner on second, or on second and third, it makes possible a force at any base.

In setting up a double play, the pitcher should consider that the following batter will be much easier to double up if he swings right-handed, especially when he is a pull hitter who may drive the ball sharply to either the third baseman or the shortstop.

Occasionally a batter will be passed to get at the pitcher or to force the other team to pinch hit for him if he is pitching a strong game. The advisability of this move can be tempered by other factors, one of which is the strength of the batter who precedes the pitcher. If he is a weak batsman, it is wise to pitch to him, particularly when there are two out. In this event the pitcher, usually an "out man," may lead off the next inning, always an advantageous occurrence to the defensive team.

Another time when the intentional pass may be put to good use is with the winning run on third and either none or only one of the other bases occupied. Here, a walk will not only set up a double play but also (with one out) will eliminate the necessity of playing the infield in close, an alignment that gives the batter a much greater chance of hitting safely.

One variation on this maneuver is a partial intentional pass. Assume that first base is open, that one or more runners are in scoring positions, and that an exceptionally good hitter is at bat; if the count goes to 3-0 or 3-1, it may prove wisest to walk the man purposely rather than risk throwing him a "fat" pitch.

A more subtle variation, used by some experienced professionals, is the "hidden" intentional pass. It can be occasioned by the situation of runners on first and second or first and third, and the defensive team one or two runs behind in the late innings. Here, the pitcher should give the batter nothing good to hit. A walk in this case will not score a run, whereas a "fat" pitch can be driven out for a base hit that would put the game beyond recall. The word "hidden" is used because the batter should be tempted with carefully aimed pitches on or around the corners of the plate, but given nothing down the middle.

One of the cardinal rules of baseball is "never intentionally walk the tying or winning run." This should not be considered as an ironclad principle, however, for there are situations in which such a maneuver can be justified. Nevertheless, the percentages must be heavily in the pitcher's favor if he is to issue an intentional walk to a batter who represents the tying run, and they must be overwhelmingly in his favor if it is the winning run that is involved.

## WORKING ON THE HITTER

The primary aim of every pitcher should be to get the ball over the plate with something on it. Percentages definitely favor the pitcher, since even the finest of batsmen rarely hit safely more than once every three times at the plate. It follows that if the pitcher can avoid the base on balls and if he has reserved something extra for the tight spots, the odds will be greatly in his favor.

The secret of good hitting is timing; consequently, the pitcher should constantly endeavor to upset the batter's timing.

This, of course, brings us back to one of the fundamental rules: every pitch should have a purpose. The smart hurler will use a sequence of pitches, each of which will set up the batter for the next one and be, perhaps, a pitch that he is not expecting. If successful in his intentions, the pitcher will be able to keep the batter slightly off balance and will upset his timing sufficiently to keep him from getting good wood on the ball.

There are so many ideas on the subject of working on the hitter— ones that seem only loosely connected, though they fit into one overall method of operation—that categorizing them is difficult. In studying them, the reader should be aware of the basic theory behind them and should make it part of his own approach to pitching tactics. That theory is, a pitcher's greatest asset is the batter's imagination.

### Establishing a Pattern

Each pitch delivered during a ball game should form part of a definite sequence. As a consequence of the variable factors upon which it is dependent, the pitching pattern can and should be varied from pitch to pitch. A real mound artist has a carefully planned method of operation, yet is, at the same time, an astute improviser. He employs psychology and guile in the overall aspect of his sequence and remains alert to any momentary change that can be turned to his advantage.

The time for concentration on the batter's weakness is when the pitcher is ahead of him in the count and he is forced to swing at a ball that is close to or in the strike zone. It may be added that if the batter is given nothing but pitches on which he is weak, he will be given enough practice to eventually overcome the weakness. Furthermore, he will be expecting the pitch that gives him trouble. For these reasons the batter's weakness should be exploited primarily when the pitcher wants him to hit the ball.

The sequence or pattern should be so arranged as to take full advantage of the batter's weakness. Of course, it is desirable to retire the hitter on the first pitch (or on any one, for that matter), but this is a rare occurrence. Consequently, each pitch should have some element of surprise, and the overall pattern should be designed to build to a climax, or "out pitch," the one on which the batter is weakest. It need not be a single delivery—a particular pitch can certainly be used more than once on each batter. The idea is to operate in such a way that, by setting him up for it, a ball geared to his weakness will make him even more vulnerable.

Specialty pitchers operate in this fashion. These are the hurlers who rely primarily on one of the "off" pitches for their effectiveness. They set up the batter for the delivery that is their specialty and use it when they want the batter to hit the ball.

During the early innings of a ball game a pitcher should feel more free to throw what he wishes. If for no other reason than the psychological one, he should use the pitch in which he himself has the greatest confidence. As the game progresses, however, the situation undergoes a natural alteration. The catcher is in a better position to judge the effectiveness of each of the various deliveries, and his proximity gives him a better "feel" of the batter. Thus, his judgment should be relied on more heavily in the late innings. This does not mean that the pitcher should relinquish whatever control he has over the selection of pitches. It is still a joint undertaking; the catcher's influence at this point should simply be the stronger of the two.

A simple example of an effective pitching sequence might go like this. With a good pull-hitter at bat, the pitcher tries to cut the outside corner of the plate with two or three pitches, then fires one in under the hands of the hitter, who will probably have geared his swing for another outside pitch. Or after throwing a medium-speed and a slow pitch, the hurler throws a good fast ball over the plate, finding that even the best hitters are not fully prepared for it.

Observation, imagination, and an intelligent approach will enable any pitcher to work out effective patterns for dealing with each batter. Among the factors that should be borne in mind and that can materially affect the sequence of pitches are the following:

1. With men on base the ball should be kept low. This needs little elucidation since, in this case, it is desirable and advisable to make the batter hit the ball on the ground.

2. With first base open and either or both of the other two bases occupied, the batter should not be given a "fat" pitch. This is one case in which a pitcher can take extra care in working on the hitter and not be too concerned should he walk the man.

3. With runners in scoring position, an exceptionally good hitter should not be fed the same pitch that has retired him early in the game. He will be expecting it.

4. When ahead of the pitcher, a smart hitter will set himself for "his pitch," one in his strong zone; he may pass up a good pitch if it is not just what he wants, since he can afford to take a strike.

5. A first-ball hitter generally does not like the curve and is set to swing at the fast ball. Because he is overanxious, the pitcher can easily make him go for a bad ball (but it should not be so bad that he will pass it up).

6. Most young and inexperienced batters fall into the overanxious category and will have a tendency to swing at anything. Bad balls should be used on them.

7. A waste pitch should not literally be wasted—it should be off the plate but close enough to the strike zone to tempt the batter. This is one more application of the principle that every pitch should have a purpose, and demonstrates cognizance of the fact that a bad ball is far more difficult to hit than is a good one. However, even though the pitcher gets ahead of the batter and can afford to waste a pitch, his main purpose should still be to get the man out. Thus, the pitch should be neither too good nor too bad.

8. Regardless of the pitch selected or the sequence developed, a sudden change—often in mid-motion—is demanded whenever a bunt, squeeze, or steal of home is detected. An unhittable fast ball is in order.

### Varying the Pattern

The pitching sequence should never be rigidly set. Momentary changes in the pitcher-batter relationship make sudden alterations in plans advisable at times. The working speed, velocity of pitches, and method of operation should be varied so as to keep the batter off balance.

When the "book" on a hitter is followed too closely and without deviation, he will become adjusted to it. Furthermore, a pitcher's stuff varies in its behavior, and he may find, therefore, that the "right pitch" is the wrong one.

This is particularly so when dealing with good hitters. There are certain batters, however (never the strongest ones), who can be retired in the same way over and over again. Any pitch near their weakness will dispose of them with little trouble. This type of hitter hangs on in professional baseball primarily because he succeeds in getting an occasional base hit when a pitcher suffers a lapse in his control or the quality of his stuff.

One special situation in which the pattern can be ignored should be recognized by all pitchers. This occurs when the batter is taking a pitch. The pitcher should try to anticipate when the take is on—and should throw a strike. If the batter shows his intentions and squares away or moves around in an attempt to rattle the pitcher, he is giving away a strike, and the pitcher should be sure to get the ball over the plate. In this case he should use a fast ball. An arrangement can be made with the catcher that will make this an automatic fast ball situation.

One other qualification in establishing a pattern bears repetition. When he finds himself in a tight spot, a pitcher should employ his best pitch. In other words, he should attempt to get out of difficulty by "pitching to his own strength."

### Varying the Delivery

It is wise for a pitcher to perfect both an overhand (or three-quarters) and a sidearm delivery. This will not only lend variety to his pitching but also enable him to cope more effectively with otherwise troublesome hitters.

A pitcher who uses both an overhand and a sidearm delivery should have both a fast ball and a curve with each motion and should mix up the two pitches. The batter should be made aware that the pitcher has both so that he will not be able to take a toehold in anticipation of a particular pitch every time the hurler changes from overhand to sidearm and vice versa. Mixing up the fast ball and curve applies also to different times at bat for the same man: he'll remember the last time.

Ordinarily it is bad practice for a right-hander to pitch sidearm to a left-handed batter, because the latter can follow the ball so well when it is delivered that way, and because a sidearm curve ball breaks directly in to him. This applies equally well to a left-handed pitcher and a right-handed batter.

On the other hand, because the pitch is so well hidden and difficult to pick up and follow, a right-handed pitcher should throw plenty of sidearm stuff to a right-handed batter and a left-handed pitcher should do the same to a lefty batter. Most hitters have trouble with a sidearm delivery when it is used by a pitcher who throws from the same side on which they bat. This is particularly so of left-handed hitters, possibly because facing a southpaw is a relatively unusual experience for them. There are sound baseball men who maintain that a left-handed batter will never consistently hit a left-handed sidearm delivery.

Likewise, a right-hander's curve to a left-handed batter (and a lefty's curve to a right-handed batter) is most effective when thrown "over the top," that is, directly overhand. Thrown in this manner, the curve will break primarily downward, rather than into the batter, and will be more difficult for him to hit squarely.

An extreme example of the sidearm delivery is the crossfire. The technique of throwing it has been explained in the section on mechanics. The crossfire should be kept away from the batter, who, in the vast majority of cases, will pull back from the plate.

### Psychology and Pitching

"He pitches with his head as well as his arm" is a highly complimentary phrase when used to describe a pitcher. Anyone familiar with baseball has heard it used in reference to an exceptionally smart moundsman. It is a fitting commentary on the skill of a polished performer, for one who belongs in this category is both a strategist and a psychologist. By a well-conceived plan of operation, by disarming mechanical moves, and by taking advantage of the batter's emotions and thought processes, the pitcher succeeds in nullifying the batter's power by outthinking him.

Guess-hitting is a bad habit for a batsman, but it is only natural that batters try to outguess the pitcher. Therein lies one of the big advantages enjoyed by a hurler. Baseball's outstanding hitters do not try to outguess the pitcher; yet even they can be maneuvered into a position in which they will more or less anticipate a certain pitch in a certain situation. It is up to the pitcher to try to stay one jump ahead of the batter in his reasoning and to exploit the perfectly normal reactions that any ballplayer will evidence in response to a given situation—in this case one that can be conceived and, to some extent, controlled by the pitcher. The poorer hitters can be outsmarted with greater frequency because they are more likely to guess. Thus, the pitcher who combines psychology with his physical skills is a tough man to beat.

Mound psychology is a very difficult thing to teach. Game situations are so numerous and have so many ramifications that rigid policies to cope with each of them could not possibly be delineated. The solution, then, is to make the pitcher think along certain lines by citing examples used by smart moundsmen. Through imitation modified by improvisation, he can profit greatly by exploring only a few of the methods employed by masters of the trade. Here are a few examples:

1. Carl Hubbell was one of baseball's all-time greats. Although expert at pacing himself, he always exerted extra effort to hold the opposition scoreless until his team had gone ahead. He was a firm believer in the theory that having a lead gives the pitcher a definite psychological advantage.

2. If a pitcher's success over the early innings of a game has been achieved by his principal reliance on a particular pitch, he will have the opposition looking for it. Switching the emphasis to another pitch will give him a valuable extra weapon in outsmarting enemy batsmen.

3. Most batters set themselves for the fast ball when the pitcher is behind in the count. This is only natural, since most hurlers have better control with the fast ball than with any other pitch. Consequently, a curve or change of pace will often catch the hitter off balance in this situation. The fact that he tends to become overanxious is another good reason for changing up on him at this time.

4. The change-up or curve should be thrown for a strike in this case because it is the element of surprise that makes it effective. The change-up, in particular, is difficult to control; so the pitcher should concentrate on getting it into the strike zone on the 2-0 or 3-1 pitch since a smart hitter, when fooled, will often pass it up.

5. Many smart pitchers will go to the curve when behind the batter and the fast ball when ahead of him, knowing that most ballplayers do not expect such tactics.

6. When the first pitch is a curve and misses the plate, for a ball, the next pitch should be another curve ball, right over the middle of the plate. Nine times out of ten the batter will take it for a strike.

7. If the batter takes a strike with men in scoring position, the pitcher should come back with the identical pitch. In this case the batter is up there to hit, and if he lets a strike go by without offering at it, he is looking for "his pitch," the one that he wants to hit. The fact that he passed up a strike indicates that he does not want to hit that particular pitch.

8. A batter's nervous characteristics can serve as a good guide to the right method of dealing with him. The pitcher should wait on a ner-

vous hitter, taking the full time allotted to him by the rules. Conversely, he should work rapidly when facing an especially calm batter or one who waves his bat in pronounced fashion, the idea being to catch this type of hitter before he is set for the pitch.

9. Occasionally the pitcher will encounter a batter who is a sign-stealer; that is, he sneaks frequent glances at the catcher in an attempt to see the signal. The logical way to handle this man is to quick-pitch him, both to catch him unawares and to discourage this habit.

10. Shaking off the catcher can prove an effective weapon to a pitcher because it can make a guess-hitter of almost any man he faces. This instance of psychology should not be limited to those times when the pitcher gets a signal for a delivery that he does not want to throw. On occasion he should shake off the sign for the pitch that he wants to use and continue to shake off each subsequent signal until the catcher returns to the original one.

### The Brush-back Pitch

Brushing the hitter back from the plate can be classed under the psychological phase of pitching. A hurler must occasionally throw close to the batter in order to be successful. If he does nothing but keep the ball out over the plate, he is inviting his opponents to dig in and swing from the heels.

Although intimidation is a motivating factor in using the brush-back pitch, its real purpose is to keep the hitter off balance and to prevent him from taking a toehold and a full swing, safe in the knowledge that every pitch will be over the middle of the plate. A pitcher who tends to be wild has no need to resort to these tactics and should not do so.

When the batter digs in at the plate, setting himself to step in to the ball and hit it out of sight, it may be a good idea to brush him back. The best time to do this is with two strikes and no balls, when a waste pitch is in order.

To "brush back" a hitter means that a pitcher, when he sees a batter digging in and looking for his pitch, will throw a waste pitch high and tight, or under the chin. Such pitches are very difficult to hit solidly and will also serve to "keep him loose" and make him less anxious to take a toehold.

In professional baseball, umpires are empowered to eject from the game any pitcher who, in their judgment, throws at a batter intentionally. The umpires can recommend a fine and suspension for him. A baseball hurled at great speed can be a deadly weapon and no pitcher should, under any circumstances, throw at a batter with intent to hit him.

When the brush-back is used on a good hitter he may, quite possibly, become both angry and overanxious. In this case he will generally be vulnerable to a change of pace. Whatever pitch he uses, the pitcher should keep the ball away from the batter since he will now stand back from the plate at least slightly.

### Pace and Pitching

The importance of pacing oneself in order to conserve strength and save something extra for the tight spots has been stressed, and rightly so. Its value in coping with the batter makes its mastery another imperative.

Varying the speeds of his pitches is the most effective way for a pitcher to keep the batter off balance and upset his timing. Since the majority of pitches are fast balls, they will be considered as the normal speed, and the slower pitches or the change of pace will be the deviations. The change-up, sometimes described by the words "taking something off the ball," can be a pitcher's best weapon if properly used.

Although much mention has already been made of the change of pace, a few additional ideas can give it the refinement needed to make it really effective:

(1) It is rarely wise to change up on a late swinger, whether he is simply a man whose reflexes are slow or one with exceptionally good wrists who can wait longer on a pitch and still get around on the ball.

(2) Another type of hitter who is rarely bothered by a change of pace is the nonstrider, who is usually well planted, with a wide stance. This man is not a lunger, and he generally maintains good balance at the plate; consequently, a change is merely a slow pitch to him, and he will be ready for it. This does not mean, however, that every pitch to him should be thrown as hard as possible—variety is still an effective tool— but it means that he is less likely to be caught off balance by a change of pace.

(3) It is seldom good practice to change up with two strikes on the hitter. This is a spot in which the pitcher has his opponent at a disadvantage, and he should call on his best stuff to get the out. An exception to this occurs when a batter has fouled off several fast balls and is used to that speed.

(4) The pitcher should not throw a weak hitter a change of pace. The fact that this man usually likes slow and high pitches and the fact that his timing is inconsistent are closely related. He is a poor batsman because of his inability to hit the fast ball and curve, the pitches he most often sees in a game. A slow pitch will seem like batting practice to him.

This last point is important because it pertains directly to one of the cardinal rules of good pitching: a pitcher should never "get cute" with a weak hitter. A poor batsman is an out, and because achieving that is the pitcher's main objective, he should go to work on him and get the out as quickly as possible.

**Operating Speed.** The pitcher's pace and the variations thereof—factors that constitute his operating speed—can also be used to upset the batter's timing. Varying the interval between pitches, hesitating momentarily at some point in the motion, adding an extra body twist, and speeding the delivery are all methods that can be employed to attain this purpose.

For example, using an extra pump before delivering to a batter who is obviously "digging in" can throw him off stride. Conversely, a speeded-up, no-pump fast ball to a batter who has just seen one or more off-speed pitches dealt with a deliberate or normally paced motion would also be effective. Such devices mean that the batter cannot afford to relax and must keep himself in constant readiness for the pitch. The pitcher also benefits from the psychological effect on the batter who, remaining constantly alert, is apt to become tense.

## Setting Up the Hitter

In formulating his operating method and sequence of pitches, a hurler should fully understand two general principles upon which the majority of outstanding mound artists base their approach to the art of setting up the hitter.

First, there is the effect that changes of speed have on a batter when they are properly applied and catch him off balance. If he is expecting a slow pitch or curve ball, a fast ball will either get by him or cause him to swing late and hit the ball without full power behind his swing. When he is set for a fast pitch, a change of pace will cause him to place his weight on his front foot too soon, making him hit the ball with an "arm swing" rather than with the weight of his entire body behind the blow. In either case no great reliance is placed on his missing the ball completely; the basic principle is to nullify the power of his swings by upsetting his timing.

Second, there is the reasoning behind the definition of the strike zone, which includes all of that space over the 17-inch-wide plate between the batter's knees and his arm pits when he assumes his normal stance. It was drawn up to embrace that area in which the batter has the greatest likelihood of hitting the ball. Theoretically, the closer to the center of that area a pitch is, the greater will be the batter's chances of hitting it. It follows that if a pitcher can induce a man to swing at balls outside the strike zone, his possibilities of getting an out are greatly enhanced.

Basing his approach to the job on these well-founded theories, a pitcher should endeavor to set up the hitter by combining pace and control in knowledgeable fashion.

The various segments of this section on pitching to the batter have a strong tendency to overlap, and many of the salient points are difficult to categorize; yet all the important points have been covered, and many ideas on tactics have been advanced. In an effort to provide tactical examples as a guide to setting up the hitter, several additional tricks of the trade are included here at the conclusion of this section:

1. The pitcher should pay close attention to where the batter stands, how he stands, how he holds his bat, how he strides, and to his attitude at the plate. These things can help in developing effective short- and long-range strategy.

2. The pitcher should move the ball around on the batter. When done from one pitch to the next, this will keep the hitter from setting himself for a ball in one location. When done after delivering several pitches to one section of the strike zone, it will set him up for a pitch to another spot.

3. If a batter likes a certain pitch, he will more than likely bite at bad balls in his strong zone. For instance, a man who is a decided high-ball hitter is usually so anxious to get his favorite pitch that he will go for a bad ball in that general area. A shoulder-high fast ball will probably induce him to swing and will prove a very difficult pitch to hit solidly. The same thing applies to hitters who have other definite strong zones, whether they be low-ball hitters or hitters who like an inside or outside pitch.

4. A bad ball in the batter's strong zone has the added advantage of setting him up for a pitch to his weakness. If he takes the intentional bad one for a ball, the next one should be delivered to his weak spot.

5. If the pitcher goes to a 3-2 count using only one pitch, he should resort to another delivery for the payoff pitch. The element of surprise in the switch will often fool the batter.

6. If he goes to a 2-2 count using one pitch, he can also try this change in deliveries. Should that one be a ball, he should come back with the same pitch. The batter will expect him to return to his original pitch if the sudden switch goes astray and thus often will be badly fooled.

7. Many times even a good curve ball hitter will miss the first curve he sees after being fed only pitches other than curves. This holds true primarily in the late innings after this batter has received one type of treatment in several trips to the plate. It also applies, though not quite

so strongly, to the good fast ball hitter and the first swift one he sees.

8. The change-up is most effective when the batter has been maneuvered into setting himself for a fast pitch. It can also be used with good results when the pitcher detects any sign of overanxiousness. A logical time for this to occur is when the pitcher is behind in the count. Another example is a first-pitch change-up to a good hitter when runners are in scoring position. In this situation a good hitter is at the plate with one primary purpose—to score the runners—and he may be overanxious on the first ball pitched to him.

9. An old pitching adage is, "When in doubt, curve him." In other words, if a hitter poses a particular problem and the pitcher has difficulty deciding how to deal with him on a particular pitch, relying on the curve ball is probably the safest procedure.

Because most batters have more trouble with the curve than with the fast ball and because a breaking ball is generally more difficult to meet squarely, this advice seems logical.

10. A bad ball hitter presents a peculiar problem: a waste pitch or a calculated bad ball has little effect on him. For that reason the pitcher should try to get every ball into the strike zone—with good stuff on it. Changing speeds and moving the ball around should be done within the confines of the strike zone. His unpredictability is what makes this batter troublesome. Fortunately, bad ball hitters are uncommon.

11. Most ballplayers are fast ball hitters. It is the ability to hit the curve ball that generally differentiates good batsmen from mediocre ones. Consequently, pitching sequence is of paramount importance in dealing with them. Whatever the delivery and whatever the pitch, a good hitter must be properly set up for it if real effectiveness is to be achieved.

12. An instance involving Whitey Ford and Ted Williams comes to mind as an example of how even the greatest of hitters can fall prey to the guile of a master craftsman. Williams, of course, could hit even the fastest of pitchers with authority, and Ford was not overpowering. Yet in a game some years back, the wily left-hander blew a third strike by this master batsman by setting him up perfectly. Williams had taken a curve for strike one and had fouled off a fast ball for strike two. Ford's third pitch was a belt-high fast ball through the heart of the plate, and Williams took it for a called strike-three. Ford had set him up perfectly and made only a fairly good fast ball seem like a bullet by *not* throwing his bread-and-butter curve when it was most expected.

Any or all of these suggestions can be applied with necessary alterations and embellishments according to any pitcher's particular needs. They should help make him a much more successful operator on the mound. If he remembers and puts into practice only the more basic procedures outlined in this section—that every pitch should have a purpose, that his primary aim should be to get the ball over the plate (preferably low) with good stuff on it, and that he should save a little extra for the tight spots—a pitcher will be able to perform with far greater effectiveness and should win more than his share of games.

## TYPES OF HITTERS

In the last section we considered pitching strategy in a general sense and as it applied to all hitters. The suggestions listed above are good practices to follow under any circumstance, regardless of the hitter.

There are certain mannerisms and characteristics shown by some hitters that are fairly reliable indications of their potentialities and possible weaknesses at the plate. A number of these peculiarities are discussed here, but their interpretation or significance cannot, of course, be wholly accurate. They do, nevertheless, apply to the large majority of hitters who fall into these various classifications.

First, it must be recognized that a really good hitter cannot easily be categorized and that he is going to get his share of hits regularly, no matter how he is pitched. Applying the general rules already mentioned (in other words, using good common sense from a pitching standpoint) is the best method to follow against a particularly good hitter. Fortunately, outstanding hitters constitute only a small minority of those who will be faced in the course of a game or, for that matter, a full season.

Following is a brief description of, and a pitching guide to, specific types of hitters:

1. A man who carries his bat particularly high is usually a low ball hitter. His swing is started by a downward movement of the bat, and it is usually easier for him to continue the motion that he has already begun and meet a low ball than to check the downward motion of the bat and begin his forward swing in a separate motion.

Similarly, a man who carries his bat particularly low is usually a high ball hitter.

2. A batter who stands away from the plate is usually an opposite-field hitter. He strides toward the plate to meet the ball and, following the line of motion established by his stride, he should drive the ball toward the opposite field.

This type of hitter stands away from the plate because he likes to hit an outside pitch. Since he has an exaggerated stride into the ball, an inside pitch would seem troublesome, although a wide curve ball or a fast ball on the outside corner may elude the sweep of his bat.

This category also covers any right-handed batter who attempts to hit behind the runner on a hit-and-run play. If the pitcher suspects the hit-and-run, he should pitch a right-handed batter in on the fists, making it almost impossible for him to push the ball to right field.

3. An open-stance hitter, unlike the man who steps toward the plate, almost invariably likes inside pitches. His very stance, stride, and swing indicate that only the very end of his bat will cover the outside corner of the plate and that he is a pull hitter whose power will be greatest on an inside pitch. The ball should be kept away from an open-stance hitter.

4. A batter who takes a long stride is usually a low ball hitter and will have more trouble with a high pitch because his long stride lowers the center of his body weight and means that a high strike will be a bad ball for him to hit.

Conversely, a short strider generally hits high pitching well and should be pitched low.

The overstrider fits in here, too. He is a quick, as well as long, strider and will have difficulty timing the ball if the pitcher changes speeds on him.

5. A batter who drops his rear shoulder is an uppercutter with a golfing swing and is a low ball hitter. He should be pitched high and tight. This will give him trouble since he is swinging up at a ball that is already high.

6. A man who crouches usually does so for a good reason. He likes low pitching and wants the pitcher to bring the ball down to him. It follows that he should be pitched high.

7. Some batters have a tendency to lunge at the ball. Thus, they commit themselves too soon, and a change of pace will catch them off balance. A high, tight fast ball will also give this type of hitter trouble because his stride is a long one, and the ball, when pitched high, will be above his strike zone after his stride has been completed.

8. The batter who has a pronounced hitch in his swing must time the hitch as well as the swing. Changing speeds will cause him trouble. However, pitching him tight and fast is probably the most effective method (particularly when he is set up for it with a low change of pace) since he will have difficulty getting around on the ball.

9. The nervous, jittery type of hitter is very eager to hit the ball and get his job over with. The pitcher should take his time and wait on this man—he will become overanxious and lose some of his hitting ability.

10. The batter who turns his head when taking his cut is usually weak on curve ball pitching since he does not follow the ball well. The

turn of the head also pulls his front shoulder away from the plate. Consequently, this man will have trouble hitting an outside pitch.

11. The "bucket-hitter" (one who steps away from the plate) will have trouble with outside pitches and curve balls breaking away from him unless he compensates for his foot-in-the-bucket stride by moving the upper part of his body into the pitch. If he does this, he can occasionally be pitched tight.

12. The sweep-hitter is one who brings his bat through on the swing with a sweeping motion of his arms and does not break his wrists properly, if at all. He is invariably weak on inside fast balls, especially high ones.

13. A "guess-hitter" is one who continually anticipates the pitch. He usually looks for the fast ball. Quite obviously, the way to fool him is to give him a pitch that he is not expecting. It is to this man, in particular, that a pitcher can put into practice some of the strategy previously discussed—such as a curve or change of pace when behind in the count, or a fast ball when the batter is "in the hole" and likely to be expecting a curve. Mixing up his deliveries in general is a good method for a pitcher to follow in dealing with a guess-hitter since this very characteristic all but eliminates the possibility of using a set pattern of pitching against him.

14. *General Categories*: Although all hitters do not fall into one of the above-mentioned groupings, they all can be categorized under one of several more general headings—pull, straightaway, or opposite-field hitters.

The pull hitter is usually a free swinger who takes a good cut at the ball. He is more apt than other hitters to strike out, but is also more apt to hit the long ball.

The straightaway hitter sprays his hits to all fields, hitting the ball where it is pitched. That is, he will hit an outside pitch to the opposite field, pull an inside pitch, and hit a pitch directly over the plate to center field. He usually has good control of the bat.

The opposite-field hitter waits on the ball a little longer than the other types and is generally a "slice-hitter" who merely pokes at the ball rather than taking a full cut. He is the toughest man to strike out but the least likely to hit for distance.

Close observation by both the pitcher and catcher, in batting practice and during the game, will help them to categorize the hitters and compile a guide for pitching to them.

For general purposes low-ball pitching is still the most effective. The lively baseball in use today and the short fences that are found in most enclosed parks make this a particularly apt principle because a low ball is relatively difficult to hit for distance.

## REORDERING PRIORITIES—
## A NEW THEORY OF PITCHING

Even a slight familiarity with baseball at its various levels of competition can lead to but one valid conclusion about pitching—that the outstanding fast ball is indeed a rarity in amateur baseball.

Yet the fact remains that pitching theory still considers the fast ball as the number-one pitch. This flies in the face of logic when one considers, in addition to the paucity of good fast balls found outside of the professional ranks, the fact that all hitters prefer the fast ball (particularly a mediocre one) to a curve ball.

Sal Maglie, a recognized authority on the breaking ball, claims that there is no such thing as a good curve ball hitter. If this observation by an all-time great is applicable to major league hitters, its wisdom should be greatly magnified at the scholastic level.

It thus behooves scholastic coaches and the overwhelming majority of aspiring pitchers to stress the importance of the curve ball. Development of a good one becomes essential for two basic reasons: (1) to serve as the number-one pitch in the preponderance of cases in which the big fast ball does not exist; (2) to make even a mediocre fast ball a valuable weapon from the tactical standpoint.

To lend credence to this theory, consider the inescapable conclusion that observation of hitters, whether in practice or during games, shows that the most prevalent and flagrant batting flaw is turning the head, or, in other words, taking one's eye off the ball. Think how difficult this renders a man's ability to meet a relatively small, rapidly moving object with "good wood"—if at all. Then visualize the virtual impossibility of hitting this same object when it changes course.

### The Tactical Approach

The thesis being advanced and emphasized is that wisdom decrees far greater use of the curve ball for all but the small minority of hurlers who are blessed with the big fast ball. The validity of this theory would seem to be reinforced when one ponders a basic question, Why would any pitcher rely primarily on a mediocre fast ball and inevitably turn to it in the clutch when it is the one pitch that any hitter prefers? After all, it is the mediocre fast ball that is thrown most often in batting practice—so that the hitter can meet the ball solidly.

The youngster who develops and specializes in the curve ball will have acquired two vital weapons in the batter-pitcher contest. Physically, he will have command of the most difficult pitch to hit well. Tactically, he will be able to make the batter hit *his* pitch the vast majority of times. In addition, he may react with far greater confidence on those occasions when a strike must be thrown to a good hitter, secure in the knowledge that a potent batsman, expecting a pitch in the strike zone, will have to contend with a curve, rather than a fast ball.

In the course of any ball game (especially in its early stages) and with only occasional variation, it pays to start an amateur hitter with a curve. Knowing that the pitcher is anxious to get the first one over for a strike, he will, in most cases, be expecting a fast ball. Furthermore, first-ball hitters are invariably fast ball hitters. Should the first one be a ball, the second pitch should be another curve—right through the middle. That it will be taken for a called strike can almost be guaranteed.

This is an example of one tactical curve ball classification—*taking*. In other words, when the batter is least expecting a curve and most likely to take it for a strike, the pitcher can afford to cut the middle of the plate with it, knowing that the element of surprise will often give him a called strike. Other categories may be labelled *swinging* and *wasting*. The former refers to those occasions when the pitcher wants the batter to hit the ball (or, at least, to swing at it) and deals him his best curve, trying to hit a corner with it. The other genre, wasting, is called for when the pitcher is ahead in the count and can afford to waste a pitch. In this case he can throw his curve plateward in such a way that it will break outside of the strike zone, yet stand a good chance of luring the batter into swinging at a bad ball.

The curve-baller has another advantage—he does not have to concern himself greatly with developing a carefully devised pattern of operation for setting-up a hitter; nor does he have to rely too heavily on pitching with finesse to a man's weakness, for his predominant use of the curve ball, in all but the rarest of cases, is accomplishing those two things —a strategic pattern develops itself, and a weakness (the curve ball) is being exploited.

Let us assume that a pitcher uses his curve ball on 60 percent of his pitches. The inevitable result is that the opposition will be constantly looking for the curve, not only because of its repeated use but also because it is generally more difficult to hit. Consider the effectiveness that this now adds to the fast ball, even a mediocre one. Being set for the curve, a slower pitch, the batter will experience difficulty in making the instantaneous adjustment necessary to handle the fast ball. (Even a good fast ball hitter often has trouble with the first one he sees after a steady diet of curve balls.) Furthermore, because he presumably prefers a fast ball, he will often chase a bad one. This is particularly so of a bad ball in his strong zone, further suggesting the wisdom of using the fast ball as a waste pitch (the poorer its quality, the more often it should be used for strictly show purposes). Even should he not chase a bad ball, the batter is now at an even greater tactical disadvantage. He is aware that the pitcher does have a fast ball and must be prepared for it, adding to the element of guessing and the resulting pitfalls. Of course, the pitcher has also tended to set him up further for the curve ball, and this is now the number-one pitch.

### Maximizing the Fast Ball

Although this is essentially a discussion of the curve ball, it has now become apparent that the fast ball has taken on greater effectiveness and importance as a weapon in the curve-baller's tactical arsenal. Thus, a few additional ideas on the use of the fast ball by a breaking-ball pitcher seems warranted. Obviously, even a mediocre fast ball takes on an explosive quality when the batter is not expecting it. A pattern has now been established in which the fast ball is rarely expected. A fairly obvious tip-off may be provided by the batter who edges forward in the box. He is not only thinking "curve" but also giving the pitcher an extra two or three feet of velocity on his fast ball.

The batter will be given much more trouble if, after throwing curves breaking away from him, the pitcher throws the fast ball in on his fists. This type of pitch can be made yet more effective if the pitcher learns to "turn it over" (release it off the side of the middle finger while twisting the hand slightly in a direction opposite that used in throwing the curve). Such a technique provides an added degree of variety to the repertoire since it means that the fast ball will move "the other way" in contrast to the curve. This renders more effective a right-hander's attempts to "jam" a right-handed batter. Care must be exercised in pitching the opposite-side hitter tight lest the movement of the ball carry it out over the plate, where he can get good wood on it. This leads logically to the idea of keeping this type of fast ball on the outside corner when facing a man who bats from the opposite side of the plate. This practice is even more important when the pitcher is ahead in the count and can afford to waste one—in this case, a fast ball that heads for the outside corner and moves out of the strike zone as the batter swings.

The desirability of working with a used baseball is obvious, especially when the curve ball is being thrown. Since there are times when this is impossible, it is propitious for the breaking-ball pitcher to consider and prepare for the ramifications thereof. When a slick, new ball is introduced into the game, a good curve is more difficult to throw. For this reason and because a new ball has a tendency to sail that adds to its effectiveness, the pitcher can risk more reliance on the fast ball until conditions are more favorable for a full return to the basic curve ball strategy. This does not imply that a new baseball automatically calls for exclusive use of the fast ball. The curve, being the basic pitch, should be employed, albeit slightly more judiciously. Because its break will not be so sharp, the pitcher must take extra care to keep it low. Throwing it at a slower speed can also enhance its possibility of fooling the hitter, for the horizontal (change-of-speed) element is now added to the vertical, meaning that even the poorer curve probable under these conditions has been augmented by another device that can render meeting the ball solidly a more difficult task.

Changing speeds on one's pitches as a means of upsetting a batter's timing can be enhanced by varying one's working speed. This can also be particularly effective when the basic intention is to make the fast ball seem faster. The curve ball pitcher should eliminate motion and quicken his actions when throwing a fast ball, thereby adding to the element of surprise. If, for example, he uses a pump or modified windup in the normal delivery of his curve ball, his fast ball will benefit greatly if he eliminates extraneous motion or the pump. Merely accelerating his pitching motion is, in fact, often sufficient to throw the batter off stride. What is being advocated for the breaking-ball specialist is, in effect, a perfectly legal quick-pitch.

The use of a decoy shake-off in situations similar to that described in the last paragraph is an additional ploy used in an effort to confuse the hitter and upset his timing. This involves shaking off the catcher several times, even though he may have signalled whatever the pitcher wants to throw. The catcher will soon be aware of the little game that is being played and do his part, eventually returning to the desired sign. More important, each shake-off means one more time that the batter will be conned into guessing what pitch will be thrown. This gimmick can be employed on any occasion and is particularly effective in the type of setup under consideration here.

### Teamwork *and* Cooperation

Mention has already been made of several game situations in which the fast ball should be automatic (for example, when the batter squares around with no one on base and is obviously taking a pitch or when the suicide squeeze or steal of home is detected), whatever pitch has been signalled and with little cause for concern over whether the batter will be fooled by it. In the case of a probable sacrifice it has been suggested that the batter be started with a high fast ball. After the first pitch in this situation, however, the pitcher will benefit by going back to his basic curve ball strategy. For contrary to popular opinion, it is the curve ball— not the high fast ball—that is most difficult to bunt, because the batter must follow the break of the ball with his bat and, in many cases, even bend his knees to adjust to it properly for a good bunt.

The fact that it is easier to throw and control a good curve with a used baseball than with a slick, new one has also been discussed. For this reason a coach would be well advised to instruct all his players, especially the first and third baseman and catcher, that their pitcher will benefit if the same ball is kept in play whenever possible. They should retrieve foul balls in an effort to give their pitcher this advantage. If a new ball is introduced and feels too slick for the pitcher, he can request a different one from the umpire or at least take the time to rub some of the sheen off the new one.

The team should also be aware that the curve ball is more likely to be pulled than the fast ball. Their positioning should take this into consideration. Furthermore, it is desirable for a team to know when the fast ball will be thrown, especially because the curve-baller's use of it is generally as a surprise pitch that will either sneak by the hitter or cause him to swing late. Professional clubs have pitching signals relayed to all players. Although this may not be essential at the scholastic level, certainly the short-second combination should be aware of the pitch to be thrown (they, of course, should read the catcher's signs along with the pitcher).

### A Different Angle

Most pitchers throw with a three-quarter overhand delivery. For the curve this is ideal since one thrown in this fashion will break both down and to the side. Whatever the angle of delivery normally used, the curve ball specialist should master all three—overhand, three-quarters, and sidearm—for variety as well as for specific tactical use. If the pitcher learns to to throw the fast ball and the curve from these angles and at only two speeds, he will have enlarged his repertoire tremendously—simply by mastering the two basic pitches.

It is only natural that a curve ball breaking in to him is the one most easily hit by any batter. Therein lies the value of developing a curve thrown straight over the top. One device that a pitcher may find helpful in imparting a sharper break to his overhand curve is to raise himself up on the toes of his pivot foot. This automatically shortens the stride and brings the ball down at a sharper angle and with a better break (a curve ball delivered over the top rarely breaks as sharply as that thrown three-quarters overhand). This pitch should be used extensively on the man who bats from the opposite side of the plate.

The righty versus lefty situation does not preclude use of the normal (three-quarter arm) curve. It can still be an effective pitch, particularly when spotted correctly. Aimed for the outside corner, it can suddenly change from a ball to a strike, in which case the batter is quite likely to take it. When it is a foregone conclusion that an opposite-side hitter will swing at a strike, the pitcher should spot his best curve low and on the inside corner, under his hands. When an aspiring moundsman has reached this stage of proficiency, he will be operating like a real pitcher, working the hitter in and out, and with a breaking ball, at that.

The sidearm curve is a valuable tool when mixed with a fast ball thrown from the same angle. It usually has a more sweeping and less sharp break than the three-quarter variety. Since its action is flat, its value against an opposite-side hitter is doubtful. Yet it can prove a potent weapon, not only because it adds variety to a pitcher's arsenal but also because it can be spotted for either the swinging or taking situation described previously. Furthermore, its very existence can transform a sidearm fast ball into a devastating weapon. Suppose, for example, that the batter has been started with a sidearm curve. Should the count reach two strikes, the pitcher can return to his sidearm delivery—this time with a fast ball. The odds are overwhelming that he will catch the batter by surprise; in fact, in many cases, he will be able to sneak a sidearm fast ball through the middle for a called third strike. The strategy of mixing the sidearm fast ball and curve also applies to different times at bat for the same man —he'll remember the last time.

Many schoolboy pitchers would prefer to throw the fast ball from one angle and the curve from another (usually an overhand fast ball and a sidearm curve) because they can get better stuff on each of the two pitches this way. Obviously, this is not desirable; yet even without developing all the pitches previously discussed, it can be made to work to a pitcher's advantage. On one of my better ball clubs, for example, one of our young pitchers had only a fair natural overhand fast ball. Experimentation showed that his fast ball, when delivered sidearm, was far superior in both velocity and movement. Naturally, he was converted to a sidearmer. For some reason, however, he could not throw a satisfactory sidearm curve, whereas delivered overhand, it was a good pitch. Hence, he became a sidearm fast-baller who threw his curve overhand. He was a winner because of one simple device: he threw an occasional overhand fast ball, primarily for show purposes, although, of course, he was establishing a pattern that would enable him to sneak it by the hitter occasionally for a strike.

### General Curve Ball Strategy

Quite obviously, a major factor in determining pitching tactics is the count on the batter. Paul Richards once said that in the game of baseball there is no such word as *never*. Likewise, it stands to reason that the term *always* should be eschewed. Yet if one rule could be formulated and safely applied to simplify the art of pitching it would be: When you are ahead of the batter, throw him the fast ball; when behind, throw him the curve. The vast majority of hitters do not expect such tactics. Ted Williams says that he always looked for the fast ball on the 2-0 count and often did so at 3-1.

Obviously, this is not an inflexible rule of thumb, particularly in view of the fact that the basic purpose of this school of pitching is to promote greater general usage of the curve. It is, nevertheless, sound operating theory.

A perfect example of the value of using the curve ball when behind in the count was provided late in the 1971 season by one of baseball's true greats, Tom Seaver. In a game against the world champion Pittsburgh Pirates, Seaver afforded an opportunity to observe what a master crafts-man does when he gets behind the batter on his first pitch. Eleven times in that game Seaver had a one ball, no strike count. On all eleven occa-sions his next pitch was a curve ball—ten of them for *called* strikes. In the remaining instance he missed with his curve, eventually falling behind three-and-one and being reached for a hit, the only one he allowed in the game.

There are many special situations involving the ball-and-strike count. Two of them will be cited here as food for thought and as a spur to the development of additional strategy.

1. If the pitcher goes to a 3-2 count using only one pitch, he should resort to another delivery for the pay-off pitch.

2. If he goes to a 2-2 count using only one pitch, he can try the same tactic. Should that one be a ball, he should come right back with the same pitch. The batter will expect him to return to his original pitch if the sudden switch has gone astray and thus often will be badly fooled.

As for general strategy to be used in spotting the curve ball—When he is ahead of the batter, the pitcher can afford to be finer in his attempts to hit spots. In fact, this is one occasion in which an effort should be made not to throw a *fat* pitch. On the other hand, when behind the bat-ter, the pitcher can afford to be fatter with his curve because of the ele-ment of surprise involved, and, of course, he should not attempt to be too fine lest he miss the strike zone and fall further behind in the count.

In essence, then, the pitcher who relies primarily on the curve ball has many advantages in his favor. Probably none is more important than that he has demonstrated an understanding of how he must pitch in order to win. Thus, he is the type of pitcher most likely to have the assurance that contributes so to mound success and the self-discipline that is most conducive to making the batters hit his pitch. No other qualities are more essential in winning.

## *A PITCHING CHECKLIST*

To help a pitcher master the various mechanical moves that pertain to good pitching and to improve his overall performance thereby, we offer the following checklist. In rating himself he should consult with his catcher and coach and should work hard to perfect each phase of the pitching game in which he is deficient. When he checks out with a passing grade on each of these items, the pitcher will be well on his way to becoming a finished performer on the mound.

1. Condition: Is he in shape to make the most of his natural ability? To bear down with something extra in the clutch? To go nine innings at full speed?
2. Grip: Is he choking the ball? Does he telegraph his pitches by the grip?
3. Stance: Is it correct in accordance with the rules? Is it conducive to maximum stuff and good control?
4. Hiding the Ball: Does he hide the ball from the batter and cover it properly to prevent detection by the coaches?
5. Eyes on Target: Does he sight his target properly and keep his eyes glued to it throughout his entire motion?
6. The Push-off: Is it powerful enough to get his full weight into the pitch?
7. Stride: Is it free from the serious defect of throwing across the body? Of landing on the heel? Of being too long?
8. Follow-through: Is it complete, with fully bent waist and squared-away finish?
9. Spin: Is proper backspin being imparted to the fast ball and maximum rotation to the curve?
10. Control: Can he throw seven out of ten pitches for strikes with each of his deliveries? Can he consistently get the ball close to where he wants it?
11. Curve: Is it effective when used, and can it be thrown with control and confidence on any ball-and-strike count?

12. Change of Pace: Is it similar in appearance to the fast ball? Is it neither too fast nor too slow? Can it be controlled?
13. Holding the Runner: Has he developed a good head move? Does he prevent runners from getting a big jump on the ball?
14. Pick-off: Has he developed a deceptive move to first? Can he make the pick-off play at second?
15. Fielding: Does he protect his position adequately against ground balls? Does he perform well his allied duties, such as backing up bases, covering first, and starting the double play?
16. Bunts: Does he get off the mound quickly, handle the ball cleanly, and make the various plays properly?

# *General Defense*

Defensively a ballplayer must think of himself as part of a unit, and his moves must be considered in relation to what each of his eight teammates is doing. Thus, team defense is a matter of coordinating the individual skills of nine different players.

Good hands, a strong arm, and speed of foot are important assets in the fielding skill of any player. Yet many men have overcome the lack of one of these attributes and have become sound defensive players.

Hustle, the ability to anticipate a play, knowing where to throw the ball and getting rid of it quickly, and the practice of consistently sound habits are qualities that, if developed, will turn a mediocre natural ballplayer into a valuable defensive performer.

## GENERAL RULES

Each defensive player should give careful consideration on every pitch to the game situation and the ability of the batter. His positioning and subsequent actions will be dictated by these factors.

Defensive alignment of the team as a whole should be decided upon by the coach. The individual player can adopt certain principles that will enable him to be fully prepared for almost any play.

1. Every player should figure that the next ball will be hit to him and should know what to do with the ball when he gets it.

2. Baseball is a team game—players should help each other at all times. All should be aware of what the others will be doing on every play.

3. There should be a good reason for every throw. The more throws, the more chance a base runner has to advance.

4. Each player should have a mental plan of action in case of an error.

5. Defensive players should shift position according to the game situation so that they will have the best possible chance to get to the ball and make the proper play. The pitch being thrown is another indicator—the slower the pitch, the greater the chance of its being pulled. These shifts should be done subtly so that the pitch is not tipped.

*(a) Field ground balls from the ground up (Bud Harrelson)*

*(b) Watch the ball into the glove*

*Catching the ball*

*Starting for the ball (front, right)*        *Starting for the ball (front, left)*

6. Any time a fly ball is hit, it should be called for—in loud, clear tones—by the man who intends to take it. Other nearby players should call the name of the man who is to make the play.

7. On a high fly in the sun, the fielder should glance toward the ground once he has the ball located, then look back at the ball. He should shield his eyes with his glove, even when wearing sunglasses.

8. Whenever possible, two hands should be used to catch the ball. A ball below the waist should be caught with the little fingers together; above the waist, with the thumbs together.

9. To play a ball directly in front of him, a fielder can start on either foot. If the ball is to the right and in front of him, he should use a crossover step with his left foot; if it is to the left and in front of him, he should use a crossover step with the right foot.

10. To play a ball behind him and to his right, the fielder should start with his right foot; on one behind him to the left, he should start with his left foot.

11. A defensive player should always play the ball, not let it play him. Whenever feasible, he should make an attempt to move in on it.

12. The use of the voice is very important both in lending encouragement and giving directions to a teammate and in providing an "audible target" for a throw when his attention is focused on the ball.

A team is rarely stronger than its infield. Individual skills should be perfected, but it is coordinated effort and team play that are the real essentials to an infield. Nevertheless, as each player improves the mechanics of his game through sound practices, he not only helps himself but also contributes to cohesive team play by making the work of every player predictably uniform and doubly effective.

*Defensive set position*

*Fielding a ground ball to the right*

## The Ready Position

The objective of the initial stance is to assure a quick start in any direction. An infielder should assume a position with his feet comfortably spread; his shoulders, knees, and hips relaxed; and his breathing deep until the pitcher is ready. He should then become alert, his knees bent, weight forward on his toes in a modified crouch, his arms between his knees and slightly bent (the hands-on-knees stance can push the spikes into the ground). In order to get the best possible jump on the ball, he should keep his eyes on the batter rather than the pitcher.

## The Fielding Position

As the ball nears him, an infielder should be bent at the waist and knees; his feet should be staggered and spread, with his right foot at a slight angle outward for balance; and his weight should be forward. The wrists should always be loose and flexible, with the face of the glove and bare palm toward the ball. For a ground ball the glove should be touching the ground and in front of the left foot. An infielder should keep his head down on a grounder (when lifted it pulls the entire body up) and try to follow the ball into his glove with his eyes. The ball should always be fielded from the ground up.

When an infielder plays the ball in front of him, it will be easier to handle, easier to recover if fumbled, and less likely to roll through him.

If possible, an infielder should be in correct throwing position before the ball arrives. When going far to either side, he cannot pay close attention to the position of his feet and concentrate fully on getting the ball. Even then he should try to set himself for the throw before the ball hits his glove—every split second is important in infield play—by coming to a stop in throwing position. This is done by sliding on the inside of the foot nearest the ball. After "braking" to the right, he will be in position to step

*Fielding a ground ball to the left*

with his left foot and throw. On a ball to his left, he should perform a hop-step action for the throw since he will have come to a momentary stop with his weight on his left foot (see illustrations).

### Playing the Ball

Catching the ball and throwing it should be combined in one continuous motion. In order to achieve this, one's glove should give with the impact and circle toward the throwing side. As the arms start upward, the throwing hand should be removing the ball from the glove. At the same time (as ball hits glove), the right foot should move forward in a short step.

Timing is of the utmost importance in playing the ball. Timing consists of perfect balance while moving and can be defined as fielding the ball at the top of its hop, with one's weight forward. Use of a rubber ball in practice helps develop this knack.

A slowly-hit ball should be fielded with two hands. The throw should be made as the ball is fielded and the infielder begins to straighten up; the body continues on in the direction of his approach to the ball. A slow roller inevitably involves a close play; thus, any move that wastes time should be eliminated.

### Getting the Out

The throw should go to a spot that will best enable its receiver to handle it and make the play. The throw for a force play should be above the belt; for a tag, below the belt.

In order to make the ball easy to follow, an infielder should pull his glove away from it when making a throw, especially a short one. On a long throw the fingers should be spread to reduce the curve of the ball.

An infielder should not hesitate in throwing a man out at first. He

should "fire the ball"—in relaxed, unhurried fashion. This makes the out easier and is important for two reasons:

1. Whenever a defensive player takes a step to complete a play, a base runner is being allowed a step toward his objective.

2. The more quickly the ball arrives, the greater will be the chances of recovering a fumble in time to retire the runner.

## Fly Balls

The man who will take a fly ball should call for it in unmistakable tones and should be guided by the other infielders. If two men can handle the ball, the one who can take it while coming in on it is the one who should make the catch. This is especially so on a fly that can be caught by either an infielder or outfielder. The outfielder should always call for it since he is coming in on the ball, has the play in front of him, and is in good position to make a throw. This rule also applies to any fly ball near the mound. The pitcher should never take a high fly in fair territory.

Fly balls or relays handled by an infielder in outfield territory should be run—not thrown—into the infield, unless the ball is specifically called for by another player.

It is extremely important that all players, especially infielders, realize that a fly ball to the infield will always drift away from home plate.

## Tagging the Runner

In making the tag an infielder should straddle the bag. This ensures the runner's sliding into the ball instead of into the defensive player's feet. When the ball is placed between the runner and the bag, he will, in effect, tag himself. An experienced player will not reach for the runner, for this simply makes it easier to avoid the tag.

The ball should be held in the gloved hand, which affords greater

**163**

*Position for the tag—let the runner tag himself (Julian Javier)*

protection, and it should be pulled away from the runner as the tag is made, thereby reducing the danger of losing the ball from the force of the base runner's slide. When the glove is folded, a kick will drive the ball into the pocket. For a quick, safe tag the motion should be down, then up—not the sweep, often wildly made, that may seem more natural.

When the throw is wild, the infielder should try to get the ball at the expense of losing the runner.

### Backing Up the Play

One of the infielders should back up every throw to another, the second baseman moving toward first on a throw to that base from the catcher, the shortstop or second baseman backing up the play at second depending on who covers the bag, and the shortstop backing up throws from the catcher to third base.

### Defensive Alignment

Correct infield depth depends entirely on the game situation. A tight infield should be played only when a run cannot be given; that is, if the man on third is the tying or winning run late in the game. Otherwise, it is best to play at normal depth and take a chance on the batter, since a normal .200 hitter becomes a .600 hitter with the infield drawn in.

Several rules of thumb for infield positioning can be adhered to with little deviation and to good effect.

1. Early in the game or when more than two runs ahead, play deep and give up a run.

2. With men on first and third and fewer than two out, play for two—unless the man on third is the winning run.

3. A tight infield is less risky with one out than with no outs since there is less chance of a big inning should the batter hit safely.

4. With men on second and third play at normal depth (unless the man at third is the winning run) since only one run will score when the ball is hit to the infield.

5. Cut off the tying run at the plate unless a single will put the winning run in scoring position.

## Tactics

An infielder should occasionally be a groundskeeper, smoothing the ground and removing pebbles in his territory. This can prevent the bad bounce that may cost his team an out or even a run.

This "tending" also applies to the bases. First and third should be nudged toward the infield after every play, giving the batter slightly less fair territory at which to shoot. Second base should be as far toward left field as it will go. The extra inch or so that a runner must slide may be the one that saves an out.

The infielders should make sure that a runner touches every base. If he does not do so, a defensive player should call for the ball and touch the base. The omission must be called to the umpire's attention since this is an appeal play.

In shifting with the pitch, infielders should avoid obvious moves that will tip off the pitch to the batter. An effective way of using advance knowledge of the pitch for getting a jump on the ball is simply to lean to the appropriate side. Placing one's weight on the right foot for a curve ball to a right-handed hitter, for example, will mean a difference of a step in getting to the spot where the ball is most likely to be hit, yet will in no way telegraph the pitch to the batter.

If the catcher has called for a pitch-out, the infielder involved in a pick-off play should give a return signal. This avoids confusion and assures the catcher that someone will be in position to receive his throw.

With rare exceptions an infielder should not make a long throw for the out when a short one will do. The safer and surer out is the one that should be played—especially with two outs.

When an infielder takes a ground ball with a man on third, he should "look him back" (drive him back to the base with a quick glance before throwing). This also applies to a runner on second base when a ball is hit to the left side of the infield.

A good rule for all ballplayers to follow is, "Keep the winning run as far from home as possible."

# Special Defensive Plays

Every player should make himself a part of every play. Even if he does not actually handle the ball, he performs a vital function for his team when he assumes a backup, cut-off, or relay position, one of which may be needed if his teammates' execution is not perfect.

Several specific defensive plays have been perfected over the years and have proved to be the most effective methods of combatting the offensive moves of the opposing team. They are used by professional teams with only occasional slight variations and operate on the principle that a well-conceived team maneuver is far more effective than loosely coordinated individual efforts in keeping the other team from gaining any unwarranted advantage. At the scholastic level all these plays should be practiced to the point of proficiency—with absolute perfection of three of them as the primary goal. The team that masters the first-and-third double steal, the run-down, and the force-out will be a strong defensive unit.

## The Cut-off

This series of alignments has two purposes—to provide a target for the throw from the outfield and to allow the interception of a throw that

*The cut-off at third*

will not get the lead runner but may cut down or check the advance of another runner.

A long hit calls for an infielder to go to the outfield to serve as relay man. Since *the second throw should be the short one, the relay man* (almost always the second baseman or shortstop) should not go too far from the infield.

The use of the voice is very important in the cut-off play. All along the line, from the outfield to the final destination of the ball, instructions should be shouted to any player who throws or handles the ball. The man at the end of the line calls the cut-off play, shouting "cut" or "let it go" as the situation warrants. Both relay and cut-off men should wave their arms to give a better target.

Here are some hints that will help the effectiveness of the cut-off man:

1. Catch the ball on your throwing side.
2. Fake a catch when letting the ball go through.
3. If no call has been made and the runner passes you before the ball arrives, the run should be conceded and the throw cut off.
4. Rush forward to intercept a wide or late throw.

### Cut-off Situations

1. Single, no one on base; or fly on which the throw goes to second: The shortstop covers; the second baseman backs him up on a ball to left field (positions are reversed on a ball to right field). When the ball goes to center field, the man nearest the base covers it. This gives the outfielders practice in throwing, and if the ball gets through, the man covering the base can get out there in time to serve as relay man.

2. Single with a man on second; or fly ball to the outfield with a man on third and at least one other base occupied:

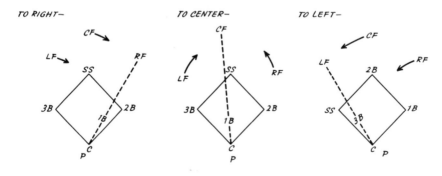

3. Single with a man on first (cover second only on the batter); or fly ball with men on first and second:

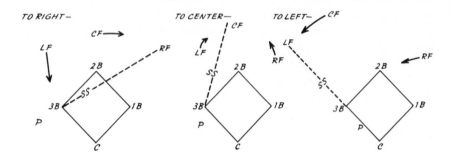

4. Extra-base hits: The second baseman is the relay man when the ball goes to right, the shortstop when it goes to left; the man with the stronger arm when it goes to center; and the first baseman when it goes down the right field foul line.

On a sure double, both second baseman and shortstop should go out for the relay, one backing up the other, since the cut-off man does little good here and two relay men prevent an extra base on a fumble.

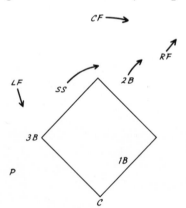

5. A variation: When the first baseman is the cut-off man, the pitcher should consider covering first base. Then, when the ball is cut off by the first baseman, someone will be in position to take a throw to retire a runner who has taken a wide turn at first. This play involves a calculated risk because of the possible overthrow of home. Yet in amateur competition, there are very few outfielders with arms powerful enough to propel the ball far past the catcher.

6. General rules:

(a) The *second* throw should be the short one.
(b) The cut-off man's head is the target.
(c) With the bases loaded, the throw should go home.
(d) The pitcher's position is in foul territory, backing up the play. He should not serve as cut-off man.

## The Double Play

Infield depths:

(a) Deep—normal position; 2B and SS move two steps in for DP setup

(b) Modified—1B and 3B in on grass; SS and 2B at DP depth

1. *Man on First*: The first baseman ordinarily holds the runner close to first. The second baseman and shortstop play two steps in; the throw to second should be chest high and directly over the bag.

The moves involved around second base are discussed at length in the section on the second base combination.

A notable exception to standard procedure occurs when the ball is hit to the third baseman by a left-handed batter. When this occurs at the amateur level of play, the throw should go to first base since no one will be in position to cover second properly.

2. *Men on First and Second*: The first baseman plays off the bag; the second baseman and shortstop play two steps in.

The double play with men on first and second should be made second to first, except in the following instances:

When the ball is hit to the shortstop's right, the throw goes to third.

When a ball is hit directly to the third baseman or to his right, he should step on third, then throw to first.

When a ball is hit directly to the pitcher or to his right, the throw goes to third.

On balls fielded by the catcher, except those toward first base, the throw goes to third (time permitting).

When a force play is made at second but the batter will definitely be safe, a throw to third may catch the runner rounding that base.

These are maneuvers designed primarily for scholastic baseball. They strongly imply the desirability of forcing the runner at third whenever possible. The value of this approach is twofold: it keeps a runner from reaching third, from which there are nine ways to score (there are only two from second); it eliminates the troublesome first-and-third situation, should the double play attempt fail.

3. *Men on First and Third*: The infield should be in normal double play positions, with the first baseman holding the runner close to the base. The attempt to play for two should be made by way of second unless the runner on third represents the tying or winning run. If the play is made on the runner going home, the third baseman should follow him in toward the plate for a quick put out in case he attempts to get caught in a rundown and delay the out until the other two runners reach second and third. At the same time, the shortstop should cover third.

4. *Bases Loaded*: If the run at third is an important one, a tight infield should be played and an attempt made to cut off the run at the plate. Otherwise, a modified infield is employed. The second baseman and shortstop then make the play by way of second. The double play goes from home to first on a ball hit to the pitcher, first baseman, or third baseman. An exception to this rule is the case in which a ball is hit directly over either first base or third base. In these instances the bag should be touched and the throw then made to home plate. Remember that the force is off after the bag is touched, and the runner must be tagged at home.

5. The second and third basemen, when fielding a grounder, should always look at the runner advancing toward them before making a throw. He may be giving them an easy out by running into a tag.

6. Above all, a team should constantly think: Get the first out; lose it, and you get nothing. Thus, the force out, not the double play, is the real key.

### The Sacrifice

The most effective weapons in combatting the sacrifice are the alertness of the infielders and anticipation by the pitcher and catcher.

Only rarely will the signal for this play be picked up. However, with the bunt in order, when the runner fails to look alternately at the third base coach and the batter, it is probable that a signal has been given.

Pitcher-catcher strategy is covered in detail in other sections.

*Man on First*: The pitcher moves forward; the first and third basemen charge the plate, returning to their bases if they do not field the ball.

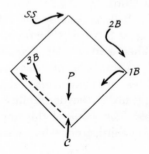

*Defense against the sacrifice (second baseman covers first)*

The second baseman covers first, and the shortstop covers second. Their initial steps should be toward home. This enables them to cover their positions should the ball be hit in that direction, while still allowing them to shorten the distance to the bases they must cover. The catcher pursues the ball and covers third base if the third baseman fields it.

*Men on First and Second*: The batter should be allowed to bunt the ball. The pitcher charges the third base line; the third baseman covers the bag; the shortstop fakes the runner back to second and continues in to cover the mound. The second baseman covers first, and the first baseman charges the plate. Worked properly, the play will be at third, then possibly to first.

An alternate method, tried experimentally by some professional teams, brings in an outfielder to cover third, while the third baseman plays halfway to the plate. This method, risky at best, should be used only with a weak hitter at bat and the bunt almost certain.

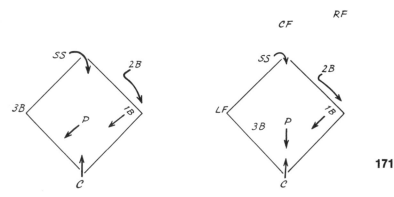

*Man on Second:* This is likely to be encountered only with a weak batsman at the plate. Assignments are the same as for the sacrifice with men on first and second. Care must be exercised not to break with the pitch—alertness is the answer. A play at third requires the tagging of the runner.

### The Squeeze Play

The only practical defense against the squeeze play is an unbuntable pitch that will catch the runner trying to score. The key to foiling it is spotting the runner's break for the plate. The pitcher should then throw high and outside to a left-handed batter, at the shoulder of a right-hander. When the play becomes apparent, the pitcher and the first and third basemen advance toward home plate, and the second baseman covers first.

When the squeeze is worked with runners on second and third and the play for the out must be at first base, the defensive team must be alert for the double squeeze (the man on second base continuing around third and in to score).

If the squeeze is detected in time for the pitcher to step off the rubber before throwing home, he will have become an infielder. Should the batter then bunt the ball, he will be guilty of interference and the runner declared out. This is an unusual and smart play that may be possible on occasion.

### The Hit-and-Run

This play is most effectively thwarted by anticipation of it, followed by a pitch-out that cannot be hit but should enable the catcher to throw out the runner at second base. Unfortunately, this can be accomplished only occasionally; thus, the second baseman and shortstop must decide on their assignments as soon as they suspect a hit-and-run. Since the batter usually tries to hit behind the runner (to right field), the shortstop will cover second base most of the time. (A left-handed batter is the one most likely to try to hit toward left field.) The man who covers second should edge toward the base as the pitcher throws, playing the ball as best he can if it is hit to his position.

This is most likely to occur in a tight game with a good hitter at bat—especially with one out, and even more so when the pitcher is behind the batter in the count and must throw a strike.

## The Steal

There are definite times when a steal should be anticipated: with no outs or two outs, a fast man on first and a good hitter at bat in a close game; or with one out and a weak hitter at the plate. The defense should be doubly alert for a steal of second in those situations in which the count goes to 3-1 or, especially, 3-2. In addition to the role of the pitcher and catcher, an important factor in thwarting a steal of second is the base-covering assignments of the shortstop and second baseman. (See "The Second Base Combination.")

A steal of third base is relatively rare since the runner is already in scoring position. It should never be tried with two out. Nevertheless, the defense should be prepared for it. The third baseman should move toward his base after the ball passes the batter; the catcher should be in position to throw on every pitch; and the pitcher, shortstop, and second baseman should cooperate to hold the runner close to his base since he is unlikely to attempt a steal of third unless he gets a good jump on the pitch.

Above all, the infielders should let the catcher know whenever a runner attempts to steal.

## The Double Steal

Mastery of the first-and-third situation is one of the keys to successful defense. It is devoted chiefly to combatting the double steal, of which there are two varieties—on the catcher and on the pitcher.

**On the Catcher.** This is the most common double steal attempt. In most cases the primary objective of the offense is to place two men in scoring position. Yet the defense should obviously concern itself principally with preventing the runner on third from scoring.

The cut-off assignment is extremely important. At the amateur level, where few hitters can place the ball in open spots, the defense can avoid confusion by using one man, either the shortstop or second baseman, in the cut-off spot on all double steal attempts, the man with the better arm being the logical choice.

The pitcher should hold the runners close; after delivering the ball, he should straighten up—arms over head—for a dual purpose: to provide a target for the catcher, who must glance at the runner on third and then throw hurriedly; and to help freeze the runner at third, his probable reaction being that the pitcher will cut off the throw.

The catcher should take firm, aggressive action. He *must* glance at third while striding into his throw. The third baseman, with a better view of the action, should call for the ball if the runner wanders too far off the bag.

The catcher's throw to second should be directly to the bag, waist high to facilitate handling and a return throw if necessary. The cut-off man should be one step in front of the bag, facing home, where he will be in position to tag the runner with a leftward pivot to the rear on a play at second, or to step forward to cut off the ball and make the return throw with good momentum directly toward the plate when the runner tries to score from third.

The uninvolved member of the second base duo should back up the play and offer verbal assistance. Both first and third basemen should follow the runner breaking from their respective bases in order to be in position for a quick tag should a run-down ensue. The outfielders also become involved, with the left fielder covering third base and the right fielder protecting first.

At the scholastic level, when the man on third represents the winning run, the throw to second becomes too risky with fewer than two out. Three other possibilities are open to the defense.

1. Use the pitcher as cut-off man. This is safest, but rarely draws the runner off third.

2. Throw to the shortstop, playing shallow in his normal alignment. From third it is quite difficult to tell that the ball is not going to second. This may lure the runner into breaking for home. With the relatively easy return throw from shortstop, the chances of cutting him down are greatly increased.

3. Use a fake to second and throw to third. To draw the runner on third off his base, the catcher should make a full-arm fake to second without even glancing at third. A good follow-through should leave him in front of the plate with an unobstructed view of third and far greater likelihood of a good throw to that base.

**On the Pitcher.** In all probability the double steal attempt on the pitcher is a maneuver in which the offense has definite designs on scoring a run—either through a forced balk or mishandling of the play by the defense. Yet with practice, combatting it can be relatively easy.

As soon as the runner breaks from first, the first baseman should shout, "Step off." The pitcher should then back off the rubber and pivot toward second *by way of third base*, thus freezing the runner on third. The throw goes to the shortstop covering second. He charges hard at the runner from first, forcing him back, while carefully keeping an eye on the runner at third.

If the lead runner moves more than a third of the way toward home, he becomes the target. The shortstop, however, should throw only to prevent the lead runner from scoring and, in such cases, should throw *home* for the out since throwing behind the runner becomes dangerous when a potential run is involved.

The double steal with runners on successive bases should be treated like an ordinary steal of the lead base.

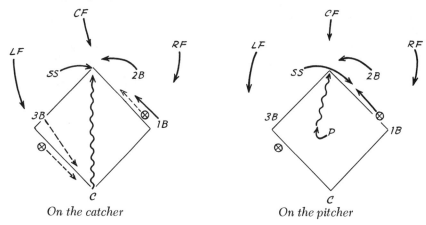

On the catcher                    On the pitcher

### The Pick-off Play

**From the Catcher.** For maximum chance of success and minimum risk of a misplay, a pitch-out should be signalled and a play put on with an infielder. When this is done, the infielder involved should sneak behind the runner and go to the base as the pitcher delivers the ball to the batter. A missed swing or bunt should be construed as an automatic pick-off signal.

The throw to first or third should be on the inside of the diamond; on a missed bunt the second baseman handles a pick-off throw to first. Second base should be covered according to the batter, the shortstop taking it with a left-hander at the plate, the second baseman with a right-hander.

The outfielders should move into position to back up the throw as soon as they see that a pick-off is being attempted.

**From the Pitcher.** The technique of this pick-off play has been thoroughly discussed in previous sections. The pitcher can make a throw to first at his discretion; a signal play should be used at second base; but an attempt to pick a runner off third base should rarely, if ever, be made.

The outfielders as usual should be moving into backup positions on the throw.

### The Run-down

When a run-down develops, the baseman at the base from which the play started should return there after he throws the ball. The runner should always be forced back to the base from which he came, and it should take not more than two throws to get him.

The man with the ball should hold it high, in plain view, and should use a modified overhand or sidearm throw to lessen the danger of hitting the runner with the ball. The man receiving the throw should move slightly to the side so there will be no bodily contact with the runner as the tag is applied, with the possible loss of the ball resulting. Furthermore, the runner is entitled to the base line as long as the fielder does not have possession of the ball.

The ball should not be thrown until the runner commits himself and then only when he is slightly more than halfway to the man who will get the ball. This will keep him from ducking safely back past the thrower. On the other hand, the throw should not be delayed so long that the runner will be past the infielder receiving the ball before it reaches him.

When a runner is hung up (caught between bases), the man with the ball should rush directly at him and force him to commit himself. Once the runner makes his move, it is time to head him off with a throw.

The pitcher is strictly a backup man on this play and should stay out of it unless he is needed to retrieve an overthrow or to take the ball for a last-second tag in case the runner gets by one of the infielders and is close to the base.

These three points should be borne in mind as an effective run-down procedure:

1. A fake throw can make the runner commit himself.
2. With two men on base, run the first one down fast, and keep an eye on the lead runner if he is the other one.
3. A man should not be allowed to escape from a run-down. This is a gift out presented you by the other team.

**Philosophy for an Effective Defense.** Baseball games are not won, they are lost. At every level of competition, a sound defensive team can usually hang on long enough to let the opposition beat itself. In amateur baseball this strategy involves three principles:

1. Get one out at a time.
2. Allow only three outs per inning.
3. Make no unnecessary throws.

*Effective run-down technique (note thrower moves out of base-runner's path)*

# The Catcher

His ability as a handler of pitchers, a receiver, and a field general far overshadow any other factors in measuring the value of a catcher to his ball club. A good man at this position will have an alert mind, keen powers of observation, and the ability to make split-second decisions, even as a play is in progress. The fact that he participates on every pitch and is the one player with the entire field in front of him means that he should be able to "take charge" and direct the play of his team.

Not only his pitchers but also every one of his teammates should be able to rely on the catcher as the solid man on the ball club.

## PREPARING FOR THE PITCH

### Signals

The catcher's initial position is a squat, from which he surveys the situation and gives his signal to the pitcher.

Signals should be given *well back in the crotch* and should be *covered from the third base side with the glove*. The fingers should be spread and "squared" with the pitcher. Two basic ideas guide the philosophy behind these measures:

1. The catcher must know precisely what his pitcher is throwing, for a missed signal can result in a passed ball and possibly even a broken finger for the catcher. Obviously, then, the pitcher must know, see, and understand the set of signals being used.

2. He must hide his signals from the opposition. The batter will be concentrating on the pitcher; so the catcher must guard against the coaches. As a precautionary move the first and third basemen should report the fact whenever either can see the signal.

The catcher should also watch the position of his arm and elbow, which can give away signals unless held in the same position every time a sign is flashed. Natural movements and a fair degree of precaution can protect even the simplest set of signals from detection.

Signals themselves can be very simple—such as one finger for the fast ball, two for the curve, three for the change, and combinations for the off-pitches (more than three fingers may be misread)—as long as they are

178

not picked up by the opposition. When a runner is on second base, they can, of course, easily be seen; here a more complicated set, or a switch-signal, should be used to confuse the runner and keep him from flashing the sign to the batter.

Probably the safest (if not the simplest) set of signals is multiple signs. For example, the catcher will always give three signs, a predetermined one signalling the actual pitch.

## Stance

The catcher should come up from his squat rapidly, be ready for the pitch, and give a stationary target. Remaining in a squat or resting on one knee is bad practice simply because a raised position presents a better target and facilitates easier shifting and quicker starts.

The stance should be balanced and comfortable with the weight forward, right foot back slightly, knees flexed, and rump high for mobility (the hips should be above the knees). The catcher's correct position is squarely behind the plate and close enough to the hitter so that his arm, if extended, will touch the batter's shoulder. (There is little cause for worry about the bat since the hitter strides forward.) Thus, he will be closer to second base (inches count) and to a bunted ball, will find low pitches easier to handle, and *will catch more pitches in the strike zone.*

The same stance should be used for both fast ball and curve so as not to telegraph the pitch to the opposition (the feet should not be shifted until the pitcher is delivering the ball). There is often a tendency to shift one foot to the side or to widen the stance when a curve ball is to be thrown,

*Catcher's stance—normal*

*Catcher's stance—man-on-base*

or to hold the glove flat for the fast ball and facing down for the curve. These telltale mannerisms must be eliminated.

With a bunt or steal in order, a more erect position—with the rear foot further back—should be assumed. This is a modified sprinter's stance and allows a quick start. The full-target stance, however, should be retained when the pitcher is wild.

### Target

Giving a good target is one of the catcher's most important functions. His target should be prominent and stationary.

The pitcher should concentrate on a fixed object. Thus, the catcher should not move *noticeably* until the ball is being delivered, because the target will probably be some part of his anatomy. He should also make his target a large one, facing the widest part of his glove directly at the pitcher. Alternatively he can stand so that his body will present a wide target if he knows that the pitcher is sighting on it. Above all, he should make sure that the target being used is in the strike zone.

For a pitcher who is very wild, or exceptionally fast, the catcher should assume a wider stance. In this way he will have less difficulty in handling wild or very fast pitches, while at the same time making a slightly larger target. This in no way violates the idea of not tipping off the pitch. It is merely a precautionary measure to cut down the number of wild pitches and passed balls.

## RECEIVING THE BALL

### Basics

The fingers of the catcher's right hand should be flexed, with the thumb resting against the index finger, prepared to receive the pitch. As the ball hits the glove, the right hand should be brought over it. Catching the ball with fingers extended or pointing toward the pitcher invites injury.

Every pitch should ideally be caught in the middle of the body. In fact, no ball should be caught by backhanding or reaching for it unless absolutely necessary. This marks one of the chief differences between a good and a bad receiver. The shifting with the pitch that it implies must be practiced diligently until it becomes a well-ingrained habit.

The ball should be *met* with the mitt (not received), with the arms extended to a point where the catcher can see the ball hit his glove. In this way he can help himself in performing his main task.

*Receiving an outside pitch*

*Receiving a wide pitch*

*Receiving a low pitch*

*Blocking a low pitch*

*Receiving a high pitch*

*Blocking a low pitch to the side*

### The Main Task

The catcher's number-one duty is to *catch every strike in the strike zone*. One method of achieving this is to bring every pitch *toward the belt buckle* as it is caught. Done smoothly, this prevents borderline pitches from being moved out of the strike zone—in effect, it allows a strike to speak for itself. A hinge-like wrist flick is sufficient without being too flagrant. Using this movement, he should naturally catch a low pitch from underneath, a high one from above; he should bring corner pitches in toward the center of the plate. The belt-high delivery may be handled from either above or below. Manipulating the knees (slightly bent for a high pitch, more erect on a low one) can also help keep the ball in the strike zone.

Another and probably more effective means of assuring the pitcher of a strike whenever he throws one requires not only meeting the ball so that it is caught in the strike zone but also holding it there for the umpire to see that it is a strike. This method is best when no possibility of a steal exists, whereas the first technique is advisable when a throw may be needed to catch a runner.

At the same time the catcher should take care not to block the umpire's view of the ball by excessive jumping movements or by raising his body. A strike should be called a strike, and the catcher can help his pitcher get what he has earned.

### Shifting with the Pitch

In order to get his body in front of the pitch, the catcher should shift his position by stepping in its direction with the foot nearest the ball. Naturally, this has reference only to a bad pitch.

On a wide pitch he should move forward as well as to the side, so that there is less chance of a mishandled ball rolling behind the catcher. This is especially so with a runner on base. The forward and lateral move is no problem on an outside pitch, since the batter will not be in the way.

A different move is called for on an inside pitch. With a right-hander at bat a quick step or hop should be used, replacing the left foot with the right, followed by a short, sideward step with the left foot. This will get the catcher in front of the pitch quickly, well balanced, and in position to throw if necessary. The reverse is used for a left-handed batter, the right foot being replaced by the left on the first step.

For low pitches a definite forward move should accompany the lateral shift (this shortens the hop) and is made by going down on both knees— left leg first on a pitch to the right side; right leg first on a pitch to the left side. In this way the catcher can move further to the side, making him a greater barrier against a wild pitch. The body should face the ball directly to prevent its being deflected to the side rather than in front of the plate. A high bounce should be blocked with the body, a low bounce with the glove. This helps to make the catcher impregnable when in front of the ball.

### After the Pitch

From a physical standpoint the catcher's first move after receiving the pitch should be to take the ball in his bare hand and bring it into throwing position. This should be done on every pitch, for then it will come automatically with men on base.

The return throw to the pitcher should be crisp and accurate, at chest level. A good throw will keep the pitcher on his toes. On the other hand, a poor throw, repeated often, may allow a runner to advance and definitely will use up too much of the pitcher's energy.

## THROWING

In amateur baseball, as opposed to the professional game, most bases are stolen on the catcher, not on the pitcher. Thus, it is essential that a catcher develop a strong, quick, and accurate throw.

For a strong throw it is imperative that a catcher "cock his arm" properly. His elbow should be as high as his shoulder in order to get power behind the ball (with a drooping elbow the major force will be upward). A good drill for developing this technique and for strengthening the arm is to practice the throw to second from a kneeling position for a few minutes every day.

For accuracy (and added power) the catcher should step directly toward his target. This, along with quickness, can be mastered only through concentration and practice.

### Getting the Ball Away

With a man on base the catcher should make doubly sure that he is as close to the batter as possible without interfering with the swing. The few inches saved may mean an out rather than a stolen base.

The first move should be to "cock the arm" by bringing the ball up to a point behind the right ear. An across-the-seams grip and overhand throw will create backspin and impart greater "carry" to the ball.

As he receives the pitch, the catcher should quickly shift his weight

Catcher's throw to second—
cocking the arm

Catcher's throw to second—
stepping toward the target

to his right foot while maintaining good balance. He will then be in position to get off a good throw with only one step. The left foot simply serves to guide the throw, doing so with a stride directly toward the target.

On a pitch to his right, the catcher's right foot should step toward the ball, shifting his weight so that only a slight pivot on the right foot is necessary to make the throw with a single step. For a pitch to his left, he should go back on his right foot as he receives the ball (he has shifted toward it on his left foot) and then forward on the left for the throw.

In order to keep the runner from gaining an extra step and to facilitate easy ball-handling and a quick tag by the infielders, a catcher should keep in mind the following:

1. If every pitch is caught in the middle of the body, throwing will come more easily.
2. Only *one step* should be taken in throwing to a base.
3. The throw should be directly over the bag at knee level.
4. With a man on base, every pitch should be caught with the intention of throwing the runner out on a steal attempt.

### Using the Pitch-out

Any premeditated pick-off attempt should involve the use of the pitch-out. It should be signalled by the catcher, with a return sign from the infielder who is to take the throw.

A pitch-out should be wide of the plate to prevent the batter's interference with the catcher's view of the play or his throw. In this way the ball can be thrown without obstruction to catch a runner stealing or wandering too far off base, or to break up the hit-and-run.

For easy handling of the ball and little wasted motion and lost time in making the throw, the pitch-out should be chest high as well as away from the batter. With a right-handed batter the catcher should place his left foot behind his right as the ball is delivered. Next is a step to the outside of the plate with the right foot. This prepares him to throw by taking his normal stride forward with his left foot. An exception to this is possible with a man on third, at which time

*Receiving a pitch-out*

a brush-back pitch-out may be used since it may divert the runner's attention.

With a left-hander at bat the pitch-out will be to the catcher's left. As the ball is delivered, he should replace the left foot with the right, step to the side on his left foot, pivot on the right one, and step forward on the left as he throws. To ensure that the weight will be behind the throw and be moving directly toward the target, he should make the catch with his head to the outside of the ball; that is, on the right side for a pitch-out to the catcher's right, to the left side for one to his left.

To increase its effectiveness, the batterymen should employ the pitch-out intelligently in accordance with the following principles:

1. The best time for the pitch-out is with two out and the count in the pitcher's favor.

2. It should not be employed unless the run is important—then the catcher can call for it if he anticipates a steal or hit-and-run or thinks that he can pick off a runner who is taking too big a lead.

3. A pitcher who is having control trouble cannot afford to waste a pitch; so a pitch-out should not be used at this time. In fact, in high school ball, with the hit-and-run unlikely, the wisest strategy is probably for all pitchers to use a high strike rather than a pitch-out when the steal is anticipated.

4. With a sacrifice in order, a curve ball pitch-out is good strategy, not only as a clue to the batter's intentions but also (since he will lean with the pitch as it curves) as a lure to make the runner wander too far off the bag, making himself an inviting target for a pick-off throw. *A missed sacrifice bunt* is a good indication that a pitch-out should be signalled and the runner picked off.

5. The pitch-out signal should precede finger signs, rendering them meaningless. It should be an "outside" sign, one that the first and third

basemen can read. The coach may start the chain with a vocal signal; the baseman should end it with a return signal.

### The Pick-off Throw

A random throw to a base should never be made. The catcher should throw only when he sees a definite chance to get the runner and if he is sure that one of his infielders will be moving toward the base to take the throw. This applies even when a pitch-out has been signalled. A throw with little chance to get the runner is a needless one and risks an advance by the runner if the ball is mishandled.

If the runner has strayed too far from his base, the catcher should not hesitate to throw him out, even if no play has been prearranged. A bluff throw should be used to drive the runner back to his base when no one is in position to take a throw. A realistic fake will keep the runner honest without risking a wild throw.

Should the runner be hung up between bases, the catcher should run toward him, ready to throw if he makes a break in either direction. Here the runner would have gained such a jump toward either base that the catcher should not throw until he has made the runner commit himself.

*To second base:* This throw should be used by amateur ballplayers only on very rare occasions. Bluffing the throw or running toward the man on base would be wiser moves at this level of play.

*To first base:* To eliminate the danger of obstructing the throw by a left-handed batter, the catcher should make this peg sidearm and to the right of the batter. When it is hurled sidearm, the ball should be started higher to allow for its natural sinking to the right.

With men on first and second, a throw to first should be made only if that runner is a sure out, since this is an invitation for the man on second base to advance to third.

*To third base:* This throw should be on the inside of the diamond so that the third baseman can catch the ball in stride, make the tag with little lost motion, and avoid hitting the runner or having him obscure the throw. With a left-hander at bat the stride and throw are perfectly natural ones. With a right-hander the catcher's first move should be a step to his right on his right foot to afford him a clear view of the base. The stride and throw come easily after this initial move. For added quickness a sidearm throw with no stride is permissible here, but its use should be restricted to experienced catchers.

A pick-off throw with a man on third should be automatic when the batter swings and misses, since the runner is most likely to be careless at this time. An arrangement for this play should be made with the third baseman and shortstop so that they will expect a throw whenever the situation arises.

## The Double Steal

This play is usually tried with runners on first and third. Since the man on first invariably makes the initial break, the catcher will generally throw toward second base. The defense must attempt to prevent a run from scoring—and to get an out, either at second base or home plate.

The catcher's throw should be to the base at second. Then it will get that runner if allowed to go through, yet will be easy to intercept if taken by the cut-off man.

The assignments for this maneuver should be prearranged. Occasionally the pitcher is used for this purpose. Naturally, he should be fully informed of his role when involved in the play, and a throw to him should be a hard, head-high one, made to look as much as possible like a throw to second.

The entire procedure is discussed in the section on defensive plays. From the catcher's viewpoint it will be more effective if these four basic ideas are kept in mind.

1. The throw should hit the cut-off man in the chest; then, if not intercepted, it will be a good peg to second.

2. There are only two possible plays by the catcher—the throw to second, *always* preceded by a head and shoulder fake toward third; a full-motion bluff toward second and the throw to third.

3. If the runner on third is too far off his base, get him; if the other runner has second made easily, forget him. (This is an exception to the second point.)

4. Ordinarily, the man on third is the catcher's chief concern. However, if either of the runners represents the winning run, he is definitely the one on whom to make the play.

## *FIELDING*

### Grounders and Bunts

All batted balls on the ground should be fielded with both hands, even if the ball has stopped rolling. The glove should be placed in front of a rolling ball to stop it and in front of a stationary ball as a precaution and to facilitate scooping it up.

*Catcher fielding a bunt and making the quicker sidearm throw to first base*

In fielding a batted ball, the catcher should try to position himself with his face toward the base at which the play will be made. This keeps the play in front of him and enables him to throw without having to make a blind pivot.

Since he has the entire field in front of him, the catcher should call the play on any bunt or grounder in the home-plate area, directing the throw to the proper base. This is especially so in the case of the pitcher, whose back is to the play.

The catcher's throw to first or third on a ground ball should be on the inside of the diamond—to third, so that the play on the runner will be easier for the third baseman; to first, to avoid hitting the runner. In fact, on a ball close to the first base line, the catcher should step well into the diamond before throwing to first.

A dropped third strike, on the other hand, should be thrown to the outside of the base when the ball rolls behind the catcher. In this case the first baseman's target should be given in foul territory.

An underhand or sidearm throw (used to save time) is permissible on a play to first or third, but the throw should be overhand on the longer peg to second (on which the ball has a tendency to curve or sink if thrown sidearm or underhand).

When the catcher, after fielding the ball, is able to tag out the batter, he should let his infielders know that the force is off and that they must tag the runner if a play is to be made at any base.

On a sacrifice bunt toward third, the catcher should chase the ball and, if the third baseman makes the play, should continue to third and cover the base—but not if the play began with a man on second base, since his responsibility in that case is to cover home. All throws to first base should be backed up by the catcher unless a runner is in scoring position. This, in effect, means following the batter to first on ground balls, at a distance of about forty feet from the base line. When the ball goes through the right side to the outfield, the catcher should cover the bag for a possible pick-off throw from the right fielder after the runner has taken his turn.

Finally, a catcher should never leave home plate unguarded with a runner in scoring position and should always look him back before throwing to first should he field a batted ball.

## Double Play by Way of Home

This play ordinarily arises only with the bases loaded. Almost invariably it goes home and then to first. In this way the run is cut off, and the attempt to complete the double play is made on the batter, who has to recover from his swing and run the full ninety feet to first base, whereas the other runners have started with substantial leads.

In making this play, the catcher should keep his left foot in contact with the plate while awaiting the ball. Then a short step and pivot with the right foot will lead naturally into the throwing stride, which is made with the left foot.

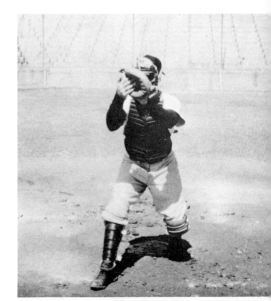

*Catcher ready to receive ball for double play by way of home (note his left foot in contact with the plate)*

The throw to first should be on the inside of the diamond, away from the batter, who must stay in the three-foot lane. With a runner rounding third base and fewer than two out, the catcher should use a full-motion bluff throw to first before heaving the ball to third to nail that runner.

### Tagging the Runner

This job is made difficult by its dual nature: the catcher must concentrate on the ball and handle it cleanly while simultaneously setting himself to block and tag the oncoming runner. Fortunately, his equipment affords adequate protection, and by learning certain fundamentals, he can be prepared, in all respects, to perform the task efficiently.

The correct position for receiving the throw places the catcher to the side of the plate—the third base side on a throw from right field or right center, the first base side (with the foot in front of the plate) on a throw from left field or left center, as illustrated in the diagrams.

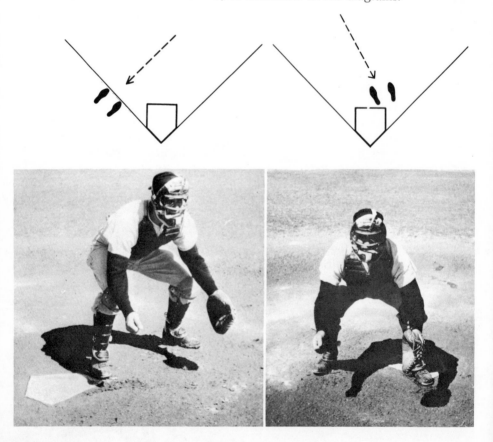

As he receives the ball, the catcher can either drop to one or both knees and hold the ball in front of the plate, where the runner will slide into it, or he can put his left leg in front of the plate and allow the runner to hit his shinguard, making the tag as the man slides into him.

When he has acquired sufficient experience, the catcher may prefer to take all throws on the first base side of the plate. The technique is to expose the plate, square off with the throw,

*Preparing for the tag (note ball in bare hand, behind and protected by glove)*

and pivot to the left (dropping the left foot back while catching the ball) —then the runner cannot elude the tag.

The tag should be made with two hands to lessen the danger of losing the ball as the runner slides in. It is best to hold the ball in the right hand and keep the back of the glove toward the runner. The hands themselves should be close to the ground to prevent a foot from going under the tag; the ball should be pulled away as soon as contact has been made with the runner, to lessen the possibility of losing possession of it.

The catcher may not block the plate unless already in possession of the ball. In fact, an attempt should be made to block the plate only if the play will be close. It is wise to give the runner a clear view of the plate while remaining in such a position that the man cannot slide straight into home but must hook to reach it. This in no way interferes with the runner; yet it keeps him from having a completely unobstructed path to the plate.

Compliance with the dictates of alert play demands that the catcher follow three basic tactical principles:

1. Don't reach for the ball too soon if the throw is a good one. Decoy the runner into slowing up by remaining motionless until the ball arrives.
2. With other men on base, leave your position to intercept a wide throw or bad bounce.
3. Play the ball, then the runner—you can do nothing until you have the ball in your hands.

### Pop Flies

Pop flies are very difficult to play since they go almost straight up and have both a tremendous spin and a tendency to curve. They are especially tough for the catcher since he must get out from under the bat, locate the

**191**

ball, and discard his mask before giving chase to it. He should *call for* and take all those in the home-plate area that cannot easily be handled by the first or third baseman coming in on the ball.

The mask should be whipped off quickly, but not discarded until the ball is sighted. It should be tossed away from the ball so as not to get in the catcher's path. If he must make a long run, the catcher can simply hook the bottom of the mask with his thumb, lift it over his head, and let it slide over his shoulder as he pursues the ball.

When the ball is hit behind him, the catcher, his back to the infield, should get under it so that it appears that it will hit him on the head, then take one step back for the catch. To field a fly hit straight up or in front of home plate, he should still position himself directly under it (facing the infield), but he needn't take a backward step, for the natural drift of the ball will be away from him, leaving him in good position for the catch. If there is anyone on base, the catcher should run the ball back to the infield in order to check the runner's advance without risking a long throw.

The principles behind these methods will be more clearly understood if two factors, based on the laws of physics, are borne in mind:

1. A pitch thrown on the right side of the plate will be fouled to the catcher's right; one thrown on the left side will be fouled to his left. Thus the path of the ball can be determined as soon as it leaves the bat.
2. A pop fly will always drift toward the infield. The higher the ball is hit, the greater will be the curve.

### CATCHING PHILOSOPHY

#### Morale

The catcher must, in a sense, assume a selfless role since it is the pitcher who should look impressive—not his receiver. The primary function of the latter is to make the pitcher look good.

The catcher alone is in front of the pitcher and is the one to whom the latter will naturally look for help and encouragement. He must be both the pitcher's brains and his eyes. He can see the entire field of play and should pass on anything he sees that will help his batterymate.

The pitcher's confidence should be treated with care. The catcher must guide him over the rough spots as far as both morale and strategy are concerned.

The catcher should adapt himself to the temperament of his pitcher.

A significant example of this principle occurs in the area of working speed. Whether the pitcher is a fast worker or a deliberate one, his preference in tempo should be catered to.

Exceptions to this center on the pitcher's control and the disposition of the batter. A most important aspect of the catcher's influence on his pitcher's working speed is the effect that it has on the latter's control. Slowing the pitcher's pace will often help him regain control. A pause before returning the ball, a few steps toward the mound, straightening the mask and chest protector—these are maneuvers that can slow the tempo of the game and steady a pitcher who is having control trouble.

A conference on the mound (it should always be at that spot) is another effective aid, not only in slowing the tempo and discussing tactics, but also in soothing the nerves of a pitcher who finds himself in a tight spot.

If the hitter is nervous and jittery, the catcher should slow his pitcher's working speed. Conversely the catcher should make his pitcher work faster to the batter who likes to take his time.

## Strategy

Pitching strategy and the most effective ways of coping with the various types of hitters are discussed in detail in the section on pitching. This material should be studied carefully by catchers since they should work in close harmony with their pitchers and, in most cases, call every pitch.

Catching strategy, however, embraces far more than this. Many stratagems of a more general nature, some of them incorporating psychology, are practiced by smart receivers in an attempt to ease the task of the pitcher.

The catcher should handle the latter part of the pitcher's pregame warm-up, taking over from the practice catcher when the pitcher is ready to throw at full-speed. In this way he will get the feel of the particular pitcher on the particular day and can begin plotting strategy accordingly. He can also begin to exert his influence as a steadying factor, thereby giving his pitcher the little extra confidence that is sometimes necessary to start the game in top form.

There may be a difference between the pitcher's warm-up throws and his pitches from the mound, particularly if (as is so often the case) the warm-up must be taken on flat ground. Whatever the situation, the catcher should discover as soon as possible which pitch is working best on that day.

If all the deliveries in a pitcher's repertoire are working properly, the catcher can, of course, call his pitches according to normal operating procedure. However, if one pitch is working considerably better than the other, that one should be called for when the pitcher is in a tight spot—that is, it is the one the batter should be made to hit. Conversely, if one pitch is not working, the catcher should allow his pitcher to do no more than show it to the batter—it should not be thrown where the batter can hit it solidly.

The catcher should rely heavily on any pitch in which his pitcher has exhibited confidence on that day. Particularly in the early innings, he should call for the pitch that he thinks the pitcher wants to throw. By setting up the hitter wisely and by making his partner believe in the wisdom of his tactics, the catcher can guide the pitcher tactfully and in a way designed to build confidence in himself—and his catcher.

In considering the tactics to be used on a certain batter, the catcher should put himself in the batter's shoes and try to imagine what pitch is anticipated. Then, quite obviously, another one should be called.

There is really no such thing as a set "book" on any hitter. Strategy, though it should be dictated to a great extent by "the book," should be strongly influenced by what a pitcher has on a certain day, as well as by any indication that the batter may give of his intentions on a particular time at bat or pitch.

In other words, the catcher cannot always go by "the book"; it is often better to work according to the pitcher's strength rather than the batter's weakness.

A batter will often tip off his intentions by his movements in the batter's box. For instance, he may move closer to the plate when expecting a curve ball or outside pitch; he may "dig in" and appear overanxious when intending to go for the long ball or when eager to hit the next pitch; or he may move his rear foot away from the plate when he is going for the opposite field. There are several other moves, made with both the hands and feet, that are made by a great many batters and that can help the catcher anticipate the man's intentions in time to signal for an appropriate pitch.

Although the catcher actually calls the pitches, his batterymate can veto those calls. His goal should be to call pitches in the same pattern in which the pitcher is thinking.

### Leadership

The catcher is the field general and should direct the play on all batted balls.

His position gives him a full view of the field and allows him to watch all aspects of a play as it develops. He should let all his teammates know the situation and the play to be made; if any development dictates a sudden change in tactics, he should make sure that the man (or men) making the play is aware of it.

Another of the catcher's duties is to keep the pitcher informed on the position of base runners while the pitcher is concentrating on the plate.

In short, the complete catcher is at once a field general, tactician, psychologist, and a hard-working mechanical receiver.

# The First Baseman

The first baseman is too often lightly regarded from a defensive standpoint. Although it is true that his bat has come to be regarded as more important than his glove, the first baseman's defensive ability will greatly enhance his value to his team.

The ideal man for this position is tall and rangy and has a good pair of hands. If, in addition, he is agile, alert, and possessed of a strong arm, he is truly well equipped for the job.

Regardless of his physical qualities, a first baseman is not stationed at that position merely to serve as a target for the other infielders and to catch their throws. When he has perfected his footwork, acquired the knack of digging low throws out of the dirt, and learned the correct tactical maneuvers, he will be a *ballplayer*—and worthy of his place on the team.

## GOOD HANDS

Good hands are, of course, a natural physical attribute. Although a player's awkward or weak hands can be improved in dexterity and strength, it is doubtful whether he will ever develop into a good defensive first baseman; his hands must be well possessed of these qualities at the outset.

The importance of good hands lies in the fact that they are indispensable to maximum effectiveness in catching the many and varied throws that a first baseman is called on to handle. They are especially important for pick-ups (he should rarely have to step back to receive a low throw) and for fielding the ball properly when he is endeavoring to use the maximum length of his reach while still keeping his toe on the bag.

By "good hands" we also mean that both should be used to catch the ball whenever possible.

## AGILITY

Agility at this position means the ability to go backward, forward, and to either side, as well as to shift smoothly and naturally for a throw, thus making the catch easier.

There have been big, naturally ungainly men who have become efficient first basemen by developing their agility through exercises and mastery of correct techniques.

Agility, then, is not a prerequisite, but can be developed; in fact it must be developed if a man is to be an outstanding defensive first baseman.

The simplest way in which to develop an agile first baseman, aside from teaching him the correct moves, is to throw at him from a short distance. He should be given practice repeatedly at handling balls thrown at him from every conceivable angle and at every logical trajectory. Familiarity alone will breed both know-how and ability.

## MAKING THE PLAYS

Knowledge of correct techniques lifts first base play out of the realm of the purely mechanical and enables a man to develop his physical attributes to a point of utmost effectiveness. The maneuvers involved are logical, relatively simple, and based on the practice of reducing seemingly intricate physical moves to a point at which their correct performance will be virtually automatic.

### Position

Proper positioning depends on several variables—the batter, pitcher, base runners, and game situation. Under normal circumstances the distance that the first baseman plays from the bag should be in accordance with his speed. Although he has to station himself at a distance from the base sufficient to allow the coverage of adequate ground, he should not be so far removed that his natural speed will not allow him ample time to reach the bag and position himself for the throw.

With a runner on first the first baseman should, in most instances, face the pitcher with his right foot against the inside corner of the base. There are occasions when a position behind the runner is justifiable. These moves will be dealt with in detail when we discuss the specific play situation to which they pertain.

When the bases are empty with two out, the first baseman should play deep and shaded toward the foul line to guard against an extra-base hit. This is especially applicable with a left-hander at the plate.

The tight infield alignment is called for when an attempt must be made to cut off a run at the plate. Here the first baseman should play at the edge of the the infield grass approximately twenty feet wide of the base. A ball hit to his left in this situation may call for a quick play at the base before the throw to the plate. If so, the runner will have to be tagged out at home, so that an accurate throw is essential (knee high and slightly to the catcher's left). Experience at making the play should promote the judgment needed to decide on the right move.

## Footwork

Probably the most important facet of first base play is the footwork involved in taking the throw. Shifting his feet in the correct fashion will allow the first baseman to handle the ball with a minimum of difficulty and to save a few feet and a little time in retiring the runner.

Properly, after a quick start, the first baseman will go to the base and place his *left foot* on it. He should then turn to watch the ball and shift as necessary. This implies that, rather than leave his left foot planted on the bag and field the ball as best he can, he will shift toward the ball when he sees on which side of him it is coming, leaving one foot on the bag. In this initial position he will both serve as a target for the throw and be ready to shift whichever way is necessary to handle the ball. A contingent benefit is that this will position him in front of the ball and cut down his tendency to lunge for it, a smooth stretch being far more effective.

To facilitate the catching of the ball, shifting of the feet (and body) should be natural and smooth. On a throw to the left side, a natural jumping motion, replacing the left foot with the right, is the correct practice. When the ball arrives on the right side of the base, the left foot should maintain contact with the bag while the body shifts to the right. Either foot can be used on a throw directly to the base. In any case, the

*First baseman in position to receive throw*

*First baseman's stretch*

*First baseman's shift to the right*

*First baseman's shift to the left; cross-over step for wide throw*

secret lies in the ability to shift naturally in the right direction at the right time.

The actual shift, though a natural jumping motion, is somewhat akin to a waltz step. The first baseman should practice it repeatedly until it is done automatically and in a smooth manner.

## Handling Throws

Regardless of the footwork required, the first baseman should stretch as far as he can toward the ball, extending his body and his arms to their fullest extent, while still maintaining contact with the bag. This will save valuable time and can often mean the difference between the runner's being safe or out.

A maximum reach is possible for a right-handed first baseman who touches the bag with his right foot and for the left-hander who anchors his left foot. This usage is primarily for a throw straight to the base.

For the longest possible stretch the first baseman's toe is the last part of the foot to reach the bag, his heel the first. Then, as the stretch is made, the heel leaves the base, and the toe remains anchored to it.

A good stretch not only saves time but also serves to shorten the hop of a throw into the dirt and facilitate its handling. Only occasionally will the hop be so big and difficult to handle that the first baseman must step back into foul territory on one foot to play the bounce, while touching the outside of the bag with the other foot.

Sometimes a very wide throw necessitates the use of a crossover step and stretch. A right-hander will employ this only for throws to his right, touching the base with his right foot, taking a long crossover step with his left, and backhanding the ball for the catch. A left-hander, conversely, will use this maneuver only on a very wide throw to his left, backhanding the ball after a crossover step with the right foot, the left one remaining on the bag.

When a throw is wild, the first baseman should leave the base to get the ball. In this case the runner will be safe, so that the primary concern is to cut off a wild throw and prevent the runner's advancing a base.

A throw into the runner is obviously quite difficult to handle well. There are two facets of this play, each demanding a different technique. A high throw to the left side of the bag, if it is not too wide, can still result in a put out—but in all probability, the runner will have to be tagged. In this case the first baseman leaps for the ball and tags the runner as he goes by, being careful to hold the ball firmly in his gloved hand as the tag is applied.

A throw into the dirt in the runner's path is quite another matter. Here a put out is all but impossible. The aim of the first baseman should be to get the ball and prevent the runner's taking an extra base. A natural tendency to back up on the ball must be resisted since it greatly increases the chances of the ball's hitting the ground or the runner, thus becoming unplayable. The first baseman should get in front of the base and the runner. He must play the ball, not let it play him.

A throw from the catcher demands still another technique. The first baseman should give a target on all throws from the home-plate area. On a dropped third strike he should give the target in foul territory since the ball will, in most cases, roll behind the catcher, thus making a throw to the outside of the base less likely to hit the runner. A bunt or dribbler in front of the plate demands that the target be given in fair territory, where the throw to first will be unobstructed. The target, properly given for this play, is both hands cupped to the side of the first baseman's face. His left foot should be on the inside corner of the bag, his right approximately three feet in fair territory.

### Holding the Runner

The proper stance with a runner on first is another aspect of position play that must be mastered. The correct station for holding the runner close to the base is the first baseman facing the pitcher, his *right* foot on the inside corner of the base, slightly crouched, and with his gloved hand extended as a target at waist level. From this position he is able to handle throws to either side and tag the runner's foot in the same motion—a sweeping one—by turning to his *right*. Thus, he will be able to make a difficult play with relative ease while keeping the runner and the diamond in his field of vision.

A tendency on the part of first basemen to take a position facing second base (with most of the back toward home) seems too prevalent and goes uncorrected by many coaches. This is a very bad stance since it greatly impedes maneuverability on a bad throw and involves a pivot toward home before the first step can be made in coming off the bag to fielding position.

When returning the ball to the pitcher, the first baseman can occasionally fake a throw, perhaps catching the runner moving off the base. At the least, it will keep him honest.

There are instances in which it is wise for the first baseman to play two or three steps behind the runner, but still close enough to hold him near the base. A particularly slow runner furnishes one such opportunity. Another occurs when the defensive team has a comfortable lead in the late innings. One more such case is encountered when a strong left-handed pull hitter is at bat, meaning that too much space should not be left through which he can hit the ball.

*First baseman's technique for holding the runner, taking a pick-off throw, and making the tag*

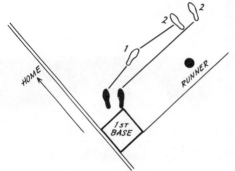

Holding the runner close to the base means that the first baseman will not be able to cover as much ground on a batted ball as he normally does. He should, however, move a few steps into the infield (toward second) with the pitch in order to position himself better to defend against a batted ball.

In moving off the bag after holding a runner, the first baseman should take a step with his left foot and then a long jump into the defensive position, facing the batter.

### Fielding Ground Balls

A ground ball to the first baseman, if it is hit hard, should be blocked as long as no quick throw is needed to retire a runner already on base. The first baseman is fortunate in that he has only a few feet to go to the bag in order to retire the batter. Thus, he can afford to block the ball rather than try for a quick, clean pick-up. This helps make sure that the ball does not go through him, allowing the runner to make first base safely and possibly advance to second.

On a ground ball hit to the first baseman, he should make the play himself if possible. When he races the runner for the bag, the first baseman should touch the infield side of the base with his left foot. By so doing he all but eliminates the danger of being spiked or of colliding with the runner.

### Feeding the Pitcher

When the first baseman cannot reach the bag in time to retire the runner himself, he will have to throw to the pitcher covering the base in order to get the out. Feeding the pitcher is an intricate maneuver and must be practiced repeatedly until its timing is mastered.

On a ball hit straight to the first baseman or to his left, he should *toss* the ball to the pitcher (not the bag), chest high and about two steps in front of the base. The chest high toss will enable the pitcher to catch the ball without looking up or down, then locate the bag.

On most fumbled grounders or balls hit to his right, the first baseman's *throw* should be chest high and to the bag, for in most such cases the pitcher will have arrived at the base and be waiting for the ball.

## The 3-6-3 Double Play

The 3-6-3 double play—from the first baseman to the shortstop, then back to first—is a very difficult one to execute successfully and a very impressive maneuver to watch when it is worked properly. The first baseman has a threefold task on this play: he must field the ball, make his throw to second, and return to the base to take the shortstop's throw. His throw should be a sidearm, accurate one, and he should return to the base and then find the ball.

A left-handed first baseman has a decided advantage over a right-hander on the 3-6-3 double play since he can throw to second without pivoting and can do so with a normal step toward that base. Furthermore, as he picks up the ball, he is in good position to make a quick underhand or sidearm throw.

After fielding the ball, a right-hander generally must pivot to his right, step, and throw. Occasionally he will be called upon to make this play on a ball hit to his left. In this instance he should pivot to his left for the throw. The rhythm should not be broken on this play—it should be made in one continuous motion.

The first baseman's throw on a double-play attempt should be on the inside of the diamond when he has been holding the runner and is inside or on the base line. If he has not been holding the runner (playing behind him), he should logically make a throw to the outside or directly to the base, the exact target depending on how quickly the shortstop gets to the base. These maneuvers minimize the danger of the runner's interfering with the play, which makes it an easier one for the shortstop. Timing is an important factor in making the throw. The ball should go to the shortstop at chest level, and the play should be timed so that the ball reaches him about one-half step before he gets to the bag, except for the outside pivot, as noted.

*First baseman's throw on a 3-6-3 double play*

The first baseman should always try to return to the base to take the throw. If the ball is hit to his right, he will have trouble getting back in time to make the play, and the pitcher, who should be covering, will probably be in better position to take the throw from the shortstop. Nevertheless, this is usually the first baseman's play.

When the ball is fielded by the first baseman directly over or close to the base, he should step on the bag to retire the batter and then make his throw to second, making sure to shout to the shortstop that the runner must be tagged, the force having been removed.

### Playing Bunts

Fielding a bunt with one hand is too uncertain. Rather, the ball should be scooped with both hands, and the throw, regardless of the base to which it goes, should be made while straightening up. The pivot for the throw should be on the left foot for a left-handed first baseman, the right foot for a right-hander.

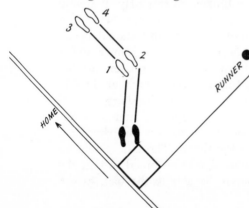

The first baseman will be called upon to play on the base and hold the runner close to it when first base is occupied and the sacrifice bunt is in order. In this case he also must move off to field the ball if it is bunted toward first.

To charge a bunt properly in this situation, the first baseman should take his first two steps toward home plate at a forty-five-degree angle. The move should be made with the left foot first.

When a sacrifice bunt goes toward third or the mound, the first baseman should try to get back to the base to take the throw. After making the put out, he should rush toward third with the ball to prevent a further advance by the runner(s).

### ALERTNESS

It is alertness that sets the good first baseman apart from the mediocre one. A first baseman should always be in a position to help out someplace else. This includes performing the backup and cut-off duties correctly, knowing when to go for a ball, and knowing the right spot to be in any given circumstance.

## Backing Up the Play

After a runner has passed first, the first baseman is no longer needed at that spot. With this in mind, he should back up any base whenever he can safely leave his position.

Three play situations that call for alertness on the part of the first baseman involve a runner going from first to second:

1. When a runner makes a break for second base, the first baseman should be sure to alert the catcher. Shouting "There he goes" will allow the catcher to set himself for a quick throw.

2. If, with men on first and third, the runner on first breaks for second, the first baseman should follow that man so that he will be in position to get a quick put out if a run-down develops. In that way he will have time to hold the other runner at third or to throw him out at the plate if he tries to score.

3. If the batter tries for two bases on a hit to left or center field, the first baseman should trail the runner until he is in position to back up second base.

## The Cut-off Play

The first baseman is an important part of a team's cut-off plays. On balls hit to right and center field with a man on second base, the first baseman is the cut-off man. He should station himself about forty-five feet in front of home in a direct line between the thrower and the plate. He should let the ball go through or cut it off according to the catcher's instructions, and, if the throw is wide or short, he should rush up to catch the ball before it gets past him. When he lets the ball go through, he should feign catching it in order to check the progress of the other runners, at least momentarily.

## The Run-down

Proper handling of this situation is discussed in the section on in-field play. A first baseman should know his role no matter where the run-down takes place. If it is between first and second, the first baseman should return to his base as soon as practicable since the runner should be run toward first by the other infielders involved.

**Pop Flies**

A smart ballplayer knows that any high pop fly will drift away from home plate. Realizing this, the first baseman should call for and take any pop fly to the right side on which he will be moving in on the ball to make the catch.

The primary requisites of first base play, then, are that a man aspiring to that position concentrate intently on the job, exercise to keep agile, and try to anticipate the play when his team is in the field. Compliance with these requirements will help greatly in making a complete first baseman.

# The Second Baseman

The second baseman is responsible for a very vital position. His duties are many and varied and include one of baseball's most difficult and most important roles—pivot man on the double play.

Ideally a second baseman is fast on his feet, has good hands and an accurate arm, and possesses raw courage. The knack of playing second base depends upon a sound knowledge of baseball percentages and the correct tactical maneuvers, the practice of effective mechanical moves, and familiarity with several tricks of the trade designed to make a difficult job a much easier one.

## COVERING GROUND

**Ground Balls.** The second baseman should try for every ball hit to the right side, including balls that the first baseman may be in a better position to handle. By so doing, he will be in position to back up the play on balls that get through the first baseman, even though he doesn't play the ball directly off the bat.

The second baseman should call for any balls hit to his left that he can handle so that the first baseman does not make an unnecessary try for the ball and leave first base uncovered.

A slow roller can be difficult because the ball must be fielded on the run and thrown while the infielder is off balance. An underhand throw is essential to catch a fast runner, particularly a left-handed batter. A barehanded scoop and throw is used by many experienced professionals; yet, if one hand must be used, the gloved hand will be much safer until the play is completely mastered. The throw should be made as the player is straightening up and while he is on the run.

The second baseman, because he has a short throw to first, can block the ball on occasion. This is particularly true of hard-hit balls, on which there will be even more time to make the play on the batter. Once the ball is fielded, however, it should be played to first with as little lost time as possible.

### Getting the Jump

Knowledge of two factors—the batter and the pitch that is to be thrown—can enable an infielder to get a good jump on the ball by anticipating the play. A left-handed pull hitter will probably hit to the second baseman's left; a curve ball or change is more likely to be pulled; and so forth. If he uses such information judiciously, the second baseman can actually be in motion as the ball is hit.

An anticipatory move must not be obvious lest it tip off the pitch. The knack of getting the jump involves starting to move (or, at least, to lean) as the ball is delivered. Too pronounced a start can catch a man completely out of position if the ball is not hit to the right spot. In mastering this technique, an infielder must act with restraint and must practice close observation of both his own pitchers and the opposing hitters.

The start for a ground ball should be made quickly, with a slowing of actions as the infielder nears the ball and an adjustment of his stride so as to receive it on the right hop.

### Playing the Arc

This means going back in a slight curve on ground balls hit to either side and coming in on the ball to field it. It can be particularly helpful to the second baseman on one of his most difficult plays—the ball hit far to his right—in which he must field the ball on the run, apply the brakes, and make his throw in the direction opposite that in which he was running. Coming in on the ball in an arc makes the stop-and-throw maneuver much easier. Playing the arc not only allows for slightly greater effective range, but also permits continuity of motion—a desirable practice regardless of the play.

### Positioning

After making the necessary allowance for the game situation, the second baseman can usually afford to play closer to his base than may seem wise. The base can be shaded in this way for two reasons: he can go to his left more easily than to his right; and more hits go through the middle than through the hole.

### Fly Balls

In addition to handling flies hit near his normal position, the second baseman must range from behind second base, into the outfield, and behind first base into foul territory.

He should take flies behind first because, unlike the first baseman, he is coming in on the ball. If, on the other hand, he hears an outfielder call for a ball, the second baseman should allow that man to take it, acknowledging the call to avoid confusion. Shouting "You take it" will let the outfielder know that he has a clear path to the ball.

On any pop fly that is handled by the shortstop with runners on first or second, or both, the second baseman covers the base. On a pop fly to the first baseman, the second baseman should move toward first, either to help out on the fly if it is too difficult for the first baseman to handle easily, or to cover first base if that baseman has no trouble in playing the ball.

### Balls to Right Field

If, on a fly ball to right field or right center, the ball is over the outfielder's head, the second baseman should trail him as long as he is going back on the ball. Then, if the ball gets past the outfielder, the second baseman will be in position to act as relay man. If the outfielder sets himself to make the catch, the second baseman should return to the infield.

### Covering First

In covering first base on a sacrifice, the second baseman's first two steps should be toward home to enable adequate coverage of his territory should the batter swing and drive one toward his position. At the same time he is reducing the distance to first. He should then make a slight arc in an attempt to come to the bag from the outfield side of the diamond near the foul line, touching the bag with his left foot. Time permitting, he should anchor his left foot on the base and give an inside target for a throw from the home-plate area. This mode of approach will also help to avoid a collision with the runner. Circling behind the runner is preferable on a pick-off throw to first from the catcher and can safely be used when the play has been signalled.

### Feeding the Pitcher

When the first baseman tries but fails to get a ball fielded by the second baseman, the pitcher must cover first. He will go directly to the bag and anchor himself there, awaiting the throw. In this case the second baseman's throw should be directly over the bag, chest high. If the pitcher is still in motion, the throw should be at the same height but timed to reach the pitcher about two steps before he reaches the bag.

## THE DOUBLE PLAY

With a double play in prospect, the second baseman should move about two steps in toward home and a step or so closer to second than is normal for the hitter at bat. This saves steps and time in getting to second base to serve as middle man in the double play, yet will not cut seriously into his fielding range.

With men on first and second, the double play should go by way of second, as it should with men on first and third—unless the runner on third represents the winning run.

The most important rule concerning the double play is—Make sure of the first out. This implies that the fielder should try to take the play himself whenever possible.

### Feeding the Shortstop

The second baseman should try to be in position to make his throw to second without taking a step. The ball should go to the base (not the shortstop), chest high. The throw is not a particularly difficult one, since the shortstop is moving toward first.

1. An underhand toss should be used on a ball hit toward the base, with the second baseman placing his right foot directly in the path of the ball while fielding it and pulling his glove away when tossing it.

2. The backhand flip, used for short- and medium-length throws, is the quickest method for the 4-6-3 double play. Rather than pivot for the

*Second baseman feeding the shortstop (half-pivot for long throw)*

*Second baseman feeding the shortstop (backhand toss for medium range throw)*

*Second baseman feeding the shortstop (underhand toss for short throw)*

throw, the second baseman simply tosses the ball with a backhand motion. This must be practiced diligently.

3. A hip pivot to the right should be used on balls to the second baseman's left and on any other play involving a throw of more than fifteen feet. (The pivot should never be to the left—if one to the right is not feasible, the play should be at first.) Here the second baseman pivots quickly to his right and throws with power from a position in which both feet are solidly planted. The speed of the pivot and accuracy of the throw are both important factors.

### The Tag Play

On a ball to his left and slow enough to be fielded in the base line, the second baseman should tag the runner and complete the play at first. If the runner stops to delay the tag, he should not be chased. Instead, the throw to first should be made to retire the batter—then the play made on the runner. If the latter runs out of the base line to avoid the tag, he should not be chased; this would defeat a double play, for the runner is automatically out.

### Making the Pivot

Competence in this maneuver is the main difference between a good second baseman and a mediocre one.

Whenever possible the second baseman should approach the base in a direct line with the throw. This will put the second baseman in good position to take the throw and make the pivot. The approach should be at full speed, but the last two steps should be taken slowly, with knees bent for lateral mobility. The pivot should *not* be made on the run—the second baseman should be set for the throw to first.

The pivot should be made in accordance with the path of the runner, who will attempt to break up the double play. If his slide is to the outfield side, the pivot should be made into the diamond; if his approach is to the inside, the pivot should be toward the outfield. If the ball is hit hard, allowing ample time to complete the play, the pivot can be made directly toward first base.

Another consideration, of course, is the direction of the throw. If the ball is wide in either direction, the pivot will have to be made to the side on which the throw comes.

The second baseman's task is very difficult since he must be concerned with both the runner and the ball, which are coming at him from opposite directions. When not in position to anticipate the path of the runner, he should vary the direction of his pivot from time to time so as to make the runner's intentions more difficult to achieve.

**To the Inside.** The pivot into the infield can be made with either foot touching the base. If the right foot is used, the step with the left one should be toward a spot about halfway between home and first, the throw being made across the body. When the left foot is used to touch the base, the right one crosses it in a step toward home, and a normal step toward first is made with the left foot for the throw. Both of these methods should carry the second baseman out of the runner's path.

It should be added here that a base runner is permitted to slide only as far out of the base line as he can go while still able to touch the bag with some part of his body. However, umpires are very lenient in calling interference on a runner who slides in an attempt to break up a double play.

**To the Outside.** The second baseman's pivot toward the outfield is

*Second baseman's double play pivot—across the bag (Bill Mazeroski)*

*Second baseman's double play pivot—straddle (Bill Mazeroski)*

made by hitting the outside of the base with the left foot, pushing back on the right, and using a moderately open step toward first with the left foot for the throw.

**Straight Ahead.** If the runner is not close to second, the pivot can be directly toward first base. The natural method is to hit the side of the base with the right foot and stride toward first for the throw. An alternative and especially safe version is to straddle the bag and drag the right foot across it on the throw. This makes touching the base automatic and is consequently the recommended method.

If the runner is close when the second baseman is straddling the bag, the latter can make a fast flip-like throw to first, leaping into the air off his left foot to avoid the slide of the runner.

It is rare that the second baseman is taken out in scholastic baseball. For that reason, as well as for safety and ease of execution, a second baseman could hardly be faulted if he made all double-play attempts by stepping directly toward first. Should the runner be close enough to make contact, the second baseman should not make the throw, the major objective—the force at second—having been attained.

**Backing Off.** If the throw is to the left-field side of the bag, the second baseman should hop to his right, drag his left foot over the bag, and make his throw from behind the base.

*Second baseman's double play pivot—jump (Bill Mazeroski)*

**Shortstop Behind the Bag.** When the shortstop goes behind the bag for a ball, the second baseman should plant his left foot against the right field side of the base and face left field. He will then be in a better position to shift for a bad toss, especially one to his right—where the shortstop's throw in this situation is most likely to be. The throw to first will then have to be made after a step back toward the outfield on the right foot.

*Second baseman's double play pivot—push-back (Bill Mazeroski)*

**No Play at First.** No player should ever make an unnecessary throw. When the first out is made but little chance remains of completing the double play, the ball should be held, eliminating the possibility of a bad throw.

A variation of this can be worked with men on first and second. With little chance to complete the double play at first, the second baseman, after making the force at second, should throw to third, where a possible put out can be made on the runner rounding the bag.

**Throw from the Pitcher.** Ideally the shortstop should handle the pitcher's double-play throw to second. However, with a right-handed pull hitter at bat, the shortstop must play in the hole; so it falls to the second baseman to take the pitcher's throw. Even when the shortstop is able to make the play, the second baseman should be going toward the base to back up the throw.

**The Key.** Whatever method is used, the secret of a powerful and accurate throw is to shift the weight to the right foot before the throwing action starts.

## The Force Play

There are several instances in which the second baseman has to concern himself only with forcing the runner at second. One of these occurs when, with two out and a force possible at second, the play is made to that base. In this case the only problem is catching the ball and touching the base. This play is generally made only on a ground ball to the left side of the infield. In order to make certain of the out, the second baseman should take the throw straddling the bag, left foot forward, and drag the right foot across the base when he receives the ball. In this way there will be little chance of losing the out for failure to touch the bag while in possession of the ball.

In certain instances the second baseman should play his base like a first baseman: on a sacrifice bunt when the force play is attempted on the lead runner, on a fumble at short or third, and on a ground ball to deep short—in the last two cases with a man on first and no possibility of completing the double play. In these instances the play will be a close one; so the second baseman must stretch for the ball with one foot anchored on the bag in order to save the time that may be the difference between the runner's being safe or out.

After a force at second and with no possibility for a double play at first, the second baseman should take a step off the bag in the direction that will not be in line with the oncoming runner. This prevents his being taken out and the possible loss of the ball. Should the move be made properly and contact ensue, it will be a case of interference by the runner and should result in the awarding of an automatic double play by the umpire.

## THE PICK-OFF

With a runner on second base, the second baseman only serves as a decoy. He can fake the runner back toward the bag but is too plainly visible to the man on second to be very effective in picking him off the base. The best time to make the fake is immediately before the pitcher delivers the ball to the plate since this may catch the runner leaning the wrong way when the ball is hit and consequently delay his start by a step or two. The second baseman should also keep the runner from taking too big a lead when a definite right-handed pull hitter is at bat and the shortstop must play in the hole. In any of these situations the second baseman must be careful not to be out of position on a batted ball by moving too far in the direction of the base. Kicking dirt toward second or faking a start in that direction is often sufficient to accomplish the desired purpose.

One instance in which the second baseman may be useful in catching the runner off base occurs after the pitcher has thrown to the shortstop covering second and has failed to pick off the runner. The second baseman should have moved behind the base to back up the play. After the shortstop has returned the ball to the pitcher, he walks in front of the runner and back to his position. The second baseman should then move in to the base from his backup position and try to pick off the runner as he takes his lead.

A move useful in holding the runner close and possibly in achieving a pick-off is one in which the second baseman plays about fifteen feet directly behind the bag and advances toward it as the pitcher goes into his stretch. Should a pick-off be possible, the pitcher can wheel and throw. If not, the second baseman, after reaching the bag, runs to his normal position. This is more propitious with a right-hander at bat and demands that the pitcher allow the second baseman time to get into position before delivering to the plate. It is also a useful device for setting up the runner for a pick-off play with the shortstop.

The second baseman occasionally covers first base for a pick-off play when a sacrifice is expected. He will be moving toward first to cover that base in this situation and, with the first baseman charging the plate for a bunt, can duck in behind the runner to take a pick-off throw. This can be done on a pitch-out signalled by the catcher. It has even more chance of success if the batter misses a bunt attempt, for here the runner will be leaning toward second or possibly will have taken a few steps in that direction. This pick-off attempt should be automatic on a missed bunt.

# *The Shortstop*

The shortstop position is both a busy and an important one. The ideal man for the job is fast, agile, and possessed of good hands and a strong arm. Almost invariably, good shortstops are aggressive, resourceful ball-players with sound baseball sense and a well-developed talent for anticipating plays.

A shortstop has much ground to cover, and more than any other player, he must field the ball cleanly (because of the long throw to get the runner at first). He is also charged with relaying the catcher's signals (by voice to the infield, by hand signs to the outfield) and with directing strategy on many balls hit to either infield or outfield.

## *RANGE*

The shortstop should try for every ball hit to the left side of the infield. A wide-ranging shortstop enables the third baseman to guard the line and the second baseman to protect the hole to a greater degree than would normally be possible. He should call for any medium-speed ground ball to his right that he feels he can handle more easily than the third baseman; otherwise the latter will cut in front of him to play it and take advantage of his shorter throw to first.

The play in the hole (far to his right) is the most difficult one for the shortstop. To set himself properly for the long throw, he should brake himself on the inside of his right foot, take a short hop on his right foot while straightening up, stride directly toward first; and make a hard, overhand throw with a good follow-through—all this in one continuous and rapid sequence of motion.

### Fly Balls

He should take all fly balls in an area running from his normal position to the mound, to second base, and to the area behind him (except those called for by an outfielder). His fly-ball range includes ones hit behind the third baseman. The prevailing rule is that a player coming in on a fly ball has priority.

### Handling the Ball

The shortstop must "play the ball" rather than let it play him. He should always move toward it, charging it as fast as possible, slowing his actions as he approaches it, then adjusting his stride to receive the ball on the right hop. He should always endeavor to get in front of the ball and set himself for the throw before he fields it.

Because of the length of his throw, speed is of the essence. The shortstop cannot afford a fumble and must often throw without straightening up, although he should do so when time permits.

### Covering Second Base

It is the shortstop's job to protect second base on bunts and on all batted balls to the right side of the infield, including any pop fly that the second baseman attempts to play.

On a fly ball to left field, the shortstop should follow the outfielder as long as he is going back. If he sets himself for the catch, the shortstop returns to second to cover the base. On a fly ball or base hit on which the left fielder has the play in front of him, the shortstop should go directly to second base. If the ball gets past the outfielder, there is still time for the shortstop to get to the outfield to handle a relay. Although he is covering second, the shortstop must leave the base and meet a wide or late throw.

Since the second baseman has similar duties on fly balls or hits to right field, it is the shortstop's job to cover the bag when the second baseman goes to the outfield and to back him up when he covers the base.

The shortstop should generally cover second base if the second baseman's duties take him elsewhere.

Specific base-covering assignments are dealt with in sections in which the various defensive maneuvers are discussed.

## Covering Third Base

In certain situations it falls to the shortstop to cover third base. One of these is a pop fly to the third baseman with a man on base. Another is a slow roller, hit with a man on first, that the third baseman must charge.

On some ball clubs the shortstop is assigned the task of covering third base on certain throws from the outfield, the third baseman backing him up. The coach should decide upon the specific occasions for such a setup.

## Runner on Second

A man on second constitutes a twofold problem. He must not be allowed too big a lead, and his presence demands proper handling of an attempted pick-off play.

A runner on second and the attention he warrants will somewhat reduce the shortstop's ground-covering range. To cover as much of his normal territory as possible, the shortstop should take care not to be moving in the direction of the base as the pitcher is delivering to the plate.

**Distracting the Runner.** A runner on second is in perfect position to read the catcher's signals and relay them to the batter. Consequently, it is good practice for the shortstop to drive the runner back to the base just as the catcher prepares to give his signal. This will cause the runner to pay heed to his own safety, thereby diverting his attention from the catcher's signs.

**Holding the Runner.** Without straying too far from his own position, the shortstop should hold the runner close to second base. Preventing a long lead will eliminate the extra step or two that can enable a runner to score on a single or advance to third on an infield out.

A feint toward the base, timed to occur as the pitcher sets himself to deliver the ball to the batter, is the most effective method of accomplishing this purpose. The shortstop should perform his fake without taking an actual step or losing his balance.

**Grounder to Short.** After fielding a grounder, the shortstop should "look the runner back" to second before making his throw to first. If he breaks for third, the play should be at that base.

The runner will try for third on a slow roller or grounder to the shortstop's left. If the ball is fumbled, eliminating the play at first, it may be possible to catch the runner taking a wide turn at third. The shortstop should be alert for this in such a situation.

**Slow Roller to Third.** When the third baseman rushes in to field a slow roller, the shortstop should follow the runner to third, where he will be in a position to receive a pick-off throw from the third baseman in the event that the latter fumbles and cannot make a play at first.

**Pick-off with the Pitcher.** This is usually a signal play, worked in either of two ways—on a count or by the *daylight method.*

When a count is used, the shortstop gives the signal. After it is flashed, the pitcher turns toward the plate and counts "one-two," and pivots to throw on "three," the shortstop having gone to the bag to take the throw.

When the daylight play is used, the shortstop gives a signal to let the pitcher know that he is going to the base. He then moves in behind the runner, and when the pitcher sees daylight between the runner and the shortstop as the latter is going toward the bag, he makes a complete pivot and throws to second.

To make the *count play* effective, the shortstop should approach the runner, fake a move to the bag, then start back to his position as he signals the pitcher. When the pitcher's arm is at rest and he has turned back to face the hitter, the shortstop makes his break for the bag. This is a good method. Experimentation may develop other, even better ones.

This play should be made on a signal so that the pitcher is unlikely to deliver the ball to the plate after the shortstop has gone to second base. Furthermore, the shortstop should make no more than one false start to the bag on any one pitch.

One of the great values in having a good pick-off play is that the reputation of having one is often enough to keep the runner close to his base.

**Pick-off with the Catcher.** Because of the length of the throw, there is relatively little chance of a successful pick-off. The throw from the catcher, however, will keep the runner honest.

If the runner's lead is too large, the catcher should signal for this play, the sign being acknowledged by the shortstop. The latter must be at the base awaiting the catcher's throw when it arrives; yet he cannot make his break too soon lest the runner be alerted. The proper time to go to the base is as the pitcher is delivering the ball to the plate, a pitch-out having been used.

A missed swing by the batter should be construed as an automatic pick-off signal. The shortstop should be prepared for a throw to second to catch the runner. His vulnerability to the pick-off play is greatly increased by the instinctive few steps he almost invariably takes on any swing by the batter.

### The Sacrifice

The shortstop should cover second for a sacrifice bunt with a man on first. In this situation there exists little chance of completing a double play, and under any circumstances it is the lead runner who should be retired if at all possible. His first two steps should be toward home in case the batter swings and hits the ball toward short. When he reaches the base, the shortstop should play the bag as a first baseman does, stretching for the throw to increase the chance of retiring the runner.

With men on first and second and the sacrifice in order, the shortstop should drive the runner back to the base and hold him there in order to increase the chances of a successful force play at third. After the pitch is delivered, the shortstop should go in to cover the mound, which will be left unprotected for a bunt when the pitcher moves over to cover the third base line.

## THE DOUBLE PLAY

As in the case of the second baseman (with a double play in prospect), the shortstop should move about two steps in toward home and a step or so closer to second than is normal for the hitter at bat. He, too, should remember to make sure of the first out.

### Strategy

Certain basic rules guide the shortstop's approach to the double play:

1. He should make the play at second himself whenever possible.
2. If, with men on first and second, he must backhand a ball hit far to his right, the shortstop may throw to third if this is the easy play.
3. With the bases loaded, the double play should go by way of second unless the man on third represents the tying or winning run.
4. With men on first and third, the double play goes by way of second unless the man at third represents the *winning* run.
5. The shortstop, unless he has been deep in the hole for a pull hitter, should cover second on a double-play throw from the pitcher since he will be going toward the base anyway.
6. If, on a ground ball near first base, the batter is retired before the throw goes to second, the runner must be tagged.

### Feeding the Second Baseman

The shortstop's double-play throw is a difficult one to make properly because of the pivot demanded of the second baseman. It is very important that it be precise. A good one will be chest high and directly at the bag, not at the second baseman.

The throw should be made without straightening up, and the glove should be pulled away from the ball to give the pivot man a good view of it. The two-handed scoop or push-throw obscures the second baseman's view of the ball and should be avoided.

The throw to second can be either underhand or sidearm, the former being used for the short toss on a ball hit near the base. For a longer throw, or on a ball to the shortstop's right on which he must apply the

(Left) *Shortstop feeding the second baseman, underhand toss for short throw; note glove pulled away from ball for good visibility.* (Right) *Shortstop feeding the second baseman, overhand (or sidearm) for medium and long throws (Eddie Brinkman).*

*Shortstop's double play pivot—outside the bag*

brakes to set himself, a sidearm throw should be used, and the ball should be aimed at a spot about one foot on the home-plate side of second.

### The Pivot

The primary considerations in guiding the type and direction of the pivot are the path of the oncoming runner and the location of the throw to the base.

If the throw is wide in either direction, the bag should be crossed on that side. On a good throw directly to the base, the shortstop should make his play according to the path of the runner, going to the outfield side when the runner approaches on the inside of the base line and going to the infield side when the runner comes in on the outside. The distance of the runner from the base permitting, the play can be made directly toward first. In any event the object of the shortstop should be to prevent the runner's interfering with his throw to first.

The shortstop should make his approach to the base as quickly as possible. As he nears the bag, the shortstop should slow down so that the proper adjustment can be made in the stride to facilitate handling the ball. He should speed up again when he sees where the ball is. Ideally he will receive the ball one-half step before he reaches the base.

It would, of course, be preferable to hit the bag with the right foot since only a single step with the left would be required for the throw to first. But the runner being intent on breaking up the double play, an extra step or short hop is sometimes necessary if he is to be avoided. Other factors, such as the direction of the throw and the position of the shortstop's feet as he gets to the bag, make variations in method imperative. Thus, there is really no set rule for making the double play.

The techniques outlined here should be employed according to the shortstop's physical characteristics and the play situation itself.

**To the Outside.** Making the play to the outside necessitates hitting the base with the right foot. The throw should be caught with the right foot on the outside corner of the bag. A step diagonally to the left with the left foot is the next move. If the runner is too close to permit making the throw on this step, the shortstop should make a short hop or shuffle step to the left, carrying him further out of the runner's path. The throw to first is then made as the shortstop lands on his right foot and steps toward first base on his left.

The drag method can also be used when the play is made to the outside. Here the right foot is placed about four inches from the outside corner of the base and is dragged across the bag as the throw is made to first. An extra step or hop can also be used if needed to assure avoiding the runner.

**To the Inside.** When the shortstop makes the double play by going

*Shortstop's double play pivot—inside the bag*

to the inside of the base, he establishes contact with his left foot. Either the drag or a step can be used, the former ensuring the force-out at second, the latter carrying the shortstop further away from the bag and out of the runner's path.

When the shortstop steps on the inside corner of the base with his left foot, he pushes off diagonally toward home plate, landing on his right foot and making the throw as he steps toward first with his left foot.

If he prefers the drag method and time permits its use, he gets to the bag with his right foot advanced and on the inside of the bag. His left foot stays behind the base and is dragged across it as he steps to throw. A half-pivot to the right on the lead (right) foot and a step slightly in the direction of home plate as the throw to first base is made will help to take the shortstop out of the base runner's path.

**Straight Ahead.** If the runner is still far distant from second base, the shortstop can afford to follow his natural inclinations and step directly toward first as he makes his throw. He can step on the middle of the base with the right foot and throw while taking a normal stride with the left foot.

The drag method can also be used here, the shortstop taking the throw while straddling the bag—right foot forward—and dragging his left foot across the top of the base as he steps to throw. When time permits, this is the surest way for the shortstop to make the double play.

**Behind the Base.** If the shortstop can stay behind the base in making the double play, he will experience little difficulty with the oncoming runner. However, since he must go to the bag quickly and take the throw while in motion, this is rarely possible. The logical time to use this method occurs when the shortstop fields a ground ball close to second base and takes the play himself. One step away from the bag he takes a stride with

*Shortstop's double play pivot—across and back*

his left foot, releasing the ball on the throw after his foot has made contact with the near side of the base.

A variation can be employed in which the shortstop hits the bag with his left foot and backs off toward left field before stepping toward first for the throw.

**First-Second-First.** The shortstop takes the throw on the first-second-first (3-6-3) double play. If the throw is a good one, the best method of making the play is to hit the base with the left foot and step into the diamond to make the return throw. The throw to first should go directly to the bag because it must be handled by a moving player—either the first baseman or, occasionally, the pitcher—and it should be chest high.

**The Key.** At the amateur level of play, the players' arms not being so powerful, the key to a strong, accurate throw is to get the weight on the right foot before the throwing actions are started.

### The Cut-off Play

One of the shortstop's important duties is to serve as cut-off man on certain balls hit to the outfield: on a single hit with a runner on first base and on a fly ball with runners on first and second. Whether the batter hits to left, center, or right, the shortstop should station himself in a direct line between the outfielder playing the ball and third base, at a point about forty feet in front of the base. The third baseman calls the play, telling the shortstop whether to let the ball go through to the base or to cut it off.

## THE SECOND BASE COMBINATION

The second baseman and shortstop are rightfully thought of as a unit rather than simply as individual ballplayers. No team can be successful unless it is strong through the middle, and in its contribution to a team's strength through the middle, the keystone combination can live up to its name.

Continual practice together is an imperative for the second-short duo. On the double play, in particular, perfect coordination and timing are demanded since any hesitancy or failure to make a precise throw will cause the double play to be lost. Thus, they should capitalize on every possible opportunity to acquire complete familiarity with one another's habits and abilities, speed of movement, and throwing characteristics. This should be carried to the extent that the two men make it a practice always to warm up together, whether it be before an actual ball game or during an ordinary practice session.

## Covering Second

Close cooperation between the keystone pair is essential to a good defense. Each should know at all times what his partner is doing or intends to do.

Who is to cover second on a steal should be decided whenever a runner reaches first base. The shortstop gives the signal for this assignment unless the second baseman is a far more experienced ballplayer.

Hiding his mouth from the opposition with his glove, the one who gives the signal does so by either opening or closing it: an open mouth means that he will cover the base himself, a closed mouth that his partner must assume responsibility. Other signals may be used as long as they clearly convey the message without revealing it to the opposition.

A team cannot overestimate the importance of properly carrying out this assignment. Failure to do so may mean that a throw will go into center field untouched, allowing a further advance by the runner. It may at the least force the catcher to look vainly for someone to whom to throw while the runner walks into second base.

In amateur circles, with less danger of the hit-and-run, one man should be assigned the duty of covering second in order to avoid confusion. The shortstop is the logical man for the job since he can see the runner advancing from first.

When the conventional method is used, several factors determine the base-covering assignment.

**The Batter.** The bearing of the batter on this situation depends primarily upon the direction in which he is most likely to hit the ball.

Ordinarily it is the shortstop's duty to cover second base on a bunt or a steal with a right-field hitter (usually a left-hander) at the plate, on bunts and ground balls fielded by the pitcher, and all throws from the right side of the infield. The assignment falls to the second baseman when a left-field hitter (usually right-handed) is at bat, except on a sacrifice bunt, in which case second is always covered by the shortstop and first by the second baseman. The bunt is unlikely with two strikes on the batter, so normal assignments prevail.

For a straightaway hitter or one with unknown tendencies, assignments depend on the pitch being thrown. A fast ball is less likely to be pulled than a curve or change; thus, the man charged with signalling the base-covering assignment should consider this in formulating his judgment.

If either man makes an attempt to field a batted ball, the other one should cover the base. Regardless of who covers second, that man's partner should back him up whenever his own responsibilities do not take him elsewhere.

**The Pitcher.** The ability of the batter and the type of pitch have a bearing on the direction in which the ball is likely to be hit. The defensive players should recognize these factors when positioning themselves. Whenever it is practicable, they should also give consideration to the spot in which the pitcher will try to keep the ball.

The pitcher's stuff on a certain day also enters the picture. If he is particularly fast, the batters will have trouble getting around on the ball and will be less likely to pull it. If he is keeping the ball primarily in one spot—for example, low and inside to right-handed batters, outside to left-handers—chances are that the ball will be hit to the left side. As the game progresses, the smart ballplayer will observe how the other team is hitting the pitcher, and such things as position play and base-covering assignments should be arranged accordingly.

### Runner on First

With a runner on first base, both the second baseman and the shortstop should take a step or two toward second after the ball has passed the batter. By so doing they will be in good position to cover the base if the runner attempts a delayed steal.

When the catcher calls for a pitch-out, both men can leave their positions with the pitch; the one who is not going to the base to take the throw moves into backup position.

In taking the catcher's throw on an attempted steal, the man covering second should break quickly and get to the base so that he will present a stationary target and also have less difficulty in shifting for a bad throw.

While awaiting the throw he should stand in front of the base, facing home plate. This allows for greater maneuverability on a wild throw and less chance of contact with the runner than does the more conventional method of straddling the bag. When he receives the ball, he can pivot to the left and be in perfect position to place the ball between the base and the runner, allowing the man to tag himself out.

## Double Steal

When the offensive team has runners on first and third (particularly if they are fast men), there is always the possibility of an attempted double steal. If the count on the batter reaches 3-1 or 3-2, this possibility is greatly increased, and the second baseman and shortstop should move two steps in, to be in better position to combat it.

Both members of the second base combination should remember to give up the run on third if the man on first represents the winning run. This is the one to keep from scoring position.

Further details of the double steal defense can be found in the section on special defensive plays.

## The Hit-and-Run

The hit-and-run is more likely to be attempted with fewer than two outs, a runner on first base, and the batter ahead of the pitcher in the count. It should never be tried when the offensive team is behind by more than one run.

If they suspect the hit-and-run, the second baseman and shortstop should position themselves accordingly. The shortstop normally covers the base with a left-hander at bat, and the second baseman does so when the hitter is right-handed.

Going to the base to cover it as the pitcher is delivering the ball to the plate will leave too big a gap for the batter to shoot at. The best procedure is to shift slightly closer to second before the pitch and to move toward the plate as the pitcher delivers, then cover the base as the situation demands. If the ball is hit toward either position, the man responsible should go for it, relying on his partner to cover the base. The play will be a difficult one at best, but not nearly so tough as it would be if the defensive player had gone to the base and left his position completely unprotected.

When a runner is going from first to second on the hit-and-run or steal and the batter hits the ball in the air, the second baseman and shortstop should fake fielding a ground ball in order to lure the runner and make a double play possible after the ball has been caught.

## The Relay

On a fly ball to left field, the shortstop is responsible for serving as relay man if one is needed. The second baseman is charged with this duty when the ball is hit to right field.

On a ball hit to center field, the man who is nearer the base covers it, and the other man is responsible for helping the center fielder or for backing up the throw. However, if one of them has a much stronger arm than the other, he is the one who should serve as relay man.

The relay man should not go too far out from the diamond, bearing in mind that it is the second throw that should be the short (and accurate) one. Several other common-sense rules are germane to the relay man's tactics:

1. The pivot for the throw to a base should always be to the left.
2. If the throw is bouncing, the relay man should let it go through since it will be difficult to handle and unlikely to get the lead runner.
3. If the runner is obviously "in" at second base, the man covering the base should leave it to back up the relay man.
4. If the hit will obviously be no more than a double, the relay man should retreat and cover the bag, while the other one backs him up.

# The Third Baseman

Third base is rightfully known as the hot corner. Its guardian is so close to the batter, and the ball often reaches him so quickly, that a good part of the time he is limited to a do-or-die effort to field the ball. The difficulty of the position is compounded by its vulnerability to bunts and slow rollers.

A third baseman must be quick thinking, have sharp reflexes, sure hands, and a strong arm. Running speed is not essential, but quick reactions and movements are requisites of successful third base play.

The handling of bunts and dribblers necessitates the ability to throw from any position. Hard-hit ground balls often can only be blocked and require agility in retrieving the ball and making a play on the runner.

Once a ball is hit toward him, the third baseman has little time to react and practically none for thought. Consequently, he must be prepared to field the ball on every pitch—and with a definite plan of action in mind.

## MECHANICS

Despite the speed with which a ground ball reaches him, a third baseman should try to field the arc since this will enable him to cover a maximum area of ground. This means that he should go back in a slight curve on well-hit balls to either side of him and should move forward to field them. Conversely, on a ball hit directly to him, he should never back up, for this would, in effect, allow the ball to play him.

Fielding the arc is not possible on hard-hit balls, except in the form of a dive or lunge diagonally backward in the direction of the ball. In a sense this constitutes taking more time in playing the ball.

The third baseman should play in a crouch while awaiting the ball; his hands are near his knees, his weight forward, his eyes on the batter rather than on the pitcher. When the ball is hit on the ground to him, he should have his hands very low (scraping the dirt) so that there is no room for the ball to go through.

His throw does not have to be hurried on a cleanly handled ball, but it should be a hard one. On the many balls that he knocks down or blocks, however, the throw will have to be made quickly.

The third baseman should practice a crossover step until it becomes second nature to him. This will help him to cover more ground. This move, when made with his right foot, is particularly important since most balls hit in his direction will be to his left.

Fielding balls to his right by backhanding them is an approved technique and means that the glove will be at a right angle to the ball, an essential for consistent, proper handling of grounders.

*Third baseman's crossover step on a ball to his left*

*Third baseman fielding a slow roller*

## THE PLAYS

### Bunts and Slow Rollers

A slowly hit ball should be charged as quickly as possible. On a bunt the third baseman should be moving toward the plate as soon as the bat drops.

If at all possible, he should field the ball with two hands. When this cannot be done, the surest method, and one that loses little time, is to field the ball on the run and *off the left foot with the gloved hand.* The throw is made while straightening up and with the body still moving forward. The play should be made in this manner whether the ball is to the right, the left, or in front of the third baseman. (The barehand scoop with an underhand throw is for professionals.)

Since the batter stands a good chance of beating out a ball hit right on the line, the third baseman should allow it to roll. He should pick it up as soon as it is in foul territory. The exception to this rule occurs when a runner is on base and will be able to advance while the ball is rolling; in this case it should be picked up to check his progress.

### The Sacrifice

On those occasions when the sacrifice can be anticipated, the third baseman should be alert for a bunt. This probability often becomes a certainty by the batter's revealing his intentions, in which case the third baseman should be charging the plate by the time the ball is bunted.

The third baseman normally protects the foul line (where the bunt is most likely to go), whereas the pitcher should be able to handle balls closer to the mound. (If the pitcher is fielding a ball, the third baseman should give him directions.) However, with a slow-footed pitcher on the mound the third baseman should be prepared to field all bunts, even the sacrifice with men on first and second.

With a bunt in order, the third baseman's position is about four feet wide of third base and on the edge of the grass. By playing close to the line he will be going straight in on the ball when he fields it. It will also facilitate returning to the bag if someone else fields the ball or if the bunt is a fake one.

With a man on second, the third baseman must take care not to leave his position too quickly lest the play be a fake bunt designed to draw him in, leaving the base unprotected against a steal. In fact, he should return to his base and cover it whenever a bunt goes to someone other than himself, or when he has fielded it and thrown the ball elsewhere.

On the sacrifice with men on first and second, the third baseman should play about two steps from the bag and cover it for a force on the runner, the pitcher being responsible for fielding a bunt in the area near the third base line. If the bunt is hard and gets by the pitcher, the third baseman must field it and make the play at first base. If the batter "hits away" in this situation, the third baseman should break several steps to his left on the swing in order to cover as much of his normal territory as possible.

In taking the throw for the force, the third baseman should play his bag as a first baseman, anchoring one foot and stretching to catch the ball.

With two strikes on the batter, the third baseman can return to his normal position. He should not forget, however, that a poor-hitting pitcher may attempt a sacrifice bunt, even with two strikes.

### Pop Flies

The third baseman should take all fly balls between third base and home plate. Since he is going in on the ball, he should "run the catcher off" any fly he can handle, always calling for the ball in a loud, clear voice.

Likewise, the shortstop is in a better position to play a pop fly behind the third baseman and should be allowed to do so whenever he calls for the ball.

If, on a foul fly, the third baseman must approach a grandstand, fence, or bench, he should go to the barrier as fast as possible. Then he should locate the ball and weave his way back toward the diamond if the ball fails to reach the obstruction.

### The Double Play

The throw to second to start a double play is of the utmost importance in retiring even one of the two men. The throw should be chest high, directly over the base, and timed so that the second baseman will be arriving at the base just as the ball reaches him. In view of the speed with which a batted ball reaches him, the third baseman may have to pause before throwing, in order to allow the second baseman to get in position for the play.

With men on first and second, the third baseman's double play on balls to his left should go by way of second base for speed and ease of execution (he should look for an easy tag-out if the advancing runner is close to him). On a ball hit straight to him or to his right, he should touch the bag to force the lead runner and, if feasible, throw to first for the second out rather than attempt the 5-4-3 double play. Although professionals employ the latter tactic, amateur teams would be well advised to try the safer approach.

With the bases loaded the third baseman's double play goes home, then to first. Once again there is the exception of a ball hit near the bag, in which case the third baseman should step on the base and then throw home, making sure to let the catcher know that the force is off and that the runner going home must be tagged.

When a left-handed batter hits to third base, a double play is usually out of the question since the second baseman will be in no position to get to the base in time to take the throw. The third baseman should make his throw to first for one sure out rather than risk a throw that cannot be handled at second and will allow both runners to be safe.

If this play occurs with men on first and second, the wisest move is a force at third and a throw to first. Should the ball be to his left, the third baseman may find it easier to get the first out by tagging the runner coming to third.

The cardinal rule is, Always make sure of the first out.

### Tagging the Runner

The third baseman should straddle the base while awaiting a throw from anyone other than the catcher. When the throw is from the catcher, he should take a position at the corner of the bag nearest the pitcher, leaving the base open so that the runner can slide into it with little danger of interference or accidental spiking. At the same time he will be able to go for a wide throw with little difficulty. As he catches the ball, he should turn to his left, placing his left foot on the outfield side of the base. He will then be straddling the bag.

The ball should be held in such a position that the runner will slide into it and tag himself. The third baseman should leave the base to go for a wide throw, the ball having priority over the runner. If time still remains, he can dive at the runner to make the tag.

Once the ball is applied to the runner, it should be removed rapidly to eliminate the danger of its being jarred loose by the contact.

## The Cut-off Play

The third baseman serves as the cut-off man on a fly ball to left field with a runner on third or on a single to left with a man on second. This is a good practice since there is very little chance to get the runner at third and since the third baseman is much closer to the cut-off spot than the first baseman.

The cut-off position is in a direct line between the left fielder and home at a spot about halfway between third base and the plate. The catcher will give instructions, and the third baseman should act accordingly.

## Backup and Base-covering Duties

With men on base, the third baseman should back up the pitcher on all throws from the first baseman. He should also be alert to back up an overthrow of second base from right field on a single with no one on base, or on a fly ball with a man on first. Another backup role occurs when the shortstop covers third base, some teams using this setup on certain balls hit to the outfield.

When both the shortstop and second baseman go for a fly ball with no one on base, it is the third baseman's job to cover second. If this play occurs with a runner on first base, the third baseman should once again cover second, but should make his intentions known to the catcher and tell the latter to cover third.

Of course, with a man on second or on third, the third baseman must remain at his own base when not in cut-off position.

## *TACTICS*

A good third baseman is, of necessity, an aggressive ballplayer. His basic endeavor should be to take any ball that he can get. Unless the shortstop calls for a ground ball, the third baseman should cut in front of him and field the ball if he can, for his throw is a shorter one and has a better chance of retiring the runner.

To help guide his actions and enable him to gain the advantage of an extra step whenever possible, the third baseman should watch the hitter, not the pitcher. Doing so will give him a better jump on the ball as well as aid in the early detection of a bunt.

There are several tactical maneuvers that should be adopted by the third baseman under specific defensive situations:

1. When the opposition has a runner on second base, the third baseman should take a step toward third after the ball passes the batter, preparing himself to cover the base on a steal. At the same time he should be wary of a fake bunt, which will draw him in toward the plate and leave the base open for a steal.

2. With a runner on third, a missed swing by the batter is an automatic signal for a pick-off throw from the catcher. The runner has a tendency to take a step or two when the batter swings and, thus, may fall victim to a pick-off throw. If the throw does not succeed in getting an out at third, it will at least keep the runner honest.

3. A runner on third base should not be allowed to take too long a lead—the third baseman should feign a play on him if he appears to be getting too big a jump on the pitcher.

4. If, with no force play possible, the third baseman fields a ground ball with a man on third base or on second, he should "look the runner back" to his base before marking his throw to first for the out.

5. A different problem is presented when, with men on first and third, a medium-speed ground ball (one not hard enough to assure a good chance for a double play) is hit to the infield. If the runner on third breaks for the plate and a play is made on him, he will often try to get caught in a run-down, enabling the other runners to advance to second and third. In order to prevent this, the third baseman should follow the runner home so that he will be in position to take a throw from the catcher and make a quick tag on the runner—getting the out in time to prevent a further advance by the other base runner. If the ball is hit to the third baseman and the runner makes a break for home, the play should definitely be made on him.

6. If, in those situations in which the third baseman covers his base on throws from the outfield, the throw is wide or late and there is no chance to get the runner coming to third, he must rush to the ball and catch it on the fly for a possible play at first or second.

7. The third baseman must be prepared to take the proper action on an appeal play. He should watch each runner rounding the base on his way home and should check the men tagging up to score after a fly ball is caught. If a runner misses the base or leaves it too soon on a fly ball that is caught, the third baseman should call for the ball, step on the base, and call the umpire's attention to the violation. Alertness on the appeal plays, especially at third base, can occasionally prevent a run.

8. On a throw to his base, the third baseman should always consider getting the ball his major responsibility. He is, in a sense, the last line of defense against a base runner attempting to score: if the ball gets by him, the opposition will score a run on 90 percent of such occurrences.

The third baseman should observe one other important tactic pertaining to positioning: with two out he should guard the foul line in an effort to prevent an extra-base hit. He should station himself deep and to the right of his regular position so that there is less chance of a batted ball's getting between him and the line and going through for extra bases.

# The Outfielders

There has long been a theory held by the casual observer that outfielders should pay their way into the ball park. Although the occasional eye-catching feats of a particularly brilliant outfielder tend, at times, to dispel this belief, the impression seems to prevail that an outfielder is merely a bat-wielding brute who must take his place in the field since, by convention, nine men are stationed at various points around the diamond.

As we go down the ladder of the various classes of baseball, too often we find that coaches and even players themselves consider the outfielders as excess baggage and the three positions as posts that must be filled by men not good enough to make the team as infielders, pitchers, or catchers.

That this is a completely erroneous impression will be claimed by all outfielders and attested to by the vast majority of pitchers. A good outfield is demonstrably a very important essential in the success of any team.

The center fielder is ordinarily the best outfielder of the three and must cover the most territory. The right fielder should have a particularly strong arm for the long throw to third when he fields a base hit with a runner on first. A left-hander will best fit into right field since his most difficult throws will be on balls hit to his left. Conversely, a right-handed thrower should play left field since his most difficult throws will be on balls hit to his right.

Natural outfielding ability—that is, speed, sure hands, and a good arm —is an important factor in the making of an outfielder; but certain skills that can be developed, such as getting the jump on the ball, position play, judgment, quick and accurate throwing, and correct maneuvers, are almost equally important and will unquestionably ensure more effective play on the part of any outfielder. To this must be added the important duty of assisting his teammates at all times by backing up both the infielders and the other outfielders whenever he can and by calling the play for another outfielder who is concentrating on the ball.

### Conditioning Hints

During his regular preseason conditioning routine, an outfielder should "shadow box" while doing his running, simulating the chasing of a fly ball while conditioning his legs.

At all stages of the season, he should use his arm as an outfielder's, not a pitcher's. The two positions require vastly different throws, and trying to combine them invites arm trouble.

### Preparing for the Play

One of the most difficult problems encountered by some outfielders is their lack of activity. This leads to an impatience that must be resisted. An outfielder should learn to wait—calm, yet alert—fully prepared in mind and body to make the correct play properly.

An outfielder should always assume that the next ball will be hit to him and should be prepared to make the play when he does field the ball. He should check the direction and strength of the wind at the start of every inning since it can greatly affect the flight of any ball hit in the air.

An outfielder should know his pitcher as well as the hitter. An outfielder's knowledge of the pitcher's speed and his use of various deliveries can be a big help in allowing him to station himself properly before the pitch. The shortstop and the second baseman can relay the catcher's signals so that the outfielders will have an even better idea of where the ball may be hit.

Position before the pitch is very important to an outfielder, and any information that will help him gain an extra step or two on the ball can mean the difference between a hit and an out.

Furthermore, the speed of any base runners should be taken into consideration so that the right play will be made when the ball is hit to the outfield. Knowledge of his speed will not only give an indication of the runner's daring and his probable intentions, but also will be a guide to where a throw will go (either to catch a runner or to keep him from taking an extra base).

## Making the Catch

When going toward a ball to catch it, an outfielder should run on his toes. Running on the heels will make the ball seem to jump and dance.

To play a ball directly in front of him, the outfielder can start on either foot. If it is to the right and in front of him, starting with a crossover step on the left foot will enable him to get a better jump on the ball; if it is to the left and in front of him, he should start with his right foot. When the ball is hit behind him and to the right, the proper start is made with the right foot; if it is to the left and behind him, he should start on his left foot.

In going for a ball hit away from him, the outfielder will find his task made easier if he runs to the spot where he thinks the ball is going to land and waits for it. This will enable him to be in good position for the catch by simply shifting a few feet according to the exact location of the ball.

The catch itself should be made facing directly toward the ball if at all possible. This involves the safety factor and makes for greater vision and maneuverability.

An outfielder should try to make all catches in throwing position since a fraction of a second gained or lost can be of tremendous importance in heading off a runner. This is one more reason that two hands should be used in making the catch. Using two hands will allow the outfielder to have his throwing hand on the ball as soon as he catches it. An outfielder should put these ideas into practice even with the bases empty since constant use will develop these moves into well-ingrained habits.

With men on base, the ball should be played closer to the throwing side so that the throw can be made in a hurry. If a long throw is needed to head off a runner and is at all possible, the outfielder should position himself to make the catch while moving in on the ball in order to get extra power into the throw.

*Outfielder going back on a fly to his left.*  *Outfielder going back on a fly to his right.*

*Catching a fly ball (note hands in position to shield eyes from the sun)*

If a ball hit in the air to either left or right field curves, it will always curve toward the foul line. This seems to be a rarely discussed fact and one that can be of great importance in enabling an outfielder to handle fly balls. This fact is covered by the laws of physics and is thus an irrefutable one. The words "if it curves" have been added to make allowance for the occasional strong wind that can affect the flight of any batted ball.

The problem posed by the sun can also affect an outfielder's attempting to make a catch. Sunglasses are beneficial but are not always available. Whether or not sunglasses are used, the eyes should be shielded with the glove—the bare hand is of little help because it is too small. If the ball is high and in the sun, the outfielder (once he has sighted the ball) should glance toward the ground, then back at the ball. This will help eliminate the danger of losing the ball in the sun.

If the background in general is bad, the problem will usually be the result of too much light color behind the hitter. In such a situation outfielders should play as low as possible, taking advantage of what little dark area there is. This, of course, will most likely be found close to the ground.

### Position Play

An outfielder should shift according to the count and the situation. Outfielding is not a stationary job; the situation varies with each pitch, so that in order to be properly positioned, the outfielder should move occasionally. For example, when the batter is ahead in the count, he should play that man to pull; with a big lead he should play a little deeper; and so forth. He can shift according to whether a fast ball or curve has been called for by the catcher, remembering that the slower the pitch, the more likely the batter is to pull the ball.

With two strikes on the batter, the outfielders should move away from pull positions since the hitter will be guarding the plate and trying only to get a piece of the ball, rather than taking a full cut, which would mean a greater likelihood of his pulling the ball.

The outfield should play deep early in the game when a single won't hurt. This cuts down the possibility of an extra-base hit and means keeping runners from scoring position. This also applies late in the game when the defensive team has a substantial lead.

The depth of the infield should also influence the position play of the outfield. When the infield plays in to cut off an important run at the plate, particularly late in the game, the outfielders should play closer to the infield since a fly ball will allow the run to score easily and since they will be in position to field an ordinary single quickly enough to make a throw home that may cut off the run.

With a left-hander at bat, the left fielder should move closer to the infield as well as to his left; and with a right-hander at the plate, the right-fielder should move in a few steps as well as to his right. This is occasioned by the fact that a hitter's power lies primarily in pulling the ball. A ball hit to the opposite field is far less likely to go for distance than one that is pulled.

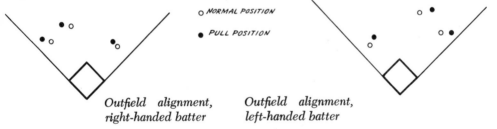

Outfield alignment,          Outfield alignment,
right-handed batter          left-handed batter

In amateur ball there is a tendency for outfielders to play deeper than is warranted by the power of the batters they encounter. Playing a shallower position will allow them to cut off many bloop hits. Because the Texas league hit is far more prevalent at this level of play than the long clout, playing shallow is a calculated risk in which the percentages would seem to favor the defensive team.

### Playing the Fence

Fields that are enclosed by a fence present problems of their own to the outfielders. If they are not accustomed to playing in a certain ball park, the outfielders should try to become familiar with it before the game starts. They should note the distances from their normal positions to the fence at all parts of the field, and each one of the trio should throw a ball against different parts of the fence in his territory to familiarize himself with the way in which a ball will rebound.

To catch a fly ball hit over his head and in the vicinity of the fence, an outfielder should try to avoid charging directly toward the spot where the ball will land. Rather, he should run to the fence and then along it to the spot where he will field the ball. This greatly reduces the danger of crashing into the fence and risking possible injury.

If it appears obvious to the outfielder that he will be unable to catch the ball and that it will hit the fence, he should position himself facing the fence, ready to play the rebound.

### When to Make the Play

An outfielder should call loudly and clearly for all fly balls that he intends to handle if there is any doubt about who will make the play. After he has called for the ball, he should take it unless shouted off by a man in better position to call the play.

"I've got it" is the conventional call for the ball, and it should be answered by the other player(s) near the play. "Take it" will suffice since this cannot be confused with the original call. The answering player should then get in position to back up the man who is preparing to catch the ball.

A fly ball that can be handled by either an infielder or an outfielder should be taken by the outfielder. He is coming in on the ball and is in much better position to call the play and to catch the ball. This is especially so with runners on base, in which case a throw may be needed to keep one of them from advancing.

As a general rule the center fielder should handle any ball that he can reach. Furthermore, if two outfielders call for a ball, the center fielder should take it. Using this rule as a guide will help greatly in avoiding confusion, and the reasoning behind it is apparent: the center fielder is usually the best of the three outfielders, and he generally plays deeper and has the play more in front of him than the other two. However, with men on base the man with the stronger arm should be allowed to make the play on a ball that is between two outfielders (the other man should call the play).

### Fielding Ground Balls

Outfielders should work out in the infield as often as possible in order to learn how to handle ground balls more effectively. Clean handling will prevent many an extra base and more than a few runs.

The outfielder should play the ball in such a way that, if he misses a clean pick-up, he can block the ball with his body—and in such a way that it will bounce in front of him.

When his team is leading by more than one run, an outfielder should play safe on ground balls by blocking them. In this situation a quick return to the infield is not imperative, and blocking the ball will keep it from getting through for extra bases.

*Outfielder blocking a ground ball*

When a game is being played in a ball park with a rough outfield, the outfielder would be wise to block all ground balls, regardless of the situation.

An outfielder should charge all ground balls, even those he intends to block. Once again, doing so can prevent the runner from taking an extra base and may, in some cases, mean an out at the plate rather than a run.

One exception that should be noted is the ball that gets by an outfielder on his gloved-hand side. In this instance the most effective technique is to make a complete pivot away from his throwing side (a right-hander pivots to his left; a left-hander to his right). Although he will temporarily have his back to the infield, this is a more natural move and will produce a quicker, more accurate, and stronger throw.

## Making the Throw

In dealing with the problem of coping with base runners, a good rule for all outfielders to follow is, Always throw ahead of the runner. For

*Outfielder throwing after a catch*

example, a throw to second base when the runner has already arrived at, or is about to reach, that base will allow him to advance to third quite easily. Throwing ahead of the runner (to third) will keep him on second base.

A ball handled by the outfield should be returned to the infield immediately—that is where the play will be. On most long balls the second baseman or shortstop will come out to assist, and if there is no specific base to which the ball must go, the outfielder should throw it to one of them. Short fly balls should be run into the infield as soon as they are caught, and the outfielder who has the ball should be ready to throw it if the runner tries to advance.

When a relay is needed, the outfielder's throw should be the long one. It should go directly to the relay man, chest high. Remembering the rule that the second throw should be the short one will ensure much more accuracy in the important throw to get the runner.

When throwing the ball home or to a specific base, the outfielder should use the cut-off man as his target and should throw directly to him, head high. In that case the ball will be in the correct position to be cut off, or if the cut-off man lets it go through, it will be a perfect throw to the catcher or baseman.

The throw to home should arrive on one bounce, making the ball much easier to handle for the catcher. The outfielder should follow the same practice on throws to third base from right field and right center. Throws from left and center to second or third, on the other hand, should reach those bases on the fly unless the ball is hit very deep.

Ordinarily outfielders can set up a double play by throwing to second on a single. Even if it allows another runner to advance, the throw to second will hold the batter at first, thereby creating a double-play situation. This should always be done if the runner to be held at first represents the tying or winning run.

With the bases loaded in a close game, the outfield should throw the ball home on a single since more than one runner will be trying to score and since a cut-off man will be in a position to handle the ball if a quick throw to another base is needed.

### Exceptions

Occasionally a bluff throw to the advance base and a quick peg to the one just rounded by the runner can result in an easy out. Outfielders should use this tactic only on balls fielded at medium or shallow depth; that is, when the throw will be a short one.

At times a batter will loaf on a single to right field. If so, the outfielder should not be afraid to take advantage of the opportunity to throw him out at first. This is not a sandlot play, particularly with the catcher trailing the runner, ready to back up first base.

### A General Theory

The percentage of runners thrown out at home plate is very small. Unless the run is very important or the chance of catching the runner is very good, it is usually preferable to keep another runner from advancing to scoring position, though done at the expense of allowing a run to score.

## Backing Up the Play

The outfielders should make themselves part of the game even when the ball is in the infield. One of them should be in position to back up any throw from one infielder to another, including throws from the catcher and the pitcher on bunts and pick-offs.

It is a good idea, if a prearranged play is being used, to flash the signal to the outfield so that they can be ready to move into position to back up the play.

The right fielder should back up first base on all bunts and pick-offs. He should back up second base on all throws from the left side of the infield.

The center fielder should back up second base on all bunts and plays at that bag.

The left fielder should back up second base on all plays from the right side of the infield and should back up third on all bunts and pick-offs at that base.

Observing these assignments will ensure that a team will not lose many bases on overthrows. It is part of the principle that outfielding is not a stationary job.

The outfielders should be moving into position so that they are a part of every play, and they should start moving as soon as they anticipate what the play will be.

A word of caution is needed at this point: the outfielders should not leave their positions to back up a base on a steal or sacrifice until the ball has passed the batter, lest he swing at it and hit the ball to the spot that has been vacated.

## The Foul Fly

A special situation of which the left and right fielder should be aware arises when the batter hits a long *foul* fly with either the tying or winning run on third base late in the game. If there are fewer than two out, the outfielder should not catch the ball, for this would allow the runner to score after the catch.

### A Cardinal Rule

Regardless of the other factors that may affect the situation, one rule that must be kept in mind by an outfielder at all times is, Keep the tying or winning run as far from home as possible.

# Offense

# Batting—The Physical Aspect

## FUNDAMENTALS

Successful hitting is the result of developing certain skills. The good batsman is always ready to hit, swings with fast hand and wrist actions, and keeps his arms away from his body during the hitting action. He attempts to swing only at strikes, to watch the ball hit the bat, to meet the ball ahead of the plate, and to avoid swinging so hard that he loses his balance.

It is simple enough to list the qualities required for successful hitting. The problem is how an individual can best acquire those qualities and apply them to his own needs. This section will try to delineate the answers to this many-faceted problem.

The art of hitting can be divided into certain fundamentals, such as the stance, the stride, hitting actions, the swing, and the follow-through. If he is to be a successful hitter, a ballplayer must strive for a batting style that will combine these essentials in the way that is best suited to his own capabilities.

### Types of Hitters

Every ballplayer who walks up to the plate falls into one of three general categories. Basically, he is a pull hitter, a straightaway hitter, or an opposite-field hitter. These broad classifications may be further refined by individual characteristics, but they are the first groupings to which we should look in analyzing batting techniques.

**The Pull Hitter.** Most long-ball hitters, those with real power, are essentially pull hitters. This type is the free swinger who hits most balls to his respective field—that is, left field for a right-handed batter, right field for a left-hander. He does so because he meets the ball well out in front of the plate with a very rapid acceleration of his bat at the point of contact. A slugger of this kind will strike out more often than the straightaway or opposite-field hitter, but he is the man most likely to break up a ball game with one swing of his bat.

**The Straightaway Hitter.** The straightaway hitter is the batsman who hits the ball where it is pitched. He pulls an inside pitch, drives a pitch down the middle through the center of the diamond, and hits an outside pitch to the opposite field. This type is also known as a spray hitter: he sprays his hits to all fields. He has good bat control and is generally the most reliable kind of hitter. Obviously he makes it difficult for the opposition to set their defense for him.

**The Opposite-Field Hitter.** The opposite-field hitter waits longer before starting his swing and contents himself with just meeting the ball. Because he delays his swing, he gets a better look at the pitch and, as a result, seldom strikes out. However, since he slices the ball and rarely gets full wrist action into his swing, he is not a power hitter except on relatively infrequent occasions.

## The Bat

The tools of his trade are of great importance to any player, and this, of course, applies to the batter and his bat. He should use one that he can handle with ease and confidence. Length and weight will vary according to the physical characteristics of the batter, as well as to occasional varible factors, such as the weather and the pitcher. The important consideration is bat control. The bat should enable a player to cope as effectively as possible with any kind of pitch or pitcher that he may be called upon to face.

**Wood, Size, and Feel.** Good bats are made of either ash or hickory, and the consensus of learned opinion seems to be that wood of the straight-grain type is most conducive to power hitting. In addition, a player should select a bat with a knot or two in the wood of the hitting surface. This generally means that the bat is strong and, as the ballplayers say, "has a lot of meat" in it.

The majority of bats used by major leaguers vary in weight from thirty-two to thirty-eight ounces and in length from thirty-four to thirty-six inches, generally running approximately one ounce to the inch.

Recently there has been a trend to light bats, even on the part of mature and powerful professionals. Their belief is that a light bat allows them greater control and lends itself to faster hand action and a better wrist snap. However, no young ballplayer should be so influenced by a big league star that he will try to use the same size bat in spite of his entirely different physical capabilities. Rather, he should seek a bat that feels comfortable and will assure him of easy handling and good bat control. In short the bat should not be so heavy that it swings the player and, at the same time, should not be so light that it cannot be easily controlled.

The size of the bat handle is best determined by personal preference. A thin handle, which can be made even thinner by shaving and sanding, is usually preferred by the free-swinging type of hitter, who feels that a bat of this kind gives him better wrist snap and faster hand action. On the other hand, a thick handle is often preferred by both straightaway and opposite-field hitters since it allows them better bat control. Whether he uses a thick or a thin handle, a player should use a bat with a thick barrel, or, in other words, a large hitting surface.

Certain variables can influence proper bat weight. For example, facing an exceptionally fast pitcher demands the use of a lighter bat. On a particularly hot day or at a time when a player is below par physically, he should also switch to a lighter bat. John Mize was a great natural hitter and a serious student of the batting art. He followed a practice of cutting down the weight of his bat progressively as the weather became hotter. Mize also used a heavier-than-normal bat during spring training, feeling that this is a deterrent to the tendency to overswing that besets most ball-players at that stage of the season.

**Bat Care.** Several simple protective methods will enable a player to lengthen the life of his bat and to ensure its resiliency. Here are several hints for proper bat care:

1. When the bat is in use, it should be held with its label up. This corresponds with the grain of the wood and will help prevent splitting.
2. Rubbing the bat with a bone or bottle will help prevent chipping.
3. An occasional application of a light coat of oil maintains the proper condition of the wood.
4. A bat should not be carelessly tossed around since this makes it more liable to sustain chips, knicks, and dents.
5. Bats should be stored in a dry place and wiped dry when they become wet.
6. When he finds the right bat, a player should keep it for his use exclusively.

## The Approach

The role of the batter is not limited to his performance in the batter's box. To be of maximum value to his team and to help himself to better performance, he should also act as a coach, groundskeeper, morale builder, and alert observer.

*The batter as a coach—signalling the runner to slide*

**The Batter As a Coach.** A batter's duties take concrete form when he goes to the on-deck circle to await his turn at the plate. He should offer encouragement and help to the man at bat by informing him of any shift in the defensive alignment or of a telltale move revealed by the pitcher or catcher, and by letting him know when to run in case of a dropped third strike or an accidental dribbler.

The man awaiting his turn at bat should always coach a runner trying to score. Before doing this he should remove any loose bat or mask that may be in the runner's path. Then he must let the runner know whether to slide or stay up when he crosses the plate. The performance of this task should be mandatory. It can mean the difference between a run and an out, and—more importantly—it may prevent a sprained ankle or broken leg for the runner.

This coaching role should be shared by the hitter, whose duty it is to coach base runners on pitched balls that get away from the catcher; he should use hand signals to let them know whether to remain where they are or, in the event that the ball rolls far enough away from the catcher, to advance to the next base.

**Making Preparations.** The batter can also help himself by his activities while waiting to bat. When on deck, he should endeavor to get the timing of the pitches being delivered to the man at bat, going as far as to take an imaginary swing as the ball comes toward the plate.

When he is leading off an inning or batting against a pitcher who has just entered the game, the on-deck batter is in an even better position to familiarize himself with the timing of the pitcher's delivery and the speed of the pitches.

**250**

While waiting to hit, a smart batter observes the pitcher's stuff at that stage of the game, as well as his operating methods. Even as he enters the box, the batter should be watchful of changes in the positioning of the defense. As he prepares to take his position facing the pitcher, he should remove excess dirt from his spikes, dry his hands thoroughly with rosin (using dirt when no rosin bag is available), and should be swinging either a weighted bat or two regular ones (in the absence of a weighted club) for the dual purpose of making his own bat seem lighter and easier to handle and of loosening his shoulder and arm muscles.

**Taking Signals.** Another important preliminary duty is taking signs. Offensive signals, usually given by the third base coach, are the subject of constant scrutiny by the defensive team, and any indication that one has been given or received should be avoided. The hitter should look to the coach for a signal—first as he steps into the batter's box, then immediately after a pitch has been received by the catcher. In order to confuse the opposition, he should take several additional glances at the coach. In this way he makes it difficult for the defense to detect the giving of a sign or to steal the signals.

## The Grip

**The Different Types.** Batting grips, as well as types of hitters, fall into three distinct categories. The classifications are the end, choke, and medium-choke grip. Free swingers generally grip the bat at the very end, their theory being that the greater length of a bat gripped in this way gives them added leverage.

The medium-choke style is used by men who desire a greater degree of bat control and who are primarily line drive hitters. Some end grippers also switch to it after the pitcher gets two strikes on them.

Choke hitters hold the bat as much as six inches from the end and by so doing achieve a greater degree of bat control. They are usually

*(Note knuckles-on-down alignment)*

| *End grip* | *Modified grip* | *Choke grip* |

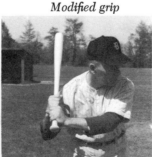

place hitters who merely try to get a piece of the ball and, as a rule, are the most difficult ones to strike out.

A few hitters grip the bat with their hands apart. Ty Cobb and Honus Wagner spread their hands on the bat. This method provides good bat control and is conducive to a level swing. In fact, some hitters who employ a conventional grip resort to the hands-apart method during spring training and retain it until satisfied that their swings are level enough to attain good results.

**Holding the Bat.** Although differences exist between ballplayers in the position of their hands relative to the end of the bat, there is great uniformity in the grip itself.

The bat should be held forward in the hands; that is, it should be gripped primarily by the fingers—not seated well back in the palms. This will provide better "feel," which provides greater responsiveness and quicker reactions to a pitched ball. The fingers of the front hand should be in control as the swing is started, ready to pull the bat through its arc of forward motion.

Establishing contact with a rapidly moving pitched ball and reversing its direction with any degree of authority requires great force of resistance on the part of the bat, and this, in turn, demands a firm grip. Although the initial grip should be firm, it should not be so tight as to cause a tension that will impair proper coordination and a fluid swing. It is as the hitting stroke begins that the grip should tighten, reaching a point at which it is very firm at the moment of impact with the ball.

**Avoiding Tension.** If too tense while awaiting the pitch, the batter will lose coordination, and his hitting will suffer. Furthermore, there will be a marked increase in his tendency to go for bad balls. As stated above, a prematurely tight grip on the bat causes increased tension. For this reason the batter should open and close his top hand before the pitcher delivers the ball, assuring himself of a loose initial grip and an attendant reduction in tension.

**Checking the Swing.** A perplexing problem for a ballplayer is how to check his swing completely once it has been started. The need for this arises when the batsman decides that the pitch is not to his liking or has fooled him, and the maneuver can be quite difficult to accomplish. John Mize recommends extra pressure applied by the top hand as a great boon to checking a swing that has already been started. Mize's exceptional ability to wait for his pitch can attest to the effectiveness of the method that he suggests.

**The Proper Grip.** Most professionals employ the *knuckles-on-down* grip in holding the bat, and its use is strongly recommended for two important reasons: first, it automatically cocks the wrists, and relaxes the hands; second, it assures the proper rolling of the wrists that provides a fluid, whip-like swing and a good follow-through. As a matter of fact, a batter will find it virtually impossible to swing without a proper roll of his wrists and good follow-through if he uses this grip. The term knuckles-on-down means that the knuckles are aligned in such a way that they form a straight line, the second and third knuckles being so aligned that the backs of the two hands come together to form a flat surface. Both bat control and power are improved when this method is employed.

**Cocking the Wrists.** We will say more later concerning the importance of cocking the wrists. At this point it is sufficient to state that the wrists should be cocked in readiness for the pitch. This is imperative if no motion is to be lost in starting the swing and whipping the bat into the ball.

**The Hands.** The hands should, of course, be well away from the body during the swing so that it will not be choked but will have the necessary degree of freedom and fluidity. While awaiting the pitch, however, batters can display a wide variety of styles with equally good results. Stan Musial, for example, held his hands more than a foot from his body; Ted Williams held his quite close.

The young ballplayer would be well advised to hold his hands fairly close to his body, with the bat pointing back over his shoulder and fairly erect (possibly even perpendicular to the ground). These practices give the batter quicker hands and better bat control since the arc of the swing will be smaller. Above all, the bat should not be "wound around the neck."

Good hitters almost invariably have "quiet hands"; that is, regardless of their preliminary motions and body movements, the batter holds his hands as still as possible just before the start of the hitting stroke and until the swing is actually begun. By observing this policy the hitter will experience little of the lost motion that delays the hitting actions and none of the countermovements that disrupt the fluidity of the swing.

### The Stance

It has often been rightfully said that a ballplayer hits with his legs. This maxim is usually meant to imply that a man's batting ability is generally no better than the condition of his legs—and they must be in shape if he is to perform at his best with the bat.

This idea should include the batter's stance—the position of his feet and the distribution of his weight thereon as he faces the pitcher. Any flaw or imbalance in the batsman's initial stance, no matter how slight, is progressively magnified through the successive steps of his pattern of action as he swings at the ball and can seriously impede his attempts to hit with effectiveness and power. For this reason the batter should give serious consideration to his stance and should make every effort to follow the principles that will make it a well-balanced one, conducive to good and efficient form.

**The Main Essential.** Two words constitute the key to the best stance for any ballplayer. They are "be comfortable." A wide variety of stances can be found among the game's better hitters; yet they all have something in common. Although they allow for individual differences in physique and mechanical ability, the stances adopted by good hitters are ones that ensure good balance and permit a feeling of comfort and ease at the plate. Unless he is successful with it (and this is rare), a batter should discard any stance with which he does not feel completely comfortable. For the best results at bat, a ballplayer should prepare for the pitch by assuming a stance that will make him physically relaxed, yet mentally alert.

**The Three Types.** There are three basic types of stance used by ballplayers, which have little effect on their other batting characteristics—the open, the normal, and the closed stance.

The open stance is one in which the batter's rear foot is closer to the plate than his front foot. He takes a stance almost facing the pitcher, which enables him to get a better look at the ball. The open-stance hitter has a decided tendency to meet the ball well out in front of the plate and is usually particularly strong on inside pitches.

The so-called normal stance is one in which the batter's feet are in an almost parallel line, with his front hip and shoulder facing the pitcher. The majority of major leaguers use a normal stance.

The closed stance is one in which the front foot is closer to the plate than the rear one. In this case the batter must watch the pitcher by looking over his front shoulder.

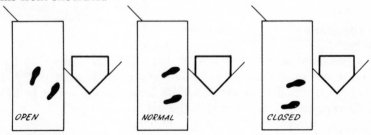

OPEN            NORMAL            CLOSED

**Vision and the Stance.** Regardless of the stance a batter finds most to his liking, it should be one that affords him a maximum view of the pitcher. Thus, it can prove helpful to alter the stance according to whether the pitcher is right- or left-handed. A left-handed batter may open his stance slightly when facing a left-handed pitcher and close it when opposed by a right-hander. Likewise, a right-handed batter may find that his vision is sharper when he opens his stance against a right-handed pitcher and closes it slightly when a southpaw is on the mound.

**Position in the Batter's Box.** Position in the batter's box has two facets —distance from the plate, which is determined primarily by personal preference; and position behind, even with, or in front of the plate, which is dictated by the pitcher's characteristics as well as by the batter's preference.

The personal preference of the batter with reference to position depends primarily on whether he desires to meet the ball before it breaks, in which case he stands in front of the plate, or wishes to have more time to judge the flight of the ball, in which case he stands behind the plate.

The type of pitcher can, of course, have a strong bearing on the position that the batter takes in the box. If the pitcher is particularly fast, a hitter should probably stand as far in back of the plate as the lines of the batter's box allow. If the pitcher specializes in slow or breaking stuff, a hitter will probably be most effective if he assumes a position in front of the plate. Most good hitters stand at the rear of the batter's box on the assumption that the slight fraction of a second gained thereby will enable them to have greater success in judging the flight of the ball and meeting it solidly.

No one position in the batter's box is used by all good hitters alike, individual style and preference being the chief determinant. They run to wide extremes, ranging from that of the great Rogers Hornsby, who stood at the outside rear corner of the box, as far from the plate as possible, and stepped into the ball, to that of the former National League star Rube Bressler, who stood well in front of the plate, with his rear foot on the inside line of the batter's box, and met the ball in a flat-footed manner with practically no stride.

However, the batter should usually stand in back of the plate and far enough away from it that the fat part of the bat is directly over the middle of the plate. This will enable him to get "good wood" on an inside pitch simply by shifting slightly, while allowing him to protect the outside corner by stepping into the ball. He should never have to *reach for a strike*. Guarding the plate in this manner is advocated because the batter should be able to hit with the fat part of his bat all pitches thrown over any part of the plate and should be able to do so with a natural and completely unhampered swing.

**The Importance of Balance.** As the batter assumes his stance in readiness to hit, with his attention focused on the pitcher, his hips and shoulders should be level and his weight evenly distributed. The importance of good balance cannot be overestimated, and it should be maintained throughout the swing. Consistently good hitting demands an essentially level swing, and in order to achieve one, the hitting stroke must be preceded by a level stance and accompanied by good overall equilibrium. Each phase of the batter's pattern of action leads to the next, and there is a definite carryover of habits, both good and bad, from one phase to the next.

For this reason a batter should adopt a moderately wide initial stance. Most good hitters use a fairly wide spread of the feet since it permits good balance, helps maintain the hips and shoulders on a level plane, and promotes a smooth shifting of the body weight into the swing. Because it gives rise to these desirable qualities in a batter's form, it is fortunate that a moderately wide stance is almost invariably a comfortable one.

**Centering the Weight.** Ty Cobb, the smartest and possibly greatest of all ballplayers, believed that slightly more weight should be placed on the front foot than on the back one. He believed that this promotes good balance. In addition, and of almost equal importance, it greatly reduces the tendency to pull away from the curve ball. Finally, placing slightly more weight on the front foot serves as a strong deterrent to lunging, overstriding, and uppercutting.

The batter's feet should be firmly planted and relatively flat on the ground when he assumes his stance at the plate. His weight should be centered mostly on the front part of the feet, not in an exaggerated manner, but comfortably and in a way that promotes a quick, smooth stride and shifting of the weight into the swing. The importance of keeping the weight forward, on the balls of the feet, cannot be stressed too strongly. It is conducive to alertness and quick reactions and is absolutely essential to good hitting. Ted Williams, the greatest of modern hitters, has stated flatly that a man who stands on his heels when he bats has no business playing baseball.

**The Knees.** The fact that good hitters are invariably intent in purpose yet basically relaxed is a theme that recurs regularly in this study of the batting art. The batsman's intentness should start with his approach to the plate. He should keep his eyes focused on the pitcher while he is awaiting the pitch but should, at the same time, be loose—with his arms relaxed and his knees flexed. The flexure of the knees need not be pronounced, but it should definitely be present in order to prevent the tension that is so detrimental to successful hitting.

**The Arms and the Stance.** The position of the arms is an important facet of the stance. That they should not be jammed against the body has already been acknowledged. The rear elbow, in fact, should be cocked away from the body. Both arms should be flexed but fairly firm. The front arm is the guiding one, both in "pushing" the bat into hitting position and in pulling it through the batting stroke; the rear arm provides the bulk of the power. The hands should be held in a relatively high position (certainly above the waist) at all times during the initial stance so that they can be properly adjusted to the height of the pitch. This principle is based on the fact that it is easier to drop the bat in order to hit low balls than to raise it into position to hit high pitches.

**Correcting the Stance.** The important consideration in this fundamental of batting is not the stance itself, but how the batter reacts from his stance. Our discussion has advanced ideas that, put into practice, will lead to a proper reaction from the stance. If, after adopting these principles, a batter finds that he cannot hit certain pitches, an adjustment is necessary. The corrective measures that may be needed can be determined by surveying the results achieved by the batting style employed. Observation and advice by an experienced coach or ballplayer is the best source of help for the batter who needs assistance; yet in the absence of such help he can often take the proper steps himself. If, for example, the batter finds that he is "getting around" too far ahead of the ball, he can rectify the situation by closing his stance. If he is not "getting around" on the ball quickly enough he can attempt to open his stance. After analysis of his trouble, experimentation will show him the amount of alteration that is needed in his stance.

There is a decided tendency among young ballplayers to overstride, pull away from the ball, and, worst of all, turn their heads and lose sight of the ball before contact is made. This often arises from having the feet too close together in the initial stance and is added reason for using a wide (but comfortable) stance at the plate.

### The Eyes

In all probability, the very first words of instruction that any youngster receives when taking up a sport are, "Keep your eye on the ball." This advice can be applied to all sports and is especially pertinent to baseball in general and batting in particular. Establishing contact between the bat and a ball thrown with great velocity and occasional changes in course and speed is difficult at best, and unless the batter concentrates with great intensity on the ball, his best efforts will go for naught—no matter how nearly perfect his form.

The ball should be picked up visually as soon as the pitcher grasps it in his throwing hand—even before his windup begins. The batter should concentrate on the ball from the time he first assumes his stance facing the pitcher, regardless of what motions he goes through before taking his swing.

An experienced pitcher will, in most cases, keep the ball well hidden until he actually releases it from his hand. Consequently, eyeing the ball during the entire windup will often prove difficult for the batter. Yet he should make an effort to do so and definitely must pick up the ball as soon as it comes into view. One method of ensuring this is to watch a square of about fifteen inches just above and to the side of the pitcher's throwing shoulder.

**The Importance of a Quiet Head.** A *quiet head* is the term used by ballplayers to describe the stillness of that part of the body that is necessary to ensure the steady, even look at the ball that is such a vital part of good hitting. The head will invariably move on a vertical plane with the stride since the stride has the effect of lowering the entire body slightly as the front foot moves ahead and the weight is shifted forward. On the horizontal plane, however, the eyes should remain fixed. At all times— while idling, on the slight twist to the rear, during the stride, with the hitting stroke, through the completion of the forward body pivot, and well into the follow-through—the head should be steady and the eyes focused intently on the ball. A familiar picture on sports pages is the one that shows an expert golfer with his eyes still fixed on the spot where the ball lay, long after it has been hit. This practice is one that ballplayers can borrow with great profit. The batter's eyes should remain fixed on the spot where ball and bat have met until he is well into his follow-through and almost ready to take off for first base. Maintaining a quiet head is the first step in effecting this good habit.

**Sighting the Ball—the Double Look.** The importance of visually picking up the ball at the earliest possible instant is quite obvious. The initial glimpse of it should come while it is still in the pitcher's hand and may be called the first (or, quick) look. Equally important to good hitting is what we shall call the second (or, long) look. This is the good look that the batter should take as the ball approaches the hitting zone. He should take it immediately after the stride and just before the hitting stroke begins. Although it must be an almost instantaneous act, it is that important glimpse of the ball during which the batter must judge its line of flight and decide on any split-second adjustment in bat elevation necessary to meet the ball solidly and with a level swing. The fleeting pause that immediately precedes the swing of the bat is of great significance to accomplished batsmen, and it is made doubly so by the opportunity it affords for the essential second look.

**Following the Ball—the Sine Qua Non.** There are some outstanding hitters who maintain that they can actually see the ball hit the bat. Whether or not this claim is literally true, it does emphasize the point that their eyes follow the ball as closely as possible during its entire flight to the plate.

Too often a batter will follow the ball as it starts toward him and then lose sight of it because he allows his stride, swing, and body pivot to cause his head to turn and his eyes to wander. Nothing can be more detrimental to good hitting. The last few feet of the ball's flight are the ones in which it curves or changes course, and it is here that the second look takes on its importance.

Thus, it seems quite logical that the batter should always follow the ball carefully from the pitcher's hand to the plate and should make a determined effort to watch the ball hit the bat. The longer the batter looks at the ball before his bat makes contact with it, the less chance there is of his being fooled by the pitch.

Good hitters go as far as to follow bad balls all the way to the catcher's glove, so highly do they esteem the principle of watching the ball during its entire flight. This practice serves a twofold purpose. It is a form of self-discipline by which a man acquires a good habit; in addition, it means that he will be prepared to hit the ball in the event that it should catch part of the plate with a last-second break or curve.

Following the pitch all the way to the bat is quite possibly the most important fundamental in the entire study of batting. No man can be a consistently good hitter unless he practices it rigorously.

## The Stride

As in most other phases of hitting, the stride varies according to the physical characteristics and the personal preference of each batter. Through experimentation every ballplayer can find the stride that will give him the most satisfactory results.

There are accomplished batsmen who take fairly long strides; there are others who use practically none—and with good results in each case. For example, two-time National League batting champion Ernie Lombardi employed a wide stance and took no stride at all; Hall-of-Fame star Mel Ott lifted his front foot in exaggerated fashion and took his stride much like a pitcher does in delivering the ball. These two extremes, however, were exceptional cases.

A player seeking the proper stride should consider the important factors of maintaining good balance and taking the stride in such a way that he feels completely natural and comfortable. It is more than mere coincidence that very few, if any, accomplished hitters use an exaggerated stride.

**Its Purpose.** When a batter strides, he is quite obviously shifting his weight into the pitch. Good hitters accomplish this in a manner that does not interfere with a smooth, level swing.

Careful analysis of successful hitting styles shows quite conclusively that the real purpose of the stride is to force the batter's weight to be centered on his rear foot and to keep it there until the hitting stroke is started. Further study demonstrates that, in order to hit with any measure of power and authority, the batter's body weight must stay behind the swing. When this practice is scrupulously followed, the needed resistance against the swinging force of the bat will have been provided.

**How It Is Done.** Our discussion thus far has indicated rather emphatically that the stride, in order to achieve its purpose effectively, must be well controlled. This quality is invariably present in the batting styles of the game's best hitters, regardless of the wide disparity found in the exact manner and length of stride used.

Although no one style is properly suited to all hitters, a batter should avoid an exaggerated stride. The ideal stride, one that is conducive to good balance, is a short one. To set an arbitrary figure, we will say that it should be anywhere from four to twelve inches in length, with virtually all hitters being able to find the stride best suited to their own needs within those limits.

The stride is made off the inside of the rear foot, and the striding foot should move into position in sliding fashion, rather than in a pronounced step. Literally sliding the foot is practically impossible because this will cause the spikes to catch in the ground. What actually should be used may be called a modified sliding step.

In order to assure the most effective shifting of the weight into the pitch, the batter's rear knee should be bent slightly, and the swing itself should be against a firm front leg.

Taking the stride in this fashion and keeping it short, with as little forward movement of the head and body as possible, means steady vision and little loss of motion. It will also allow the batter to maintain balance throughout the swing and actually enable him to adjust his timing after the pitch is on its way to the plate.

**Step to Hit.** Authorities on batting give strong emphasis to the three words that head this section. Accomplished batsmen definitely "step *to* hit," unlike the weak ones who "step *and* hit." This really means that good hitters shift their balance and body weight in the direction of the ball—stepping in on an outside pitch, stepping straight ahead on a pitch directly over the plate, and pulling slightly away from an inside pitch. It also implies that the bat is actually swung against the stride, a fact that gives purpose to the previously mentioned principle of swinging against a firm front leg.

For the inexperienced ballplayer a sound rule to follow is to step toward the pitcher to hit. This will, in most instances, assure his stepping into the ball with his full weight behind the swing. Slight adjustments can be made for inside and outside pitches, the principle to follow being the closer the pitch, the shorter the stride and the quicker the hitting actions. When experience has made him a good judge of a pitched ball, the batter can discard the generalized theory of stepping toward the pitcher and take his stride in accordance with the ball's line of flight. Until that time the more rudimentary method is a sounder practice.

**Timing the Stride.** The physical action of striding should start at the exact time that the batter sees the ball leaving the pitcher's hand. Ideally executed, it will commence no sooner than at this instant. At the same time, the batter must never wait to see where the ball is going before beginning his stride. Intricate though the element of timing involved here may sound, this exact pattern of movement is essential to hitting the ball with authority.

The double look has been described in the section entitled *The Eyes* and is closely allied to all phases of hitting, including this one. As it pertains to the stride, the double look is applied as follows: there should be a split-second wait immediately following the completion of the stride and backswing, and immediately before the hitting stroke begins. This minute pause should occur while the weight is on the rear foot. This manner of execution will help to eliminate the frequent and damaging tendency to guess at the pitch. In addition, since the level of the batter's eyes is lowered by the stride, this split-second wait gives him the second look at the pitch that allows him to make the necessary adjustment of the eyes to the line of flight of the ball.

As the step is taken with the striding foot, the weight should shift forward, with the hips, shoulders, and head remaining as nearly level as possible and the eyes concentrating directly on the ball. At the same time the hands should be moving away from the stride as it is started, putting them in good position to move forward into the swing with the shifting of the weight. Transferring the weight too soon means that arm power alone will be behind the swing, the force that can be provided by the legs and body being almost completely wasted. This tendency is quite pronounced on the curve ball and change of pace and must be guarded against on these slow pitches in particular.

One more advantage of the delayed stride is that it provides great help to the batter in learning to step into or away from the ball properly.

**Overstriding.** Probably the chief fault found in inexperienced ballplayers is the tendency to overstride. It robs a man of the advantages of a polished batting form: it lowers the arms, shoulders, and eyes; slows up the swing; robs the hitting stroke of power; and impedes the start for first base once the ball has been hit.

The batter who overstrides is easy prey for a smart pitcher, who will have little trouble in upsetting his timing. Furthermore, even when he does connect solidly, the batter will not get good results, since his power will have been dissipated in the stride rather than concentrated in the swing.

The best method of avoiding the tendency to overstride is to abide by the principle with which this section was begun—a good hitter does not use an exaggerated stride.

### Hitting Actions

The *hitting actions* are almost inseparable from the swing, and there is much overlapping between the two categories. However, a slight differentiation should be made. The hitting actions are those mechanical moves that occur between the stride and the hitting swing, serving as a connecting link between the two.

**The Preliminaries.** The techniques and maneuvers described thus far form the basis for the hitting actions. To them should be added three more ideas that give a more solid foundation to the hitting stroke in coping with certain pitches.

The batter's front shoulder should remain facing the pitcher until the swing is started. Doing so will aid the batter in hitting the curve ball and outside pitches since it serves as a deterrent to pulling away from the pitch. In addition, it will prevent the loss of power that results from getting out too far ahead of the ball (shifting the body weight too soon).

The theory behind holding the bat in a high position has already been covered. This is a means of being well prepared to handle high pitches. To make it easier for the batter to hit balls on the inside of the plate, he should exercise a quick turn of the hips slightly before the swing.

**The Backswing.** Even before the bat is moved back into hitting position, the wrists should be cocked. This is one of the most essential fundamentals in the art of hitting. By cocking his wrists the batter is actually getting ready to hit. This move should be made as the pitcher prepares to deliver the ball. If the batter waits beyond this point, he will be unprepared to meet a fast pitch.

Good hitters almost literally push the bat back into hitting position. The batter's front hand and fingers must be in control as he pushes the bat back as far as possible while still permitting a feeling of comfort. The batter must not "wrap the bat around the neck," but push it back in a plane that is parallel to a line drawn from the pitcher's mound to home plate.

The hip pivot, which is of great importance, should in reality be a two-way affair. In the backswing this move is not pronounced, but in order to ensure the good pivot that leads the way into the hitting swing, the hips must pivot backward slightly. This shifts the weight to the rear foot and is the action that results in the necessary opposite reaction—the forward pivot of the hips.

The end of the backswing is the point at which the vital split-second wait (for the second look) takes place. At this stage of his batting form, the hitter should have completed the stride and should have his weight centered on his rear foot. The bat should be at a right angle to the shoulders (not parallel to them—in other words, it should remain fairly erect; its end should never be permitted to droop as far down as the shoulders themselves; and pressure should be felt on the front forearm at the end of the backswing, almost as though it were a signal to move forward into the hitting stroke.

**The Start of the Swing.** Rotary hip action is absolutely essential to a good swing: it actually starts the forward shift of the weight and the movement of the shoulders and arms. It is the key link in the chain of action extending from the start to the finish of the swing. The rotation of the hips not only starts the movement of the shoulders and "pulls" the weight into the swing properly so that the ball is met with full power, but also leads the body through the continuous flow of motion that has its ultimate conclusion in a good follow-through.

When the hitting stroke is begun, the weight, which has been centered on the rear foot (the back-pivot heel), is shifted to the entire foot so that it will be resting equally on both feet when the bat meets the ball. Batters should avoid hitting with the weight on their heels—remember Ted Williams's words on this subject.

**The Hitting Zone and Maximum Power.** The hitting zone is that area in which each batter can meet the ball with best results. The proper hitting zone in relation to the position of the hands at the moment of impact is behind the center of the body. The oft-repeated advice that the batter should meet the ball in front of the plate may lead to some confusion now that the other statement has been advanced. To clarify the matter in his mind, the reader must take into account that the stride and the rotation of the hips precede the hitting stroke in such a way that, because of the partial completion of the body pivot, the batter can meet the ball in front of the plate while his hands are still behind the center of the body.

One of the most important batting fundamentals is hitting immediately after the stride. Intentionally or not, every good hitter puts this into practice. To facilitate the performance of this essential, the batter should allow his arms to lag slightly behind his stride. When this is done, the ball will be met a slight fraction of a second after the stride—not with it. The lagging of the arms also permits adjustments in timing the pitch to be made at the last instant and enables the hitter to capitalize fully on his wrist snap for obtaining maximum power. When bat meets ball a split second after the stride, all the power generated by the shift of body weight will go into the swing and will not be wasted on the stride alone. This is another way of saying that the full power of the entire batting action should reach its peak at the exact instant of impact with the ball.

The ability to keep the wrists cocked until the hands reach the center of the body, important in imparting power to the swing, is a technique that demands a great deal of practice—so much so that it may be considered an art in itself.

In addition to remaining cocked in this manner, the wrists should be held back in the hitting zone as long as possible. The combination of these two principles helps to assure maximum power both by delaying the wrist snap so that it occurs at the moment of impact with the ball and by making the batter increase the speed of the snap in order to get around on the ball while it is still in front of the plate.

Another necessary feature of good batting form is holding back the weight until the last possible moment so that its shifting takes place at the very instant that bat meets ball. The firm front leg against which the stride is made will keep the weight from shifting too soon and, at the same time, will help prevent the head from turning before the ball is hit.

In brief, then, the secret of power hitting is for the batter to get his weight behind the swing, while delaying as long as he can before committing himself.

### The Swing

The climax in batting is quite obviously reached when bat meets ball. Our discussion of fundamentals has been aimed at helping the hitter to contact the ball with the most telling effect possible. Thus far we have endeavored to establish a sound base for the hitting stroke, or swing. Now we are ready to take up the important business of hitting the ball.

**Starting the Hitting Stroke.** At this point the hands have moved away from the body. They are in a raised position. If they have been held high in the first place, they will have to be raised less now that the swing is about to start. This eliminates waste motion and saves precious time in the sequence of rapid physical actions needed to meet a ball hurled at great speed.

The bat, which has been pushed back into hitting position, should be "pulled" forward in order to start the swing properly. This technique gives the batter "live hands," a must in adjusting quickly to the ball's line of flight and its speed. It is the forward hand that should pull the bat across the body. This method serves to delay the uncocking of the wrists far more effectively than does a swing or push-motion.

As the bat moves forward, the hands should be whipped into the swing. To help in achieving this, the batter should visualize himself swinging a rope the same length as his bat—with a weight tied to the end of it. The motion needed to swing the weighted rope is similar to the one that will best whip the bat into the oncoming pitch. In this imagined situation, the fat part of the bat is analogous to the weight at the end of the rope.

**The Level Swing.** The ideal swing is a level one in the sense that it is parallel to the ball's line of flight. This means that it is not parallel to the ground itself, since the pitcher's mound causes the ball to come down at the hitter to a slight degree. In effect, the level swing is slightly upward in its arc. The position of the hands at the start of the hitting stroke can be adjusted according to the height of the pitch so that the sweep of the bat will always be level. Then the ball can be contacted with a level bat and level wrists and with the weight evenly distributed on both feet at the moment of impact.

The hips and shoulders, which were level during the original stance and at the start of the stride, should continue so during the swing. As the bat moves out across the plate, the front arm should be held firm and should be straightening out until it is perfectly straight at the moment of impact. When the arms have reached this position, the swing is at its point of maximum power. The wrists are firm and square at this point. After the ball has been met, the roll of the wrists takes place and carries this chain of action through to its ultimate conclusion.

In order to achieve a level swing, the rear elbow should be pointed down and held fairly close to the body at the start of the hitting stroke. This refers to the right arm of a right-handed batter and the left arm of a left-hander. A study of good hitters will demonstrate conclusively that all begin the swing with the rear elbow pointed down.

Ted Williams, one of the game's great perfectionists, states: "The ideal swing is a level swing but I don't worry about this too much because, if the other fundamentals are right, the swing will be almost perfectly level. On pitches which are higher than the belt buckle, I have the feeling that I'm hitting down on the ball slightly. On pitches that are below the belt buckle, I have the feeling that I'm hitting up.

I think of it as though I were a woodsman cutting down a tree and chopping the classic 'V' in the trunk of the tree.

On the high pitches in the strike zone you seem to be hitting down and as a result you hit the ball on a line. On low pitches in the strike zone, if you think of your swing as though you were cutting up in the 'V,' the result is to hit the ball on a line.

Perhaps it would be well to enter a word of caution here. Don't try to 'golf' the low pitches (to prevent this one should bend his rear knee to swing at the ball). And, don't try to pound the high pitches down into the dirt. Just remember the woodsman's 'V.'"

**Rolling the Wrists.** The swing should come down and across the plate, leveling out before it meets the ball. The wrists are rolled immediately *after* the ball is met, ensuring a good wrist snap and the proper follow-through.

Rolling the wrists is essential to a good swing. In order to achieve the correct roll of the wrists, the bat should be held with the second and third knuckles aligned (knuckles-on-down) as described in the section on the grip. When the batter employs this method, it will be practically impossible to swing the bat without rolling the wrists.

**Meeting the Ball.** The ball should be hit well out in front of the batter and when it is in his strike zone. When a batsman does this, the ball will not always be over the plate at the point where the bat meets it. However, the ball should be contacted at a point in which its course will carry it over the plate between the knees and the shoulders. This is particularly true of a breaking ball that need pass over only one corner of the plate in order to be a strike and that may well have curved outside the strike zone by the time it has passed the plate.

The batter should not try to overpower the ball. Rather, he should concentrate on meeting it squarely. The lively baseball in use today will go for great distances when "hit on the nose," and if it is met solidly, extra-base hits will necessarily result. In fact, the home run swing is usually seen only when the batter misses the ball. It is bad in itself since overswinging makes the batter turn his head and drop his shoulder, both damaging to the batting swing.

## The Follow-through

Batting does not end with the act of hitting the ball. It must reach a more natural conclusion than the impact of bat and ball if maximum results are to be achieved. Thus, we come to the follow-through, which is the culmination of the fundamentals that pertain directly to the art of hitting a baseball.

**The Basic Principle.** As the idea of keeping one's eye on the ball, so the principle of following-through is instilled in would-be athletes from the time of their introduction to sports. It applies to every form of athletic endeavor, as well as to each phase of the various games. It is particularly important to batting, in which failure to follow through properly can almost completely nullify the good effect that has been achieved by practicing the fundamentals covered thus far.

Even a stationary object cannot be driven very far or with any appreciable degree of force and speed if the propelling implement is stopped in flight at the point of contact. If the object is a rapidly moving body that meets an implement whose contrary movement ceases after the contact, then the rapid movement of the former will be only partially checked when the two meet. Such is the case when a pitched ball is hit by a bat. Before the flight of the ball can be reversed, a very powerful resisting force must be encountered, and this force cannot be sufficiently strong unless the bat continues right on "through the ball" in its hitting arc. In a sense, the result of an incomplete swing is analogous to a ball that has been bunted rather than hit with a full sweep of the bat.

This application of physical laws gives validity to the principle that a good follow-through is absolutely essential to attaining maximum power in hitting the ball.

**Completion of the Swing.** The forward pivot of the hips has started the hitting stroke. It is a rotary motion that must be allowed to go through to its proper conclusion if good hitting is to become a matter of course. One of the things gained by a full follow-through is a complete hip pivot. At the end of his swing, the batter's rear shoulder and hip will have come around to a point at which they are facing toward the pitcher whenever the follow-through has been a good one.

A good follow-through has another important feature. The batter's rear hip and shoulder will have swung around to a point at which they

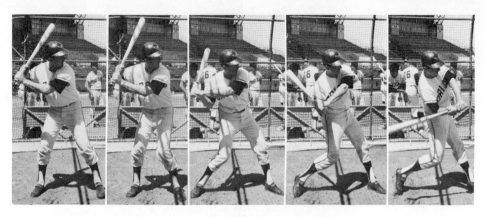

Good batting form. Note (1) Cocked wrists; bat near shoulder; hands slightly away from body and held fairly high; and even, spread stance. (2) Short, controlled stride; front shoulder in; hands held high until swing starts. (3) Hips open as hitting action starts; bat lags behind hands. (4) Ball is met as weight shifts; wrists are firm at impact; ball is hit in front of plate; bat is thrown forward; then wrists roll. (5) Above all, note that the eyes follow the ball right to the bat and remain there even after the ball is hit.

are facing the infield, and the body weight will also be leaning in the direction in which the ball has been hit, following the ball and giving it an added push, as it were.

Ideally, the bat should complete its arc of motion at a spot that coincides with the middle of the hitter's back. When the bat terminates its stroke in this position—in the middle of the back, from both a horizontal and vertical standpoint—the swing has been a fairly level one, full enough to assure the batter of his full power if he meets the ball well.

### Becoming a Base Runner

The primary concern of the batter is to hit the ball safely. Yet when he has driven it into fair territory, his responsibilities do not cease. Nor should he dismiss them with the attitude that his duties call for him simply to start running. On the contrary, the batter becomes a base runner as soon as he hits a fair ball and then must consider his actions from the viewpoint of a base runner.

The adoption of correct base-running techniques is at least as important for the trip to first base from home plate as it is in the remainder of the circuit around the bases. It is covered in detail in the section on base-running.

### Clarification

The elements of batting that have been discussed encompass the essentials and are of the utmost importance to any ballplayer who would be a better hitter. They are, moreover, so closely related that they should be thought of in their entirety—as one continuous flow of motion.

Timing, in its overall aspect, is the most important element in batting. As it pertains to the synchronization of the various phases of the batter's pattern of action, it can be an intricate process. Because an attempt has been made to break down batting form into its integral segments, some confusion may understandably have arisen. However, the reader should realize that each of these fundamental parts of hitting takes place within a fraction of a second and that there is both a strong connection between and a definite overlapping of them in their sequence.

### The Therapeutic Method

Both singly and as a continuous whole, the physical moves previously described are correct ones, practiced by major leaguers almost without exception. These mechanics comprise the most effective method of hitting a baseball well—and with consistency.

Unfortunately, not all ballplayers are able to develop the hoped-for knack of meeting the ball well, even when they make a conscientious effort to master correct techniques.

The aim of the *therapeutic method* is to eliminate those flaws most prevalent in the batting forms of men who fail to achieve their own maximum hitting effectiveness.

This method prevents the development of basic flaws by eliminating their causes. Therefore, it can be used not only as a means of therapy but also as a positive measure in teaching the art of batting—particularly to young and inexperienced players.

**The Technique.** The therapeutic method concerns itself chiefly with the position of the hands while awaiting the pitch and with the importance of rotary hip action in giving impetus to the swing.

The bat is held close to or just touching the shoulder, but with the hands away from the body. The entire pattern of action is started by a hip pivot. The body then turns smoothly, and the bat follows quite naturally in a level, compact swing. As the bat moves out over the plate, the wrists should be whipped through the ball.

The efficiency of this style arises from the elimination of extraneous movements, particularly of the hands, and the preclusion of the incorrect shifting of the body weight.

**Corrective Action.** The therapeutic effects achieved by such a swing are the—

1. elimination of hand-hitching;
2. reduction of the tendency to overstride;
3. cutting down of head movement;
4. prevention of pulling away from the ball;
5. curbing of the premature shifting of the body weight.

Positive Results. This method of batting enables a player to effect several positive achievements:

1. Meeting the ball "out in front" but with the hands behind the center of the body
2. Getting the body behind the swing
3. Promoting a good follow-through

## THE STRIKE ZONE

A constant theme of this study of the art of hitting is that the batter should offer only at good pitches and that he should make a determined attempt to hit the ball while it is in the strike zone. This insistence is motivated by the belief that no batter should help the pitcher and make that man's task any easier. Percentages definitely favor the pitcher as long as he stays ahead in the count (even the best hitters connect safely only about once in every three times at bat). For that reason the batter must avoid giving the pitcher any extra advantage. One of the principal ways in which a batsman can safeguard his own interests is to know the strike zone and realize fully its importance in the game of baseball.

### The Reasoning Behind It

A thorough understanding of the reasons for which the dimensions of the strike zone have been so defined should help all ballplayers to appreciate its significance.

The founders of the game were sound in their reasoning when they outlined the limits of the zone through which a ball must pass to be considered a strike. A ball that passes over the plate within this area is far more easy for the batter to hit than one that fails to enter it as it goes by him.

Home plate is seventeen inches wide. Any pitched ball that passes over the plate at a point above the batter's knees and below his armpits when he assumes his normal stance is considered to be a strike. The umpires interpret the strike zone to be three dimensional, and all ball players should realize this fact. It is not simply a flat-space area seventeen inches wide extending vertically from the batter's chest to his knees. It also has depth and, if extended to its extreme limits in all directions, forms a five-sided column of space that can be measured in cubic inches. It is shaped much like a pentagonal box kite.

Every cubic inch of that space is in the strike zone, and, figuratively speaking, belongs to the pitcher. In order to throw a strike, he has only to make the ball touch any part of this space. The batter must protect all parts of that solid area—top, bottom, side, front, and back.

### Ted Williams's Theory

We can place a great deal of stress on the opinions voiced by Ted Williams, for Williams was the finest hitter of the modern era and, more important to this discussion, one of the keenest students of the art of batting. His studies have been exhaustive and have been carried out with astute observation and keen insight. Although a great natural hitter, he has an approach to batting that is scientific in its method and attention to detail. Ted Williams's theory on the significance of the strike zone is well worth passing along. To paraphrase his exact words: Get a good ball to hit. In order to pick out a good ball to hit, you've got to learn your strike zone.

Reduced to mathematics, the zone into which the pitcher must throw the ball for a strike measures approximately 4¼ square feet (allowing seventeen inches for the width of the plate, three feet for the distance from the batter's knees to his armpits).

If the hitter develops the habit of swinging at balls that are only two inches above, below, outside, or inside his normal strike zone, he enlarges the target that the pitcher must hit by two inches all around. Instead of a 4¼ square-foot target, the pitcher now has one of almost six square feet at which to shoot—an increase of 37 percent in target size. Give a good pitcher an advantage like that, and he'll make a monkey out of you.

Master your *own* strike zone. It's something you've got to keep working at, and it's the one advantage you have that keeps the pitcher "honest." He has to get the ball into your strike zone, or he's going to give you a base on balls.

### Knowing the Strike Zone

Rogers Hornsby is considered by most baseball men to have been the greatest of all right-handed batters. His theory regarding his art was brief and to the point: "The secret of good hitting is hitting only good balls."

This is probably an oversimplification, but it does give weight to the importance of knowing the strike zone and selecting a good pitch to hit.

A batter who offers at bad balls is only helping the pitcher. Many smart moundsmen operate on the theory that the simplest way to retire the hitter is to make him go for bad balls. The batter who does so is actually falling into a trap.

In the case of pitchers who are wild, swinging at a bad ball eliminates the advantage that can be gained from their lack of control. A base on balls not only provides the offensive team with a base runner but also often harms the pitcher's confidence in his control and makes him throw "fat" pitches that greatly simplify the batter's task.

Experience and practice are the best teachers for a batter endeavoring to learn his strike zone. One concrete method of acquiring this knowledge is to stand at the "strings" (see the section on drills) when a pitcher is throwing at them. In the absence of strings, an ambitious batter can take a position "at the plate" while the pitcher is warming up and have the catcher serve as an umpire, calling balls and strikes. The batter should not swing at the ball but simply stand in his normal hitting position, giving him excellent practice in judging a pitched ball.

One qualification is needed. A batter should know his own strike zone —some strikes are not in his strike zone. Only when he has two strikes on him must he swing at any strike.

Perhaps the main cause of swinging at bad balls is tension on the part of the batter. The overanxious hitter is a source of comfort to a smart pitcher. When he finds himself in this state, the batter can help to alleviate the situation by stepping out of the batter's box and taking more time in getting ready to hit. He should bear in mind that if patient but always prepared for it, he will get "his pitch" in three out of four times at bat.

## POWER

Every ballplayer has the yearning to be a power hitter, the big man in his team's attack, the slugger who can clear the bases with one mighty swing of his bat. Unfortunately, nature has endowed very few with the ability to deliver the long ball with any great degree of consistency. That too few players realize this fact is also unfortunate because, in their desire to wield the big stick, they attempt to knock the cover off the ball and thereby sacrifice base hits—and power.

This is not meant to discourage aspiring ballplayers by giving them the impression that only a Henry Aaron can hit the long ball. A look at major league home run statistics will dispel this belief. What it is intended to convey is the idea that each man should realize his own capabilities and limitations and handle himself accordingly. Aaron has great natural power, but he knows that swinging too hard will impair his hitting; consequently, he goes intentionally for the long ball only upon occasion. The average ballplayer should do likewise, contenting himself with good overall hitting performance and the occasional long ball that will come quite naturally to the man who meets the ball well.

### The Lively Ball

The jack-rabbit baseball in use today has actually been a detriment to hitting. The fact that even weak hitters can pound the ball out of the park has given all of them the urge to be home run sluggers. As a result home run production has increased, but batting consistency has declined sharply. In their attempts to overpower the ball, present-day hitters are robbing themselves of both good timing and a smooth, level swing.

Today's ball may not differ in specifications from the one that has been in use for the last thirty years. However, improvements in the manufacturing process have unquestionably added to its resiliency. Furthermore, bats seem to be greatly improved in quality and driving power. This combination has placed an emphasis on the long ball and made it much more common in the modern game.

The most important fact that batters should realize is that they need not overpower the ball to hit for distance. Stan Musial, for example, met the ball with a smooth, rhythmical swing. He did not try to tear the cover off of it. As a result Musial hit for consistently high averages and, at the same time, amassed a goodly share of extra-base blows.

The lively ball will definitely go for greater distances when "hit on the nose." If the batter simply concentrates on meeting the ball squarely, the extra-base hits will follow, and his batting average should show a definite improvement.

### Providing Power

The premise has been advanced that meeting the ball well is the main causative factor in achieving power with the bat. This statement is, to all intents and purposes, irrefutable. For a fuller appreciation of the techniques by which the desired result is attained, however, further investigation and a more detailed breakdown are required.

Although meeting the ball squarely should be a batter's primary goal, that alone is not sufficient to give him maximum power. The speed with which the bat is brought forward is at least the second most important element in hitting for distance. This is, in reality, another way of saying that maximum driving power is brought about by quick action of the arms and hips and is dependent upon rapid acceleration of the swing of the bat at the moment of impact.

The batter's body balance is too often upset by a hard, forceful swing. This means that poor timing results from most attempts to overpower the ball. The vast majority of good hitters use a moderately hard swing, one that is smooth and basically level and that features good, quick wrist action. They believe in letting the bat do some of the work and try to achieve the feeling of having put about 90 percent of the shoulder and arm strength and a full 100 percent of the wrist strength into the hitting stroke. The addition of the follow-through and body-lean, which should ensue, will place the entire weight behind the swing.

All this signifies that the correct adaptation of the fundamentals discussed heretofore and the use of a slight degree of moderation in their application will enable any ballplayer to hit with the power that will most closely approach his own potential.

## Hitting Line Drives

The line drive is the best kind of hit. The hitter who can deliver this type of blow consistently is the one most feared by pitchers. Although many home runs have considerable loft, the big sluggers are primarily line drive hitters. Their solid liners most frequently produce base hits, and their especially well-hit balls have sufficient carry to clear the fences.

When the ball is hit solidly (that is, contacted in its center by the fat part of the bat) with a level swing and good follow-through, the result will be a low-trajectory ball (line drive).

Ty Cobb, in discussing batting in general and the desirability of hitting line drives in particular, said, "Don't slug at full speed; learn to meet them firmly and you will be surprised at the results."

What Cobb was saying is that rapping out line drives greatly increases the chances of hitting safely and that the best way to do this is to concentrate on meeting the ball squarely.

## Timing and Power

No matter how far or in what direction this book leads, it seems impossible to get away from the element of timing. Every fundamental of batting involves it and, at the same time, is dependent upon it. Certainly power hitting depends almost entirely upon it. The various techniques suggested as aids to the batter have, as their ultimate purpose, the improvement of his timing. On those occasions when it approaches the point of perfection, batting power follows almost naturally.

Good timing comes through practice and with experience. A discussion of the ingredients that contribute to it alludes to almost all the fundamentals discussed thus far. For example, in order to synchronize the wrist snap and the shift of body weight with requisite precision, the wrists should remain cocked until the hands reach the center of the body as the bat is brought forward in its hitting arc.

In a well-timed swing the bat meets the ball in front of the plate as the weight is transferred to the front foot. The hitting swing reaches its zenith with the complete transfer of weight, while the wrist snap at the moment of impact can be likened to a sudden explosion of energy. To ensure good timing, the batter should observe the same hitting zone for all pitches, fast or slow. This means that an adjustment in stride and swing must be made in such a way that the point of impact will always be in the same area relative to the plate and reaffirms the importance of the principle that the batter should step *to* hit.

### Uppercutting—Pro and Con

Some hitters intentionally swing with a slight uppercut for the purpose of giving loft and carry to a batted ball. Although it is true that their method occasionally bears fruit, the fact remains that this imposes upon them a handicap of inconsistency. A pitched ball is much easier to hit solidly when the swing is level. Furthermore, the uppercut swinger will usually have trouble with anything other than a low pitch, hitting the high ones straight into the air. When this kind of hitter does drive out a high pitch with authority, it is generally because he has altered his style and has met the ball with a level swing.

Line drives are still the most desirable hit for a batter, and they are best achieved by a swing that is slightly downward, or completely level. This practice (the downswing) should be avoided on low pitches—the hitter should remember Ted Williams and his woodsman's "V" and try to meet a high pitch with a slight downswing. When this is done, the swing will be essentially level, and line drives will be the result.

### The Wrists and Power

Although the arms, shoulders, hips, and legs all give force to the swing, it is the wrist snap that produces the real driving power and propels the ball with speed and for distance.

Rolling the wrists is of paramount importance in imparting this desired snap to its fullest degree. After the ball leaves the bat, the roll of the wrists takes place as a continuation of the swing. The opposite of this is the sweep-hitter, whose stiff-armed hitting stroke does not utilize the wrists and, consequently, deprives itself of much power. A sweep-hitter swings at the ball instead of hitting at it as does the man who rolls his wrists properly, and a great difference results in both the distance of the batted ball and the speed with which it leaves the bat.

Some hitters follow through with only one hand on the bat. This leads to the conclusion that batting power is attained primarily in the first half of the swing, receiving its greatest impetus from the wrist snap. It must be noted, however, that even batters who finish the swing with only one hand on the bat follow through properly in order to achieve maximum driving power.

### The Bat and Power

There has long been a rather widespread belief in the idea that the size of a bat, both its length and weight, has a strong bearing on the driving power of the man who wields it; the feeling is that the larger the bat, the greater the distance the ball will travel when hit.

It is true to a certain extent that a longer and heavier bat will enable a hitter to drive the ball further—depending upon his ability to control that bat. Unfortunately, it is extremely unlikely that any but the strongest batsmen can handle an extra-large bat with adequate control. Thus, the big stick frequently makes perfect timing impossible to all but a small minority of ballplayers.

Most long-ball hitters hold the bat at the very end. The extra length afforded by the end grip provides more leverage by enlarging the arc in which the bat moves, and this, of course, provides greater driving power. It also means that for every movement of the bat handle, there is proportionately greater movement of the hitting surface, making complete bat control more difficult to attain.

To gain added leverage, some outstanding hitters have resorted to tucking the little finger of the lower hand under the knob of the bat. Lou Gehrig and Jimmy Foxx were two who used this method to increase the length of their bats and gain that added leverage.

On the other hand, bat control is more essential than the size of the bat. Even Babe Ruth, although he ordinarily employed the end grip, would occasionally work his hands up the handle when the pitcher got two strikes on him. A good power hitter of recent years, Sal Bando, also uses a choke grip in which his hands are about two inches from the knob.

The trend today is definitely toward lighter bats. Present-day ballplayers seem to feel that a smaller bat, one that can be handled easily, lends itself not only to adequate bat control but also to the rapid acceleration of the swing and the forceful wrist snap that are the main contributors to power hitting.

### PULLING THE BALL

Most long-ball specialists are primarily pull hitters. There are two good reasons that this is true: First, a pull hitter meets the ball well out in front of the plate, driving his bat forward very rapidly and with a pronounced wrist snap in order to do so. In so doing he has performed two of the essentials that promote power hitting.

Second, the physical construction of ballparks is such that the fences close to the foul lines are generally far shorter than they are in center field and its bordering areas. Although the straightaway hitter keeps the defenses spread, allowing a greater number of base hits to fall safely, many of his hardest blows can be caught and merely go for long outs.

If he hopes to clear the fences for home runs, the batter will obviously have much greater chances of success when he pulls the ball. As a consequence young ballplayers who give evidence of developing good power are both encouraged and taught to pull the ball.

### Basic Theory

Most ballplayers are natural opposite-field hitters. This characteristic stems from an innate fear of the ball and the resultant instinctive urge for self-protection. Following this line of reasoning, a youngster will step into a slow pitch and is likely to pull the bat. Fast deliveries, however, bring out his self-protective instincts and tend to make him look for the ball before he even thinks of swinging at it. Therefore, his batting stroke is a more or less defensive gesture and, combined with the delay in his actions, will cause him to hit to the opposite field, if at all.

### Acquiring the Knack

The problem, then, is learning how to pull the ball. Some young ballplayers, through experience and the growth of confidence that often follows, develop the ability to pull the ball without specialized coaching. Others must work hard at it. Practice and experience provide the first steps in overcoming fear of the ball and gaining confidence. A player simply cannot get too much of them. In addition, other more mechanical means can be employed to help a man acquire the knack of pulling the ball.

All hitters are more likely to pull an inside pitch than one on the outside of the plate. For that reason a man who has difficulty in pulling the ball should stand close to the plate, thereby making almost any ball in the strike zone an inside pitch. As a matter of fact, a batter should never have to reach for a strike in order to hit it, whether or not he desires to pull the ball.

An open stance is another device that facilitates pulling the ball. Open-stance batters are almost invariably pull hitters because they naturally meet the ball well in front of the plate. Furthermore, they are usually low-ball hitters who particularly like inside pitching. Would-be pull hitters should likewise develop a preference for low and inside pitching.

Additional measures that can be of help are a slight bending at the waist—but not at the knees—and the use of the knuckles-on-down grip, which both speeds the wrist snap and increases its strength.

A definite pull hitter will drive a wide pitch through the box and will often have trouble keeping an inside one in fair territory. In batting practice, during which the pitching is not so fast as it is in game competition, the batter should almost invariably pull inside pitches foul. By game time, then, the batter's well-hit drives should travel to the desired field.

## ADVANCING THE RUNNER

Theoretically, every ball should be hit where it is pitched. There are times, however, when it is desirable to place-hit to a general area so as to increase greatly the chances of advancing the runner to scoring position. In practically all cases this involves hitting the ball to right field, and it takes two forms: the hit-and-run, in which it is imperative to hit the ball; and hitting behind the runner, in which case the element of compulsion is eliminated, though the ball should be driven toward right field if it is hit.

### The Hit-and-Run

The hit-and-run is a do-or-die type of play. In it, the runner takes off for second base with the pitcher's initial motion toward home plate, just as he does on a steal. The batter must hit the ball in order to protect the runner and should try to hit toward right field so as to improve the runner's chances of reaching scoring position safely.

**Why and When It Is Used.** Probably the primary objective of the hit-and-run as it is practiced in professional baseball is to decrease the possibility of a double play. The idea behind this practice is that a ball hit between the first and second basemen is more difficult to turn into a double play because of the long and usually awkward throw involved in retiring the lead runner. That the runner is well on his way to second base when the ball is fielded is possibly an even more important consideration. Furthermore, if the ball goes through to the outfield, the runner will more than likely be able to advance to third base with little trouble.

The hit-and-run is mainly for right-handed batters, since a left-hander usually hits toward right field and is more difficult to double at first because of the better start he gets after hitting the ball.

Occasionally it is best to hit toward the shortstop position. Naturally, this is dependent on who will cover second base. To determine this beforehand, the batter should notice the positions of the shortstop and second baseman relative to the bag. The man who is playing closer to it will almost invariably cover the base. Another and even surer method of determining this is for the batter to take a pitch and have the runner bluff a steal of second. The man who is to cover will usually fall into the trap and start for the base.

It takes an accomplished batsman to execute the hit-and-run in theoretically correct fashion. For that reason an inexperienced batter should simply hit away, the important consideration being the prevention of a double play.

The play should not be used by a long-ball hitter, who stands a good chance of moving the runner into scoring position whenever he meets the ball well. The hit-and-run is also a poor maneuver to use with a runner on second or third because he is already in scoring position. Furthermore, in order to keep the opposition from setting its defenses for the hit-and-run, it should not be overused.

Protection of the runner being of vital importance, there will be times when the hitter should throw his bat at the ball in order to safeguard the man on base. When the defensive team is prepared for the hit-and-run, for instance, they will often resort to a pitch-out in order to upset the play. If this occurs, the batter must endeavor to protect the runner at all costs.

When the hit-and-run is on, most batters should usually try only to meet the ball and hit it on the ground. With a two-ball, no-strike count the batter should definitely hit away since the pitcher is in the hole and will often come in with a "fat" pitch.

**How It Is Done.** The points above should not discourage the average ballplayer from acquiring the knack of hitting to right. It is a skill that can be of tremendous value to both a player and his team and is worthwhile mastering.

Obviously, much practice is needed to become adept at it. Hall-of-Fame member Luke Appling, a two-time American League batting champion, was one of the game's great hit-and-run men. Accomplished as he was, Appling never ceased working to perfect his artistry. In batting practice he would have the catcher call out at irregular intervals, "There he goes," after the pitch was on its way to the plate and would then attempt to hit the ball to right field no matter where it was pitched. A ballplayer need not go quite as far, but he should regularly practice driving the ball to right field if he desires to become an effective hit-and-run man.

There are several methods by which a right-handed batter can hit to right field. All should be tried until the proper one is found. Thereafter, that particular way should be practiced to the point of perfection. These various techniques can be summarized as follows:

1. Align the *third* knuckles: This prevents a complete roll of the wrists and makes pulling the ball very difficult.

2. Spread the hands: This should not be done so noticeably that it tips off the opposition as to the batter's intentions. Spreading the hands facilitates a push-type swing that almost naturally will send the ball to right field.

3. Move the right foot back several inches, and stride toward right field: For purposes of masking his intentions, the batter should move his right foot as the pitcher is about to release the ball, not any sooner. This method permits a relatively normal swing that more or less aims the ball toward right field, the direction in which the body weight will be moving.

4. Keep the hands ahead of the bat on the swing: This is actually a relatively safe method of swinging late. Because of the position of the bat behind the hands, the ball cannot be pulled but will be hit behind the plate, which (combined with the angle of the bat when it meets the ball) will cause it to go toward the opposite field.

5. Keep the right elbow close to the body on the swing: This is another method of meeting the ball with the hands ahead of the bat, thereby bringing it into the pitch late and causing it to go toward the opposite field.

Any one of these techniques can help the batter to accomplish his purpose.

These tactics should occasionally be varied if the defensive team gives a good indication of who will cover second base. At times a batter should hit toward the shortstop position, particularly with a left-hander at bat, in which case the shortstop is most likely to cover the base. A left-hander can use any of the enumerated methods to hit to the opposite field when the opposition indicates that the shortstop will cover second base on the hit-and-run.

**Two Variations.** The bunt-and-run and the run-and-hit are two variations on the hit-and-run theme; they do not alter the original to a great extent and can prove of value to a player seeking to advance a teammate to scoring position with less risk than is involved in the hit-and-run.

1. *The Bunt-and-Run:* This is a version of the sacrifice in which the runner does not wait until the ball is on the ground before starting for second base. As on the hit-and-run, he breaks with the pitch, and the batter must meet the ball in order to afford him the necessary protection. In this case, however, the batter will bunt the ball rather than hit it with

a full swing. The bunt should go toward third base. When the third base-man comes in to field the ball, he leaves his base unprotected. Thus, if the runner has succeeded in getting a good jump on the ball, he will probably be able to reach third.

An alert shortstop can upset this play by covering third base. Outside of the major leagues, however, there are very few shortstops who are able to anticipate it. Furthermore, the play is made to order for a left-handed batter since the shortstop will almost invariably cover second base with a lefty at bat, leaving third wide open when the third baseman fields the bunt.

Whether or not the bunt draws in the third baseman, this play stands a better chance in the matter of protecting the runner, for the batter will have less trouble in bunting the ball than in hitting it with a full swing.

2. *The Run-and-Hit*: This is a play in which the runner breaks for second with the pitch and the batter swings at the ball at his own discretion. It is most effective when attempted with a 3-1 or 3-2 count. In this way the batter swings at a strike in order to protect the runner (and himself on 3-2) but passes up this pitch if it is a ball since this gives him a base on balls and allows the runner to advance automatically. It is attempted quite often with fewer than two out and almost invariably with two out, in which case it is a perfectly natural maneuver.

### Hitting Behind the Runner

This play differs from the hit-and-run because only the batter is concerned with the actual execution. Then, too, no element of compulsion is present. What is implicit here is the desirability, at certain times, of driving the ball toward right field with men on base.

The object is to advance the runner to second base by hitting the ball on the ground toward the opening between first and second, this gap being larger than usual with the first baseman holding the runner close to the base. When the ball is hit in the desired direction, the second baseman will in most cases have to field it, going to his left to do so. This means that a double play will be very difficult to effect. If hit hard, many of these balls roll through to the outfield for base hits, allowing the runner to reach third with little trouble.

This play is strictly a no-out maneuver. It is generally attempted only with a man on first base. It is, however, a good move with a runner on second base since it can move him to third, from where (with one out) he will have at least two opportunities to score. Even with runners on both first and second, the use of this play can be justified since as mentioned, a double play is unlikely on a ball hit to the second baseman's left. Then, with men now on first and third, the first baseman will probably play on the base with the runner, and of course the man on third will be easier to bring home than he was when on second base.

The batter is not compelled to swing at any particular ball and can, in fact, wait for an outside pitch, which is more easily hit toward right field. He should, however, hit away with a count of two balls and no strikes, when the pitcher is likely to come in with a fat pitch, or when he has two strikes charged against him and must guard the plate.

The batter should be concerned mainly with just meeting the ball, preferably by bringing his arms down so as to increase his chance of hitting the ball on the ground.

Any of the methods described under the hit-and-run can serve the batter's purpose in hitting behind the runner. The nearer to the plate the batter makes his hitting zone (that is, not out in front as it ordinarily is), the easier it will be for him to place the ball toward right field.

## BATTING FAULTS AND THEIR REMEDIES

Every ballplayer should have a twofold batting goal. He should strive to hit as well as his physical capabilities allow, and he should try to avoid slumps. The former can be achieved; the latter is a more difficult task.

### Slumps

Even the best of hitters fall into occasional batting slumps, which are usually of a temporary nature. They seem to be inevitable and are generally caused by unknowingly acquiring one or more bad habits. When in the throes of a slump, the smart ballplayer will turn to a coach or teammate for assistance. This disinterested observer can often detect a fault that has inexplicably arisen to impair the batter's best efforts. In most cases the batter is completely unaware of its existence and is conscious only of the fact that something is causing a flaw in his hitting. Once discovered, the underlying cause of a slump can be eliminated by applying the proper therapy.

The psychological effects of a slump often prove more damaging than the causative fault itself. A batter beset by such a lapse should realize that discouragement in the face of it can be his worst stumbling block and that he should, at all times, keep swinging naturally with the assurance that sooner or later the base hits will start dropping in for him.

More specifically, when his batting suffers a temporary decline, a

*A good method of breaking a slump—use the compact inside-out swing and try to hit to the opposite field*

ballplayer should observe three "don'ts": don't keep the bat on your shoulder; don't lean with the pitch; and don't swing at the pitcher's motion rather than at the ball itself. Furthermore, and probably even more important, the batter should try to hit every ball back at the pitcher until he starts to meet them well once more. He will not actually accomplish this, but merely trying to do so will make him follow the ball closely and will help him to meet it solidly. In fact, the amateur ballplayer would be well advised to go as far as to try to hit to the opposite field, this entails a push-type swing that provides greater bat control and, most importantly, it automatically ensures that he will keep his eye on the ball, thus eliminating the most damaging of all batting flaws.

### Basic Faults

The bad habits that cause occasional slumps are the same common faults that keep some ballplayers from achieving maximum results from their natural hitting ability.

As a general rule men who are poor hitters should make an extra effort to follow the ball closely and to avoid swinging at bad balls. They should also concentrate on learning to meet the curve ball squarely and, all else failing, may try hitting to the opposite field until they are watching the ball closely and meeting it well.

The most common, definable batting faults are listed below with suggested remedies for rectifying them:

**Overstriding.** This is one of the most prevalent and damaging of bad habits. The batter who overstrides loses balance, wastes power, and will have serious difficulty in adjusting his timing to pitches of varying speeds. The best remedy for this fault is to widen the stance, put more weight on the front foot, and concentrate on starting the swing with a hip pivot.

**Lunging.** Lunging at the ball is a common fault that seems to be a natural move on the part of some hitters. It is an exaggerated form of overstriding in which the body weight shifts suddenly and awkwardly, rather than smoothly and with equilibrium. It can be eliminated to a considerable extent by employing a slight inward (to the rear) turn of the body as the pitcher is about to release the ball. This is especially applicable to slow and breaking pitches, on which the tendency to lunge is at its height.

**Foot-in-the-Bucket.** Fear of the ball is probably the main contributing factor to the habit of pulling away from the pitch. The best suggestion that can be offered to overcome it is for the batter to step toward the pitcher to hit. If it persists, the foot-in-the-bucket fault can be compensated for to some degree by the batter's shifting his weight to the front foot with his stride, thereby getting the full weight of his body into the swing by means of his hip pivot.

**Hitching.** A hitch in the swing is caused by a movement of the hands, arms, or both just as the pitcher is releasing the ball. It not only hampers a smooth swing but also makes it difficult for the batter to get his bat around on fast pitches. The important asset of "quiet hands" is missing here. Holding the bat so that it barely touches the outer part of the shoulder will lessen the inclination to hitch. Some form of hitch is present in the styles of all hitters—good and bad. The damaging one is that in which the hands are dropped. The harmless one is that in which they are pushed back into hitting position. Thus, concentration on the latter form is another boon to eliminating a bad hitch.

**Lifting the Rear Foot.** Lifting the rear foot upsets balance and both delays and upsets the smooth shifting of the weight into the pitch. This fault can be eliminated by placing more weight on the rear foot.

**Uppercutting.** Long-ball hitters often uppercut intentionally, hoping to give the ball added loft and distance. This is, however, a bad practice when it reaches the point of becoming a habit. The uppercutter is strictly a low-ball hitter and can be expected to hit high pitching straight up.

The first thing that an uppercut swinger should do to overcome this fault is to widen his stance, giving him better balance and more even distribution of his weight. He should also open his stance. This will shift the center of his body weight forward, greatly reducing the tendency to uppercut.

Employing the knuckles-on-down grip not only facilitates a proper rolling of the wrists and follow-through but also, in the case of the uppercutter, helps him achieve a more level swing.

A good drill for correcting the tendency to uppercut is to have a player take practice swings with his rear knee on the ground. Also, he should be reminded to keep the fat part of the bat above his hands.

Carrying the hips and shoulders on a level plane and placing more weight on the front foot are additional aids in eliminating the uppercut swing. Furthermore, a conscious effort to complete the follow-through with the bat in the middle of the back is an aid to achieving a level swing.

**Chopping.** Chopping is the direct counterpart to uppercutting. Although it is less natural as a movement and, therefore, less prevalent in practice, it is equally damaging to good hitting. To overcome this habit, the batter should raise his front shoulder until it is level with the rear one and should place more weight on his rear foot.

**Overpulling the Ball.** If the batter pulls virtually every pitch into foul territory, he is hitting with the stride. This causes a serious loss of power. It can be remedied by closing the stance and by consciously observing the slight pause at the end of the backswing and stride. Additional help may be provided by employing the slight inward body twist that has been suggested previously and by taking care to delay the uncocking of the wrists until the swing reaches the center of the body.

**Getting Around Too Late.** The batter who consistently swings late is quite possibly the victim of hand-hitching. Other factors, such as slow reflexes or faulty position, can enter the picture. As a general rule this handicap can be alleviated by opening the stance and by having the bat well back, in position to hit—with the wrists cocked—as the pitcher goes into his motion.

The open stance may lead to an almost natural instinct to pull away from the ball (especially among young ballplayers). To offset this possibility while still assuring a more rapid opening of the hips, the batter should employ the simple device of toeing-in with the rear foot.

**Head-Turning.** The eyes should remain fixed on the ball until it is met by the bat. When the batter turns his head too soon, he loses sight of the ball and will have difficulty in meeting it solidly, if at all.

This is probably the most damaging habit that a batter can acquire. To overcome it, he should have his front shoulder facing the pitcher until the ball is well on its way to the plate; he should "keep his chin behind the ball"; and he should practice place-hitting (or, hitting the ball where it is pitched) or, better yet, try going to the opposite field.

**Sweeping the Bat.** A batter who swings in a sweeping motion gets no benefit from a wrist snap and will look very bad against tight pitches. This type of batter can overcome his fault by the full utilization of his wrists. To achieve this, he should align his second and third knuckles (the knuckles-on-down grip), should be sure that his wrists are cocked before the pitch, and should make a determined effort to roll his wrists on his swing. Carrying the bat in a high position also seems to have good effect in curbing the habit of sweeping the bat.

**Change-Up Trouble.** This affliction can be described as an inability to hit the change of pace. The change-up is most bothersome to a batter who overstrides or lunges. Thus, in order to be better prepared to hit it, he should employ a slight inward turn of the hips as the pitcher is releasing the ball.

As a further aid in overcoming difficulty in hitting the change of pace, the batter should try to hit to the opposite field, and above all he should simply try to meet the ball rather than attempt to overpower it.

**Curve Ball Trouble.** The best method of overcoming difficulty in hitting the curve ball is to follow the pitch closely right to the bat and try to hit the ball with the rotation.

This topic is discussed in detail in a later section entitled "Hitting the Curve Ball."

## BUNTING

The present-day trend toward emphasis on the long ball and the big inning has caused the art of bunting to be sadly neglected. Even experienced professionals are, in a great many cases, mediocre or poor bunters. In their defense it can be said that the lively ball and highly resilient bats make it difficult to lay down a good bunt—particularly when the opposing team expects it and the pitcher throws almost nothing but high fast balls while the first and third basemen charge the plate. However, this does not alter the fact that practice is the best means of attaining proficiency in the ability to bunt.

### The Sacrifice

The first principle to be observed in the proper execution of the sacrifice bunt is that the word *sacrifice* should be taken literally—the batter should give himself up.

As the pitcher is about to deliver the ball, the batter swings around by stepping forward with his rear foot; he should be facing the pitcher with feet squared and his body bent slightly at the waist and knees. He should be certain to move the front foot slightly to the outside so that the rear foot will not be out of the batter's box when the ball is bunted. When this play is in order, it is more important to get the ball on the ground than to disguise the bunt.

The sacrifice is best executed when the batter's weight is on the balls of his feet and slightly forward. While swinging around into the squared-away position, he should *push* the bat forward until it is well out in front of the body, with the arms fully extended. The batter should await the pitch with his bat held stationary *immediately below the shoulders.* By carrying his bat at the upper level of the strike zone, the batter will automatically know which pitches to pass up and which ones to bunt. A high ball is difficult to bunt well, and any pitch that comes toward the batter above his bat should be allowed to pass—it will be a ball. A pitch below his bat is the one to bunt since it will be pushed downward into the dirt by the batter's effort to contact it.

The upper hand should slide toward the fat part of the bat and should come to rest with the fingers behind the bat at a point slightly more than halfway to the end, or about even with the label. The upper hand should be loose, the other one tight, and the bat should be guided by the lower hand.

The height of the bat should, to a great extent, be adjusted by raising or lowering the body from the waist and knees—the less arm motion, the better the bunt in most instances. Furthermore, when the fat part of the bat is held slightly higher than the handle, there is much more likelihood that the ball will be bunted downward, into the ground.

The actual bunt should be performed in a manner similar to that used in catching the ball; that is, the bat should give with the pitch. In short, the ball should do the work.

*The two basic types of sacrifice bunt: square-around* (left) *and half-pivot* (right)

When the sacrifice is signalled, the batter is given the prerogative of picking his own pitch. It does not necessarily have to be a strike but should be one that is in a location that makes it buntable. When he is called upon to sacrifice, the batter should never take a strike.

The biggest hazard in executing the sacrifice is the danger of bunting the ball in the air. If the batter avoids the high pitch (at which he would have to bunt upward) and waits until the ball is on the ground before starting for first base, he will greatly lessen the possibilities of bunting a pop fly.

To succeed in his purpose of advancing the runner, the batter generally must bunt the ball close to either foul line—one that goes toward the pitcher is tailor-made for a force out at second and a possible double play.

More specifically, with a runner on first base the ball should be bunted toward first since the first baseman will be holding the bag against the runner, leaving him in relatively poor position to field the ball in time to make a force play at second.

With a man on second base or men on first and second, the bunt should go toward third. This often causes the third baseman to field the ball, leaving his base uncovered against the runner advancing from second. However, the batter must be careful to get the ball past the pitcher, forcing the third baseman to field it.

These tactics should be carried out only when the man at bat is an accomplished bunter. Because of the desirability of successfully advancing the runner, the inexpert bunter should lighten his task by bunting the ball where it is easiest for him to do so on any given pitch.

The expert can employ a different technique. He can give more consideration to masking his intentions and can afford to attempt his sacrifice without squaring around. In operation this maneuver is performed in

the following manner. With his feet remaining in normal hitting position, the batter pivots at the hips as the pitcher delivers the ball; his trunk and knees are bent moderately, and his weight is centered on his front foot; the fat end of the bat is pointed toward the pitcher; the bottom hand stays close to the waist, the top one grips the bat lightly—near the label; the bat should give with the ball as it is contacted.

This method should be attempted only after the "safe" way has been thoroughly mastered. Until that time it is more important to get the ball on the ground than to conceal one's intentions from the opposition.

### The Squeeze

The *safe squeeze* is performed in much the same manner as the sacrifice, with the batter picking his own pitch. The important thing is making the bunt a really good one on which the runner will be able to score from third.

The *suicide squeeze* involves compulsion. The runner breaks for home on a certain pitch, and the batter must bunt the ball—on the ground.

The technique for the suicide squeeze differs slightly. The batter delays his square-around move until the pitcher is about to release the ball lest the latter detect the play, change tactics, and throw an unbuntable pitch. Furthermore, the batter should square around by moving his front foot back until it is parallel with his rear foot. In this way he will slightly delay the catcher's efforts to get at the runner should the bunt be missed.

For safety purposes the suicide squeeze bunt should be aimed directly at the pitcher, and, again, the ball must be bunted on the ground.

### Bunting for a Hit

There are two principal methods of bunting for a hit—the drag and the push. The drag bunt is executed by sliding the upper hand up the bat and using the lower one for a fulcrum as the front foot is moved toward home plate and the rear foot dropped back. The bat is dropped (lowered) by the upper hand. The ball should be met behind the body and from a slightly crouched stance.

In the push bunt the arms are fully extended, and the ball is pushed toward the opposite field.

In either case the batter should do more than merely step back with his rear foot to position himself properly. He should also move his front foot toward the plate and shift his weight onto it. In addition, he should actually be running toward first base by the time the bat meets the ball.

*Drag bunt*                           *Push bunt (Bill Mazeroski)*

A right-handed batter can either push the ball toward first or drag it down the third base line, whereas a left-hander pushes a bunt toward third base and drags one in the direction of first base. A bunt aimed toward third should roll along the base line; one toward first should be directed at a spot between the first and second basemen and out of the pitcher's reach.

**Left-Handed Batter.** The drag bunt is used against a poor-fielding pitcher; against a left-hander who falls toward third on his follow-through; or against a first baseman who plays very deep. It should be a soft hit, out of the pitcher's reach, made while the batter is taking a crossover step toward first. In order to direct the ball to the right side, the top hand should roll as the ball is contacted.

The push bunt, most effective against a slow-moving pitcher and a third baseman who plays deep, is also executed while taking a crossover step toward first. The hands should be well away from the body, with the bat angled toward third base.

**Right-Handed Batter.** The same considerations apply in selecting the bunt to be used. The fat end of the bat should be pointed at the pitcher for the drag bunt, and the ball should roll close to the third base line.

A right-hander's push bunt is executed like a sacrifice except that the bat is pushed rather than allowed to give with the ball. The hands and elbows should be away from the body, with the fat part of the bat facing first base. The push bunt toward first can occasionally be worked with better chances of success when it is preceded by a fake toward third.

The push bunt is a play that (for tactical effectiveness) should not be used indiscriminately. It is for experts—men who have mastered the technique of bunting. Moreover, it is an ability that is well worth the time and trouble needed to acquire it. The good bunter will beat out a number of hits over the course of a season, and, of equal importance, he will keep the defense on edge and will cause the third baseman to play closer to the plate, thereby cutting down on his fielding range.

This play is not a smart move with two outs and the team at bat trailing by more than one run, with two exceptions: if the batter is a good base stealer, or a long-ball hitter is the next man at bat; or if there is a runner on third base and the first and third basemen are playing deep.

## The Fake Bunt

There are three variations of the fake bunt, all of which can prove of great value to a batter and his team.

A rarely used but potentially damaging offensive weapon that is based on the sacrifice is known in baseball circles as the *bastard play*. In it, the batter squares around as if to bunt but hits the ball with a fairly full, chop-like swing. The idea is to lure the shortstop to second base to cover it against the runner and the second baseman to first to cover it on the batter. The ball is then hit to one of the spots that have been vacated, usually toward shortstop for a right-handed batter and toward second for a left-hander. The fake must be convincing in order to draw the infielders out of position. If properly executed, this play requires no more than an ordinary ground ball hit in the general direction of one of the vacant spots in order to be successful. It is a particularly effective maneuver when worked with men on first and second and the sacrifice in order.

Another version of the fake bunt is the one in which the batter squares around to decoy the third baseman into charging the plate for a bunt, then "rams the ball down his throat." Both this and the bastard play must be practiced numerous times before a player attains proficiency in their execution. Once perfected, they can be turned into devastating offensive weapons.

The third type of fake bunt does not involve hitting the ball. It is intended solely to pull the defense, especially the third baseman, out of position. The batter squares around as if to bunt but lets the pitch go by. There are two occasions when this move is of particular value—when the batter is taking a pitch, or when a runner is attempting to steal third. In the first case the step or two closer to the plate that the third baseman may play when he is wary of a bunt will allow that much more chance of driving a hit past him. If, on the steal of third, the third baseman moves in to protect his territory against a bunt, he will leave the base uncovered against the advancing runner.

## BATTING DRILLS

Batting skill, for most ballplayers, is acquired gradually. A purposeful, systematic approach to the problem is the best means of developing hitting ability to its fullest extent. Carefully planned practice adds interest to the daily routine, and when the ultimate goal of improved performance is achieved, baseball will prove an enjoyable as well as challenging experience.

### Exercises

Preseason conditioning should be designed not only to improve a batter's eye and his timing; but also to attune his bodily movements to the proper performance of fundamentals.

The series of pivot exercises described below will accomplish this while at the same time developing the balance that is closely related to timing:

1. Assume a normal batting stance; place the hands on the hips; pivot at the hips as though swinging the body into a pitch. Go back and forth in this motion until the hip pivot seems natural and the trunk feels loose.

2. Using the heels as pivots and hanging the arms limply at the sides, pivot to the rear, shifting the weight to the back heel; pivot forward with the weight resting on the whole of both feet as the body returns to its normal position; continue the forward movement until the weight is on the front heel, which then becomes the pivot point; continue forward until the complete follow-through position is reached. This should be a back-and-forth motion with no stop.

Repeat this set of actions several times, making a determined effort to keep the head and eyes in a stationary position.

3. Go through the same routine several times with a split-second stop between its various phases.

4. Perform the same series of movements, this time with a bat; first step by step, then as a continuous pattern of action. Repeat several times and *keep your head still!*

5. Practice the still-head drill: The batter swings a bat, with a strong light (the sun, when outdoors) at his back. A coach or player then places his foot on the shadow of the batter's head. The object is to take a full cut with the "head remaining underfoot." This should be repeated many times—until the head remains still consistently—and should be continued throughout the season.

## Drills

Ballplayers should make it a rule to get themselves thoroughly loosened up before swinging a bat with full force. A series of simple bending and stretching exercises (a minute or two is sufficient) will help prevent muscular pulls and strains and will prepare a batter for the hardest of swings. This rule is particularly applicable to preseason practice, during which the muscles are not well conditioned, and to cold days, when they are slow in loosening up.

The fundamentals of batting should be worked on as separate entities, then put together as a whole. The players should practice alone in front of a mirror at home and on the field with a teammate or coach observing and making suggestions.

1. Swing a bat as often as possible. Visualizing a pitcher throwing at you, go through a normal swing repeatedly to strengthen the hands and wrists and to develop good form. The use of a batting tee whenever available greatly assists a player in learning to hit pitches in different spots and in keeping his eye on the ball.

2. When bad weather prevents outdoor work and a gym is available, have a fellow player pitch to you, using a tennis ball to eliminate the possibilities of damage to buildings and fixtures. A half-dozen swings at a ball thrown slowly will prepare you to hit fast pitches. This indoor batting practice is highly recommended in preseason training sessions. By the time outdoor workouts are held, you should be ready to hit at full speed. The use of a pitching machine with tennis balls will accustom you to fast pitching.

3. When on the ball field, practice the start to first. Do it as it has been described earlier, and be sure to include the rounding of first base. This should be performed numerous times until correct habits become second nature.

4. Many ball clubs have strings set up to outline the strike zone for the use of pitchers who are working to perfect control. Take the opportunity to learn your strike zone by assuming a normal batting stance at the strings when a pitcher is working with them. If no strings are available, stand "at the plate" when a pitcher is warming up, and have the catcher call balls and strikes. This practice will prove helpful to the pitcher as well as to the batter.

5. Play "pepper" with other ballplayers whenever the opportunity presents itself. This is a good conditioner for all hands and is of especial value to the batter. It facilitates improved bunting and place-hitting while at the same time impressing on the batter the necessity of keeping his eye on the ball and meeting it squarely. A visit to a major league

park before game time will demonstrate the importance with which big leaguers view the game of pepper.

### Batting Practice

Batting practice should never be a haphazard affair. It is a serious business and should be treated as such. It is discussed in detail in the section on coaching.

At various times during the season, ballplayers should take the time to work on the different skills that come under the general heading of "Batting." During regular workouts a batter should practice hitting to right field, selecting random pitches for the purpose. Bunts—sacrifice, squeeze, and for a hit—should be worked into practice sessions. (Bunting practice can be held in lieu of batting practice during indoor workouts.) The fake bunt and its variation, the bastard play, are maneuvers that should be tried. Finally, if troubled by a particular pitch, the batter should enlist the aid of his batting practice pitcher and have that man throw him a good sampling of the pitch on which he is weakest.

# Batting—The Mental Aspect

## ATTITUDE

The theory of hitting can be reduced to its most basic element by simplification. It involves meeting the ball with the bat and driving it to a spot where it can be neither caught nor retrieved by a fielder and thrown to first base before the batter can reach that goal. In short, batting resolves itself to that brief, pointed, and now legendary epigram of Willie Keeler's: "Hit 'em where they ain't."

Even this almost facetious definition, however, demands study from a tactical standpoint when it is realized that the so-called zones of safety for batted balls vary with the batter, the opposing pitcher, the physical characteristics of the ballpark, and the game situation that prevails at a given moment.

It has been established, thus far, that batting ability is at least partly an inherent talent and that it is comprised of a batting eye, coordination of muscles, and the correct performance of certain fundamentals.

Unfortunately, in its entirety batting is not quite so simple. One more very important piece must be fitted into place to complete the picture—the mental aspect.

Above and beyond the purely mechanical there is a wide field to which the batter may attain and in which he may develop powers quite beyond those to which nature has seemingly limited him. The mental phase of batting is the element that enables a man to make the most of his ability. Proper utilization of his talents allows a ballplayer to rise above the status of being a mere mechanical workman. The successful player is the one who numbers among his assets a combination of energy, perseverance, aggressiveness, ambition, know-how, and confidence.

It is the aim of this section to convey the means needed to develop those qualities.

### The Right Frame of Mind

The good competitor is a man who can rise to the occasion and come through with a base hit when the ball game is at stake. He is not necessarily a nerveless character, always cool and calm. As a matter of fact, he is in many cases keyed up and fired with determination; yet he is always able to turn this emotional pitch into an intentness of purpose that enables him to be relatively relaxed until he explodes with a burst of concentrated energy as he swings at the ball.

Willie Mays, one of the greatest of competitors, is the living personification of this—a pleasant, reserved man, outwardly calm and relaxed even in the heat of a ball game, yet a veritable dynamo, motivated by an intense singleness of purpose when he goes into action.

A real competitor, such as Mays, goes up to the plate to hit. Except on those rather infrequent occasions when the "take" sign is in effect, he is mentally prepared to hit every pitch. He is not afraid to "stand in there" with determination and confidence.

The ballplayer who has learned not to hurry possesses a true asset. *Two o'clock hitter* is the term used to describe a man who hits line drives in batting practice but pops up in the game. The real difference is the pressure placed on a man by game competition. A two o'clock hitter is one who tightens under that pressure; the real ballplayer is the one who, figuratively speaking, takes it easy and relies on his form.

A ballplayer who is under too much pressure to perform well at the plate should step out of the batter's box occasionally and make himself take more time. One of the benefits of slowing his pace and relaxing is that it reduces the tendency to go for bad balls. Anxiety is the chief cause of this serious fault; so the batter should take his time in the realization that he will eventually get "his pitch" and that patience and calmness will better assure him of being prepared for that pitch when it comes.

The good hitter approaches the plate in a frame of mind in which he does not care who is pitching or what is thrown. This man knows that all he must do is meet the ball when it crosses the plate, and he feels that he has the ability to do just that.

Inexperienced batters tend to exaggerate the pitcher's ability and to underestimate their own. Naturally, this is particularly so "in the clutch." To nullify this tendency, the batter should realize that the pitcher, too, is under pressure and that with runners in scoring position it is the pitcher who is in trouble. The batter should certainly adopt that attitude and should remember that as long as he swings, he is dangerous.

A batter should keep his chin up and "hang in there" at all times. Obviously, that is the best way for him to overcome the psychological effects of occasional setbacks. Yet, paradoxically, a certain amount of discouragement can be beneficial. A ballplayer should not allow himself to become too discouraged by mistakes, but a mistake can often prove the most valuable lesson that a player can have.

Aspiring hitters are usually subjected to much theorizing and instruction. Although a batter should not ignore such beneficial instruction, he should, somehow, try to stand at the plate in readiness to hit—free in both mind and body. Thus, perhaps the best attitude for the batter to adopt is one in which he does not permit the situation to become too big for him. Why should he get rattled? No more is expected of him than that he go up to the plate and do his best. If he will bear that in mind, he can rest assured that those base hits will eventually fall in for him.

### Fear of the Ball

Respect, if not fear, for hard-thrown balls exists in all players. In one sense, the difference between good and bad hitters lies in the degree of fear of the ball with which they are afflicted. A Henry Aaron or a Roberto Clemente, although he has respect for an exceptionally fast pitcher, has practically no fear of the ball and, for this reason among others, is never a target of an intentional duster. On the other hand, a .200 hitter is gun shy to a certain extent and is more liable to intimidation by close, fast pitches.

There is little reason for any batter to be plagued by a large measure of fear. Any man with average eyesight and reflexes should have no difficulty in avoiding a ball thrown at him. Furthermore, protective helmets, mandatory in most leagues, are readily available and reasonably priced. They can help greatly in allaying a man's fear of a pitched ball. Although a helmet or protective cap is no guarantee against being hit, it does eliminate most of the danger of serious injury and, as a result, can provide relative peace of mind for all but the most timid of batters.

The batter who needs reassurance about his safety at the plate should be made to realize that correct methods can reduce to a minimum the danger of his being hit.

There are several principles that, if practiced faithfully, will enable any batter to go to the plate with little worry about the possibility of being hit by a pitched ball:

1. A close pitch is easy to duck if the batter follows it carefully. It is the ball he loses sight of that can be dangerous.

2. Turning one's head greatly increases the danger of being hit.

3. The batter should not move his *rear* foot to avoid a pitch.

4. The correct method is to move his front foot back, at the same time keeping his eye on the ball. Incidentally, this also helps guard against being caught unawares by a sudden, sharp-breaking curve.

5. As a last resort the batter should hit the dirt in order to keep from being hit by the ball.

The incidence of the use of an intentional duster, or bean ball, is greatly exaggerated. There are many outstanding pitchers who go through an entire career without once resorting to this practice. Two great performers, Walter Johnson and Bob Feller, are conspicuous examples. In many cases a brush-back pitch, high and tight—designed to keep the batter from digging in at the plate—is the worst offense of which a pitcher can honestly be accused.

Dusters are thrown primarily by pitchers who are being hit hard, and, even then, serious doubt can be voiced as to malicious intent. Most bean-ball incidents or feuds are sparked by an unintentional wild pitch that sails in close to the batter's head. If the deliberate use of a duster is suspected, the practice could be eliminated immediately by an order from the manager or coach for the pitchers to throw at each other.

There are good hitters who are willing to stand at the plate and defy the pitcher to throw at them. They know that concentrated attention on the ball makes it all but impossible for them to be hit.

### Shyness

Shyness on the part of a batter can be defined as the kind of uncertainty that is the middle ground between outright fear and the air of assurance displayed by all good hitters.

Shyness is occasioned primarily by a lack of familiarity that can cause timidity even in a man whose overall courage cannot be questioned.

The obvious remedy is practice and experience to such an extent that this lack of familiarity disappears, and uncertainty along with it. The whole matter can be disposed of by emphatically stating that experience —teaching a man what he can do—eliminates shyness and promotes the confidence that is needed to capitalize fully on his physical ability.

### Confidence

With this topic we come to the most important element in the mental aspect of batting. Although in itself it may not give rise to good hitting, confidence is certainly a distinguishing characteristic of the game's better batsmen.

The spirit that wins ball games is built on confidence. Perhaps that statement and some of the platitudes included in this section sound like excerpts from a pep talk. So much the better, for the importance of confidence to a hitter cannot be overestimated. The need for it must be impressed on any ballplayer who aspires to good hitting.

Every batter wishes he could hit—this is hope. Confidence is a much stronger word—it is faith. Indeed, no manager desires the presence of a ballplayer who does not believe in himself, feeling with justification that if a man doubts his ability to do a certain thing, the chances are that he cannot.

Another way of stating the matter is to assert that confidence, in a very real sense, is the capacity to make the most of one's ability. The fact that a ballplayer should be aware of his limitations and be guided by them has been previously advanced. However, even more emphasis should be placed on the idea that faith in his capabilities is the spur that is needed to capitalize fully on them. Confidence, then, is the mental tonic that can lift batting performance above the level of mediocrity.

George Sisler is one of baseball's immortals. Twice he batted over .400, and his record of 257 hits in one season is a mark that may never be broken. Neither a vain nor conceited man, Sisler was a real student of the art of hitting. Yet consider what he said, in all sincerity, about the importance of confidence to a batter. In discussing his phenomenal success over a period of years and the reasons for it, George Sisler remarked, "At times I actually felt sorry for the pitcher when I came to bat. I could hit anything he had. I knew it and he knew it. That's the real explanation for any success I may have achieved."

The old principle that a man can swim better with the tide than against it applies here, this time in the form of the mental tide that is built up through confidence. The assurance that it provides is an important part of the proper frame of mind for a ballplayer. Relaxation at the plate, another vital asset, is based primarily on this all-important factor.

The next phase of the mental aspect of batting to be discussed is determination. It is very closely related to confidence, each of the traits having a strong effect on the other. In concluding this section and starting the next, let it be said that real determination is vital in batting. It is built through confidence, which, in turn, stems from practice, desire and ability.

## Determination

Determination to make good is the catalytic agent that motivates all the desirable mental qualities that enable a man's physical assets to bear fruit. As it pertains to batting, it is an indispensable attribute.

Quite possibly the greatest ballplayer who ever lived was Ty Cobb. The number of records credited to him gives cold, statistical evidence to his phenomenal ability. Yet perhaps his greatest value lay in his capacity to upset the opposition by taking advantage of every conceivable opening and, in many cases, by creating those openings himself. Cobb possessed good natural gifts but not those of a superstar. Cobb's greatness came from his mental approach to the game, the burning desire to excel that drove him to the pinnacle of his profession.

Thus, Ty Cobb is the proper authority on whom to call for testimony of the stress that should be placed on determination as a salient point in the mental phase of batting.

Cobb attributed his remarkable accomplishments primarily to purely mental qualities, putting special emphasis on his determination to succeed at all costs. It was his belief that he was actually a .320 hitter and that his .367 lifetime average, or a difference of almost fifty points in his batting percentage, was due to one thing—his tremendous determination.

Al Simmons, a dangerous right-handed batter and a member of baseball's Hall of Fame, credited much of his success to this burning desire to excel. Speaking of his development into one of the game's most feared hitters, Simmons said, "I developed a contempt for pitchers." Ty Cobb called this the best short definition of batting ability ever spoken, adding that, in his opinion, the most important factors pertaining thereto are concentration and determination.

As previously stated, the good competitor is the ballplayer who can rise to the occasion and come through with a base hit in the clutch. One of the reasons for this faculty is pure determination. A good hitter's determination is at its height against good pitching.

Of course, a player's natural ability is the first thing that catches the eye of a major league scout. If it is not present, the candidate will not merit a second look. More important to our consideration of this phase of batting, however, is the fact that a scout looks for more than mere mechanical skill. Attitude is a vital factor to a scout. He pays close attention to a demonstrated determination to succeed and willingness to strive for success. They are the keys that give a scout an insight into how much a man will be able to make of his natural talents.

In the final analysis determination can be defined as consistent courage (or, guts), which is actually earnest, courageous, aggressive good sportsmanship.

## TACTICS

Regardless of how well he has mastered correct batting techniques and no matter what his ability as a hitter may be, a ballplayer can get even better results at the plate if he is a smart hitter—one who is observant, who takes advantage of every opportunity to gain an edge on the pitcher, and who employs the tactics and tricks of the trade that will enable him to accomplish his dual purpose of helping himself to better performance and his team to greater success.

Throughout the text numerous references have been made to tactical maneuvers pertaining to batting. Even in a discussion of fundamentals that are basically physical in nature, batting strategy is inevitably involved as the various ramifications of the mechanics of hitting arise. The two are closely interrelated, and, consequently, many sound policies of the batting game have been explained. There are, however, several other purely tactical elements that definitely should be mentioned; these will teach inexperienced ballplayers how many smart batsmen gain the advantage over the pitcher, thereby becoming successful hitters.

### On Being Prepared

It is assumed that the batter will follow the policy, laid down at the outset as elementary and vital, of being physically relaxed—yet mentally alert—as he faces the pitcher. But what of the pitcher himself and the consideration that must be given to his working methods?

A batter should always be set for the *fast ball*. Although there are definite situations in which a pitcher will usually rely on a certain delivery and in which that pitch can be looked for with some degree of certainty, guess-hitting, which is covered in more detail in the next section, is very risky and should be discouraged from the start. Good hitters do resort to it—but more often they set themselves to be able to cope with a fast pitch. Then, rather than concentrating on where the ball is going, they endeavor simply to meet it squarely.

Because of the great speed with which a pitched ball reaches the plate (it usually covers the sixty feet in less than ½ second), a fast ball will be past the batter before he is set to swing, unless he is ready for it. Furthermore, adjustments in timing can be made that will enable the batter to handle the curve ball, change of pace, or other such pitches, all of which are slower than the fast ball. This entails the second look, or slight pause after the stride, that has been emphasized (in the section on fundamentals) as extremely important. Thus, if he is always set for the fast one, the batter will be ready for any type of pitch.

A high, tight fast ball is one of the most difficult pitches to meet solidly. If the batter has trouble with this type of pitch, he should adopt a slightly crouched stance and pass up the high ones—the pitcher will have to come down to him.

A slight crouch serves another purpose that is beneficial to the batter. It brings his strike zone a little lower and, at the same time, makes it slightly smaller, giving the pitcher less room in which to maneuver and a smaller target at which to shoot in order to throw strikes. Possibly even more important, a slight crouch brings the batter's eye level down—nearer the strike zone—affording him a much better look at the ball.

### When to Take

The obvious answer to the question of when to hit would seem to be any time a batter takes his position at the plate. If a batter could be sure of hitting safely most of the time, that answer could be accepted and further discussion would be superfluous. There are, however, certain situations in which percentage play (the law of averages) dictates that the batter should take a strike. It is generally good practice to make the pitcher throw a strike under the following conditions:

1. When the batter's team is losing by more than two runs in the late innings (the seventh, eighth, and ninth): In this situation every out (in fact, every pitch) counts, and the batter should not be too anxious to swing. Getting on base is the important consideration, and as long as the pitcher throws "balls" the batter stays alive.

2. When the preceding batter has walked or been hit by a pitched ball: Here the pitcher may have hit a wild streak or have become upset by his momentary loss of control; hence, the batter should not help him by offering at the first pitch or, especially, at a bad ball.

3. When the batter is the leadoff man in an inning or if a new pitcher takes the mound: This gives the hitter a chance to look over the pitcher's stuff and to prevent him from being in the enviable position of getting one out with one pitch.

4. When the preceding batter has been retired on one pitch: The batter should try to avoid making the pitcher's task an easy one. On the contrary, he should make the opposing hurler work hard. He should never be allowed to get two outs on two pitches.

5. When there is a strong possibility that the enervating effect of a hot day will cause the pitcher to "run out of gas": A pitcher with over-powering stuff should be made to throw as many pitches as possible in the hopes that the physical effort involved will take its inevitable toll and that he will lose some of his stuff and be easier to hit in the late innings.

The batter who takes a strike should "play out the string." In other words, until the pitcher throws a strike, the batter should continue his policy of taking the next pitch. This is what is meant by "take a strike."

The batsman should not let the pitcher know when he is taking a pitch. Doing so will allow him to throw one for an automatic strike. Faking a bunt on a first-pitch take is a good move—and it may draw the infield in a step or two.

Naturally, these tactics should be varied occasionally to keep the other team guessing. There are times when a pitcher who is plagued by a wild streak will ease up to get the ball over the plate. When he "lays the ball in there" in this fashion, it is an invitation for the batter to hit. As a general policy, however, taking a pitch under the circumstances outlined above is sound baseball.

### When to Hit

There are times when the batter should attempt to hit the first good pitch. One of these occasions occurs when he comes to bat with a runner in scoring position and the run involved is an important one; that is, it will increase a lead, make or break a tie, or reduce the opposing team's margin to a point at which the score will be close. Exceptions to this occur when the count is three balls and no strikes and when first base is open (only second or second and third are occupied), in which case a walk will not prove too damaging and the pitcher will be careful not to throw a "fat" pitch.

A batter should not take strikes when he is "up there to hit." This does not mean that he should swing at anything the pitcher throws, but it does signify that when runners are in scoring position or his team has the opposing pitcher on the ropes, he should "be a hitter" and offer at any pitch that is to his liking and in the strike zone. Under these circumstances he should take a strike only if the pitcher has been exceptionally wild or if one of the "take" situations applies.

Occasionally a batter will get the green light from his manager or coach to "hit the cripple" (the three-ball, no-strike pitch), though only when he is a good hitter who (with runners in scoring position) is likely to deliver a long ball, or when the hit-and-run has been signalled.

With two strikes on him, the batter should swing at any pitch that looks like a strike. A good attitude for any ballplayer to adopt is, "If the ball is close enough to argue about, it's close enough to hit."

### How to Hit

The manner in which the batter swings at the ball is subject to occasional alteration in accordance with the game situation. For instance, with the infield playing in to cut off a run at the plate, the batter should not try to overpower the ball but should concentrate on meeting it solidly. The advantage in this case lies in the possibility of hitting the ball through or over the infield rather than in driving it beyond the reach of the outfielders. An old baseball adage has it that when the infielders are in tight positions, a .200 hitter automatically becomes a .500 hitter, for an ordinary ground ball will, in many cases, go through the infield for a hit.

When the batter has two strikes, he should be "guarding the plate." In other words, he must concede something to the pitcher, who has him at a disadvantage. Power should be sacrificed and emphasis placed on meeting the ball rather than on knocking it out of the park. Many good hitters go as far as to shorten their grip when these circumstances prevail. On the other hand, with fewer than two strikes, the batter should pass up any pitch that has fooled him.

There are, conversely, definite occasions when the batter should attempt to hit for distance. For example, it is desirable to go for the long ball when the bases are empty with two out (here, unless the batter can reach scoring position, it may take two additional hits to score him). For a similar reason an attempt should be made to drive a man home from first when he is the only base runner with two out. It is also sound baseball, in some cases, to swing for an extra-base hit with runners on first and second and the opposition leading by more than two runs. A long ball under these conditions makes it possible to score both runs. It also eliminates the possibility of a force play at second base, whereas a single will score only one run and at the same time set up a double play with fewer than two out.

A specific example of batting tactics was covered in detail under the section *Hitting behind the runner.* This is the case in which the batter should try to drive the ball on the ground between first and second. Something that was not touched upon, however, is the role of the batter on a steal of second base. When this play is prearranged, the batter can help the runner by standing deep in the batter's box and by swinging at the ball (and missing it) so as to interfere slightly with the smooth continuity of the catcher's throw to second, or by faking a bunt as described under "The Steal." Inexperienced players who cannot afford to waste too many strikes can limit this maneuver solely to those times when the pitcher throws a strike.

The batter should step out of the box when he tends to be over-anxious; this will reduce the tension under which he finds himself and cut down on his tendency to go for bad balls. This should also be done against a pitcher who takes an excessive amount of time between deliveries. The aim is to prevent the batter's tension from mounting and possibly to cause the pitcher to become impatient or overanxious. Other occasions on which the batter should step out occur after he has hit a foul ball with a man on base (so that the runner will have a chance to catch his breath and survey the situation anew) and after the pitcher has made a pick-off attempt (so that the runner can recover his composure and assume a ready position for taking his lead). When the batter steps out of the box, he must be certain to request timeout from the umpire since the umpire alone is empowered by the rules to call time.

With a runner on base, stepping out when the pitcher is in the middle of his motion or immediately after he breaks his set position may cause him to balk.

## GUESS-HITTING

The batter who attempts to guess what pitch is coming next is playing into the hands of a smart mound artist. The pitcher *knows* what he is throwing; the batter can only guess. An experienced hurler, simply by varying his operating methods, will take full advantage of this and have the batter completely at his mercy. If the batter is lucky enough to overcome these odds and guess correctly, he *may* succeed in hitting safely. If he does not get the pitch he is expecting, he will look very foolish indeed.

Baseball's better hitters do not try to outguess the pitcher. They are always prepared for the fast ball and concentrate primarily on getting good wood on the ball, making the necessary adjustments in timing only after they see that the ball is an intermediate-speed or slow pitch.

## Looking for the Logical Pitch

Without succumbing to the pitfalls of guess-hitting, a batter can safely look for a certain type of pitch in any of several specific situations. In other words, he can expect to be pitched to in the way that is most advantageous for the opposing moundsman—that is, he can anticipate the logical pitch in a given situation.

For example, with the double play in prospect or with the infield playing in close to cut off a run at the plate, the batter can look for low pitching, particularly curve balls, since the pitcher will undoubtedly try to make him hit the ball into the dirt.

With the sacrifice in order, the batter can reasonably expect high fast balls, which are difficult to bunt; when the pitcher is unusually wild with one kind of pitch, the batter can expect to be fed another kind the greatest number of times.

This last instance is similar to the case of a pitcher who has one particularly good delivery but is mediocre with his other pitches. Hoyt Wilhelm, the great relief pitcher, fits into this category. Wilhelm has a baffling knuckle ball, which is his "out-pitch." His fast one, only fair at best, is used as a waste ball, rarely thrown over the plate and used only often enough to let the batter know that it exists. Some pitchers will resort to this strategy on certain days when one of their deliveries is not working well. Under these circumstances the batter can logically look for the "money pitch" on most occasions, particularly when the pitcher is behind in the count.

Physical characteristics of the ballpark also have a bearing on the situation. If, for example, the right-field fence is very short, a left-handed batter will, in all probability, get very few inside pitches. (However, he should not crowd the plate in exaggerated fashion, looking for an outside pitch, lest the pitcher deal him one in close and find him relatively helpless against it.) When both fences are short, the batter will probably see very few slow pitches, for they are the easiest ones to pull. And on dark days or in the twilight hours, when visibility is poor, a pitcher with a good fast ball can be expected to rely mainly on that pitch.

A smart pitcher will continually try to set up the batter for certain deliveries, and the latter must guard himself against falling into these traps. For instance, the pitcher will shoot for the outside corner a few times; if he notices the batter moving closer to the plate to protect the outside of it, he will "bust one in on his fists." When some of the better pitchers get a count of two strikes and no balls on the hitter, they will often brush him back with a high, close fast ball (or try to get him to go for a bad ball, usually high and tight) and then come in with a curve ball, low and away.

Finally, when the game situation is a tight one, with the pitcher in the hole, the batter can logically expect to get the hurler's best, or "clutch," pitch. Most pitchers operate on the principle that when in a jam, they should pitch to their own strength.

These are some of the situations in which observation of the pitcher's habits, along with common sense, can give the batter a good indication of the type of pitch for which he should be prepared.

Watching the pitcher constantly—learning what he throws, how he throws, and when he throws it—will help the batter to react, not guess.

### Positive Guessing

As a general rule, first-ball hitters are weak on the curve ball, and they lie in wait, ready to pounce on the first fast one they see. They assume that most pitchers try to get ahead of the batter with a quick strike, usually a fast ball. Furthermore, they are loath to let the pitcher get them in the hole, where he can go to work on them with his curve ball.

On the other hand, straightaway and opposite-field hitters usually anticipate the intermediate and slow pitches (curve ball and change of pace) and, because of the type of swing they favor, seem to enjoy better success against this kind of pitch.

When they guess right, batters who fall into these categories stand a good chance of hitting safely. Conversely, when their surmise is incorrect, they fare poorly. Wise batters who follow this pattern greatly improve their prospects by adopting a method that may be called *positive guessing*. In other words, they anticipate a certain pitch and swing at the ball only if they get that pitch. On the other hand, batters who rely on pure conjecture commit themselves to swinging at any ball, but in a fashion that is geared to meet one type of pitch. Then, if their guesswork is wrong, their timing is badly off, and their base hits will be few and far between.

This form of positive guessing has a variation that is occasionally practiced by good hitters when the pitcher falls behind in the count. A typical case in point would be that of a batter who likes a pitch in a certain spot. With a count of two balls and no strikes, for example, he can set himself to swing at a pitch in his strong zone. Then, if he gets that pitch, he hits away. If not, he passes it up. This is the method that is quite often used when the hitter gets the green light from his manager to hit the "cripple."

Although guess-hitting is frowned upon by most experienced baseball men, it does exist and will unquestionably continue to do so as long as the gambling instinct is present in any ballplayer. In many cases it is the catcher against whom the guessing is done. He is, after all, the man who gives the signals, the brains of the battery to a good extent. Some receivers fall into set patterns in their calling of pitches and are predictable enough to furnish the batter with a good indication of the probable pitch. There are catchers, for instance, who will rarely call for a fast ball under certain circumstances. At times this habit is so pronounced that a team can anticipate the pitch when a certain catcher works with a certain pitcher, but will abandon the idea when a different catcher is behind the plate for the same pitcher.

### Reading the Pitch

*Reading the pitch* (or *pitcher*) is the term used to describe the ability of sharp-eyed coaches to detect, from a telltale mannerism on the part of the pitcher, what he is about to throw. It also covers the stealing of the catcher's signals by either a coach or base runner. This part of the game is more a matter of observation than of mere guessing.

The reading of pitches by the batter himself is ill advised since it is based on partial knowledge at best. It should not be encouraged. A smart coach can be far more successful at this practice. On the other hand, a pitcher is occasionally so overpowering that even foreknowledge of his offerings is of little avail to the batter. In his early days Bob Feller is said to have telegraphed his pitches; nevertheless, he mowed down enemy hitters with monotonous regularity—even when they knew what was coming.

Some players refuse to accept this information, preferring to hit completely on their own. There is actually some justification for this, for an element of danger is involved in a batter's foreknowledge: a pitcher who suspects that he is being read can resort to a last-minute switch; a coach can make a mistake; and a fast ball headed for the batter can be a source of peril when he is waiting for it to curve.

It would seem that a runner on second base could be a great help in picking off the catcher's signals and relaying the information to the batter. This idea can be largely discounted, however, because a good catcher will use alternate sets of signals with a man on second base.

The catcher can, at times, be a source of visual information to an alert ball club. Some receivers have a tendency to move closer to the plate when a curve or change-up is coming. Others may turn the right foot to the outside when a curve is being thrown, or widen the stance for a fast ball. The glove, too, can be an indicator: it is often held flat for the fast ball and pointed down for the curve.

A smart batter will take advantage of every piece of information in his possession, but trying to outguess the pitcher should definitely not become his regular practice.

### Guessing—a Final Appraisal

A smart batter cannot observe pitching over a period of years without gaining a good idea of what some pitchers will do under certain circumstances. Occasions arise when guessing becomes almost a certainty. Experience, familiarity with a pitcher, and a knowledge of how he operates in a given situation can, at times, give a batter an insight into his probable working method so that the next pitch can be sensed with a good degree of accuracy. In such a case the batter would be foolish if he did not take advantage of his knowledge. Every batter who uses his eyes is guilty of guessing or, in this situation, of what could more accurately be termed *observation.*

There are other good hitters who go by the policy that, "I want my mind on the ball and nothing else. I want to feel that I can hit it no matter what happens. If the pitcher is trying to outguess me, he's wasting his time because I don't guess." The batter who follows this policy is definitely playing his percentages wisely. As long as he refrains from guessing, the probability of guessing wrong will be eliminated.

Honus Wagner was an exceptionally good batsman whose views on guessing are interesting. Wagner once said, "Outguessing the pitcher is a tough proposition. Once in a while I might have figured that a curve ball was about due, or maybe a fast one. But not often, because I was no mind-reader. My main job was not to hypnotize the pitcher but to hit the ball. So, most generally, I tried to be ready for whatever might come. That is the only safe rule in the long run."

## HITTING THE CURVE BALL

The curve ball is more troublesome for most hitters than the fast ball since a change in the course of the ball's flight is obviously quite difficult to contend with when the batter is attempting to get good wood on it. That the mound fraternity seems to be in accord with this contention is evidenced by the widely accepted pitching maxim, "When in doubt, curve him."

Nevertheless, regardless of how sharp it is, the curve ball is slower than the fast ball and thus can be hit well by any ballplayer endowed with ordinary coordination, eyesight, and intelligence.

In the case of more than a few batters, fear of the curve ball becomes pronounced. Because of this and the fact that coping with it is, in many respects, a psychological matter, we are dealing with it as part of the mental phase of hitting. Regardless of the category in which it is placed, the fact remains that hitting the curve ball with consistency demands some thought, as well as coordinated physical activity. In terms of response, the mental and physical aspects are closely related, perhaps more so than in any other facet of the game.

There are two primary reasons that ballplayers experience undue difficulty in handling the curve: first, because there is a strong tendency to pull away from it, a tendency to which many batters succumb; second, because too many hitters do not follow the ball closely all the way to the bat. If these two habits are nonexistent, almost any batter should be able to hit the curve ball.

At precisely what point it is best to try to meet the ball has long been the subject of conjecture. That is, will the batter get best results if he tries to hit the ball before, while, or after it breaks? The best suggestion that can be offered is that each player should experiment by shifting his position in the batter's box until he finds the method that best suits his own style. (Incidentally, the best curve ball hitters try to meet the ball during or after the break.)

The batter should try to hit to the opposite field a curve ball that is breaking away from him; if it is breaking in to him, he should attempt to drive it back through the pitcher's box (if he does so, in all probability he will pull the ball). In other words, and quite logically, the batter should try to hit the curve ball with the rotation. In addition to this, if the batter places more weight on his front foot, he will lessen the tendency to pull away from the ball. (Closing his stance and sighting the ball over his front shoulder will also help.) Obeying these principles will demand that the batter follow the ball closely and will aid him greatly in trying to meet it solidly.

A smart pitcher rarely telegraphs his pitches, but it is very difficult to cover up the curve ball entirely. Some of the telltale signs that usually indicate that the curve ball is coming can be listed as follows: the pitcher's free leg goes higher than usual; his wrist bends noticeably inward; and his arm is bent at the elbow in pronounced fashion. Also, as his arm comes through in the delivery, less white will be visible since the back of his hand will be toward the hitter, thus obscuring the ball.

The following ideas may prove helpful in telling a batter what type of curve ball to anticipate. A pitcher who throws from the same side (right-handed batter versus right-handed pitcher) is more likely to throw his curve three-quarters overhand or sidearm, hoping it will break away from the hitter. (The batter should try not to pull away from a sidearmer's deliveries.) One who throws from the opposite side (righty versus lefty) will probably try to throw his curve ball over the top—that is, straight overhand—in order to make the ball break down rather than in to the batter.

Two of the fundamentals of batting will help a player to spot the curve ball more easily. They are (1) trying to watch the ball meet the bat and (2) observing the split-second pause and hitting immediately after the stride. To improve his performance in general and his hitting the curve ball in particular, a batter should diligently practice both fundamentals.

### The Off Pitches

The fast ball, curve, and change of pace are the basic pitches. The batter who can hit those three consistently will be able to cope with almost any pitcher. However, we should mention the so-called off pitches that are employed by a great many moundsmen.

The one that is most commonly used is the slider. Often called a *nickle curve*, the slider is, more accurately, a variation on the fast ball. By gripping the ball off center and delivering it with a normal fast ball motion or by applying a slight last-minute twist to the ball, the pitcher can make it move sharply to the side in sliding fashion rather than break in the pronounced manner of the curve. The value of the slider lies in its being almost as swift as the fast ball and in its approaching the plate looking very much like that pitch, the one possible indication being a spiraling rotation with a "dot" in the center. Since it is difficult to detect because of its similarity to the fast ball, there are no particular measures that can be taken to hit any one slider. It is especially difficult to contact after its break. If a batter has great trouble with the slider, he can move forward in the box and concentrate on meeting the ball instead of worrying about where it is going.

The knuckle ball is another pitch that is in wide use. There are two varieties of this delivery. When thrown slowly or at half speed, the knuckler dances in such a way that it is often called a *flutter ball*. When thrown hard it acts like a "dry spitter," dropping very sharply as it nears the plate. The knuckler is unpredictable and, consequently, difficult to meet solidly. It occasionally baffles pitcher, catcher, and batter alike. Most pitchers who employ this delivery, rely very heavily on it and generally lack a good fast ball. Thus, when facing a knuckle-baller, the batter should be concerned primarily with that pitch. He should stand forward in the box, cut down on the swing, and concentrate on meeting the ball. The batter should definitely not try to overpower the knuckler. The watchword here is, hit the ball in the same way that it is pitched.

The other off pitches, such as the fork ball, screw ball, palm ball, and so forth, are used only occasionally, even by pitchers who throw them; thus, they can be passed over here without elaboration.

The sinker will not be considered here, because the way in which the term is used is somewhat misleading. The sinker is actually a fast ball that for some pitchers, moves down and in, instead of taking off. To avoid added confusion, the batter should not consider it a separate pitch but should treat it as a fast ball.

The change of pace is one of the basic pitches and has been covered in the section on batting weaknesses. However, an additional idea that may prove helpful to batters who are bothered by slow stuff was advanced by Bobby Avila, American League batting champion in 1954, who had always been troubled by slow pitching. In his championship year he adopted a successful method of coping with the "junk balls": he used a light bat against slow pitchers. This enabled him to wait until the very last moment before committing himself, for he was able to whip the light bat into the ball with an especially fast swing.

### PINCH-HITTING

A man who is called upon to pinch-hit fills a difficult role. He must come off the bench cold and enter what is generally a tight spot. There is consequently more cause for his having to contend with a certain anxiety. Thus, his problem is to some extent mental rather than physical.

Major league clubs can afford to carry men whose talents are specialized even in this relatively limited field. There are, for instance, pinch-hitters who excel at leading off an inning; ones who are particularly adept at scoring a runner from third with a long fly ball; and those who can be counted upon to move a runner from second to third when there are no outs. The initial responsibility lies with the manager, who must select the right man for the right spot, giving consideration to how each man hits against the kind of pitcher who is working and what the team will have in reserve for an even bigger situation that may arise.

Outside of the big leagues reserve strength is often questionable and the problem, therefore, more acute. The manager or coach will use the best man available at the time to serve as a pinch-hitter; consequently, more of the weight falls on the shoulders of that player.

When a player is tapped for pinch-hitting duty, he must try to be as loose as possible, both physically and mentally. All hitters should swing a weighted bat or several conventional bats in preparation for going to the plate. This is particularly important for a pinch-hitter who has been sitting down for most of the game. He should swing the weighted club until his shoulder and arm muscles feel free and supple; then he will be ready physically.

The pinch-hitter should consider what kind of hit will best serve his team's purposes and then act accordingly. If the game is close and a runner must be moved into scoring position, a ground ball to the right side may succeed. When a long ball is needed, the pinch-hitter should swing for distance. Any one of the techniques discussed earlier may be the one to employ in order to do his team the most good. Nevertheless, a clean base hit will go a long way toward providing the desired results.

Because he comes into a game cold, a pinch-hitter should have to contend with fewer restrictions than a player who is taking his regular turn at bat. Being called upon to take a "fat" pitch for a strike is a particularly bad thing for him to have to do, the only time that this is called for is when the pitcher is exceptionally wild and waiting him out seems like good strategy.

One thing that the pinch-hitter should bear in mind is the necessity of reporting to the umpire before taking his position at the plate. This is a regularly observed custom, and although no penalty will be imposed on the batter himself, his team is liable to a fine in organized baseball and certain other leagues.

A pinch-hitter should not let the situation seem to big for him; he should be well aware of the fact that the most that can reasonably be expected of him is that he make his best effort.

# Base-Running

Base-running has important factors other than speed of foot. In fact, many fine base runners are men who lack exceptional speed but who excel on the base paths because of alertness, good judgment, and thorough knowledge of sound technique and baseball percentage.

A base runner can look to a coach for advice and instructions before a play starts, but once he is in motion, he must depend on his own judgment and knowledge of proper base-running practices 90 percent of the time.

## Three Basic Principles

Good base-running depends upon three basic principles:

(a) *Know the importance of your run.* All moves by a ballplayer when on the base paths must be guided by this principle. He must be fully aware of exactly how much the run he represents means to his team and should base his actions almost entirely on this consideration. Of course, if the other team gives him an extra base, he should take advantage of it. Usually, though, a base runner should take chances only when his run is an important one, and then only to get into proper scoring position.

(b) *Always watch the runner ahead of you.* Too often, this obvious principle is neglected. A ballplayer can do little but hurt his team by breaking up a rally if he does not pay heed to the actions of any of his teammates ahead of him on the base paths. When two runners find themselves caught on the same base, one can be sure that the trailing runner has been guilty of a very serious error.

(c) *Touch every base.* And go back to touch any base you have missed.

## The Start

Getting off to a good start is highly important for any runner in any branch of athletics. This certainly applies to baseball in general and base runners in particular. Every ballplayer should make an all-out effort on the first three steps and run on his toes at all times to achieve maximum speed at the earliest possible instant.

A batter can save himself a valuable fraction of a second in getting to first base by getting a good start from home plate; in this way he can beat out infield hits that would otherwise be outs.

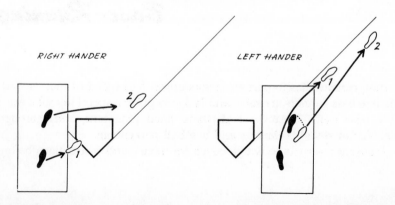

RIGHT HANDER          LEFT HANDER

A right-handed batter should take his first step with his right foot after his follow-through. At this point his right foot will actually be in better position for the initial step since his weight will have shifted to the left one.

A left-handed batter should start with his rear foot (the left one). This will be a crossover step and will give him a great jump since his weight, because of his follow-through, will already be going toward first base.

### Approaching the Base

The manner of approach to any base should be determined by the same principles that guide a runner nearing first base. When running directly to a base, the runner should touch the middle of it. This applies particularly to first base, of course, since there is no need to worry about overrunning the bag. He should, at the same time, endeavor to contact the base without altering his normal stride. Jumping for it when he nears the base will actually cause the runner to lose time in his race with the ball.

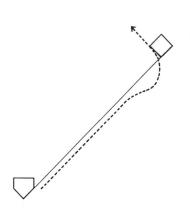

When rounding a base, the runner should touch and pivot against the corner of the bag nearest the mound. He should swing wide as he gets to within about twenty feet of the base and should hit it without breaking stride, using either foot, although the left one is preferable. Swinging wide before reaching the bag will enable the runner to be moving directly toward the next base as he rounds the one he is nearing, thereby eliminating the need to take several extra steps in order to continue on to the next base. Furthermore, when going from one base to another, he should always run in the base line; that is, directly toward the next base in a straight line.

### Taking Signals

Generally, no offensive play should be attempted unless the coach or manager signals for or gives approval of it.

A runner should return to his base to get the signal, which is usually given immediately after the pitch. If he does not get the signal, the runner should call time. Halting play to tie his shoe is one method of doing this.

Both the batter and the runner(s) should adopt the habit of taking an occasional look at the coach *after* the signal has been given. This can often prevent the other club from guessing that a signal has been given.

### Strategy

A runner *should* try for an extra base when he represents the tying or winning run. It is senseless to gamble when the run is not an important one.

Ordinarily, the time to take chances is with one out. With no outs a team should play it safe since there are usually at least three chances to get the runner around the bases to the plate. With two outs a team should also play safe lest it kill its possibilities of scoring at all.

The old adage that a runner should content himself with being at second base since he is already in scoring position should be ignored when an opportunity to reach third presents itself. He should realize not only that he is ninety feet closer to home but also that there are nine ways to score from third but only two from second.

### Guides to Action

As long as the ball is in front of the runner and within his field of vision, he is on his own. In all other cases he should look to the coach for guidance and should do so before he arrives at a base so that he will allow sufficient time to take the proper course of action.

Of course, it is not possible to look for a coach when going in to second base; here, of necessity, the runner is on his own. When breaking from first base, the runner should look for a batted ball as it is fielded, not only to guide his actions if he continues on his way around the bases but also to prevent his being doubled up on a line drive or fly ball on which he could otherwise return safely to his base. When he sees that the outfielder must play a grounder far to his glove side, an alert runner will go for an extra base.

When the throw is behind him, the runner should watch the hands and eyes of the infielder who is awaiting the throw. The slide should be made to the side of the base away from the ball; in this case, the fielder's hands and eyes are the best guide to use. If the baseman reaches toward the runner for the ball, the slide should be straight into the base, making the catch more difficult. This also applies on a force play, in which case the runner should get to the base as directly and quickly as possible.

## Tagging Up

When on first or second, a runner should tag up on any routine fly ball to the outfield with no outs. In many cases he will be able to advance after the catch. However, if the fly is a short one, no advance will be possible after a catch. Thus, the runner should go halfway, particularly when he can be forced out at the next base on a fly that is not caught.

In any case in which it is doubtful whether the ball will be caught, the runner should go halfway—until the ball is either caught or falls safe. When a fly ball is hit with one out, the runner should always go halfway. (With two outs the runner should of course be moving on any batted ball.)

When on third base, the runner should tag up on any ball hit in the air with fewer than two outs, even on a line drive that looks like an obvious base hit. This will save valuable time and enable the runner to score if the ball is caught. If it falls in for a base hit, he will have no trouble scoring anyway.

This move back to third on any ball hit in the air should become an automatic and immediate reaction on the part of any ballplayer who would become a sound base runner. As soon as the ball is hit in the air, the runner should instinctively return to third base.

## Foiling the Double Play

With a double play in prospect, the runner on first base should slide into second in such a way that he will interfere with the throw to first base.

The rules of the game state that the runner should slide so that some part of him is within reaching distance of the bag. Allowing approximately three feet on either side of the base will permit the runner to break up the double play while remaining within the bounds of legality.

To break up a double-play attempt, the runner should use a hard slide, with his knees at a forty-five-degree angle, and should endeavor to hook the striding foot of the defensive player.

We should also consider the bases-loaded double play by way of home. The runner from third should slide into the catcher when possible because this, too, constitutes breaking up a double play.

Every ballplayer, when considering such tactics, should always bear in mind that he should play the game as hard as he can but should, at all times, stay within the rules. He should never intentionally injure an opponent.

One special play that arises with the double-play setup occurs on a ground ball hit to the second baseman, on which there is a possibility of tagging the runner for the first out. The man on first base should never run into the tag on this play. If the second baseman comes at him in an attempt to make the tag, the runner should hold up and make the second baseman chase him, delaying the tag (if not avoiding it completely) long enough to prevent a double play. In fact, the runner should hold up as soon as it is apparent that this play can be made on him.

### First-and-Third Tactics

When a team has runners on first and third (or the bases loaded) with fewer than two out, there is always the possibility that the defensive club will try for a double play by way of second base. For this reason the runner on third should notice whether the left side of the infield is playing back and, in effect, giving up a run.

As a matter of fact, any time a runner reaches third base he should observe the position of the infield to see whether they are conceding him a run on a ground ball.

If, on the other hand, the infield is playing in to cut off the run at the plate, the runner on third must wait for the ball to go through the infield before attempting to score (except, of course, when the bases are loaded and he will be forced at the plate). When the infield plays in close position with runners on first and third, the man on first should take advantage of being lightly regarded by the defense and should steal second, thereby placing two runners in scoring position.

If, with men on first and third, the runner on first represents an important run, he must be especially careful not to take too big a lead and be caught off base. The defensive team will be looking for such an opportunity for they will be concentrating on the important run and paying little attention to the other runner.

In the first-and-third situation the runner on third should attempt to score on a ground ball in almost every case in which one is hit. The main goal here is to prevent a double play. Even if the throw does not go home, the runner breaking for the plate may succeed in diverting the infielder's attention enough to prevent the completion of a double play—and will have scored a run in the bargain. If the play is being made on the runner at home, he should pull up and get caught in a run-down in an attempt to permit the other runners to advance to second and third. He should move around sufficiently to put two runners in scoring position and, as a final maneuver to delay the tag, should run or even dive out of the base line at the very last moment. In nine cases out of ten, the defensive player making the tag will follow the runner or instinctively lunge at him, allowing more time for the other runners to advance to scoring position.

The exception to this practice arises when the ball is hit too slowly for the defense to complete a double play. In this case they will be playing for one out and will probably go for the runner at home. A similar instance is the medium-speed or slow ground ball with men on first and second. With no chance to complete a double play, the pivot man may try to catch the runner taking a wide turn at third after the force has been made at second. In either case the lead runner must be careful of attempts to catch him napping.

### Trying to Score

The time to take chances is with one out. For this reason, among others, it is recommended that with a runner on third, or runners on second and third, and one out, the man on third should try to score on a ground ball to the shortstop or second baseman. Unless the infield is playing in to cut off the run at the plate, this gamble is worthwhile since clean handling of the ball and a perfect throw are required to retire the runner trying to score. Over the course of a season, the percentages are with the offensive team, and many more runners should score than will be thrown out at the plate.

### Men on First and Second

When a team has runners on first and second, the man on first base can afford to take a comfortably large lead, particularly if the pitcher gets behind the batter and cannot afford to waste a pitch-out.

If the run at first is more important than the one at second, the defensive team will be playing the man at first at the expense of the other runner; so caution must be exercised by the runner at first. If, by any chance, a pick-off throw is made by the catcher to first base, the runner at second should be alert for an opportunity to steal third—he can probably make it since here, again, unusually good throws and clean ball handling will be needed to get him.

### Bases Loaded

The bases-loaded situation requires all runners to get a good jump and make an all-out effort to beat the throw on any ground ball hit to the infield. For this reason they should take substantial leads and ordinarily can afford to do so. They must, at the same time, be very careful not to get caught off base. This would be almost inexcusable since it would break up what is the definite prospect of a big inning.

The two-out, run-and-hit situation, in which the runners break with the pitch, must be handled with care. The proper time for this is, of course, on the 3-2 count with the batter swinging at his own discretion. On this maneuver the runner at third should not break for the plate, since doing so will interfere with the batter's swing. Going halfway will suffice. The other runners should only jog lest a smart catcher make a throw that catches one of them rounding the bag after a base on balls.

### Safety Rules

Any man who crosses the plate with a run should, as soon as he scores, assume a position that will enable him to coach any other runner who may be trying to score on the same play. He should let him know whether to slide or stay up as he comes in to home plate. This simple move can mean the difference between a run and an out and, even more important, may prevent an injury to the runner by keeping him from sliding unnecessarily or hesitating because of indecision.

It is also a good idea for the lead runner to pick up a loose bat or mask if it will be in the way and cause possible injury to the oncoming base runner.

### On Being Doubled Off Base

One of the pitfalls of which a base runner must be wary is getting doubled off base on a line drive. The only times that this can be justified occur when he is off with the pitch on a hit-and-run play and the batter hits a line drive to one of the infielders, and when the first baseman has been holding the runner close to his base and catches a line drive hit directly over the bag. In all other cases the runner should be able to return to his base safely. There is no rule compelling him to be further from his base than the nearest infielder, and he should make it a practice not to break for the next base until the ball is on the ground or through the infield.

A runner should never allow himself to be doubled up on a line drive or fly ball to the outfield, regardless of how spectacular the catch or how accurate the throw by the defensive player.

## On Being Picked Off Base

Any man who reaches base immediately becomes very important and valuable, both as a potential run and (in the team aspect of base-running) in upsetting the pitcher. He should be fully cognizant of this fact and must never allow himself to be picked off base. The runner guilty of this fault breaks up a potential big inning and may cost his team the ball game.

When a runner is clearly picked off, he should start immediately for the next base, hoping to force a mishandled throw or a run-down from which he can escape.

## The Run-down

When caught in a run-down, a ballplayer rarely escapes safely. Yet alert thinking and the practice of good technique can help a runner to capitalize on the run-down as a potential gain of ninety feet. Obviously, adequate drill work on this maneuver is a requisite for any ball club

A trapped runner should try to work his way toward the next base, retreating only if there is a definite avenue of escape. He should try to force as many throws as possible by changing directions as soon as the ball leaves a fielder's hand. His primary goal should be to delay the tag as long as possible, for the lengthier the delay, the greater the chance for an error. This tactic also permits other runners to advance.

A runner may occasionally resort to one of two methods to escape the out. First, since he is permitted to run in a path three feet to either side of the base line, he can use these six feet in which to maneuver. Second, he can force the defense into committing an obstruction, a violation that means not only that the runner(s) will be declared safe but also that an extra base will be awarded. Infielders often have a tendency to linger in the base line after throwing. If the runner changes directions as soon as the fielder makes his throw and rushes at him as fast as possible, contact with a fielder not in possession of the ball may ensue. And this, of course, is obstruction on the part of the defensive player.

A coach who intends to use either of these moves would be wise to give the umpires prior warning.

### Taking a Lead

When a player becomes a base runner, his job is to advance as quickly and easily as possible around the bases until he scores a run for his team. Any move that will make his task easier should be both studied and perfected.

One of the methods by which a runner can help himself is to master the correct technique of taking a lead, a maneuver that varies according to the base involved and the game situation. The runner who takes a proper lead greatly enhances his possibilities of getting a good jump on the ball and, of course, of eventually scoring a run.

**The Lead Off First.** The pitcher's move to first is the major factor in determining a safe as well as sufficient lead. Against a left-hander, especially one with a good pick-off move, a small lead is a necessary precaution. Naturally, greater liberties may be taken with a right-hander on the mound.

A lead of four steps would seem ideal. This would permit the runner two steps and a slide. Against some pitchers a bigger lead will be possible, but two steps and a slide should be used. This will prove adequate—and safe.

The runner, in taking his lead, should keep on his toes with his weight well balanced. A modified crouch with the arms slightly extended to the side will help maintain good balance and allow the runner to move quickly in either direction. When the pitcher makes a pick-off throw the runner should use a slide whenever necessary to get back safely. For a quick return to the base when a slide is not required, the most efficient method is to go straight to the base, hit it with the right foot, then step over the foul line with the left foot.

One rule that should be scrupulously observed by a base runner is never to cross his legs when taking a lead. Once he does so, he can be caught flat-footed by a pick-off throw. Backing off the base until the full lead has been reached is a good method of avoiding the tangled feet that can cause the runner to be caught off base.

The pitcher's feet and knees should be closely observed for a tip-off signalling a throw to first to pick off the runner. When a right-hander lifts his *rear heel* as his initial move, he is definitely going to first base with the ball.

A defensive lead, one in which the normal distance is used but in which the weight is leaning toward first, is a good precautionary measure. This is so against both a pitcher with a particularly good move and one who is unknown.

The so-called secondary lead is of great importance. This is the lead that the runner can take on the pitcher's motion. To assure himself of a good start on a batted ball, the runner should take a moving secondary lead of two or three steps. However, he should take it at only half speed and never in such a way that he will be retired on a pick-off throw from the catcher. Safety for a move in either direction is the keynote here.

In making a break for second base, the runner should start by pivoting on his right foot. The first step is then a crossover with the left foot. This means that almost a full step is gained in comparison with starting by a step on the right foot—and every step is important in making the next base safely.

*Base-running—the take-off*

**Going from First to Third.** Going from first to third on a single is a move that should be thought about and practiced until a player is thoroughly prepared to take full advantage of the opportunity to do so when it arises.

The runner (and coaches) should be aware of the exact position of the outfielders and the throwing ability of each. The latter includes the tendency to charge the ball, to field it cleanly, to get it away fast, and the actual strength of their arms. They should also take full cognizance of how hard the ball is hit.

With two outs the runner should be absolutely sure that he can reach third before attempting to do so. With one out he can afford to take a chance. With no outs the attempt to reach third may be worth the gamble since it may set up a big inning.

**The Lead Off Second.** Taking a lead off second differs markedly from taking one off first for two reasons: first, a runner at second is not held close to the bag as he is at first base; second, the catcher's pick-off throw is a long one, and less danger exists of being caught off base on a throw by the catcher.

For this reason a big lead is not necessary at second base even though a longer one is possible than at first. As a matter of fact, a really big lead at second should be discouraged. There is little sense in drawing a pick-off throw or in being lured into a trap for a well-timed play by the pitcher and shortstop.

The runner at second should not venture further than the distance of the shortstop or second baseman from the bases depending upon which one is closer to the bag. A lead of about four steps is a good one. A bigger one is not needed, since the runner can get fifteen to twenty feet on the pitcher's motion—and this is a moving lead, not a stop-and-go one.

The runner on second should be certain that a ball hit to the shortstop has gone through before breaking for third. However, if the ball is hit to his left, he can set out for third since there is little possibility of his being thrown out on such a ball. Furthermore, an alert runner may be able to advance to third on a long throw to first by the shortstop (and, in some cases, by the third baseman) if he gets a good jump, taking off just as the infielder throws.

**The Lead Off Third.** The first rule to be observed by a runner at third is that he should take his lead in foul territory. A runner who fails to follow this rule betrays evidence of poor coaching and inexperience. The reason for taking a lead in foul territory is to eliminate the possibility of the runner's being hit by a batted ball in fair ground. This would, of course, result in his being declared out.

In returning to base, the runner should move into fair territory so as to obstruct the vision of both the catcher and the third baseman should a pick-off throw be attempted.

The second principle is that the runner at third should return to his base and tag up on any ball hit in the air. The reason for this has been discussed previously; so suffice it to say here that a coach cannot over-emphasize the importance of an *immediate* and instinctive return to the base.

When tagging up on a fly ball, the runner should shift his weight to the advanced foot before the actual start. The first step is then taken with the rear foot (in this case, the left one), allowing him to get a much better jump on the ball—it saves almost a full step. The runner is allowed to leave his base as soon as the ball comes into contact with any part of the fielder.

Ordinarily a big lead can be taken at third base. There is more danger of a pick-off throw from the catcher than from the pitcher, and with this in mind, the runner should determine how large a lead he can get on the pitcher's motion. He should, however, avoid taking such a big lead that he will have to start back toward third before the catcher actually has possession of the ball since this can cause him to lose an opportunity to score on a passed ball.

*The lead off third* (left); *returning to third* (center); *tagging up* (right).

Faking a steal of home can occasionally disconcert the pitcher and impair his effectiveness. The false start toward the plate should be made as the pitcher reaches the top of his windup, in hopes that his concentration on the pitch to the batter will be upset.

### Sliding

The purpose of the slide is threefold: it can enable a runner to avoid being tagged and to reach base safely in many cases in which he would otherwise be put out; it is a very effective brake for a runner who must stop at a base—far more so than an erect stop; and it can serve to prevent a possible collision between the runner and an infielder.

**Technique.** Sliding should be practiced diligently by all ballplayers. Properly done, it is one of the most useful (and necessary) skills that a player can acquire. Improperly done, it can result in serious injury.

A good slide is actually a form of controlled falling, in which it is of the utmost importance to have the muscles relaxed. To provide maximum safety from leg injuries, a ballplayer should fall backward as he hits the dirt. The slide should be made on the most well-padded part of his body —the buttocks. In addition, the front foot should be raised off the ground to eliminate the danger of having the spikes catch in the dirt. The runner should be limp as he hits the bag.

**Theory.** When the runner is at all in doubt, he should slide. He cannot err by doing so, one important factor in his favor being that the braking effect of a slide will eliminate the need to slow down before reaching the base. Of course, a slightly earlier arrival at the base will result.

Once the runner makes up his mind to slide, he should do so. There should never be the least hesitation in the slide itself—hesitation or changing one's mind at the last second being the chief causes of injury to a sliding runner.

**Direction.** A runner should look to the coach for a signal to slide or stay up. A good coach will also indicate the side to which the slide should be made. At second base, where there is no coach, the runner must take his cue from the infielder who covers the bag.

The slide should be to the side opposite that on which the ball is coming. The position of the fielder's hands and eyes serve as a guide to the runner for judging the direction of the throw. When the fielder reaches directly toward the runner, the slide should be straight into the bag in an attempt to interfere with the throw. This applies also to a force play.

### The Slides

There are three basic slides, each of which should be practiced and mastered—and on both sides of the body for slides to either side of the base. They are all feet-first slides. The head-first slide should be discouraged since it not only allows very little deception but also greatly increases the danger of injury to head, face, and hands. This is so despite the increased use of it by major leaguers as the quickest means of reaching a base. Amateurs should adopt the more conventional method.

When sliding, the runner should do so in such a way that his face will be turned away from the throw. Furthermore, since there is a strong tendency to put the hands down on the ground, giving rise to cuts and scrapes, the sliding runner should make sure to carry his hands well off the ground. Picking up a handful of pebbles or dirt each time he gets on base will help a runner to rid himself of this tendency. The hands and arms can also be used to protect the head and face.

**The Bent-Leg Slide.** The bent-leg slide is usually made straight in to the bag. It serves as an effective brake and also enables a man to spring up and keep going.

The take-off can be made on either foot. When the slide is made straight in to the bag, either side can be used; the choice depends on whichever is easier for the player involved. As he starts his slide, the runner should fall back on his buttocks, tucking one foot under his body with his knee bent at approximately a right angle. The advanced foot should be kept in the air so that the spikes won't catch in the dirt, and the leg should be virtually straight. The body weight should be back on the buttocks—not on the knee.

If the runner desires to stop at the base into which he is sliding, his forward foot should go over the bag, which is then hooked with the rear foot.

In the case of an overthrow or mishandled ball, the runner may want to continue on to the next base. If so, he should hit the bag with his front foot, at the same time pushing up with the leg that is tucked under him. His momentum, as well as the added push, will enable him to spring up and get away quite easily.

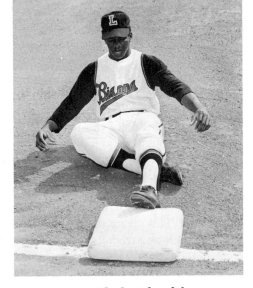

*The bent-leg slide*

The bent-leg slide can also be used to elude the tag. Here, the slide is made slightly to the side of the base, the lead foot hooking the nearest corner of the bag as the body continues on to the side away from the throw.

Primarily, however, the bent-leg slide is the one that should be used when the runner intends to go straight in to the base.

**The Hook Slide.** When a runner is attempting to avoid being tagged, he generally uses the hook slide. It can enable a runner to establish contact with the base while simultaneously falling away from the tag with his body. The hook slide should be mastered on both sides so that the runner will always be able to slide away from the ball.

In making this slide, the runner should take off on his left foot for a slide to the left and with his right foot for a slide to the right. He should

*The hook slide*

go straight in to the bag, contacting the middle of the front part of it with the left foot when sliding to the right and with the right foot when sliding to the left. The other foot should be held off the ground as it goes to the side of the base. The momentum of the slide will cause the body to hook around to the side of the base.

In short, the hook slide should be straight in to the base until contact with the bag is established; then the body falls away from the tag. This method enables the runner to save valuable time in reaching his objective. Too often, ballplayers fall away from the base before actually contacting it. This means that the runner will have travelled an extra two or three feet before arriving at the base—often the difference between being safe and out.

The whip slide is a variation of the hook slide and is used to avoid the tag when the baseman is waiting with the ball. It starts as the hook slide does, but the runner slides further to the side of the base, kicking his legs away from the base as he hits the ground. He reaches for the base with the nearer arm, and as the baseman tries to tag him, he whips his arm back and away, turning his body in. At the same time he reaches for and touches the base with his other arm. The baseman must follow the slide, and the runner gives him only his arm or hand as a target for the tag.

**The Feet-First Slide.** This is a straight-in slide used to get back to the base on a pick-off throw or to avoid being doubled up. Although not advisable, the head-first slide can also be used in this situation—a runner should use anything to get back safely.

On a straight-in slide the runner should concentrate on watching the base. Conversely, on a slide designed primarily to avoid being tagged, he should concentrate on the baseman's hands.

**Two Special Slides.** The double-play slide (the slide to break up a double play) has been described in a previous section; yet some of its salient points bear repetition.

In breaking up a double play, the runner must slide in such a way that some part of his body is within reaching distance of the base. The most effective method to use is a hard straight-in slide with the knees bent at a forty-five-degree angle. If possible, the runner should make contact with the striding foot of the defensive player.

Sliding in to first base is another special slide. The runner should slide in to first base only when it will mean avoiding a collision on a close play, or when the throw pulls the first baseman off the bag toward home plate so that he must try to tag the runner. A slide will often enable the runner to avoid being tagged and to reach first base safely.

# *Offensive Plays*

## The Steal

Running teams are usually successful ones—operating in many cases, on the theory that when the other team can be made to throw the ball, there exists the possibility of an error that will enable the runner to advance. Indiscriminate base-running, however, can be of little value to anyone but the defensive team. The steal, in particular, must be judiciously employed.

The value of the steal lies in the fact that it gives the offensive team something for nothing—the advance of a runner without sacrificing an out—and can help them to a run that would not have scored had it been left entirely to batting power. As a corollary, an indirect advantage is gained from the disconcerting effect that the threat of a steal often has on the pitcher.

**Factors Affecting Its Use.** The steal should usually be attempted only when it involves an important run—almost never to win a game but only to get a runner into scoring position. For instance, it should not be used, unless it is a gift, when—

1. a team is more than two runs behind;
2. the opposing pitcher is having control trouble;
3. a runner is on second with two outs (he's already in scoring position).

The use of the steal is precluded by a slow base runner. With the right man on base, its use must still be tempered by the ability of the man at bat. For example:

1. With a good hitter at the plate, a steal of third or home should not be risked.
2. With two outs and a weak hitter at bat, a steal is unwise since an unsuccessful one means a poor batsman will lead off in the next inning.
3. With two outs and a good hitter up, a steal of second is a good move since it can put a runner in position to score on a base hit.
4. A steal of second is more likely to succeed with a left-hander at bat (he obstructs the catcher's throw, to a certain extent).

The players involved should consider the count on the batter. The steal is more logical when the pitcher is behind and cannot risk a pitch-out. If the pitcher can be expected to throw a curve (whether or not he is behind in the count), the steal will have more chance of success because of the slightly slower speed of and relative difficulty in handling the curve ball.

In the vast majority of cases, the steal will be signalled by the coach. Very rarely should the player be on his own and then only when he is a smart and experienced base runner.

**Getting the Jump.** Although most high school teams run more on the catcher than on the pitcher, it is essential for runners to learn to get a good jump on the pitcher. Certainly his moves will be the key to successful steals as they progress to higher levels of competition.

Predictably rhythmical pitchers are the easiest ones on whom to steal. They work in a cadence in which the rhythm is almost identical on every delivery to either batter or base. A smart base runner will watch the pitcher closely to learn his rhythmic pattern and will attempt to steal "on a count." In other words, if the delivery forms a five-count rhythmic cadence, the runner will go when the count reaches four. If by any chance a pick-off throw is made to the base, the runner should keep going and try to reach his objective.

A right-hander is, of course, easier to run on than a lefty. Against a righty the key is his left heel. When he lifts his left heel after his stop, he is going home with the ball. Almost invariably, a right-hander will lift his right heel as the initial move in throwing to first.

Although more caution must be exercised against a lefty, a good jump still may be achieved. The runner should learn to go on a lefty's *first* move, whatever it may be. In most cases he will pitch to the batter, and the runner will get his jump. If the throw goes to first, the runner should head for second—delaying his slide as long as possible to hinder the shortstop. Unless the ball is handled cleanly and thrown with accuracy, the runner should be able to make it safely to second.

Other clues that indicate pretty definitely that the pitcher is delivering to the plate are dropping his rear shoulder, raising his front elbow, and bending his rear knee.

Combining these two methods—counting and tip-offs—whenever possible will provide an almost perfect way in which to get a good jump on the ball. This is the secret to successful base-stealing.

**The Batter's Role.** The batter can aid materially in effecting a successful steal.

When this play has been signalled, the batter should move to the rear of the batter's box and should swing to miss the ball if it is a strike (in scholastic ball few hitters can afford to give up a strike, and there is more likelihood of imperfect play by the defense). An even more effective device in disconcerting the catcher is to fake a bunt, drawing the bat back at the very last instant. He will be much more conscious of an obstruction with a stationary rather than moving bat and may be less prepared for a steal with "bunt" imprinted in his mind. The batter can be of considerable help to a teammate who is trying to steal third by simply bluffing a bunt. This may draw the third baseman plateward, leaving his base unguarded against the steal.

On a steal of home, the batter serves a useful purpose by crowding the plate and remaining in position until the last possible instant. He may be able to swing at the ball, missing it intentionally. If so, the swing should be an easy and high one, although it cannot be risked if the runner is too close. Faking a bunt may be a better method and could cause the catcher to commit interference in his anxiety to get the ball in time to retire the runner.

**Stealing Third.** Any discussion of base-stealing pertains primarily to the steal of second base. A steal of third is relatively rare, despite the fact that it is more easily accomplished than a steal of second. That the runner can get a much bigger lead and jump on the pitcher is partially offset by the fact that he is already in scoring position and need not risk an out by attempting to steal third. Nevertheless, it is good percentage baseball to try for third base when chances of success seem reasonably good.

A steal of third is best done with one out and a right-hander at bat. This will put the runner in position to score on a ground ball, a fly to the outfield, error, or a squeeze play. Ordinarily, an attempted steal of third with no outs is bad policy since three chances remain to bring him in from scoring position. It is very poor strategy to try a steal of third with a left-hander at bat since, in this case, the catcher has a clear view of third and an unobstructed throw to that base.

The *continuous acceleration* move in stealing third is worthy of mention. Using this move, the runner lengthens his lead with increasing speed until in full flight. It is particularly effective against a left-handed pitcher.

**A Precaution.** When a runner has had to return to his base several times because foul balls have nullified a steal, the play should be called off since his repeated efforts will have a tiring effect.

**Stealing Home.** A steal of home is a foolish play at best because of the many safer ways in which a runner can score from third. It is most logically tried with two outs, a weak right-handed batter at the plate, and after at least one fake has been made to lull the pitcher into a sense of false security. Its chances of success are directly proportionate to the length of the pitcher's windup. It stands greater chance of success against a left-hander since he has more difficulty in keeping third base within his view.

**The Delayed Steal.** The delayed steal is a play that should be attempted only by an exceptionally fast man. It is worked after the catcher has received the pitch and should be tried only if the runner has noticed laxness by the catcher (lobbing the ball back to the pitcher) or carelessness on the part of the second baseman and shortstop (failure to move toward the bag after the pitch). If he times his move properly, he should be taking off as the catcher starts his throw to the pitcher. The pitcher then must catch the ball, pivot, and throw, while the infielder who covers must come from a deep position to make the play—all aspects of the situation combining to improve the runner's chances of reaching second safely.

A delayed steal of third base is a rare occurrence. A good lead must be gained on the pitcher's motion, and the break for third should come as soon as it seems that the runner has succeeded in drawing a throw to second from the catcher. It can be worked only against a catcher who likes to throw and will not hesitate to fire the ball to second base. The runner attempting a delayed steal of second can also capitalize on luring the catcher into throwing behind him (to first base).

**The Double Steal.** A double steal of third and home does not make sense, for two runners are in scoring position, a normal double-play situation does not exist, and it is a very uncertain undertaking.

The primary aim of a double steal of second and third is to eliminate the possibility of a double play and to advance a second runner to scoring position. The most advantageous time for its use occurs when the offensive team is no more than two runs behind and there is one out. It is merely a steal of third with the man on first following. Thus, conditions pertaining to the steal of third apply here.

It is the first-and-third situation with which we are primarily concerned when discussing the double steal. It can be justified under two sets of circumstances: (1) with two out, when no more than two runs behind, and with a good hitter at bat—the objective being to advance a second runner to scoring position. Scoring the man on third is only a secondary aim; (2) with one out, when no more than two runs behind, and with a weak hitter at bat—the objective being to prevent a double play and possibly to score a run on the steal itself. It is worked as follows:

The man on first breaks for second on the pitch, and if the throw goes through to the base, he pulls up short and gets caught in a rundown. The man on third waits until the ball is over the pitcher's head before making his break for home, having moved out into the base line to obstruct the catcher's view of third base. If executed perfectly, this play can result in one run scored and a runner on second base. An alternative, when the throw is cut off, is to have the runner on third hold his base and the other runner continue on to second. This, of course, puts one more runner in scoring position, even though it is not literally a double steal.

**The Triple Steal.** This play is comparable in all respects to the steal of home except that, with two other men on base, it is an even more foolish venture.

**The Forced Balk.** With a poor hitter at bat, men on first and third, and an inexperienced pitcher on the mound, this play may succeed. The runner on first should start for second as soon as the pitcher looks away from him. The object is to induce a balk, something that will happen if he stops his motion or obeys the natural impulse to throw to second without first stepping off the rubber.

A variation may be attempted if a batter walks with a runner on third. He should jog to first and start for second if the pitcher looks the other way.

This play is best employed with fewer than two outs so that if the pitcher does not balk, a put out will not end the inning with men on base.

### The Sacrifice

The only purpose of the sacrifice is to advance a runner by sacrificing an out. The batter should give himself up, concentrating solely on getting the bunt down and in the right location. An attempt to mask his intentions will detract from the batter's ability to bunt well. Furthermore, the defensive team, especially in amateur competition, is more likely to lose its composure when it knows that a bunt is coming.

Bunting technique is described in the section on batting.

**The Pitch.** When the sacrifice is on, the batter picks his own pitch, selecting one that is "buntable" though not necessarily a strike. However, if it is a strike and the batter does not try to bunt it, he has committed a serious error.

*The first principle of the sacrifice—give yourself up and get the ball on the ground so as to advance the runner (Eddie Brinkman)*

**The Place.** Ideally, a sacrifice should go toward third and be hard enough to make the third baseman field it, leaving his base open. But unless the bunter is accomplished, he should bunt the ball where it is pitched.

If he is capable of placing his bunts well, the batter should do so according to the game situation. With a runner on first base, a bunt toward first can be effective against a right-handed first baseman. He will have been holding the runner and will be in relatively poor position for a throw to second. Of course, this will eliminate the possibility of the runner's advancing to an unguarded third base.

Ordinarily a bunt toward third is desirable with a runner on second base. However, with men on first and second and a force-out possible, the difference in fielding ability between the first baseman and pitcher should be considered. The bunt should go toward third if the pitcher is the poorer gloveman, toward first if the first baseman is more inept, with the additional qualification that the play at third is easier for a left-handed pitcher.

The distance of defensive players from home plate at the time of the play is another factor in determining the wisest target for the sacrifice bunt.

**The Time.** The strategy behind a sacrifice makes it an advisable, if not mandatory, maneuver at times. It is definitely a wise move in certain situations:

1. In the late innings of a tight game, especially with no outs and a runner on first or men on first and second.
2. With a weak hitter at bat, followed by a strong hitter. A pitcher, if he is not a good hitter, should sacrifice even with one out to eliminate the double-play possibility and to give himself a rest if he bunts successfully.
3. As a surprise play—with one out and a good hitter coming up next.
4. With a man on second, no outs, the score close, and in the late innings. The runner can then score on a fly, error, or short hit.

5. In a close game, with no outs and men on first and second, even with a good hitter at bat. Having two runners in scoring position makes the loss of the out worthwhile even though a good hitter has been sacrificed.

6. In a close game with men on first and third, and no outs—especially if the man on first is the winning run. At worst, the offensive team should wind up with men on second and third and one out; if the bunt is well placed, the man on third can score.

**The Runner.** The runner should be able to advance unless the bunt is a really poor one. He must, however, exercise caution in one respect—making sure that the bunt is on the ground before breaking for the next base. He should not allow himself to be doubled up if the bunt is popped into the air or picked off by the catcher if the bunt is missed completely.

After taking his lead, the runner should advance an additional few steps in a secondary lead as the pitcher delivers the ball. He should then hold up and delay his break for the next base until sure that the ball is on the ground.

Patience is demanded of both batter and runner. Neither should commit himself too soon, and both should remember that it is preferable to advance to second by way of a walk.

**The Bunt-and-Run.** This play can be very effective and can be a judicious substitute for the hit-and-run. Here, as in the hit-and-run, the runner breaks with the pitch. The batter, instead of swinging, lays down a sacrifice bunt. The runner should be able to reach third base if the bunt is a good one, particularly if the third baseman must field it. The runner must exercise caution, however, lest a smart third baseman throw to second and catch him rounding that base.

## The Squeeze Play

When properly executed, the squeeze play not only scores a run but also can have a demoralizing effect on the defensive team. But it cannot be used indiscriminately, and it is potentially dangerous since any indication that it is being employed will bring an unbuntable pitch and an easy out.

**The Time.** The proper time to try the squeeze is in the late innings of a close game, with *one* out. There is little sense in gambling for the run (and the risk is great on a squeeze) unless it is an important one. Moreover, with no outs there are three chances to score the runner from third.

**The Bunter.** The man at bat on a squeeze play must be a good bunter since he must get the ball on the ground in fair territory. As stated in the section on batting, the technique for the squeeze bunt involves moving the front foot back in squaring around so as to allow slightly more time to bunt, to delay the catcher, and to increase the chances of causing interference by the catcher.

**The Suicide Squeeze.** This is an all-out gamble to score a run. The runner breaks for the plate, and the batter must bunt the ball no matter where it is pitched. The runner and the batter must wait until the pitcher is in the act of throwing to the plate before making their moves. The batter has one main concern—to bunt the ball in fair territory, on the ground.

**The Double Squeeze.** This is merely a suicide squeeze with runners on second and third. The runner from second breaks with the pitch, rounds third, and continues home on the throw to first.

**The Safe Squeeze.** As on the sacrifice, the batter picks his own pitch, and the runner does not break for home until the ball is on the ground (in this case, in the right spot to allow him to score). The batter should not square around too soon, and—most importantly—the bunt must be well placed. Obviously the batter must be an excellent bunter. The surprise element and minimizing the possibility of losing the runner are factors contributing to the advantages offered by the safe squeeze. The sacrifice with men on first and third is a version of the safe squeeze.

**Two-out Squeeze.** With an outstanding bunter at bat, a drag-bunt squeeze with two out may prove successful, depending entirely on the unexpectedness of the play and the ability of the batter to bunt safely for a hit. It is a variation of the safe squeeze.

### The Hit-and-Run

The hit-and-run can be a devastating weapon, effective in advancing runners as well as in discouraging the opposition. Upon it is based the attack of a so-called running team.

**Theory.** The hit-and-run is based on the idea that the runner moving toward second will draw either the shortstop or second baseman away from his normal position. Obviously it is intended to advance the runner two bases rather than one.

Probably more important as an aim is the elimination of a possible double play on a ground ball. In this case, not only will a double play be avoided, but a runner will advance to scoring position.

**The Time.** The hit-and-run should be used only when a run is needed and with an experienced player at bat. It is always a good play when the pitcher is behind the batter and must throw a strike.

This is particularly so on the 3-1 pitch because a fourth ball does not have to be hit by the batter, a safe advance to second being automatic.

The hit-and-run is often sound policy with a weak hitter at bat—a man who is more than likely to hit a double-play ball; but it is not good policy when more than one run behind or with two outs.

**The Batter.** The runner must be protected; therefore, a good hit-and-run man is one who is capable of "getting a piece of the ball" on a given pitch. Preferably he has sufficient bat control to hit to the spot vacated by the man moving to cover second on an apparent steal. Generally he should be adept at hitting behind the runner (to right field) in order to enhance a team's chances of moving the runner from first to third.

The batter should be alert in detecting a player's edging over to cover second base. Usually the second baseman takes it for a right-handed batter, the shortstop for a lefty. The batter should use this to guide his actions. When the covering infielder cannot be detected in time, it is always safe to hit to right field (behind the runner).

**The Runner.** The runner should break for second base as soon as the pitcher is going to the plate with the ball—exactly as he would on a straight steal. After he has taken a few steps and the ball has been hit, the runner should look for it to make sure that it is not a fly ball that will be caught and on which he could be doubled up at first base.

**The Bunt-and-Run.** This play really belongs in the category of the sacrifice, where it has been discussed. It is a relatively safe maneuver with a good bunter at bat.

**The Run-and-Hit.** For a team that lacks good hit-and-run men but wishes to play a running game, the run-and-hit is a very effective weapon. "Starting the runner" involves his breaking for second on the pitch. The batter, however, swings only if it is a strike. This provides two options— a steal if the pitch is a ball, the hit-and-run if it is a strike.

The run-and-hit is particularly effective with the count at 3-2. If the pitch is a strike, the batter has a good ball to hit; if it is a ball, the runner advances automatically.

**Strategy.** For most effective results this play calls for a fast man at first base and a right-field hitter at the plate.

It can be used with men on first and second but, in this case, is not likely to open a hole at either short or second.

The hit-and-run should not be used with a slow man on base and a fast one at bat. A slow base runner stands little chance of stealing second if the batter fails to hit the ball; a fast man at bat is unlikely to hit into a double play. Thus, under these circumstances, it is both unwise and unnecessary to employ the hit-and-run.

A long-ball hitter or a man who hits sharp line drives should not be required to swing at a certain pitch, for this will greatly reduce his chances of hitting the ball solidly. The hit-and-run should not be employed with such a man at bat.

It is bad policy to employ the hit-and-run with men on first and third, no outs, and a 3-2 count on the batter for the following reasons: there are three chances to score the man from third; a line drive or strike out can result in a double play, choking off a possible rally; and the runner on third will score anyway on a ground-ball double play.

## The Run-and-Bunt—
## Key to an Aggressive Running Game

The plays and their nuances thus far described have been based on conventional baseball tactics. At the amateur level a more daring approach, based on starting the runner, has proved highly successful in my own coaching career.

The purpose of this type of running game is to pick up extra bases and runs; to force the breaks by making the opposition throw the ball. The principles on which this philosophy are based include the following:

1. Getting a good jump on the ball
2. Reducing the pressure on the batter since few schoolboys have really good bat control
3. Using multiple-choice plays to provide safety valves
4. Being aggressive yet judicious in the approach to situation strategy
5. Making every effort to advance a runner to third base, from which there are nine ways to score a run, as opposed to two from second base.

It is entirely possible to build a successful running game around the sacrifice, especially with the use of multiple-choice plays. These are run-and-bunt plays in which the runner breaks with the pitch and the batter bunts at his own discretion.

The option feature of multiple-choice plays offers many advantages:

1. When the batter squares around, the defense will think "sacrifice." This will aid any attempted steal.
2. Even if one man misses the sign, the double-option possibility can help avoid disaster.
3. A good bunt can produce a two-base sacrifice, especially if the third baseman is forced to field the ball.

In attempting to sacrifice a runner from second to third, two principles must be considered. With a lefty at bat, the runner should wait until the ball is on the ground before advancing (an attempted steal of third with a lefty at bat is unwise), which strategy makes this an ordinary sacrifice.

With a right-hander at the plate, however, it may be possible to squeeze the runner home from second, particularly when the bunt goes toward third. Here the defense will have to make the long throw to first and then a good peg to the plate to head off the runner.

This method of attack—starting the runner on a sacrifice—demands good bunting, which in turn requires careful teaching and considerable practice. Perfected, it can prove a devastating weapon in a team's offensive arsenal.

## THE BASE COACHES

The coaches at first and third base play an important role in the success of any team. Theirs is a demanding role, for they must concentrate fully on their tasks, keeping one jump ahead of the play and being prepared to make split-second decisions as various situations arise.

Whether this role is filled by a manager, coach, or player, its duties and responsibilities should be thoroughly understood by any man who occupies a coaching box.

### The Basic Rule

As a first consideration the coaches must never assume that a runner will do the right thing—they must always give him instructions.

Every offensive play and possibility should be clear in the coach's mind so that he can properly instruct the runner. It is imperative that he be aware at all times of the inning, the number of outs, the score, the count, the speed of the runner, the ability of the next hitter, and the habits of the defensive players.

### The Two Coaches

The first base coach has jurisdiction over the batter as soon as he becomes a base runner and should encourage as well as guide him as he comes to first. Once the runner passes first base, he must focus his attention ahead of him, and he becomes the responsibility of the third base coach. However, this should not prevent the first base coach from shouting warnings or advice whenever necessary.

The third base coach is the more important of the two, both because he is the one who usually gives the signals for offensive plays and because of his position in the directing of base-line traffic. After the runner has reached scoring position, it is the third base coach who must attempt to guide him safely in to home plate with a run.

### Advising the Man on Base

About 90 percent of the help that a coach can give the runner comes before the ball is hit. Such assistance includes the location of the ball, the number of outs, the alignment of the defense, any offensive play that has been signalled, when to play safe, the throwing ability of the outfielders, when to tag up or go halfway, the pick-off move of the pitcher, the catcher's throwing ability, what to do on a ground ball, the danger of a line drive, and any other information pertinent to the game situation.

To inform the runner of these things, the coach should move as close to him as possible between pitches. This helps the runner understand the coach's advice and prevents the opposition's overhearing what may prove to be valuable information to them.

### Guiding the Man in Motion

Once in motion, the runner is, for the most part, on his own. However, the coach must be depended upon almost entirely when the ball is outside the runner's field of vision. Regardless of the situation, any encouragement or instructions that the coach may give can be of assistance to the runner.

An oncoming runner should be advised of whether to keep going, take his turn and stop, or stay on the bag. He should also be urged on if the play will be close—a coach should bear in mind that a runner does not always make an all-out effort and must be reminded to do so when the occasion demands it.

*Coaching signals: stop* (left); *take your turn* (center); *slide* (right).

### Signalling the Runner

Rotating the arms in a clockwise motion is a signal to the runner to continue to the next base. The coach should step toward the base line when giving this signal so that there will be no doubt of his intent.

When the coach holds one hand in the air, palm toward the runner, and points to the next base with his other hand, he is indicating that the runner should round the base and hold up, remaining alert for the possibility of advancing an extra base.

To stop the runner, the coach should hold both hands in the air, palms toward the runner; if the play dictates that the runner should stay on the base, the coach should point to it.

The third base coach should signal a runner whether to slide or stay up. Occasionally the first base coach may be called upon to do so, but this is a relatively rare occurrence.

To stop the runner, the coach holds both hands in the air, palms toward the runner. To indicate the necessity of sliding, the coach should extend his arms toward the ground, palms down, much as an umpire does in calling a runner safe. Holding the hands toward either side of the base will let the runner know to which side the slide should be made.

As the runner approaches third base, the coach should move up the line toward home plate, enabling him to advise the runner at the last possible second. This, of course, is applicable only when there will be no play at third base.

### Whom to Watch

With a man on base, the coach should pay little attention to the pitch but should keep his eye on any infielder who may sneak in behind the runner for a pick-off attempt.

**341**

With one exception it is the baseman moving toward the base to take a throw who will tip off a throw to the base. Only at first, with the first baseman holding the runner close to the base, is it the pitcher who should be watched for a pick-off attempt.

### Tagging Up

The coach should see that a runner who has tagged up on a fly ball gets a good start. He should watch the ball and give the runner a signal to go as soon as the ball comes into contact with the fielder. With no outs it is good percentage baseball to have a runner on first or second tag up on a medium-deep fly ball, a possible exception being one hit to center field, from where the throw to second is short.

If there is one out or if it appears doubtful whether the ball will be caught, a runner at either first or second should go half-way. With two outs, of course, all runners should be moving as soon as the ball is hit.

A runner at third base should instinctively and immediately tag up on any ball hit in the air. This will save him valuable time in trying to score on a caught fly ball. If the ball falls in for a hit (even if it is a sharp line drive), he can still score easily. The coach should remind any runner who reaches third to tag up on a ball hit in the air, but this move should become automatic and instantaneous.

A special play that presents interesting possibilities is the foul fly, hit with runners on first and third. Both runners should tag up, and as soon as the ball is caught, they should both bluff a break for the next base. If this maneuver draws a throw, it will enable at least one of them to advance. In this case a throw to second base could enable the runner on third to score; a throw to the plate could permit the runner on first to move to second, thereby placing two runners in scoring position. This play is certainly worth a try if the occasion for it arises.

### Avoiding the Double Play

On only two occasions is it excusable for a runner to be doubled up on a ball hit in the air: (1) a line drive to the infield on a hit-and-run play; (2) a line drive that the first baseman catches directly over the bag with a runner on that base.

In all other instances there is no need for the runner to be further from the base than the nearest infielder. The coach should alert the runner to the danger of being doubled up on a line drive and should have him headed back to the base as soon as the play seems apparent. The runner should not leave for the next base until the ball is on the ground or has gone through the infield.

A runner should *never* be doubled up on a *fly ball*; it is the coach's duty to see that he is properly alerted at all times.

### Avoiding a Gift Out

The coach should not allow a runner to run directly into a tag on a ground ball to an infielder. The runner should be warned of this ahead of time so that he does not blunder into this situation.

For example, when, on a grounder to the second baseman with a man on first, the fielder attempts to tag the runner, the latter should stop and make the second baseman chase him. Delaying the tag in this way will often eliminate the possibility of a double play.

### The Pick-off

A runner who is picked off base breaks up a potential big inning. This should never happen, and, to a great extent, it is the coach's responsibility. The coach should keep the runner informed at all times and should prevent him from wandering so far off base that he is easy prey for a pick-off throw.

### Specific Coaching Duties

The runner is, of course, the key man when he is on the base paths, but the coach can exert a strong influence on his actions. There are several specific responsibilities that can help in this respect.

*First Base*

1. Do not allow the runner to take his lead until the pitcher is on the mound, ready to pitch.
2. Watch for a predictable rhythm in the pitcher's motion, and inform the runner if a cadence can be "counted." It can help him get a good jump on the ball.
3. With a sacrifice in order, watch the second baseman lest he sneak behind the runner for a pick-off throw.
4. Advise a runner on second only if a fielder sneaks behind him. In all other cases, a conflict with the advice from the third base coach should not be chanced.
5. Advise a runner on first of the game situation and of any signals given.

*Third Base*

1. Inform a runner on second of the number of outs and of whether to tag up or go halfway on a fly ball. Remind him to be certain that the ball has gone through the left side of the infield before advancing; to run full speed if forced on a ground ball; of whether to "play it safe" or to take a chance; and of how much room the shortstop is allowing him.
2. As a runner rounds third on his way home, the coach should let him know whether to run hard or take his time.
3. Once the runner passes third base, the coach should concentrate on the succeeding runner(s).
4. The coach should be alert for a throw intended to catch a runner who has taken his turn at third.
5. The coach should inform a runner at third of the number of outs; to tag up on any ball hit in the air; of whether the infield is playing in to cut off a run at the plate; to stay outside the base line; to be alert (and not moving back to third) on passed balls; and of any signal that may have been given (this should be done verbally).

## Signals

The signal for an offensive play is usually given by the third base coach. This is invariably so when the manager or head coach fills that role. If the manager remains on the bench, he occasionally gives direct signals himself but generally relays them through the third base coach.

On some ball clubs the third base coach gives signals to a left-handed batter, the first base coach to a right-hander. Usually, however, the third base coach gives all the signals.

**The Plays.** Signals are generally used for five offensive maneuvers. They are the take and the hit-away for the batter, and the sacrifice, steal, and hit-and-run for both runner(s) and batter. For purposes of simplicity, the hit-and-run and squeeze can be covered by the same signal.

**Types of Signals.** The signals used should be simple and should be conveyed by a natural movement or gesture on the part of the coach. They can be given by one gesture, a series of moves, or by elimination of one of the series of moves. In addition, they can be indicated by a key that precedes or follows the sign.

It is advisable to have an answering signal from both batter and runner(s). This helps avoid confusion and can eliminate costly mixups in attempted plays.

**By the Batter.** A team with a good hit-and-run man often allows him to give his own signal for the play. It should be arranged with the three men who precede him in the batting order and demands an answering signal.

**Dual-Purpose Signs.** The run-and-hit, whenever employed, is a combination play. It has the effect of a hit-and-run when the batter swings at the ball and is a steal when he takes the pitch. Some ball clubs use this in lieu of the hit-and-run when that play is signalled; others have a special sign for it. It is particularly useful with a 3-1 or 3-2 count since a fourth ball will achieve the desired result with no risk of an out.

Many teams use the same signal for both hit-and-run and suicide squeeze. The safe squeeze, on the other hand, can be indicated by using the sacrifice sign.

**Concealing Signals.** The manager or coach who gives his signals from the bench is invariably subjected to close scrutiny by the opposition. Consequently, an oft-used practice is to have one of the players on the bench give signs at the manager's bidding. Then the opposing team must discover who gives the signals before they can begin to decipher them.

The danger of a club's having its signals stolen is ever present. Some teams go as far as to have certain players on the bench concentrate on the opposing coaches, batter, and runner(s) during an entire game to accomplish this purpose. The hit-and-run sign is the only one in which professional clubs are really interested, and a knowledge of it by the defense can paralyze a team's attack. For this reason an alternate set of signals should be resorted to when the least suspicion of stolen signals is aroused.

**Sample Signals.** There are, of course, innumerable gestures and combinations thereof that can be used as offensive signals. Assuming that they are to be given by the third base coach, we will present the following sets of signals as examples of three commonly used methods of giving signs. Each is combined with a key, and resorts to occasional use of a verbal signal. Answering signs should be arranged for the hitter and runner(s) alike.

*One Gesture*

> Key: Walk toward the hitter when giving the signal
> Sacrifice: Right hand to cap
> Steal: Right hand to letters
> Hit-and-run: Right hand to belt
> Take-off (cancel): Left hand to same spot
> Take: Both hands to cap
> Hit away: Skin to skin
> Answer—batter: Step into box left foot first; runner: skin to cloth

*Series*

> Key: Hands on knees after giving signal
> Sacrifice: Touch cap, letters, and pants—in that order
> Steal: Touch letters, pants, and cap—in that order
> Hit-and-run: Touch pants, cap, and letters—in that order
> Take-off: Rub hands together
> Take: Remove cap
> Hit away—verbal: "Get yourself a hit"
> Answer—batter: Run hand up bat; runner: tip cap

*Elimination*

> Key: Cup hands to mouth, and shout at batter or runner
> General signal: Touch cap, face, letters, and belt—going down
> Sacrifice: Don't touch face
> Steal: Don't touch letters
> Hit-and-run: Don't touch belt
> Take-off: Rub upward
> Take—verbal: "Look it over"
> Hit away: Hands on knees
> Answer: Batter and runner both hitch pants

# Addenda

# *Baseball Tactics in Action*

The practical application of many of the ideas presented in this book can, perhaps, best be shown by the analysis of an actual game.

The third game of the 1956 World Series between the Dodgers and Yankees has been chosen to serve as an illustration of many of the points emphasized in the text. That this particular contest was played many years ago and that it was not a particularly memorable one are inconsequential. Important is the fact that this was an interesting game from a tactical standpoint and that it serves admirably to demonstrate how major league ballplayers practice sound techniques and tactics.

The clubs held pregame meetings in which they reviewed the capabilities and habits of their opponents, both individually and collectively. The strength, weakness, and tactics of each hitter; the speed and daring of each man when on base; the fielding and throwing ability of each player; the operating methods of the rival pitchers; the characteristics of the ball park; the prevailing weather conditions; the overall team strategy —all these points were carefully discussed.

The game was played at Yankee Stadium on October 6, 1956. It was a sunny, rather cool day as the game started, with a moderate wind blowing in from right field. Playing conditions were good.

The lineups:

| BROOKLYN | NEW YORK |
|---|---|
| Gilliam, lf | Bauer, rf |
| Reese, ss | Collins, 1b |
| Snider, cf | Mantle, cf |
| Robinson, 3b | Berra, c |
| Hodges, 1b | Slaughter, lf |
| Furillo, rf | Martin, 2b |
| Campanella, c | McDougald, ss |
| Neal, 2b | Carey, 3b |
| Craig, p | Ford, p |

*First Inning*

Whitey Ford, a left-hander, was the Yankee pitcher. He had a good fast ball and an excellent curve, which he controlled exceptionally well.

**349**

DODGERS:

Gilliam, after taking a strike, was thrown out by Carey.

**Gilliam, leading off, was playing the percentages by taking a strike.

Reese struck out after running the count to 3-2.

**Ford's first five pitches were fast ball, curve, fast ball, curve, and fast ball, in that order. On the 3-2 pitch he used the same rhythmical motion but hesitated at the top of his windup, throwing Reese's timing off sufficiently to enable him to slip a fast ball past Reese for the third strike.

Snider struck out on a bad ball.

**Ford was making his task easier by staying ahead of the hitters.

Roger Craig, a tall right-hander with a sinking fast ball and fair curve, was the Dodger pitcher. He occasionally dealt sidearm to right-handed batters.

YANKEES:

Bauer took a strike, then flied deep to Furillo on a curve ball.

**Bauer followed the ball well, hitting the curve with the rotation (to right field).

Collins flied to Snider on a 3-1 pitch.

**The outfield was playing deep since they could afford to give up a single early in the game.

Mantle beat out a bunt to the right side.

**Mantle caught the infielders playing back and laid down a perfect drag bunt, just out of Craig's reach and too soft to allow Neal to make a play at first.

Berra took two balls and a strike before grounding to Neal.

**Hodges tried for the ball but returned to cover the base when Neal, who had the easier play, called for the ball.

SCORE—New York 0, Brooklyn 0

*Second Inning*

DODGERS:

Robinson walked on five pitches.

Hodges singled to deep short.

**McDougald, seeing that he had no chance to retire the batter, tried for a force at second, but Robinson, running with the 3-1 pitch on a run-and-hit situation, beat the throw.

Furillo took a strike, then flied to Bauer, Robinson advancing to third after the catch.

**With no outs Robinson tagged up and went to third after the catch. He was now in position to score on a fly ball to the outfield. Bauer's throw went to second to keep Hodges from advancing to scoring position.

Campanella flied to Bauer, Robinson scoring after the catch.

**Once again the throw went to second to keep Hodges from scoring position.

Neal fouled out to Berra.

**Berra played the ball to allow for the drift back toward the infield. Ford went toward the ball to give advice and encouragement to Berra.

YANKEES:

Slaughter flied to Gilliam.

**Gilliam was wearing sunglasses but was prepared to shield his eyes with his glove if the ball got into the sun. He played the ball to curve toward the foul line.

Martin hit a home run into the left-field seats.

**Martin met a curve ball well out in front of him, and his normal swing enabled him to hit it out of the park since he met the ball squarely.

McDougald walked on a 3-2 pitch.

**Craig was being very careful after the home run and lost the hitter.

Carey struck out.

**There was little danger of a steal with the pitcher due up next, but Campanella, as all good catchers, caught each pitch prepared to throw out the runner.

Ford struck out on a curve ball.

**Craig took advantage of his "out man" and went right to work on the pitcher.

SCORE—New York 1, Brooklyn 1

*Third Inning*

DODGERS:

Craig singled to right field.

Gilliam hit into a double play, Martin to McDougald to Collins.

**Gilliam fouled off two bunt attempts, both high fast balls, Ford making it as difficult as possible to lay one down. Martin and McDougald moved in a few steps and were in perfect position to execute a quick double play.

Reese singled to center.

**The pitch was a high fast ball, almost a waste pitch, since Ford had a count of two strikes and one ball on the batter.

Snider fanned on three pitches.

**Ford got ahead of the batter and made him chase a wide curve ball.

YANKEES:

Bauer struck out.

**Craig was following the book by concentrating on his curve ball to Bauer.

Collins grounded out, Hodges to Craig.

**Craig broke for first as soon as he saw that the ball was hit to the right side. Since the ball was hit to Hodges's left, Craig took the throw running parallel to the foul line. The throw from Hodges was a good one— chest high, reaching Craig two steps before he hit the base.

Mantle popped out to Campanella.

**Craig got ahead of the batter and made him go for a bad ball. Campanella positioned himself with his back to the infield to allow for the drift of the ball. He discarded his mask by tossing it away from the direction in which he was running.

SCORE—New York 1, Brooklyn 1

## Fourth Inning

DODGERS:

Robinson was thrown out by Carey.

**The Dodgers had been taking a strike but suddenly changed tactics. Robinson swung at the first pitch and hit it sharply, Carey making a great play to retire him.

Hodges grounded out, Carey to Collins.

**Carey did not hesitate but fired the ball to first to retire the runner.

Furillo was called out on strikes after fouling off two pitches.

**Ford had Furillo looking for the curve ball and whipped over a quick fast ball for a called third strike.

YANKEES:

Berra flied to Neal in short right field.

**Furillo came in to make the catch and was in better position to do so, but since Neal was calling for the ball and concentrating on it, Furillo let him take it, rather than risk a collision.

Slaughter singled to left.

**Slaughter worked the count to 3-2, then hit the ball where it was pitched, driving an outside pitch to left field. Reese tried for the ball and was out of position; so Neal covered second.

Martin hit into a double play, Craig to Reese to Hodges.

**The hit-and-run was on, but Martin hit the ball sharply to Craig, and there was time for a double play. Craig turned quickly and threw deliberately—but hard—to Reese, chest high and a half-step to the left of second base. Hodges's long stretch for the ball helped complete the double play.

SCORE—New York 1, Brooklyn 1

## Fifth Inning

DODGERS:

Campanella singled to left.

**Ford got two strikes with curve balls, then tried to sneak in a fast one.

Campanella concentrated on meeting the ball and got a base hit. Slaughter blocked the ball in left field, playing it safe to ensure that the ball did not get through and allow Campanella to reach scoring position.

Neal struck out on a 2-2 curve ball.

**Carey had been playing in to guard against a possible sacrifice bunt but moved back to normal position when the count reached two strikes.

Craig missed a sacrifice attempt, and Campanella was thrown out, Berra to McDougald.

**Campanella failed to wait until the ball was on the ground before taking off for second and was an easy out. Possibly this was a bunt-and-run.

Craig grounded out, Martin to Collins.

YANKEES:

McDougald singled on the first pitch.

Carey struck out, swinging.

**The Yankees were evidently playing for a big inning and had Carey hit away rather than sacrifice. Craig, ahead of the hitter, got Carey to fan on a high fast ball.

Ford hit into a double play, Neal to Reese to Hodges.

**Ford squared around as if to bunt, hoping to draw the infielders out of position, but took a full swing, hitting an easy double-play ball to Neal.

SCORE—New York 1, Brooklyn 1

*Sixth Inning*

The skies had become cloudy, and the sun was no longer a problem.

DODGERS:

Gilliam popped to Martin.

**Martin called for the ball in loud, clear tones.

Reese tripled to right center.

**Martin went out to handle the relay; McDougald was in cut-off position; and Ford backed up third.

Snider flied to Mantle, Reese scoring after the catch.

**The infield was in close to cut off the run at the plate. Reese tagged up as soon as the ball was hit in the air and shifted his weight forward, ready to break for the plate. In short, he lost as little time as possible in scoring this important run.

Robinson grounded out, Carey to Collins.

**With two out Carey was guarding the third base line to reduce the possibility of an extra-base hit.

YANKEES:

Bauer took a strike, then singled to left.

**As the leadoff man, Bauer was taking a strike with his team behind in the late innings.

Collins flied to Snider on the first pitch.

**Bauer went halfway on the fly to center, returning to first after the catch. The Yankees did not sacrifice, playing for more than one run with their power coming up.

Mantle popped to Hodges on a 2-0 pitch.

**With the tying run on base, the Yankees had their best hitter, Mantle, hit away, even with a count of two balls, no strikes, figuring this to be their best scoring chance. Possibly anticipating this, Craig was careful not to throw a "fat" pitch. In fact, Mantle went for a bad ball and popped it up, neglecting to wait for "his pitch."

Berra singled, Bauer stopping at second.

**Craig got ahead of Berra, two strikes and no balls, but came in with too good a pitch, Berra singling cleanly. With two out and Brooklyn leading, Bauer played safe, stopping at second. Furillo threw ahead of the runner (to third), the throw being cut off by Reese.

Slaughter hit a home run into the right-field stands, scoring Bauer and Berra ahead of him.

**Slaughter worked the count to 3-1 and, with the "hit away" sign on, set himself to swing if he got his pitch (he did: a belt-high fast ball on the inside corner). Circumstances decreed that he go for the long ball, and as a result, the Yankees, who had been losing 2-1, now enjoyed a two-run lead late in the game, meaning that Brooklyn would have to play conservative baseball in an attempt to keep their chances alive.

Martin flied to Snider on the first pitch.

**Snider ran to where he thought the ball would go and was waiting for it when it came down. He was ready to adjust his position according to the exact location of the ball.

SCORE—New York 4, Brooklyn 2

*Seventh Inning*

DODGERS:

Hodges walked on five pitches.

Furillo singled off Ford's glove. Hodges advanced to second on the hit and continued on to third when Martin bobbled the ball.

**Ford used a large glove, and it enabled him to block the ball and keep it from going through to the outfield. The ball was deflected toward Martin, who fumbled it and was unable to retrieve it in time to prevent Hodges from moving to third.

Campanella's fly was taken by McDougald in short left field.

**McDougald ran the ball back to the infield after the catch. This was wise. Without risking what was really an unnecessary throw (since there was no definite play to be made), it prevented the runners from advancing.

Neal grounded to Carey, who, in his anxiety to make a play at the plate, bobbled the ball and then threw poorly to Berra. Hodges scored; Furillo reached second; and Neal was safe at first.

**Hodges was correct in breaking for the plate, for a throw home would eliminate the possibility of a double play. If the throw did beat him home, he could pull up and get caught in a run-down, giving the other two runners a chance to reach scoring position.

Carey's decision to make the play at home was a poor one. Hodges's run was relatively unimportant because, even if he had scored, the Yankees still would have been leading. The tying run should have been kept from scoring position, and in this case, an inning-ending double play might have resulted. Even a play at first seemed more justified, particularly after the fumble, since the out was a relatively sure one and would have left the Yankees still in commanding position.

The complexion of the game had suddenly changed: Brooklyn had the tying and winning runs on base with only one out.

Jackson batted for Craig and flied to Slaughter.

**Slaughter's throw went to third but was intercepted by McDougald, who was in cut-off position. With one out Furillo and Neal had gone halfway. They returned to their bases after the catch.

Gilliam grounded to McDougald. Neal was forced at second, McDougald making the play himself.

**McDougald correctly made the easiest possible play for the third out, a big one in this inning.

Clem Labine, a right-hander with a good sinking fast ball and an excellent curve, took over the pitching duties for Brooklyn.

YANKEES:

McDougald grounded to Reese on a 3-2 pitch.

**Reese charged the ball and played it cleanly. As a good shortstop should, Reese played the ball rather than let it play him.

Carey took a third strike.

Ford, too, was called out on strikes.

**Labine did not waste time with the number-eight and number-nine hitters. He got ahead of them both and came in with his best pitch, the curve ball. The result was two strike-outs, and Brooklyn was still in the ball game.

SCORE—New York 4, Brooklyn 3

*Eighth Inning*

DODGERS:

Reese took a strike, then grounded to McDougald.

**Brooklyn, behind in the late innings, was taking a strike. Perhaps aware of this, Ford was getting ahead of the hitters.

Snider was called out on strikes.

**Ford got two quick strikes with a curve and a fast ball. He had been getting Snider out with his curve ball, and sensing that Snider would be looking for that pitch, he set him up perfectly for the fast ball, which he whipped over for a called third strike, Snider was fooled completely since he made the mistake of guessing the curve ball. The batter who is always set for the fast ball is ready to hit anything since he can always adjust his timing to the other pitches, which are invariably slower than the fast one.

Robinson singled to left.

**The count went to 3-2, and Robinson fouled off several pitches before hitting a single. With two strikes he was guarding the plate and simply trying to meet the ball. Slaughter got the ball back to the infield quickly, making his throw to second base. McDougald, alert to rush out to left field if the ball got through Slaughter, returned to second base to take the throw, Martin backing him up.

Hodges flied to Mantle.

**Ford had been giving Hodges almost nothing but curve balls. He suddenly switched to his fast ball. It was a good pitch, and Hodges went for it but was unable to get good wood on the ball, lifting a harmless fly to Mantle in center.

YANKEES:

Bauer flied to Snider.

Collins grounded to Neal and was safe on the latter's wild throw to first.

**Neal, possibly overanxious, made a hurried throw that arrived just as Hodges reached the base, but before he was fully set for it. It went wild but was retrieved by Campanella before Collins could advance to second. Campanella had followed the batter to first and was in perfect position to retrieve the overthrow.

Mantle popped to Neal.

**Labine got ahead of Mantle with two quick strikes, the second one called. He then made Mantle hit his (Labine's) pitch, a good curve ball under the hands.

Berra doubled to right center, scoring Collins.

**Labine threw five consecutive curve balls, all strikes, four of which Berra fouled off. Quite logically, he then tried to sneak over a fast ball, but Berra was ready for it. His solid double gave the Yankees an insurance run.

Slaughter was purposely passed.

**This was good policy for several reasons: Slaughter was particularly hot that day; he was a left-handed batter and Martin, who followed him, batted right-handed; and, above all, it set up a force play at any base.

Martin flied to Gilliam.

**The Yankees were swinging at the first ball in this inning, figuring that Labine's control was good and that he was getting the first pitch over for a strike. Perhaps Labine was guessing with them and not making the first pitch too good. At any rate, the Yankees were not doing much with the first ball.

SCORE—New York 5, Brooklyn 3

*Ninth Inning*

DODGERS:

Furillo doubled to right center but was out trying to stretch it into a triple, Bauer to Martin to Carey.

**Furillo's attempt to stretch his hit into a triple cannot very well be justified. With no outs and his team losing in the ninth inning, his main job should have been keeping his team's chances alive. He definitely should have been playing safe (at second base he was already in scoring position). In addition, his run meant nothing at the time, for even if he had scored, Brooklyn would still have been trailing by a run.

Campanella was called out on strikes.

**Ford was getting the big outs with his best pitch, a well-controlled curve. In short, when the chips were down, he was pitching to his own strength.

Neal grounded out, Carey to Collins.

**Collins hustled to the bag, found it with his left foot, and was prepared to shift in any direction according to the location of the throw.

FINAL SCORE—New York 5, Brooklyn 3

By playing sound baseball throughout the game and by capitalizing fully on their opportunities, the Yankees won their "must" game.

A discussion of baseball tactics as employed by the two teams in the World Series of 1956 should certainly include mention of an incident that occurred in the fourth game. It serves as a good example of big league thinking at its best.

Jackie Robinson was on first base with one out in the second inning, and Sandy Amoros was the batter. Brooklyn attempted a hit-and-run play, and Robinson was more than halfway to second when Amoros hit the ball. Amoros's effort was a foul fly close to the first base stands. Billy Martin, the Yankee second baseman, was thinking every inch of the way. He faked fielding a ground ball. To complete the subterfuge, Gil McDougald, the shortstop, ran toward second base as though he were going to take the throw for a force-out and possible double play. Robinson was taken in by the ruse and continued to run hard for second. In the meantime Collins caught the ball; Sturdivant, the pitcher, covered first base; and Robinson was out by the proverbial mile. Unfortunately for the Yankees Collins threw wild, and Robinson was able to return to first safely. Regardless of the eventual outcome of the play, this was a remarkable demonstration of the smart, quick-thinking play that marks a real professional.

## RULES INTERPRETATION

A thorough knowledge of the rules is too often neglected, even by professionals, and it cannot help but improve one's play, both from an individual and team standpoint, to be completely familiar with them.

Baseball's rules are the most intricate of any sport's, and continual study is necessary if they are to be mastered.

The following discussion of the interpretation of certain rules is not designed to be comprehensive. Rather, it covers several relatively common situations that can arise in a ball game and that are too often misunderstood by players and fans alike.

1. Appeal Plays: The meaning of this term implies that certain violations of the rules must be called to the attention of the umpires before a decision can be made. Appeal plays are three in number, and every team, when in the field, should be alert for these rules infractions so that full advantage will be taken of every opportunity to get an out.

   (a) Failure to touch a base: When an opposing base runner fails to touch a base, the ball should be retrieved and the base in question touched by a defensive player in possession of the ball. If, by any chance, the ball is hit over a fence, lost, or goes out of play in like manner, the pitcher should throw the ball to the appropriate base after he has received a new ball from the umpire and taken his position on the rubber—and before delivering a pitch to the next batter.

   (b) Leaving a base too soon: If a runner leaves his base before a fly ball comes into contact with a fielder in the act of catching it, the ball should be thrown to that base. When the base has been touched by a defensive player in possession of the ball, the runner should be declared out.

   (c) Batting out of order: This violation is a tricky one and can become quite involved. It should not be called until after the batter becomes a base runner—but it must be reported to the umpire before a pitch is delivered to the next batter. It is the original batter, not the one who batted out of turn, who is declared out. Unless the violator causes a definite disadvantage to the defensive team, it is wise to refrain from appealing to the umpire. Should the other team fail to realize its mistake and repeat it later in the game when the scoring of runs may be involved, the defensive club will then be able to take advantage of this infraction of the rules.

It must be remembered that the umpire is powerless to rule on these plays unless they are appealed to him.

2. The ball is dead and no further play is possible in the following cases:

(a) The batter is hit by a pitched ball—base runners may advance only if forced to the next base.

(b) A balk is called—base runners are entitled to advance one base; the count on the batter remains the same.

(c) A ball is batted illegally (the batter hits it while not completely in the batter's box)—the batter is declared out; base runners may not advance.

(d) A foul ball is not legally caught—the ball is dead until the pitcher takes his position on the mound with the ball.

(e) Interference is called on a player—if on a runner, he is declared out; if on a defensive player, it is an obstruction play and the runner is awarded the next base.

(f) A batted ball hits a runner—he is declared out, and the batter is awarded first base and credited with a hit.

(g) A batted ball hits an umpire before passing a fielder other than the pitcher.

(h) The ball touches a spectator.

3. A ball is judged foul or fair by its position relative to the foul line, not by where a fielder is when he touches it. A ground ball is considered fair if it passes first or third base in fair territory or if, before reaching the base, it rolls dead in fair territory. A ball hit in the air is fair or foul according to its position when it lands beyond first or third base; when it is touched by a fielder; or when it leaves the ball park by clearing a fence.

4. The infield fly rule: The batter is declared out when he hits a *fair* fly ball that, in the judgment of the umpire, can be handled by an *infielder* when first and second or first, second, and third bases are occupied with *fewer* than two out. Base runners may advance at their own risk. The infield fly should be called by the umpire as soon as possible after the ball is hit. To play safe, defensive players should treat this as an ordinary fly ball.

5. If two runners are on the same base, possession of it belongs to the

man who originally occupied it. The other runner may be tagged out if he fails to return safely to his original base. Base runners should be fully aware of this rule to avoid being caught in an accidental double play. Defensive players can play safe by tagging both runners.

6. If the ball hits an umpire after passing a fielder (other than the pitcher), it is in play. Base runners should move as they would on an ordinary batted ball, and the defense should treat the play in the same fashion, retrieving the ball as quickly as possible.

7. A base runner must run around a defensive player who is in the act of fielding a batted ball. In this situation any contact between runner and fielder will result in the runner's being declared out for interference.

8. A fielder who is not in possession of the ball may not block a runner's attempt to reach a base. In this case obstruction should be called on the defensive player; the runner is awarded the base to which he was advancing.

9. On a batted ball handled by the catcher, the batter must run in the three-foot lane that is marked off from a point beginning halfway between home and first and ending at the base itself. This also applies to bunts and batted balls fielded by the pitcher in the home-plate area. Actually, it applies on all plays at first base, but there seems to be little inclination on the part of the runner to wander out of the three-foot lane on plays other than those cited. A runner who is hit by a thrown ball on such a play shall be declared out for interference if he is not in the three-foot lane when hit or if he obstructs the first baseman, causing the latter to drop the throw.

10. The dropped third strike rule: A batter may run on a dropped third strike as long as first base is unoccupied. With two out he may run even with first base occupied. The batter should be alert for a dropped third strike and should not allow himself to be tagged by the catcher in this situation, remembering that as long as he can make the other team throw the ball, there exists the possibility of an error.

11. The balk rule: A balk shall be called by the umpires; the ball becomes dead, and runners are allowed to advance one base in the following situations:

(a) The pitcher makes any motion that can be construed as a move to deliver the ball to the batter or to throw to first base without completing the throw. He can, however, fake a throw to either second base or third when occupied.

(b) If he does not step toward the base in making a throw to it. A left-hander is allowed considerable leeway in throwing to first base, his move being considered within the rules if he steps toward a point at least halfway between home and first.

(c)  If he delivers the ball to the plate while his pivot foot is not in contact with the rubber. He can, however, throw to or fake toward any base when not on the rubber.

(d)  If he pitches while not facing the batter.

(e)  If he makes a motion to pitch while not in position on the rubber.

(f)  If the pitcher holds the ball so long as to delay the game unnecessarily.

(g)  If he takes his position on the mound while not in possession of the ball.

(h)  If he moves his arm, shoulder, knee, hip, or body in such a way as to indicate that he is pitching the ball to the plate without doing so. This applies also to a move toward first base.

(i)  If he makes any motion to pitch while not in possession of the ball.

(j)  If he takes either hand off the ball after coming to his stop and does not deliver the ball.

(k)  If he throws to an unoccupied base.

(l)  If the pitcher drops the ball while on the mound and ready to pitch.

(m)  If the pitcher does not come to a *complete stop* after taking his stretch and before delivering the ball to the plate.

The pitcher may step off the rubber and call time without being guilty of a balk, but he must be careful to do so without making any motion toward home plate or first base, moves that may be considered as intending to deceive the batter or runner.

12. A balk is called on the catcher if he steps out of the catcher's box before the ball is delivered by the pitcher. This pertains primarily to the intentional pass, and the catcher must take care to delay his stepping outside the confines of the catcher's box until the ball is on its way to the plate.

## *HUSTLE*

1. Hustle is being at the right place at the right time. It is making the right play at all times. It is helping your team by helping yourself.

2. Hustle is bearing down all the way—and bearing down twice as hard when the going gets tough.

3. Hustle is playing with your head as well as with your arms and legs. It is in the doing; it is action, not mere words.

4. Hustle is taking advantage of every opening. It makes its own breaks.

5. Hustle is what separates the men from the boys, the big leaguer from the busher. It is the one element, above all others, that helps to win ball games.

6. Be a big leaguer in everything you do—hustle all the way.

### Always Know
1. The score
2. The outs
3. The inning

### Realize

You should play to win, but be willing to accept defeat gracefully, profit from today's mistakes, and go out and win tomorrow's game.

### Remember

No team ever walked to victory.

### Above All

Baseball is a team game—help one another at all times.

# *Index*